高橋 和希

I'VE BEEN THINKING THAT WRITING A MANGA SERIES IS A LOT
LIKE FLYING AN AIRPLANE. HERE ARE SOME EXAMPLES:

- IT'S HARD TO TAKE OFF.
- YOU NEED MOMENTUM TO STAY IN THE AIR.
- WHEN YOU CATCH THE WIND, YOU CAN COAST FOR A WHILE.
- YOU'RE STUCK IN A TINY SEAT WHERE YOU CAN'T MOVE
  AND THE FOOD IS BORING.
- ...AND THE FINAL OBSTACLE IS THE LANDING.

THIS STORYLINE...THE "WORLD OF MEMORY"...IS LIKE THE PART
OF THE PLANE FLIGHT WHEN YOU MAKE PREPARATIONS FOR
LANDING. I HOPE WE MAKE IT DOWN SAFELY.

—KAZUKI TAKAHASHI, 2003

Artist/author Kazuki Takahashi first tried to break into
the manga business in 1982, but success eluded him
until **Yu-Gi-Oh!** debuted in the Japanese **Weekly
Shonen Jump** magazine in 1996. **Yu-Gi-Oh!**'s themes
of friendship and fighting, together with Takahashi's
weird and wonderful art, soon became enormously
successful, spawning a real-world card game, video
games, and two anime series. A lifelong gamer,
Takahashi enjoys Shogi (Japanese chess), Mahjong,
card games, and tabletop RPGs, among other games.

YU-GI-OH!: MILLENNIUM WORLD VOL. 1
The SHONEN JUMP Graphic Novel Edition

STORY AND ART BY
KAZUKI TAKAHASHI

Translation & English Adaptation/Anita Sengupta
Touch-up Art & Lettering/Kelle Han
Additional Touch-up/Josh Simpson
Design/Sean Lee
Editor/Jason Thompson

Managing Editor/Elizabeth Kawasaki
Director of Production/Noboru Watanabe
Vice President of Publishing/Alvin Lu
Vice President & Editor in Chief/Yumi Hoashi
Sr. Director of Acquisitions/Rika Inouye
Vice President of Sales & Marketing/Liza Coppola
Publisher/Hyoe Narita

In the original Japanese edition, YU-GI-OH! and YU-GI-OH!: MILLENNIUM
WORLD are known collectively as YU-GI-OH!. The English YU-GI-OH!:
MILLENNIUM WORLD was originally volumes 32-38 of the Japanese YU-GI-OH!.

Printed in the U.S.A.

Published by VIZ Media, LLC
P.O. Box 77010
San Francisco, CA 94107

SHONEN JUMP Graphic Novel Edition
10 9 8 7 6 5 4 3 2 1
First printing, July 2005

PARENTAL ADVISORY
YU-GI-OH!: MILLENNIUM WORLD is rated T
for Teen. It contains fantasy violence. It is
recommended for ages 13 and up.

www.viz.com

THE WORLD'S
MOST POPULAR MANGA

GRAPHIC NOVEL

www.shonenjump.com

SHONEN JUMP GRAPHIC NOVEL

Yu-Gi-Oh! Millennium World

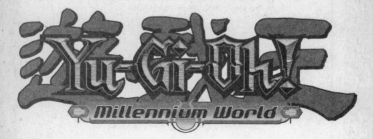

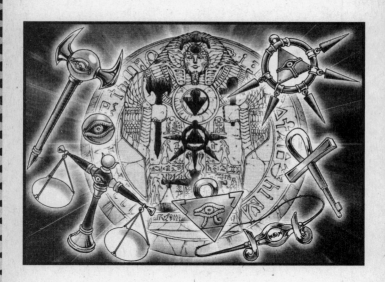

Vol. 1

THE WORLD OF MEMORY

STORY AND ART BY

KAZUKI TAKAHASHI

THE MAIN CHARACTERS

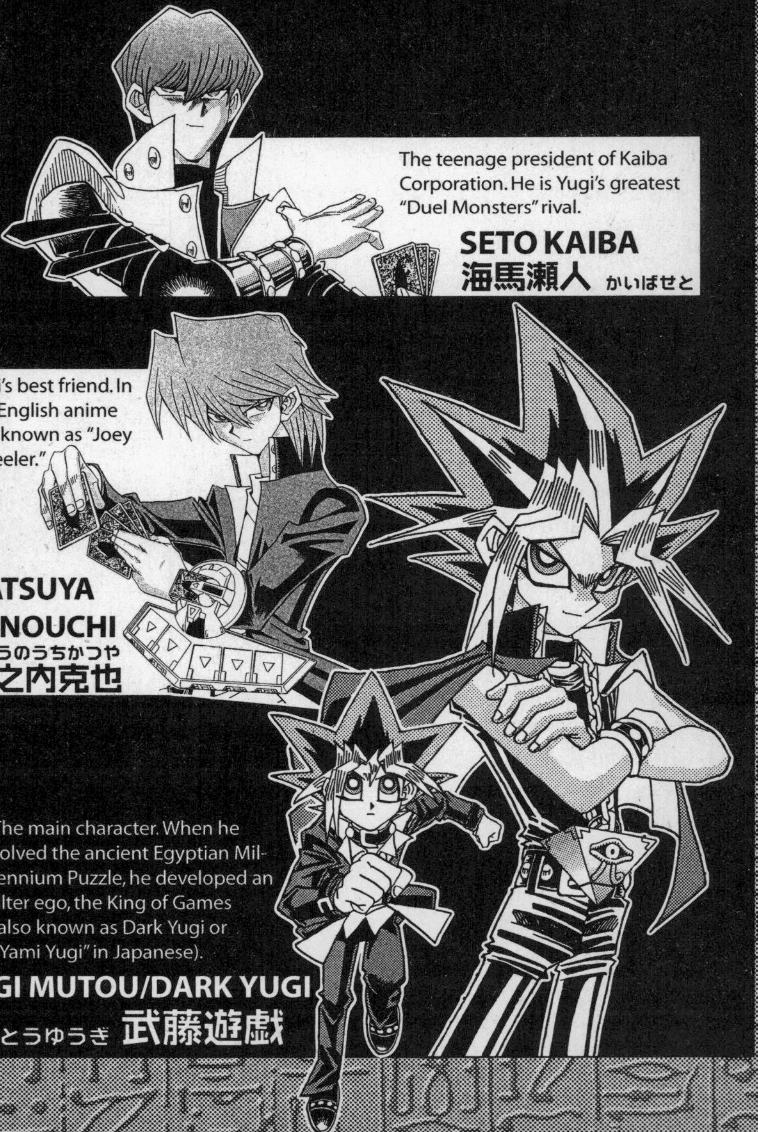

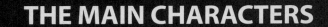

The teenage president of Kaiba Corporation. He is Yugi's greatest "Duel Monsters" rival.

SETO KAIBA
海馬瀬人 かいばせと

Yugi's best friend. In the English anime he's known as "Joey Wheeler."

KATSUYA JONOUCHI
じょうのうちかつや
城之内克也

The main character. When he solved the ancient Egyptian Millennium Puzzle, he developed an alter ego, the King of Games (also known as Dark Yugi or "Yami Yugi" in Japanese).

YUGI MUTOU/DARK YUGI
むとうゆうぎ **武藤遊戯**

THE STORY SO FAR...

Shy 10th-grader Yugi spent most of his time alone playing games...until he solved the Millennium Puzzle, a mysterious Egyptian artifact passed down from his grandfather. Possessed by the puzzle, Yugi developed an alter ego: Yu-Gi-Oh, the seemingly unbeatable King of Games!

When Yugi started playing the collectible card game "Duel Monsters," he quickly became a world champion. But what Yu-Gi-Oh most wanted was to recover his lost memories of his previous life. Discovering that "Duel Monsters" might be of Ancient Egyptian origin, Yugi entered the "Battle City" tournament sponsored by Kaiba Corporation. After many deadly duels, Yugi finally collected the three Egyptian God Cards— Slifer the Sky Dragon, the God of the Obelisk and the Sun Dragon Ra. In addition, he gathered two of the other Millennium Items—the Millennium Necklace and the Millennium Rod.

Now, Yugi has almost every piece of the puzzle. But where will his search for identity lead next?

RYO
BAKURA
ばくらりょう
獏良 了

HIROTO
HONDA
ほんだ
本田
ヒロト

ANZU
MAZAKI
まざきあんず
真崎杏子

SUGOROKU
MUTOU
武藤
むとう
すごろく
双六

Yu-Gi-Oh! Millennium World

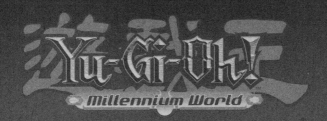

Vol. 1

CONTENTS

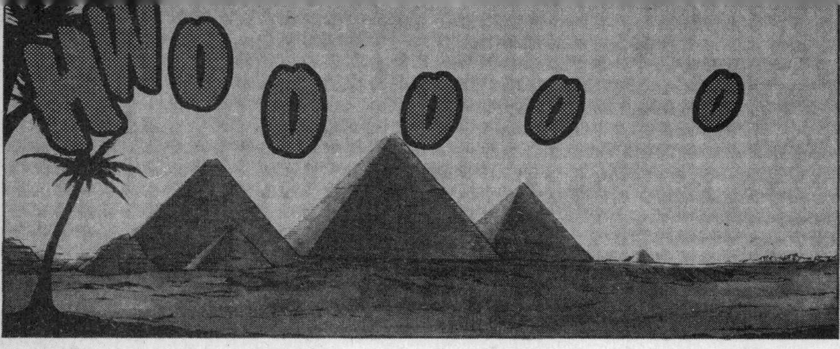
HWOOOOO

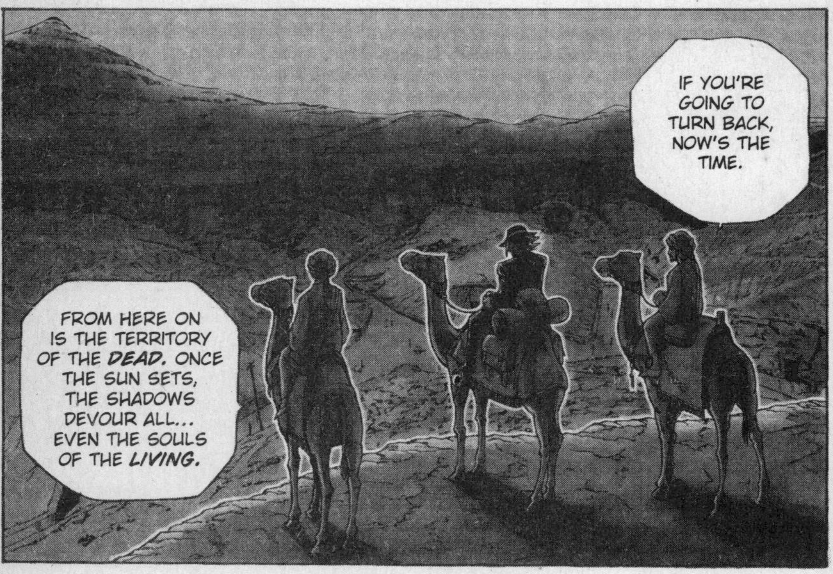
IF YOU'RE GOING TO TURN BACK, NOW'S THE TIME.
FROM HERE ON IS THE TERRITORY OF THE *DEAD.* ONCE THE SUN SETS, THE SHADOWS DEVOUR ALL... EVEN THE SOULS OF THE *LIVING.*

EGYPT • VALLEY OF THE KINGS • 1960

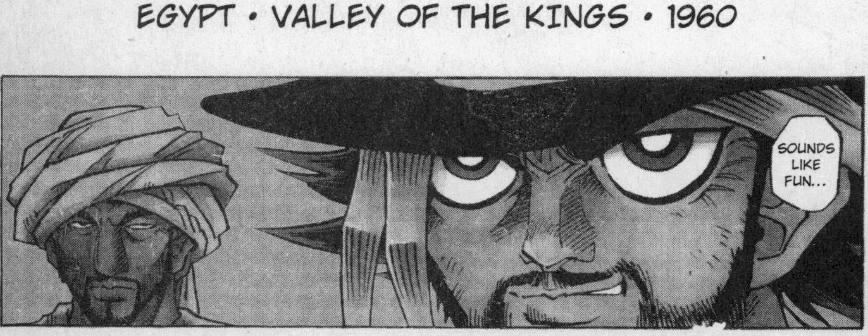
SOUNDS LIKE FUN...

Duel 1: The Millennium Treasure

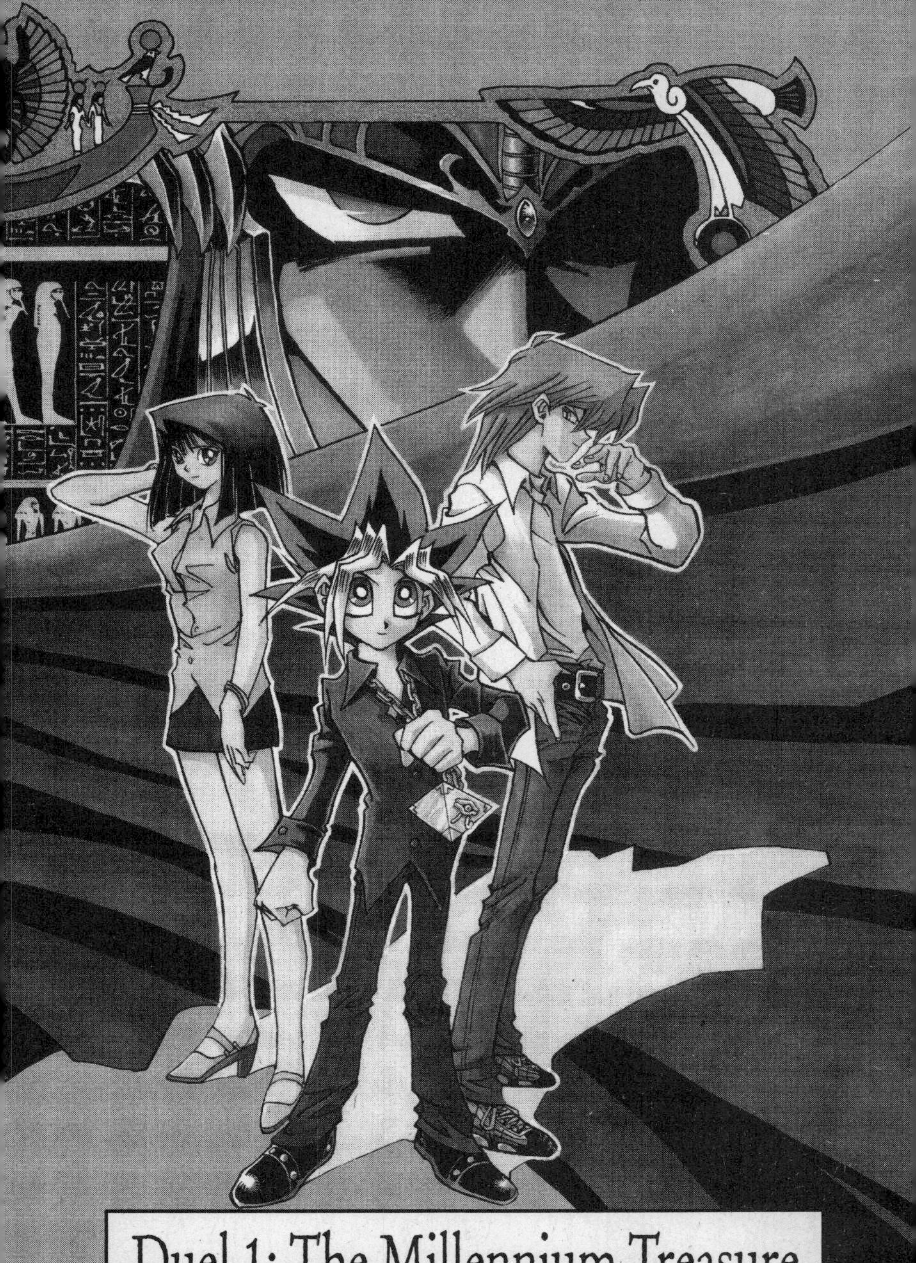

Duel 1: The Millennium Treasure

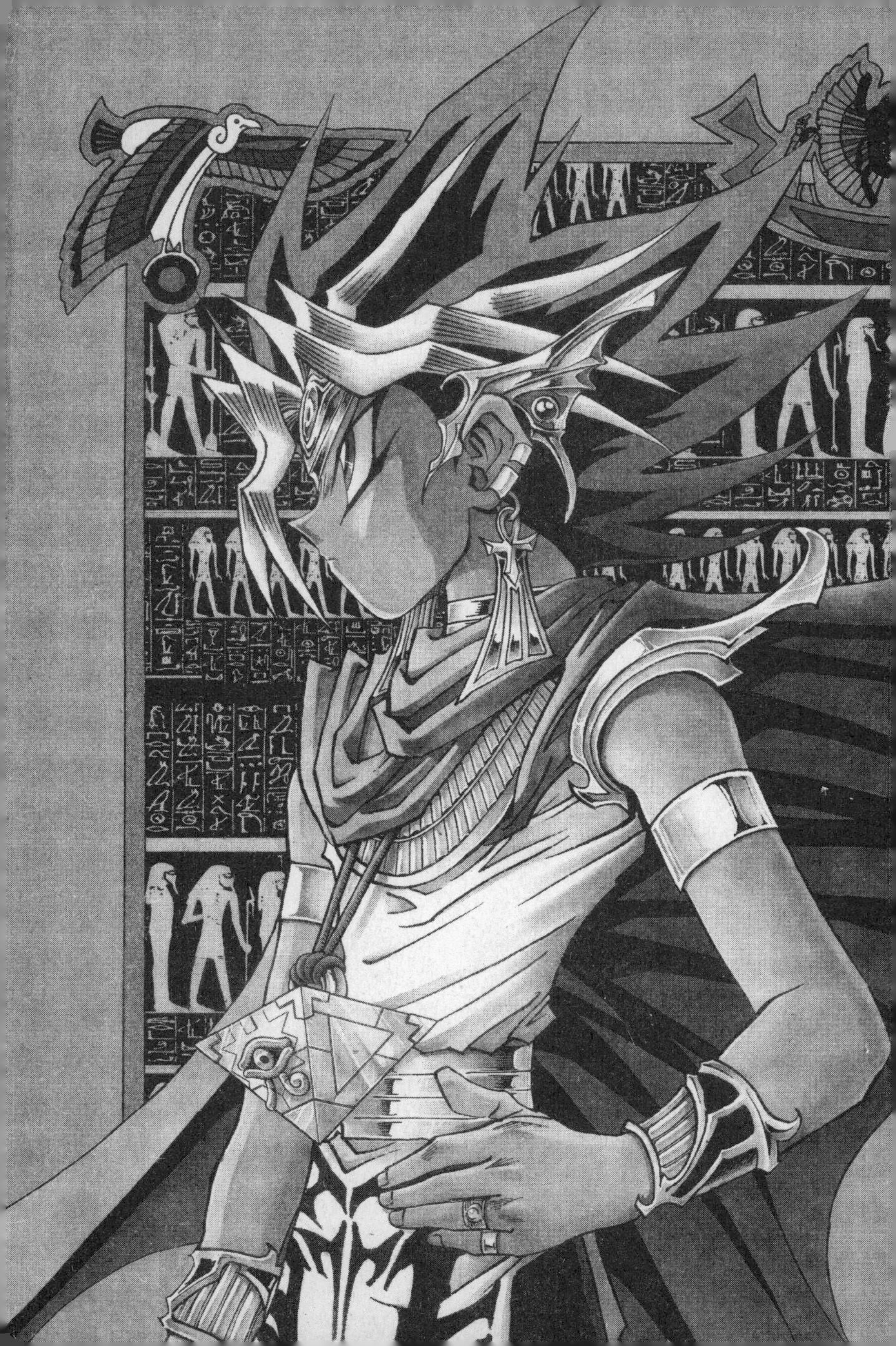

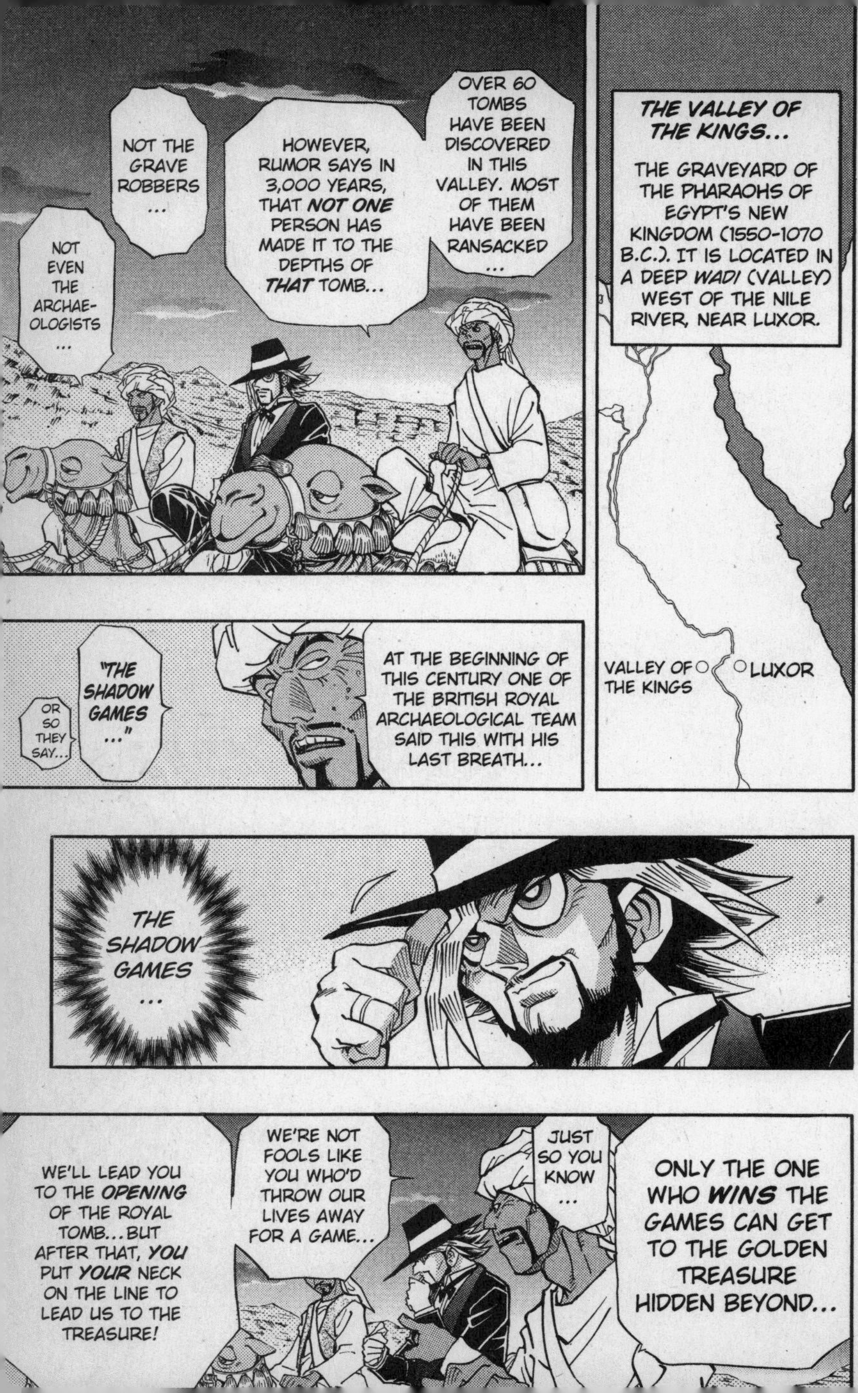
THE VALLEY OF THE KINGS...
THE GRAVEYARD OF THE PHARAOHS OF EGYPT'S NEW KINGDOM (1550-1070 B.C.). IT IS LOCATED IN A DEEP *WADI* (VALLEY) WEST OF THE NILE RIVER, NEAR LUXOR.
VALLEY OF THE KINGS
LUXOR
OVER 60 TOMBS HAVE BEEN DISCOVERED IN THIS VALLEY. MOST OF THEM HAVE BEEN RANSACKED...
HOWEVER, RUMOR SAYS IN 3,000 YEARS, THAT **NOT ONE** PERSON HAS MADE IT TO THE DEPTHS OF **THAT** TOMB...
NOT THE GRAVE ROBBERS...
NOT EVEN THE ARCHAEOLOGISTS...
AT THE BEGINNING OF THIS CENTURY ONE OF THE BRITISH ROYAL ARCHAEOLOGICAL TEAM SAID THIS WITH HIS LAST BREATH...
"THE SHADOW GAMES..."
OR SO THEY SAY...
THE SHADOW GAMES...
ONLY THE ONE WHO **WINS** THE GAMES CAN GET TO THE GOLDEN TREASURE HIDDEN BEYOND...
JUST SO YOU KNOW...
WE'RE NOT FOOLS LIKE YOU WHO'D THROW OUR LIVES AWAY FOR A GAME...
WE'LL LEAD YOU TO THE **OPENING** OF THE ROYAL TOMB...BUT AFTER THAT, **YOU** PUT **YOUR** NECK ON THE LINE TO LEAD US TO THE TREASURE!

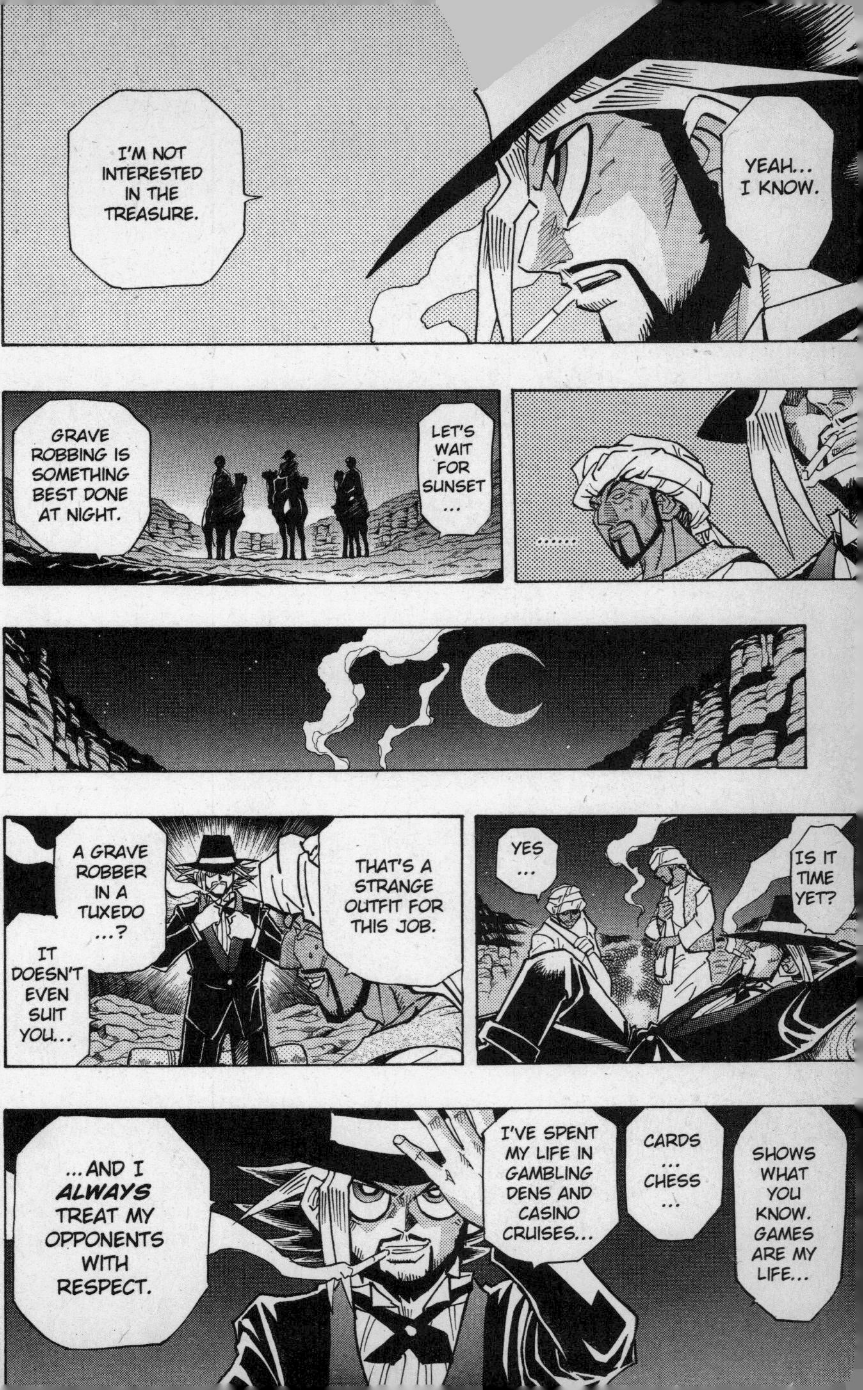
YEAH... I KNOW.
I'M NOT INTERESTED IN THE TREASURE.
......
LET'S WAIT FOR SUNSET ...
GRAVE ROBBING IS SOMETHING BEST DONE AT NIGHT.
IS IT TIME YET?
YES ...
THAT'S A STRANGE OUTFIT FOR THIS JOB.
A GRAVE ROBBER IN A TUXEDO ...?
IT DOESN'T EVEN SUIT YOU...
SHOWS WHAT YOU KNOW. GAMES ARE MY LIFE...
CARDS ... CHESS ...
I'VE SPENT MY LIFE IN GAMBLING DENS AND CASINO CRUISES...
...AND I *ALWAYS* TREAT MY OPPONENTS WITH RESPECT.

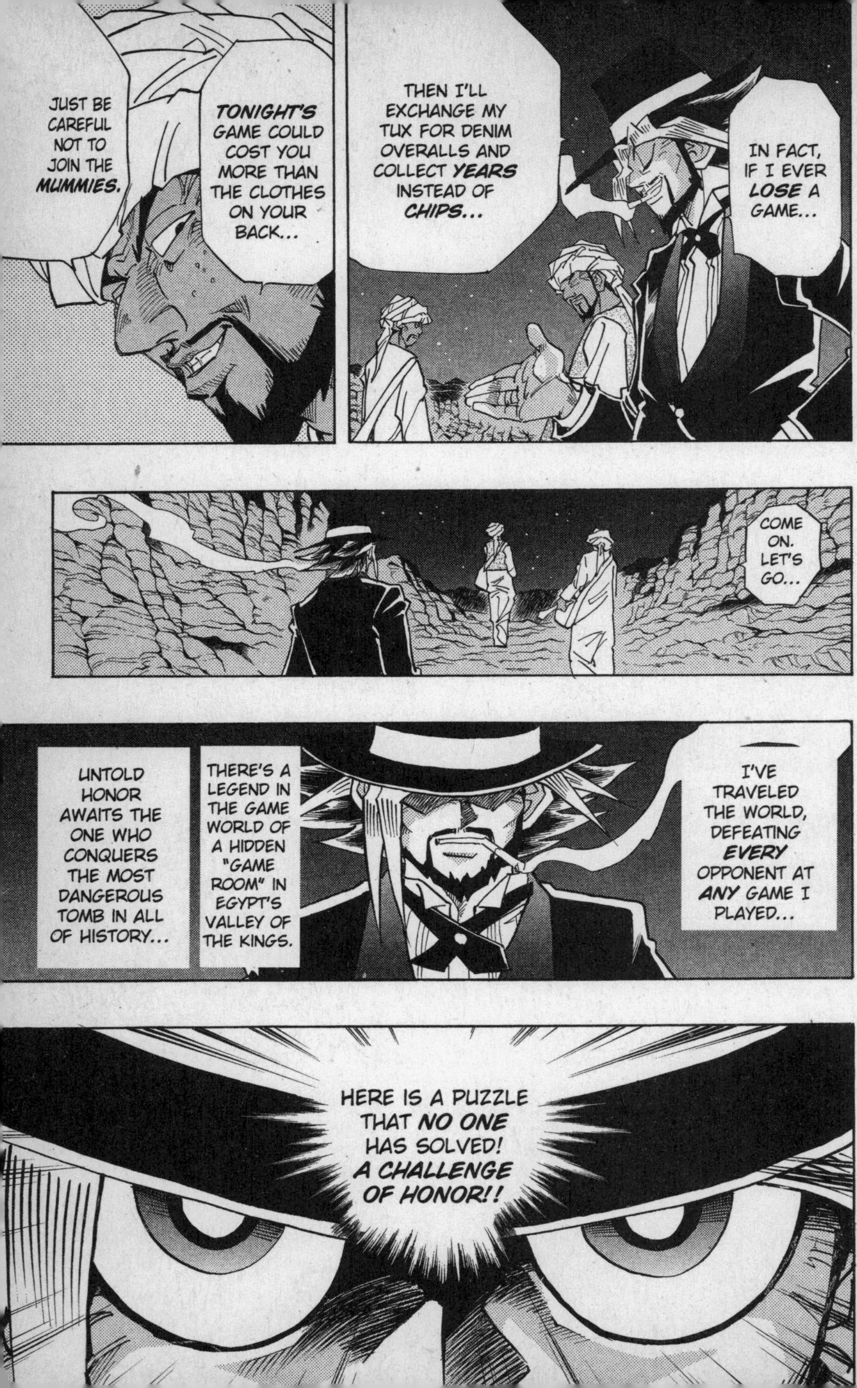
IN FACT, IF I EVER **LOSE** A GAME...
THEN I'LL EXCHANGE MY TUX FOR DENIM OVERALLS AND COLLECT **YEARS** INSTEAD OF **CHIPS...**
TONIGHT'S GAME COULD COST YOU MORE THAN THE CLOTHES ON YOUR BACK...
JUST BE CAREFUL NOT TO JOIN THE **MUMMIES.**
COME ON. LET'S GO...
I'VE TRAVELED THE WORLD, DEFEATING **EVERY** OPPONENT AT **ANY** GAME I PLAYED...
THERE'S A LEGEND IN THE GAME WORLD OF A HIDDEN "GAME ROOM" IN EGYPT'S VALLEY OF THE KINGS.
UNTOLD HONOR AWAITS THE ONE WHO CONQUERS THE MOST DANGEROUS TOMB IN ALL OF HISTORY...
HERE IS A PUZZLE THAT **NO ONE** HAS SOLVED! **A CHALLENGE OF HONOR!!**

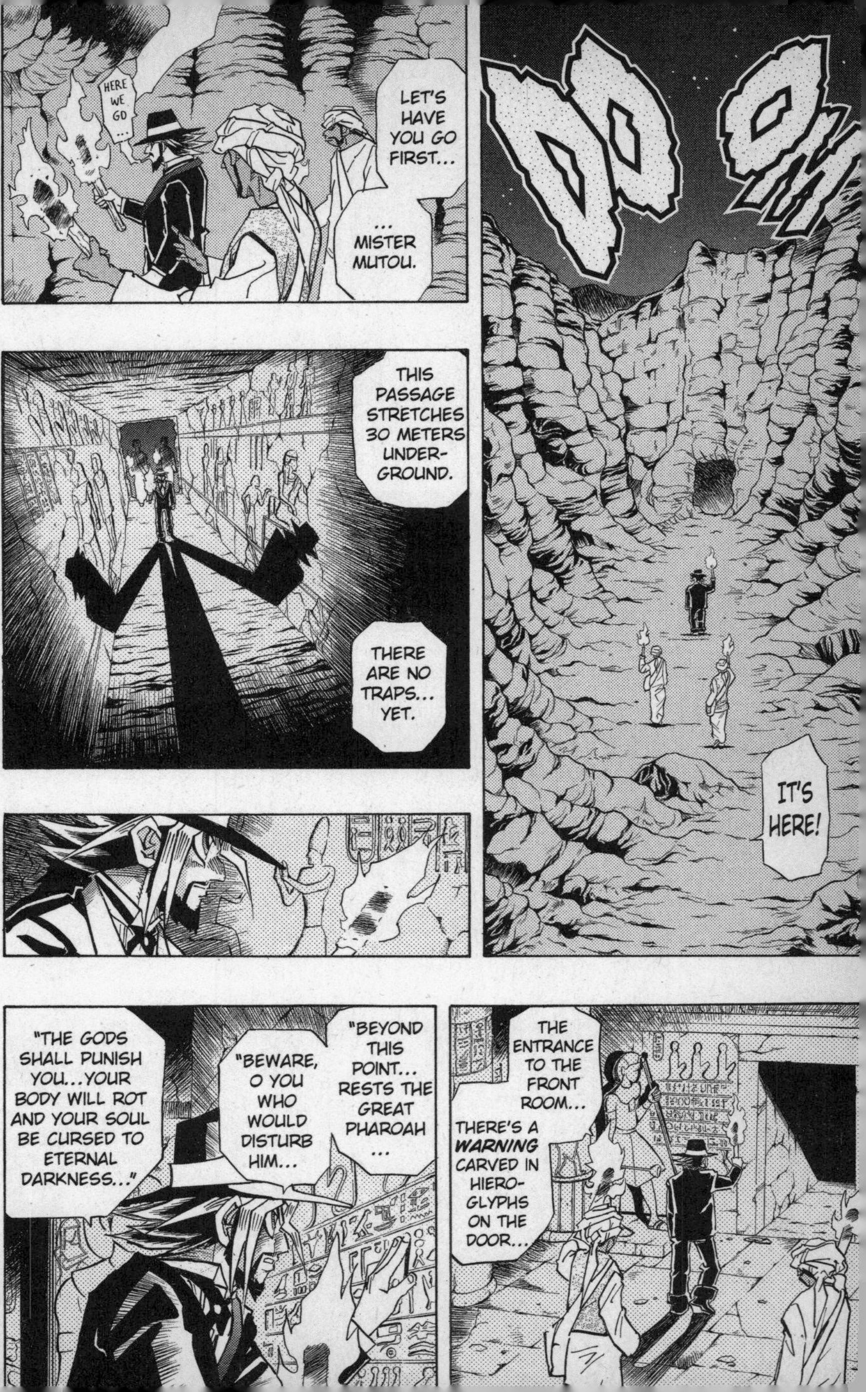
DOOM
IT'S HERE!
LET'S HAVE YOU GO FIRST...
... MISTER MUTOU.
HERE WE GO ...
THIS PASSAGE STRETCHES 30 METERS UNDER-GROUND.
THERE ARE NO TRAPS... YET.
THE ENTRANCE TO THE FRONT ROOM...
THERE'S A ***WARNING*** CARVED IN HIERO-GLYPHS ON THE DOOR...
"BEYOND THIS POINT... RESTS THE GREAT PHAROAH ...
"BEWARE, O YOU WHO WOULD DISTURB HIM...
"THE GODS SHALL PUNISH YOU...YOUR BODY WILL ROT AND YOUR SOUL BE CURSED TO ETERNAL DARKNESS..."

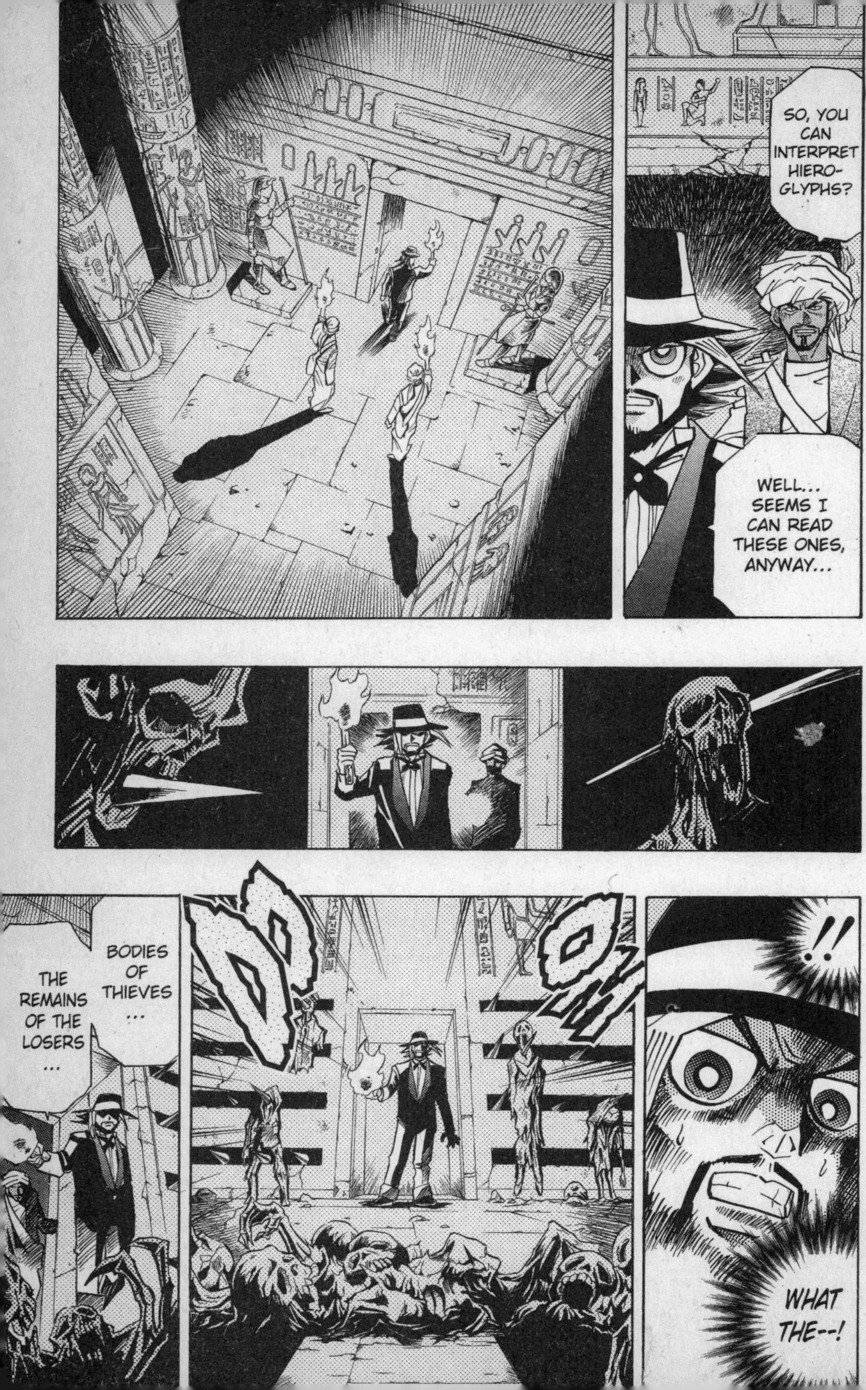
SO, YOU CAN INTERPRET HIERO-GLYPHS?
WELL... SEEMS I CAN READ THESE ONES, ANYWAY...
!!
WHAT THE--!
BODIES OF THIEVES...
THE REMAINS OF THE LOSERS...

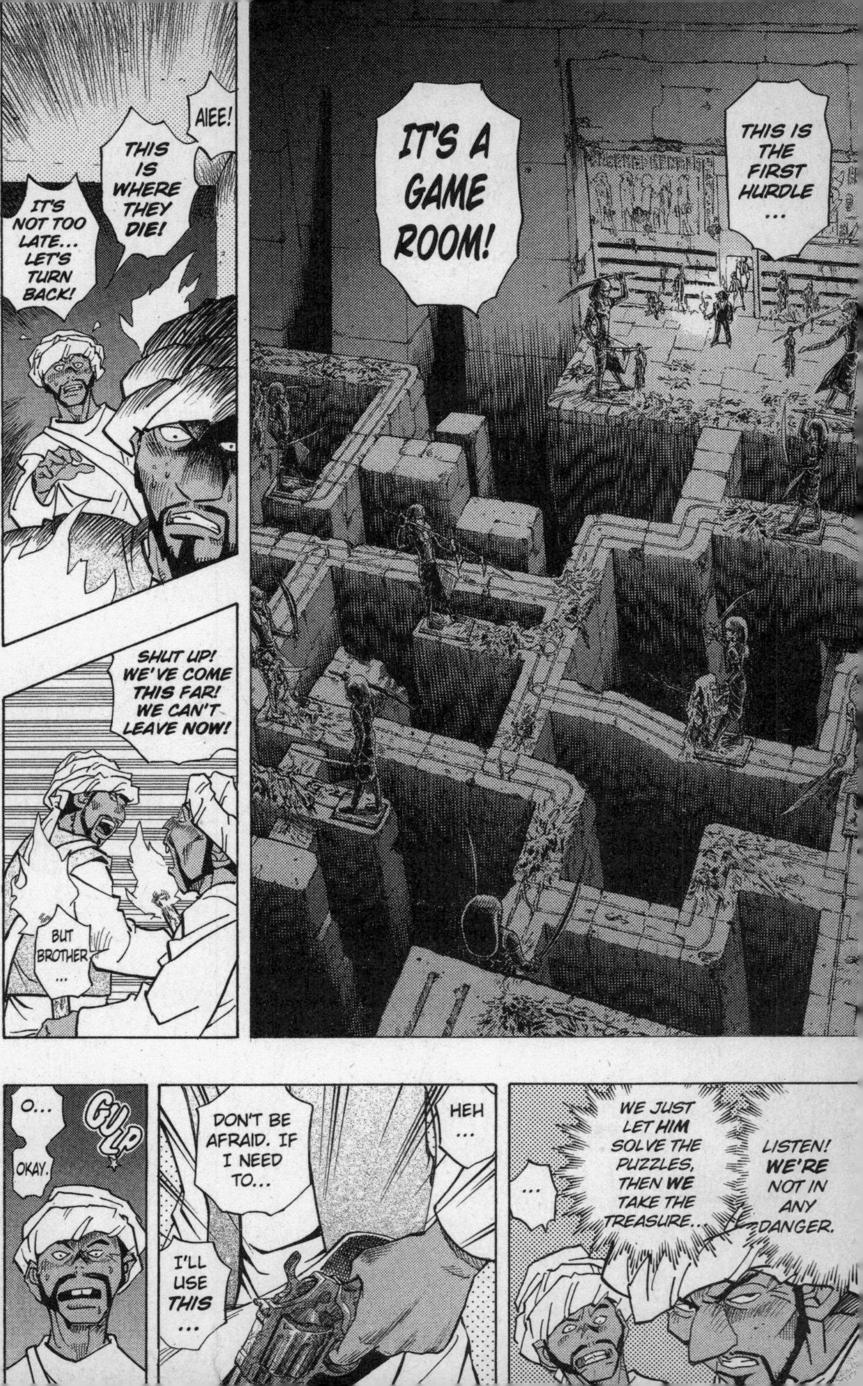
THIS IS THE FIRST HURDLE...
IT'S A GAME ROOM!
AIEE!
THIS IS WHERE THEY DIE!
IT'S NOT TOO LATE... LET'S TURN BACK!
SHUT UP! WE'VE COME THIS FAR! WE CAN'T LEAVE NOW!
BUT BROTHER...
LISTEN! WE'RE NOT IN ANY DANGER.
WE JUST LET HIM SOLVE THE PUZZLES, THEN WE TAKE THE TREASURE...
...
HEH...
DON'T BE AFRAID. IF I NEED TO...
I'LL USE THIS...
GULP
O...
OKAY.

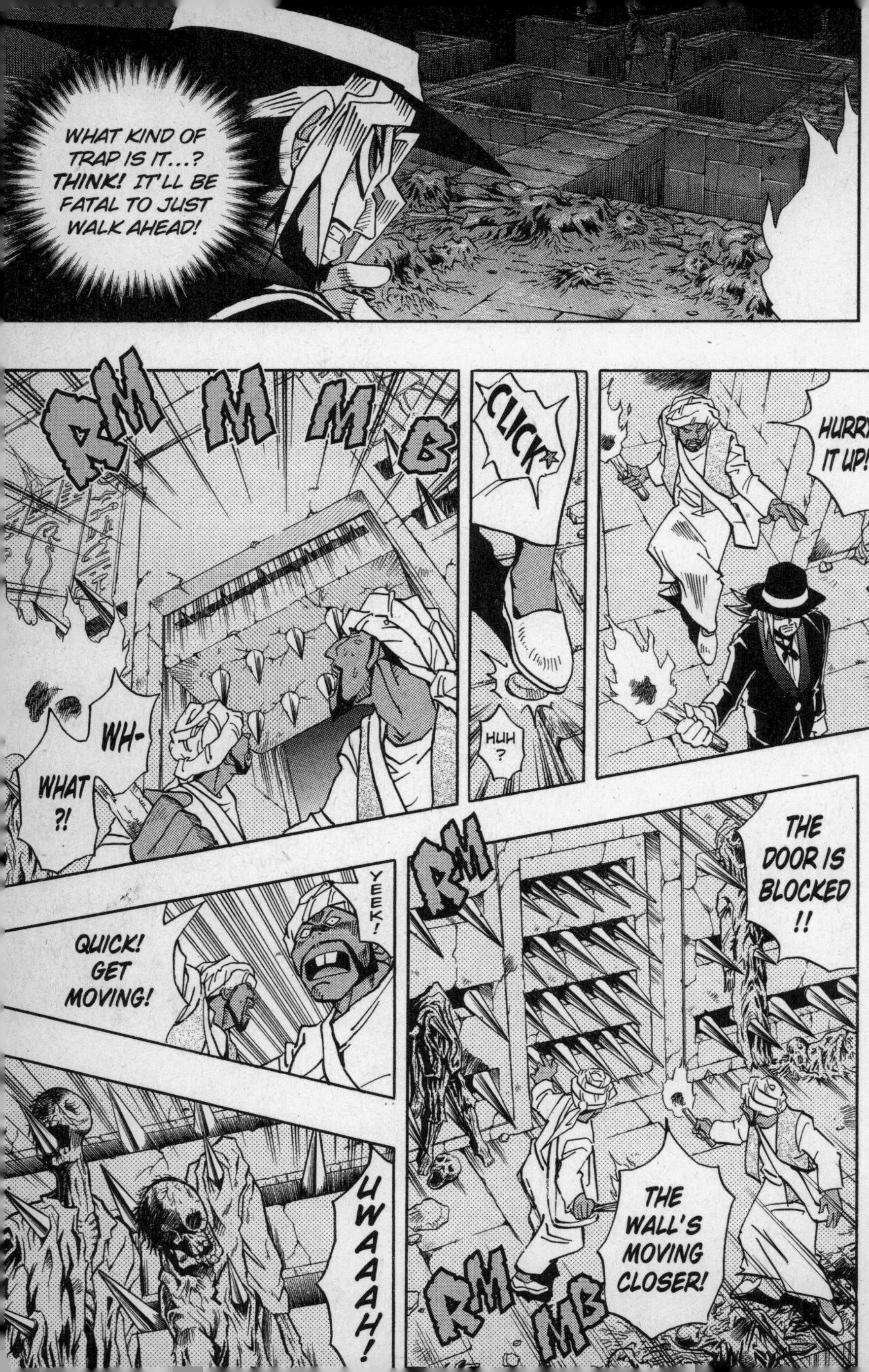
WHAT KIND OF TRAP IS IT...? THINK! IT'LL BE FATAL TO JUST WALK AHEAD!
HURRY IT UP!
CLICK
HUH ?
RM M M B
WH- WHAT ?!
THE DOOR IS BLOCKED !!
RM
THE WALL'S MOVING CLOSER!
RM MB
YEEK!
QUICK! GET MOVING!
UWAAAAH!

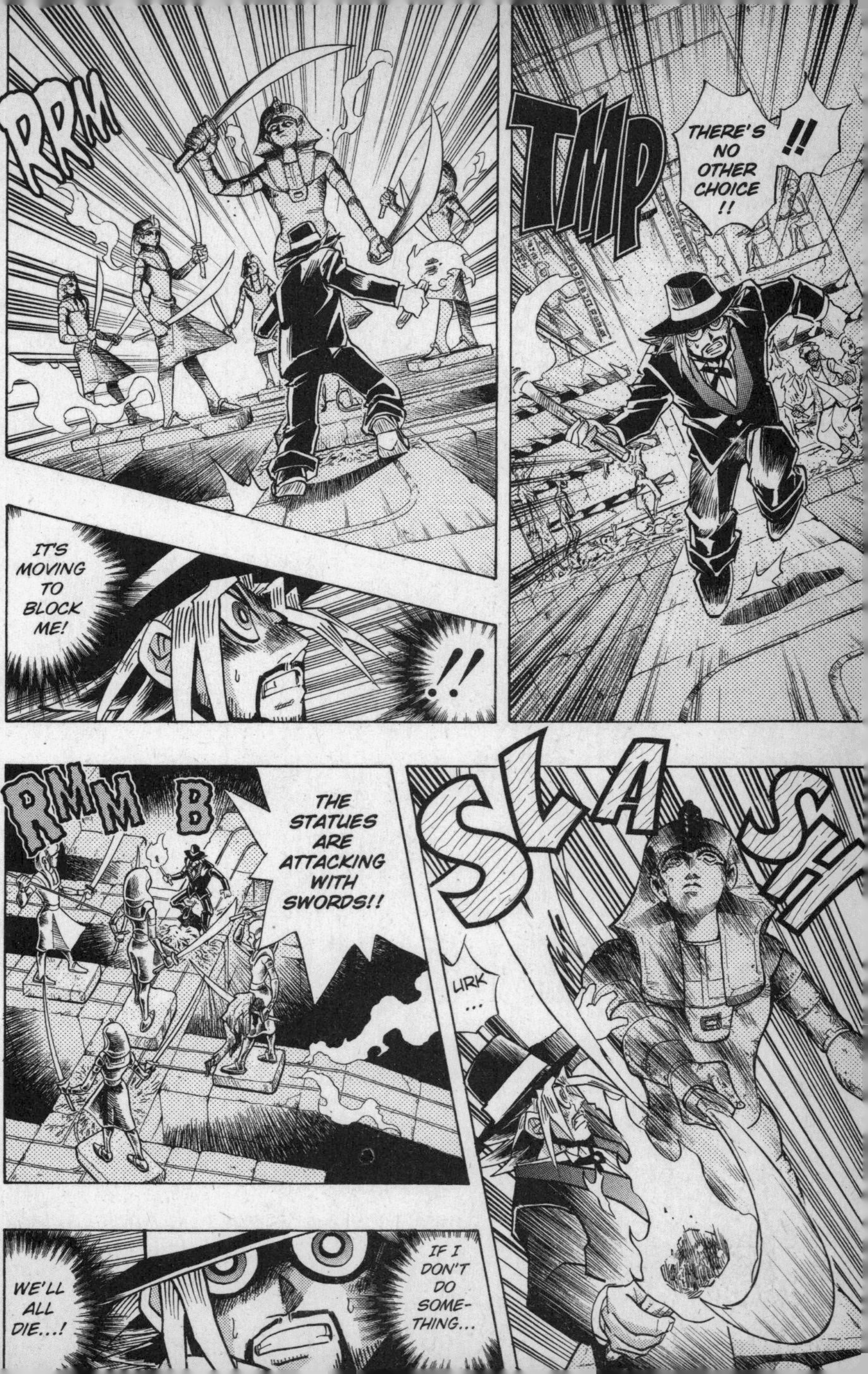
TMP
THERE'S NO OTHER CHOICE !!
!!
RRM
IT'S MOVING TO BLOCK ME!
!!
SLASH
URK ...
RMM B
THE STATUES ARE ATTACKING WITH SWORDS!!
IF I DON'T DO SOME-THING...
WE'LL ALL DIE...!

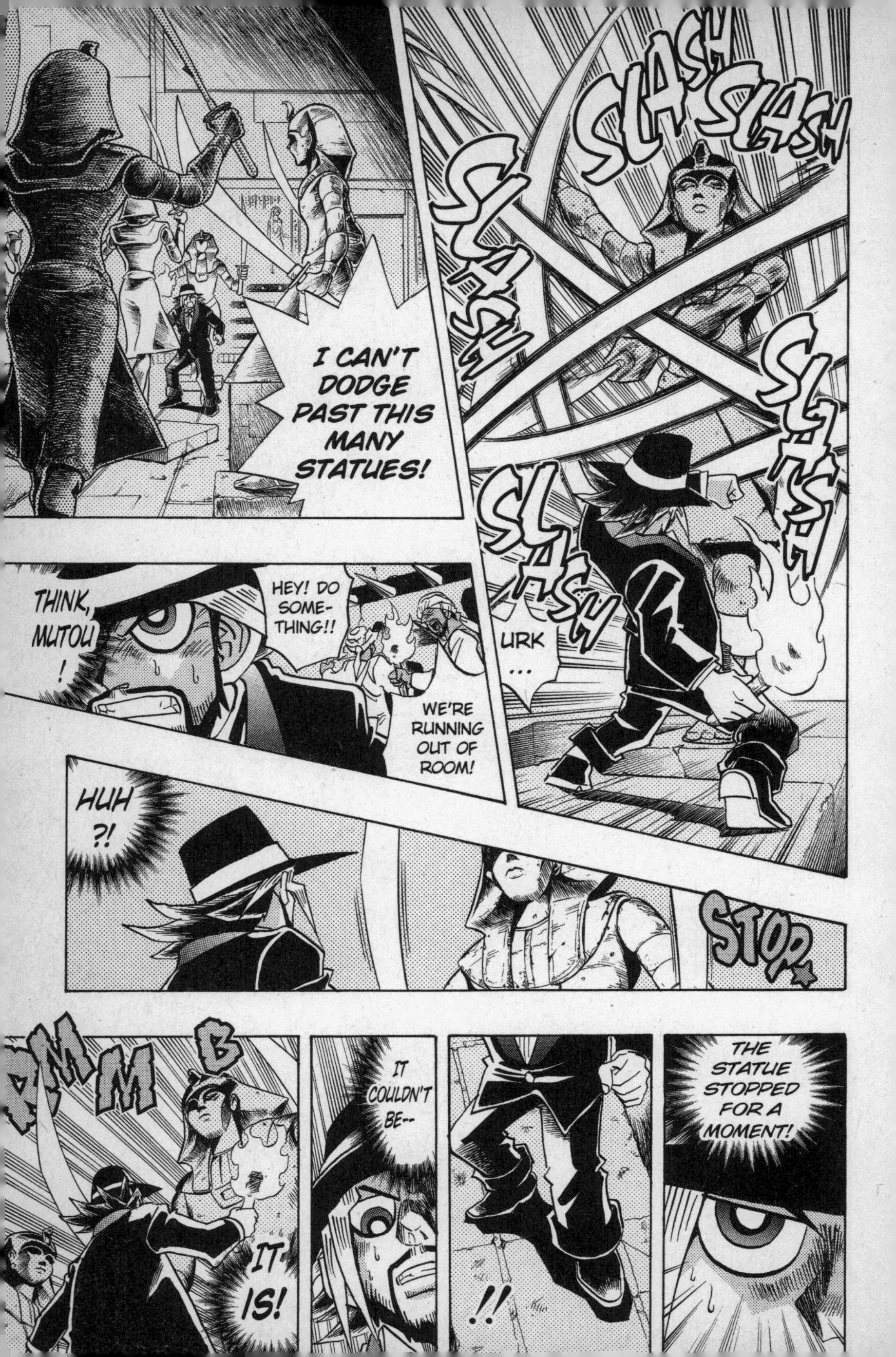
SLASH
SLASH SLASH
SLASH
SLASH
SLASH
URK ...
I CAN'T DODGE PAST THIS MANY STATUES!
THINK, MUTOU!
HEY! DO SOME-THING!!
WE'RE RUNNING OUT OF ROOM!
STOP
HUH ?!
THE STATUE STOPPED FOR A MOMENT!
!!
IT COULDN'T BE--
IT IS!

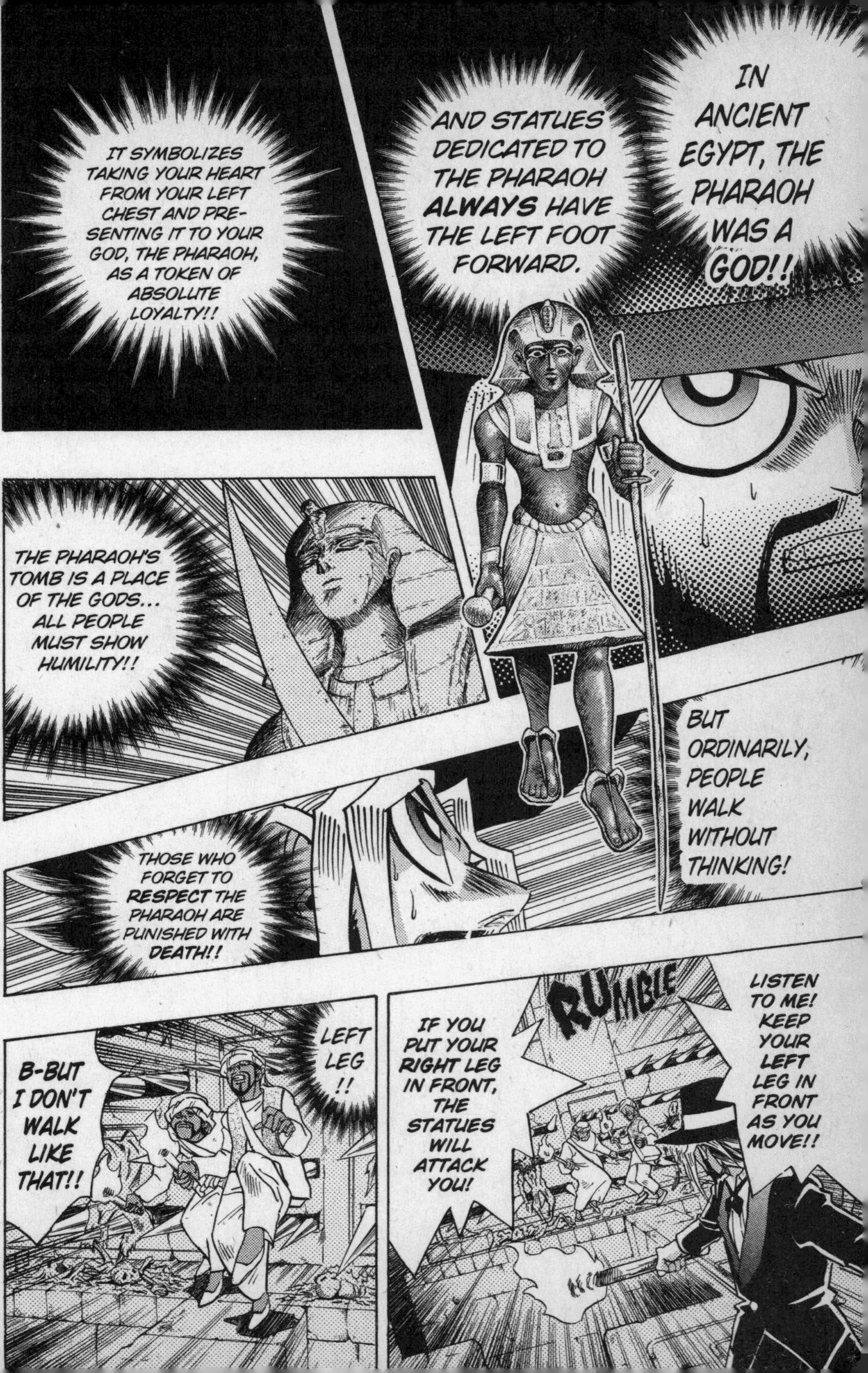
IN ANCIENT EGYPT, THE PHARAOH WAS A GOD!!
AND STATUES DEDICATED TO THE PHARAOH **ALWAYS** HAVE THE LEFT FOOT FORWARD.
IT SYMBOLIZES TAKING YOUR HEART FROM YOUR LEFT CHEST AND PRE-SENTING IT TO YOUR GOD, THE PHARAOH, AS A TOKEN OF ABSOLUTE LOYALTY!!
THE PHARAOH'S TOMB IS A PLACE OF THE GODS... ALL PEOPLE MUST SHOW HUMILITY!!
BUT ORDINARILY, PEOPLE WALK WITHOUT THINKING!
THOSE WHO FORGET TO **RESPECT** THE PHARAOH ARE PUNISHED WITH **DEATH!!**
LISTEN TO ME! KEEP YOUR LEFT LEG IN FRONT AS YOU MOVE!!
RUMBLE
IF YOU PUT YOUR **RIGHT LEG** IN FRONT, THE STATUES WILL ATTACK YOU!
LEFT LEG !!
B-BUT I DON'T WALK LIKE THAT!!

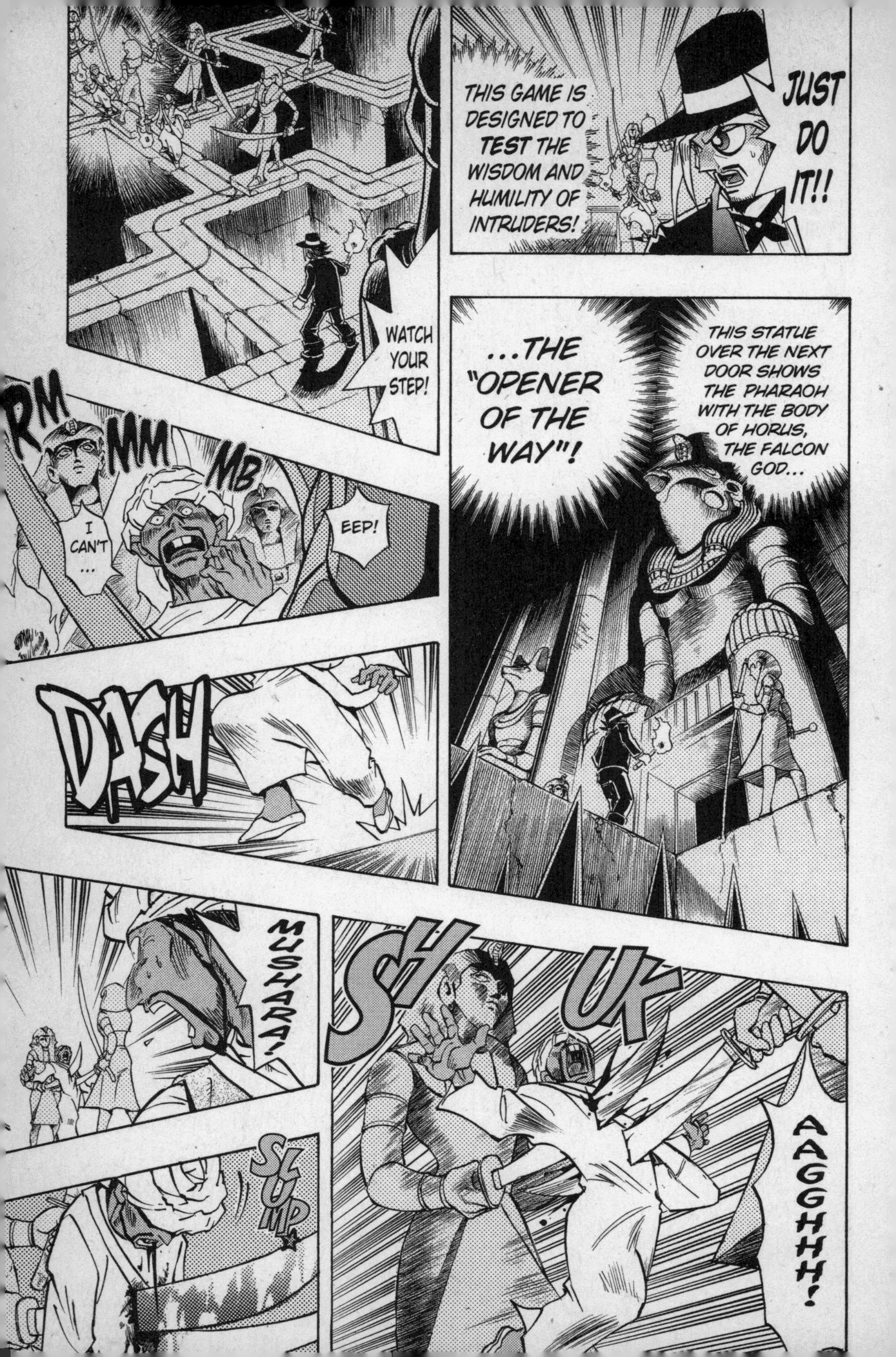
JUST DO IT!!
THIS GAME IS DESIGNED TO TEST THE WISDOM AND HUMILITY OF INTRUDERS!
WATCH YOUR STEP!
THIS STATUE OVER THE NEXT DOOR SHOWS THE PHARAOH WITH THE BODY OF HORUS, THE FALCON GOD...
...THE "OPENER OF THE WAY"!
RMMMMB
EEP!
I CAN'T...
DASH
SHUK
AAGGHHH!
MUSHARRA!
SLUMP

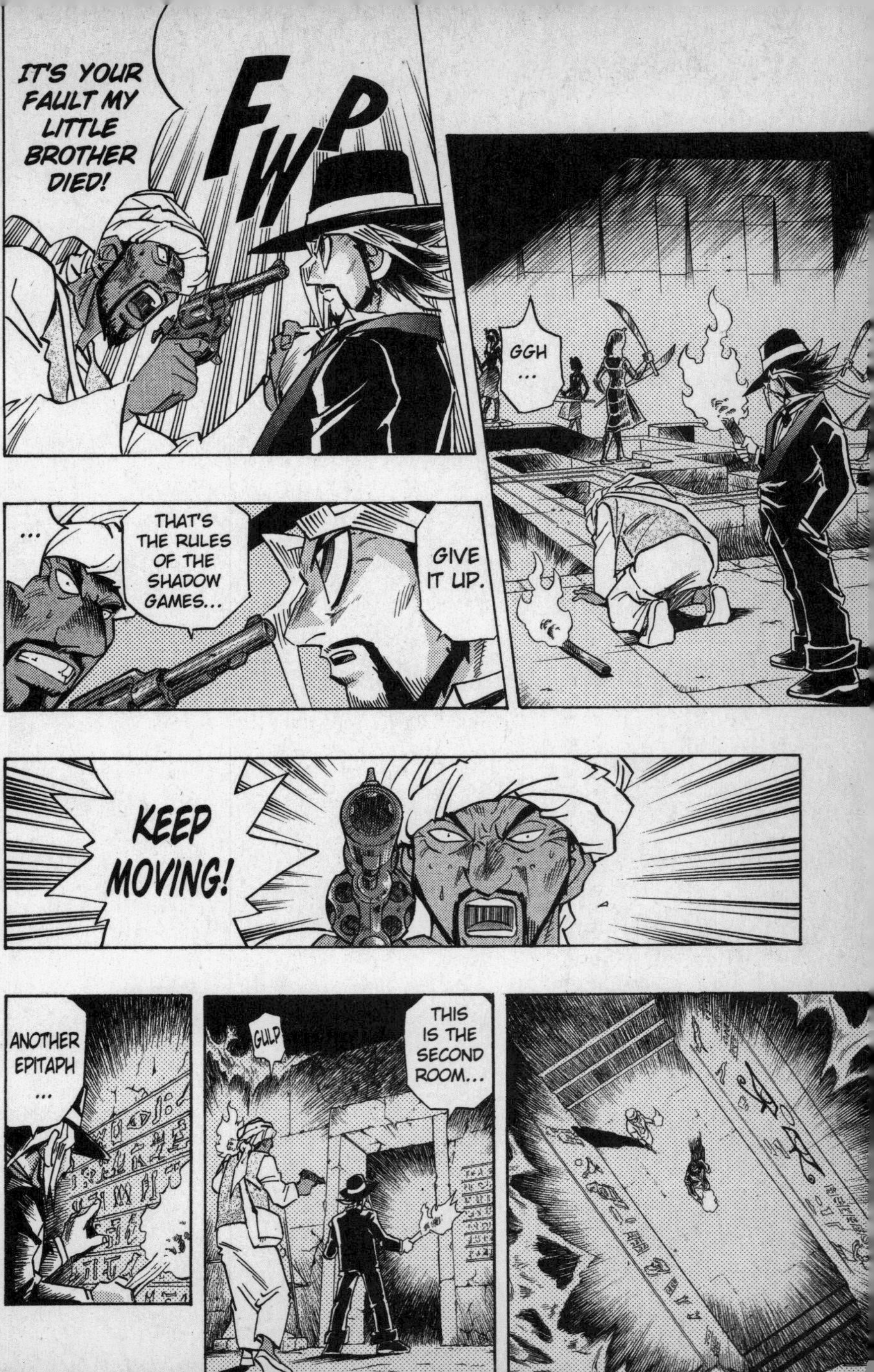

GGH ...
IT'S YOUR FAULT MY LITTLE BROTHER DIED!
FWP
GIVE IT UP.
THAT'S THE RULES OF THE SHADOW GAMES...
...
KEEP MOVING!
THIS IS THE SECOND ROOM...
GULP
ANOTHER EPITAPH ...

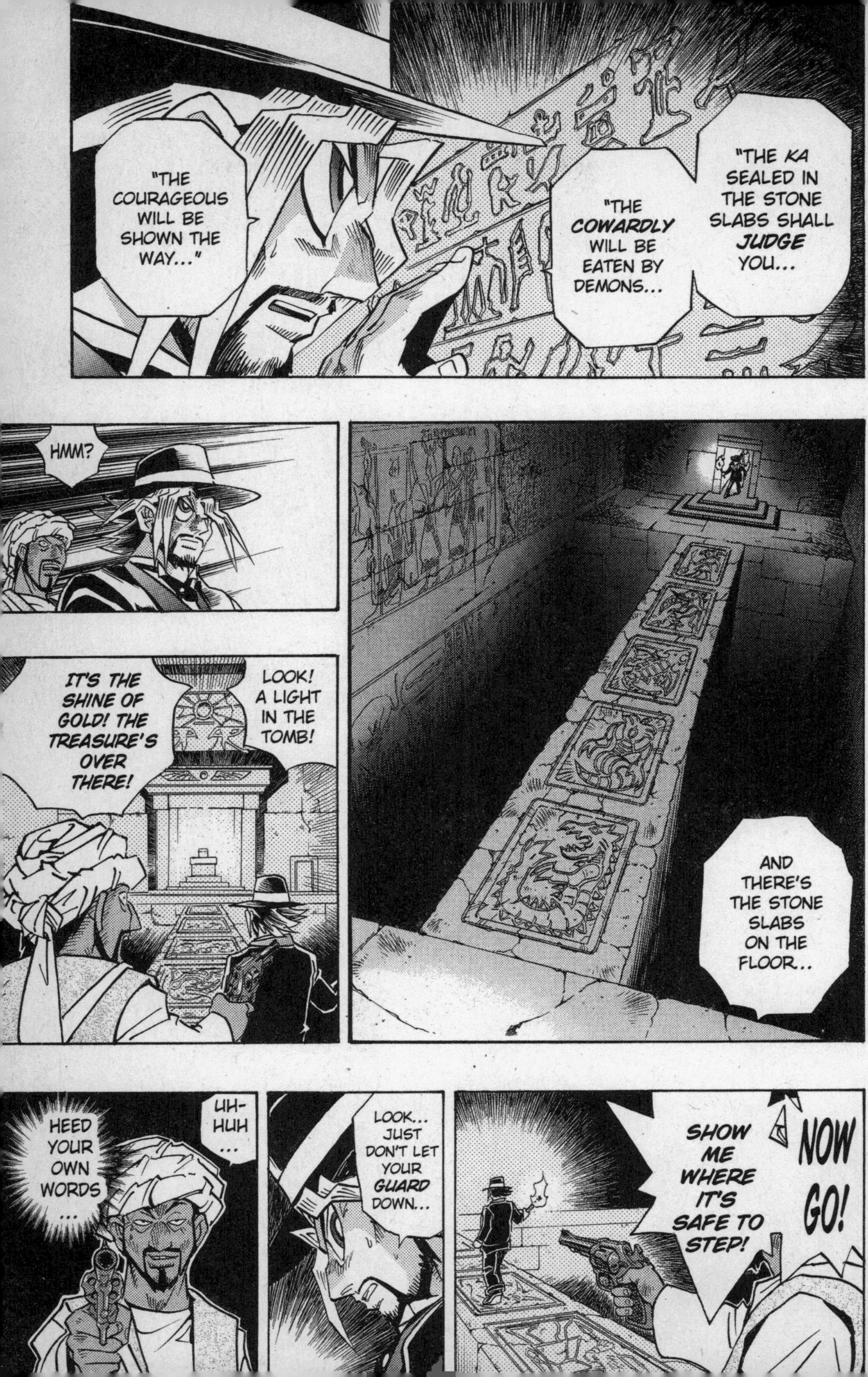
"THE KA SEALED IN THE STONE SLABS SHALL JUDGE YOU...
"THE COWARDLY WILL BE EATEN BY DEMONS...
"THE COURAGEOUS WILL BE SHOWN THE WAY..."
AND THERE'S THE STONE SLABS ON THE FLOOR...
HMM?
LOOK! A LIGHT IN THE TOMB!
IT'S THE SHINE OF GOLD! THE TREASURE'S OVER THERE!
NOW GO!
SHOW ME WHERE IT'S SAFE TO STEP!
LOOK... JUST DON'T LET YOUR GUARD DOWN...
UH-HUH...
HEED YOUR OWN WORDS...

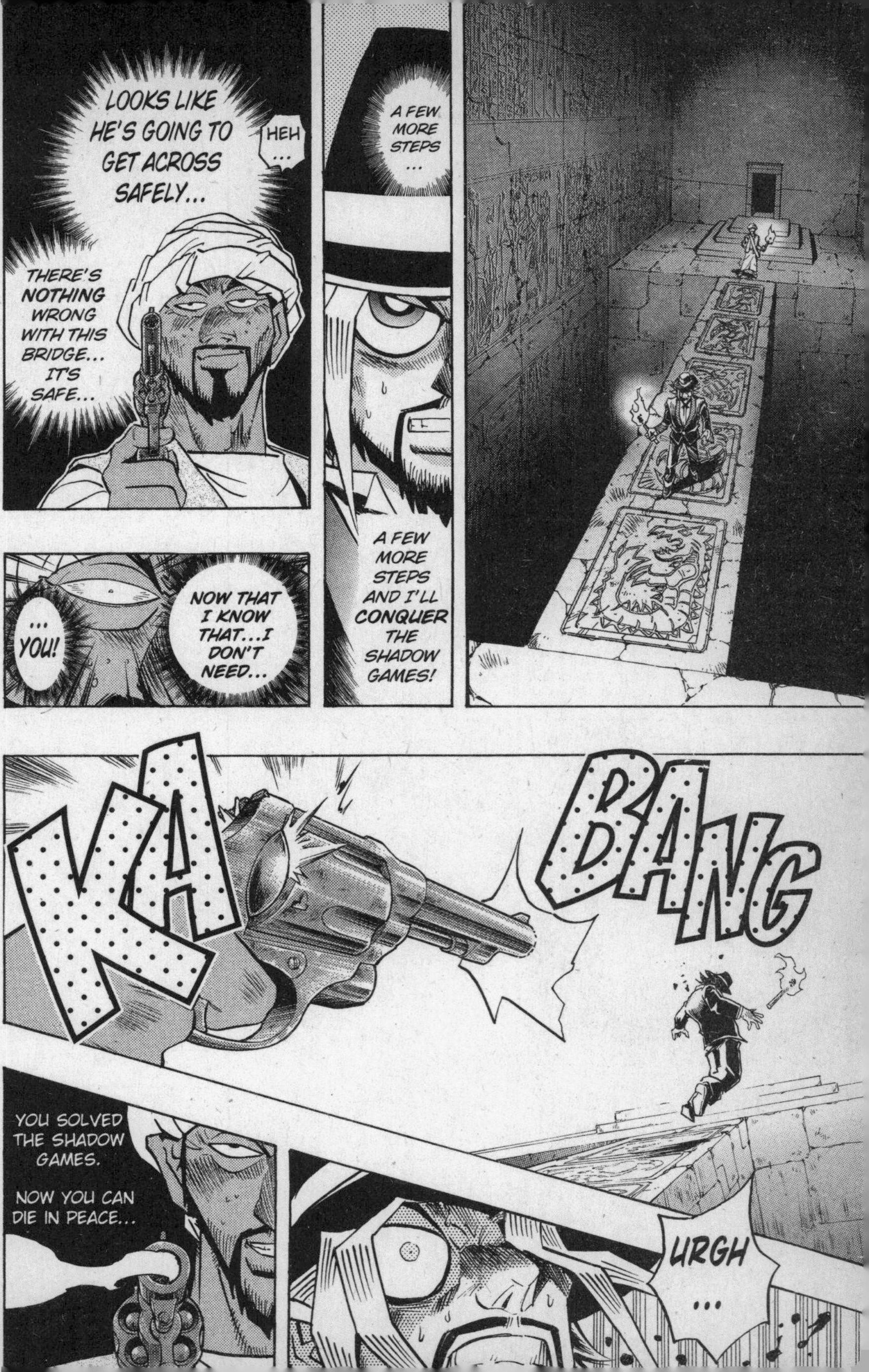
A FEW MORE STEPS ...
A FEW MORE STEPS AND I'LL CONQUER THE SHADOW GAMES!
LOOKS LIKE HE'S GOING TO GET ACROSS SAFELY...
HEH ...
THERE'S NOTHING WRONG WITH THIS BRIDGE... IT'S SAFE...
NOW THAT I KNOW THAT...I DON'T NEED...
... YOU!
KA
BANG
URGH ...
YOU SOLVED THE SHADOW GAMES.
NOW YOU CAN DIE IN PEACE...

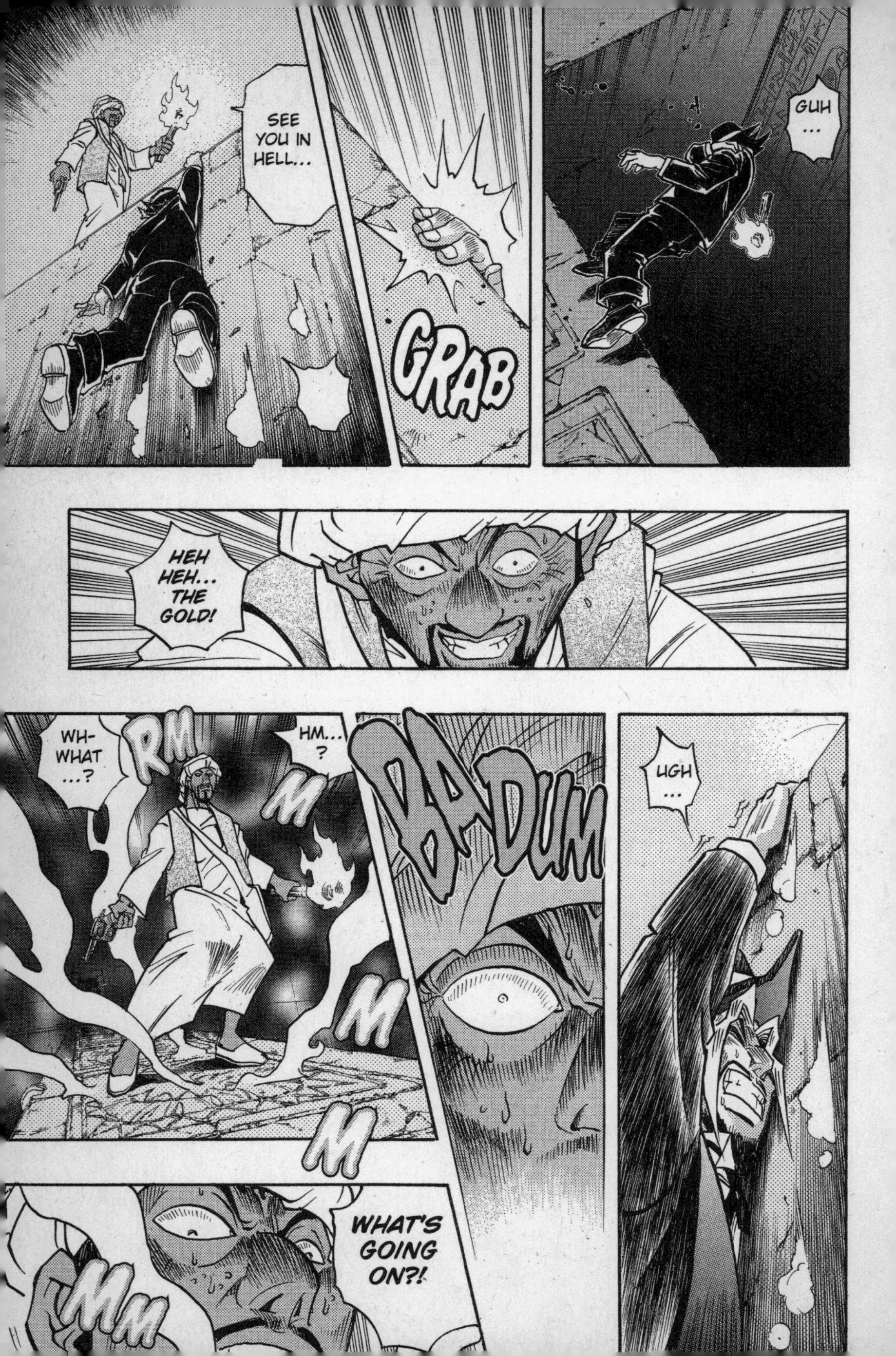
GUH ...
GRAB
SEE YOU IN HELL...
HEH HEH... THE GOLD!
UGH ...
BADUM
HM... ?
RM M M M
WH- WHAT ...?
M
WHAT'S GOING ON?!
MM

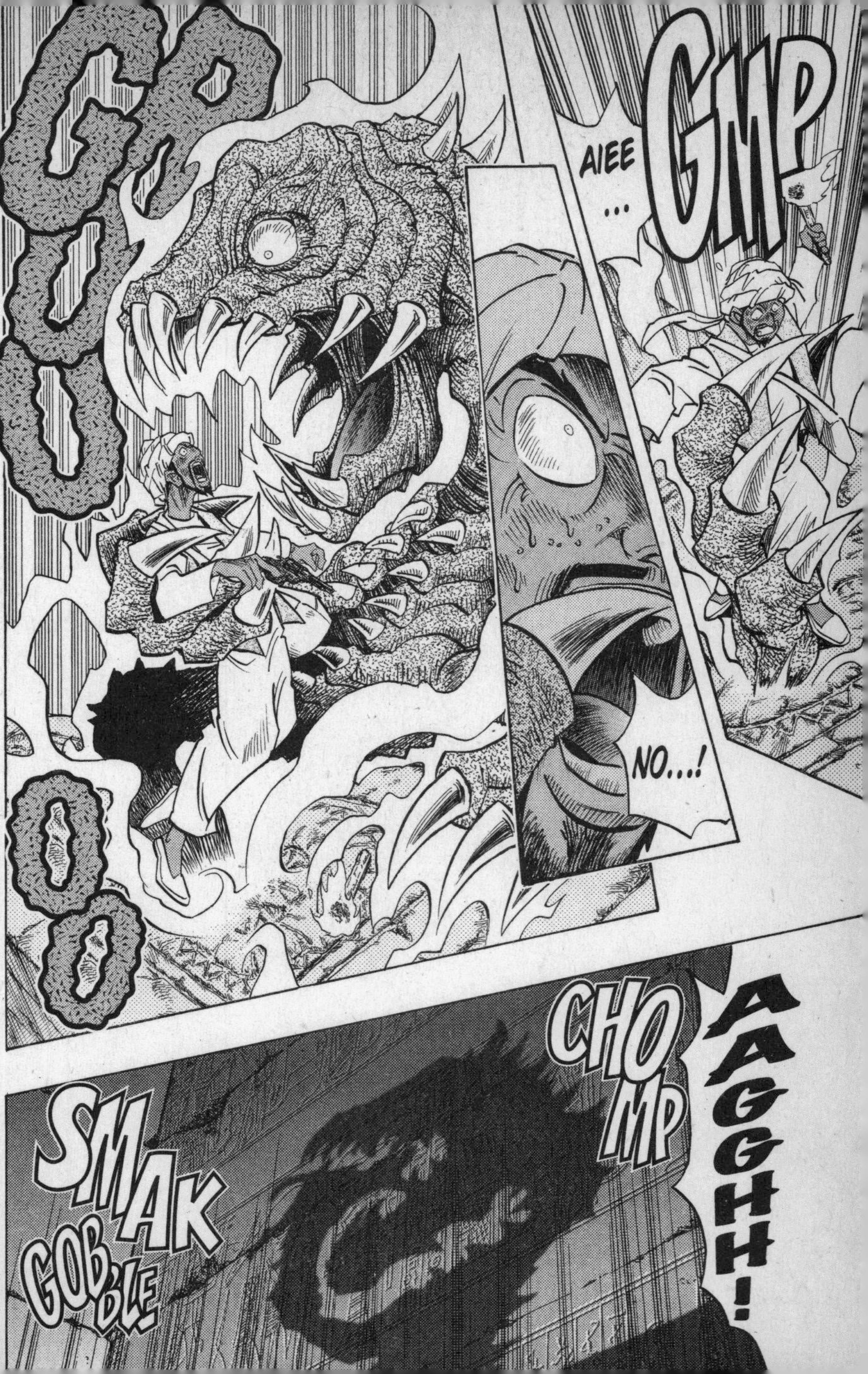
AIEE ...
GMP
NO...!
GOOOO
AAGGHH!
CHOMP
SMAK
GOBBLE

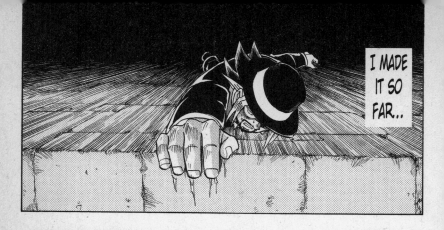

I MADE IT SO FAR...

......

IS THIS THE END ...?

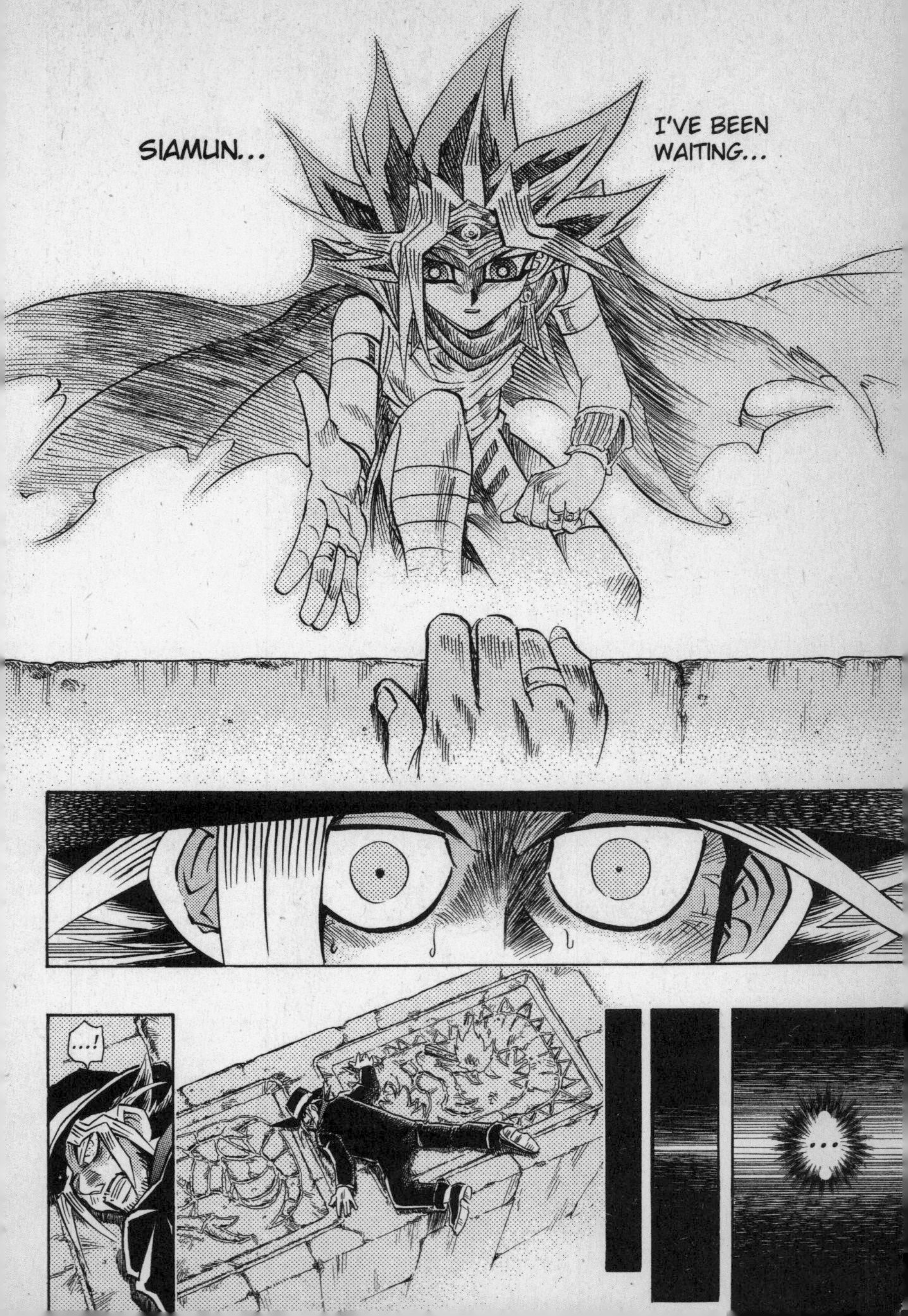
I'VE BEEN WAITING...
SIAMUN...
...
...!

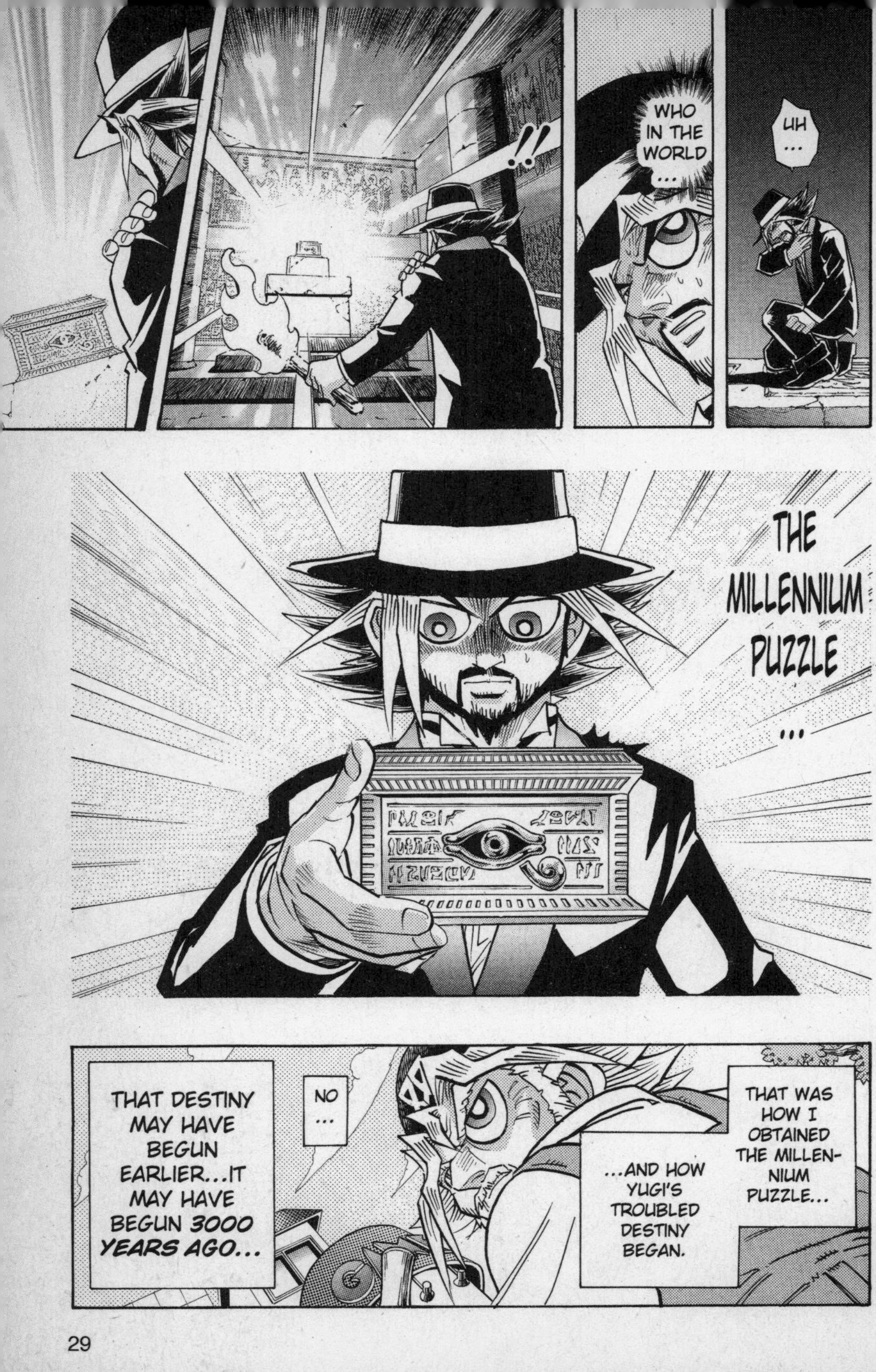
UH ...
WHO IN THE WORLD ...
!!
THE MILLENNIUM PUZZLE ...
THAT WAS HOW I OBTAINED THE MILLEN-NIUM PUZZLE...
...AND HOW YUGI'S TROUBLED DESTINY BEGAN.
NO ...
THAT DESTINY MAY HAVE BEGUN EARLIER...IT MAY HAVE BEGUN 3000 YEARS AGO...

Duel 2: A Sleepless Night

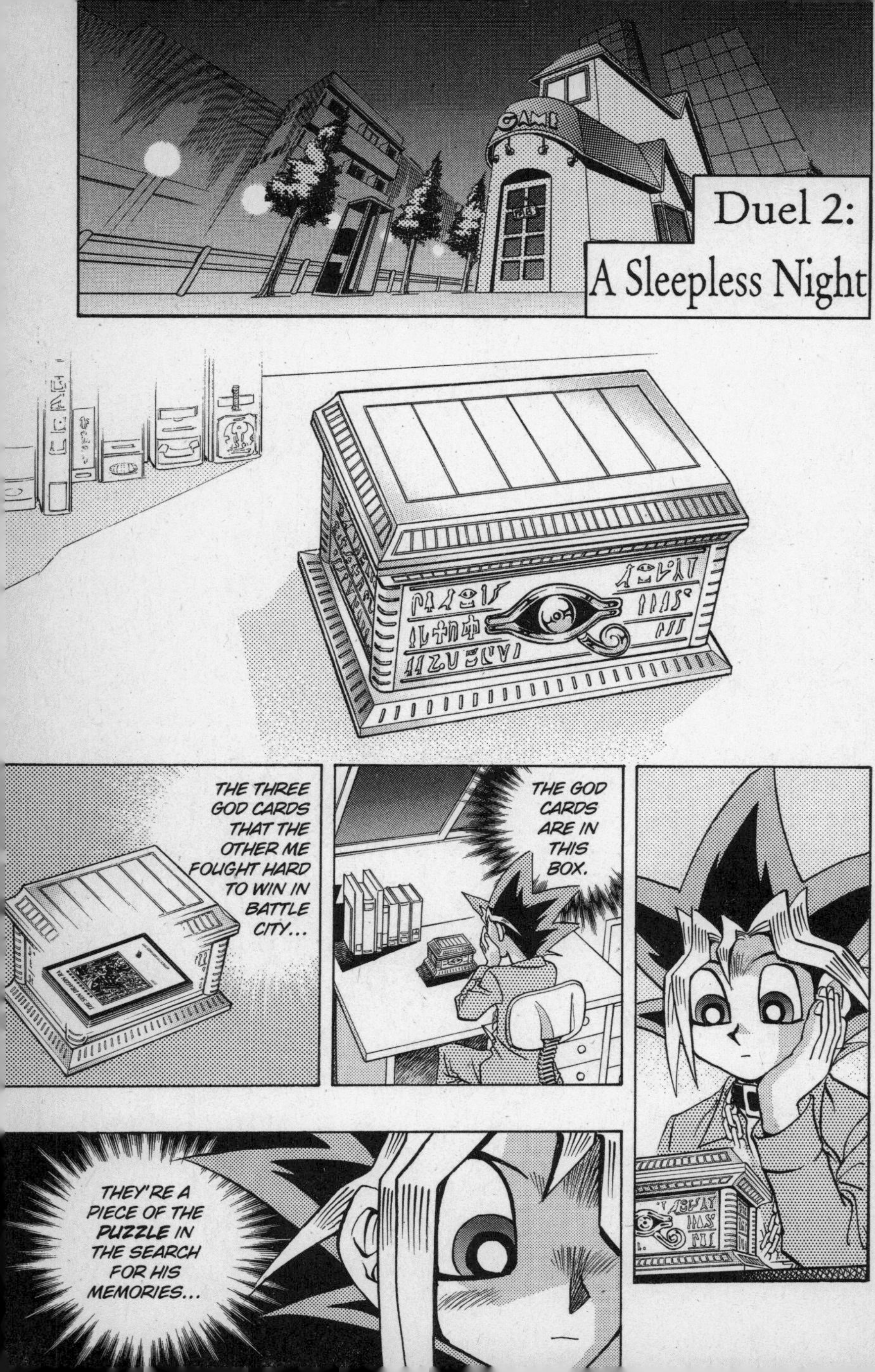
THE GOD CARDS ARE IN THIS BOX.
THE THREE GOD CARDS THAT THE OTHER ME FOUGHT HARD TO WIN IN BATTLE CITY...
THEY'RE A PIECE OF THE PUZZLE IN THE SEARCH FOR HIS MEMORIES...

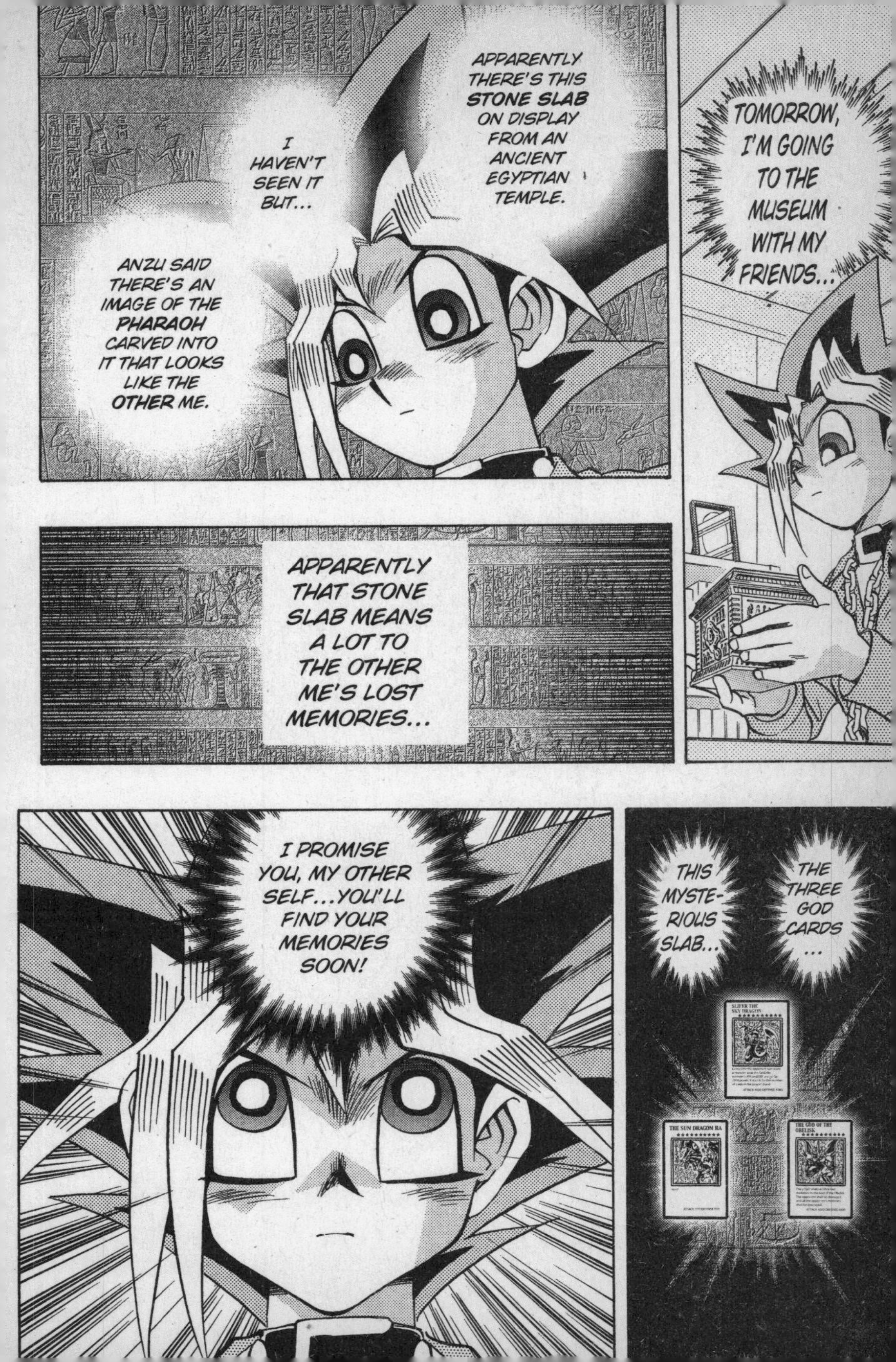
TOMORROW, I'M GOING TO THE MUSEUM WITH MY FRIENDS...
APPARENTLY THERE'S THIS STONE SLAB ON DISPLAY FROM AN ANCIENT EGYPTIAN TEMPLE.
I HAVEN'T SEEN IT BUT...
ANZU SAID THERE'S AN IMAGE OF THE PHARAOH CARVED INTO IT THAT LOOKS LIKE THE OTHER ME.
APPARENTLY THAT STONE SLAB MEANS A LOT TO THE OTHER ME'S LOST MEMORIES...
THE THREE GOD CARDS...
THIS MYSTERIOUS SLAB...
SLIFER THE SKY DRAGON
THE SUN DRAGON RA
THE GOD OF THE OBELISK
I PROMISE YOU, MY OTHER SELF...YOU'LL FIND YOUR MEMORIES SOON!

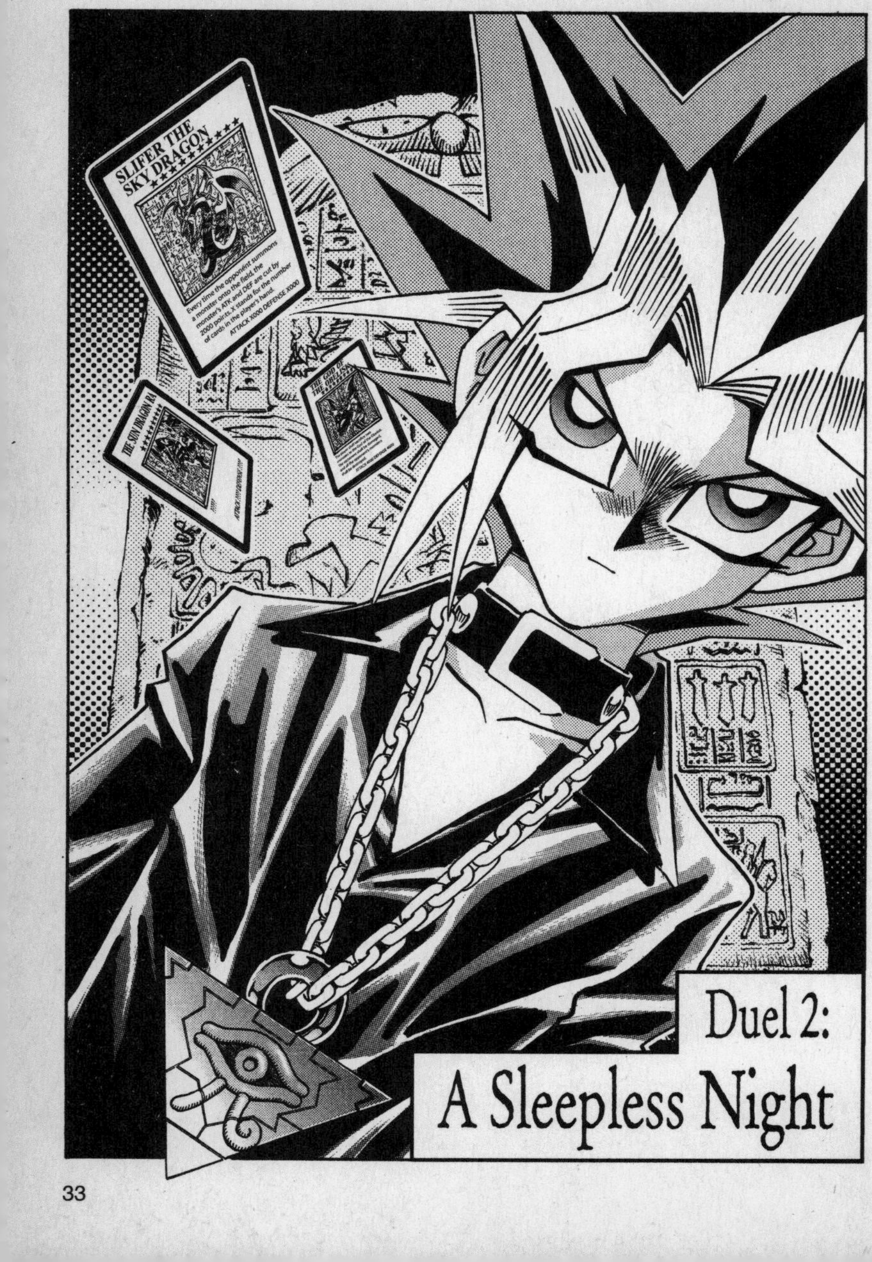
SLIFER THE SKY DRAGON
Every time the opponent summons a monster onto the field, the monster's ATK and DEF are cut by 2000 points. X stands for the number of cards in the player's hand.
ATTACK X000 DEFENSE X000
Duel 2:
A Sleepless Night

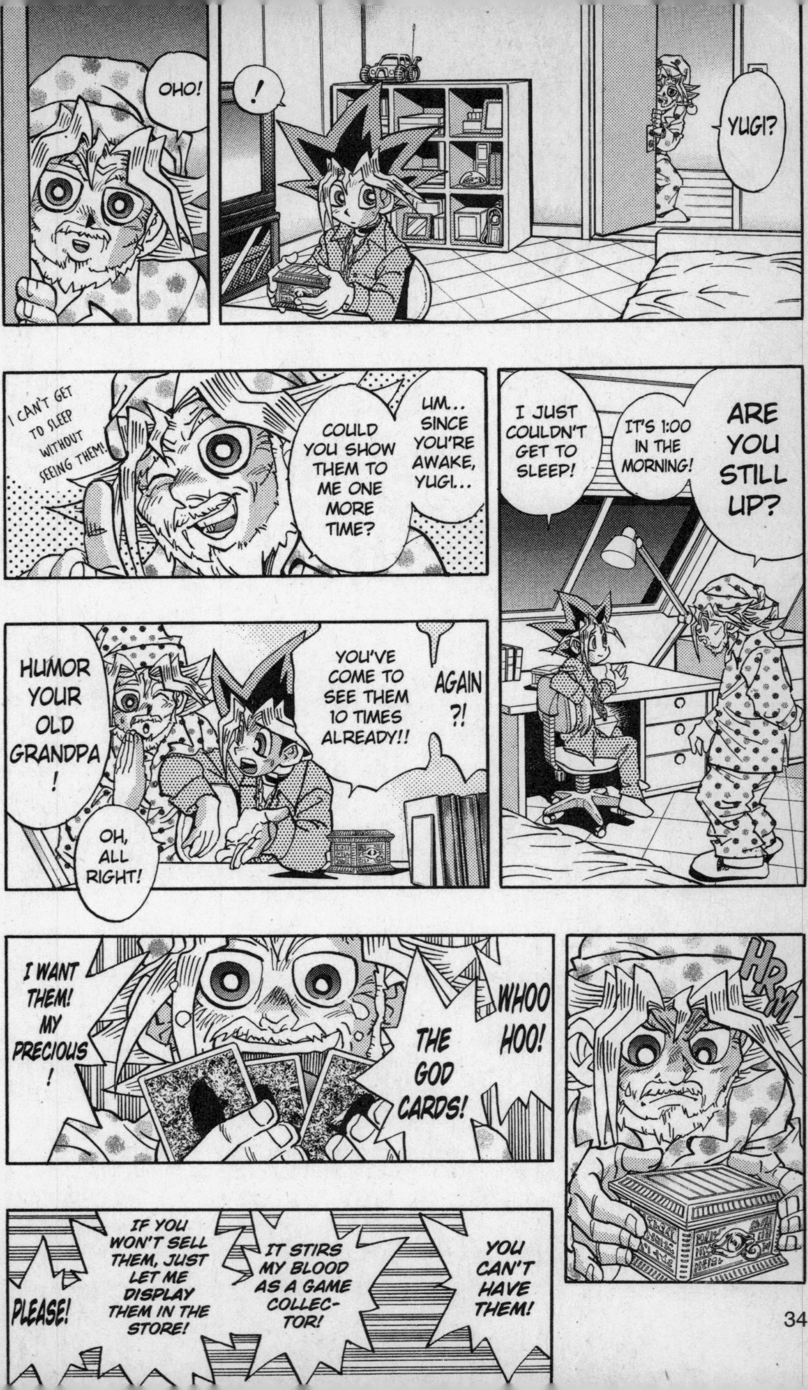
YUGI?
!
OHO!
ARE YOU STILL UP?
IT'S 1:00 IN THE MORNING!
I JUST COULDN'T GET TO SLEEP!
UM... SINCE YOU'RE AWAKE, YUGI...
COULD YOU SHOW THEM TO ME ONE MORE TIME?
I CAN'T GET TO SLEEP WITHOUT SEEING THEM!
AGAIN?!
YOU'VE COME TO SEE THEM 10 TIMES ALREADY!!
HUMOR YOUR OLD GRANDPA!
OH, ALL RIGHT!
HRM
WHOO HOO!
THE GOD CARDS!
I WANT THEM! MY PRECIOUS!
YOU CAN'T HAVE THEM!
IT STIRS MY BLOOD AS A GAME COLLECTOR!
IF YOU WON'T SELL THEM, JUST LET ME DISPLAY THEM IN THE STORE!
PLEASE!

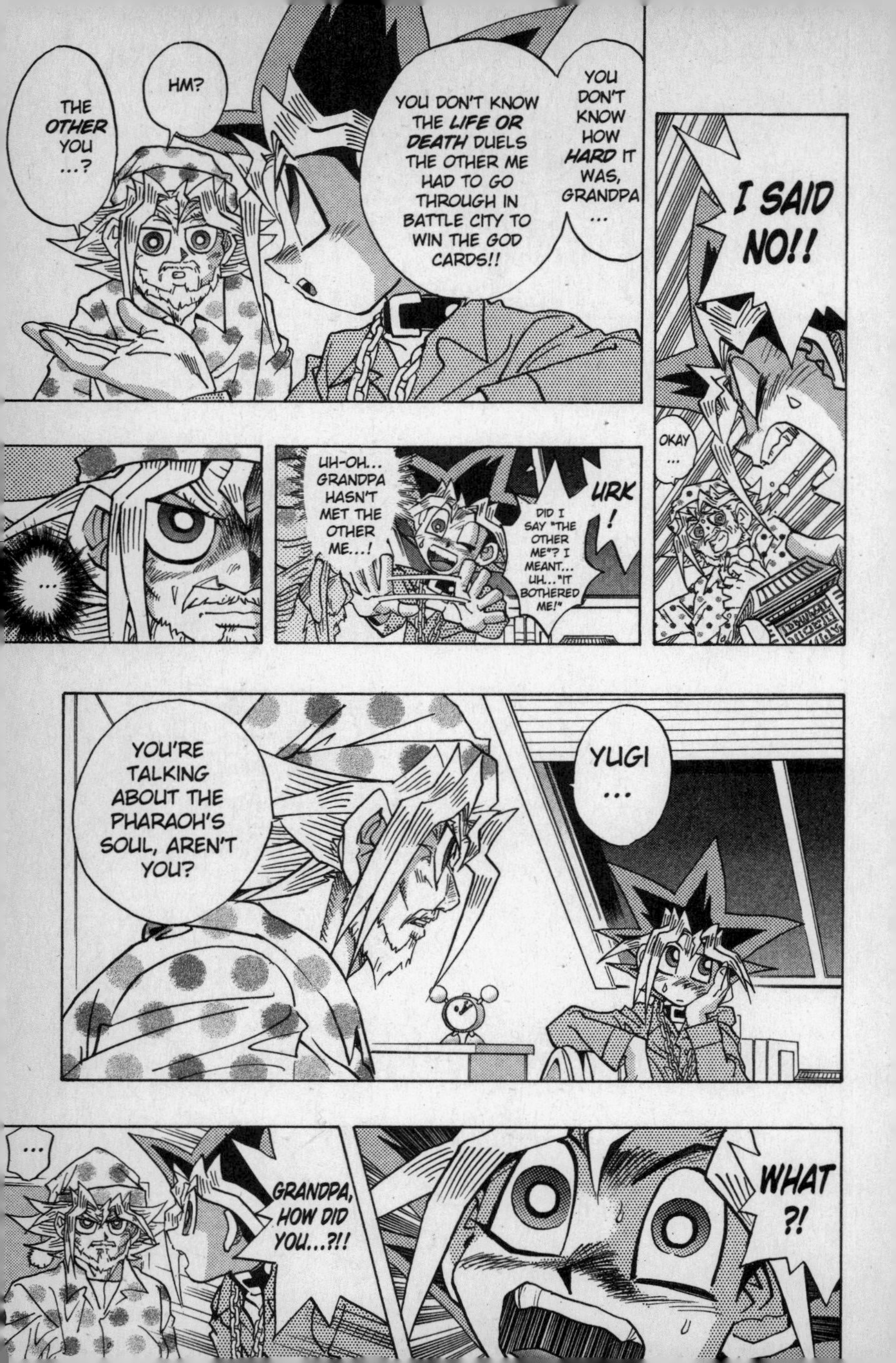
I SAID NO!!
OKAY ...
YOU DON'T KNOW HOW HARD IT WAS, GRANDPA ...
YOU DON'T KNOW THE LIFE OR DEATH DUELS THE OTHER ME HAD TO GO THROUGH IN BATTLE CITY TO WIN THE GOD CARDS!!
HM?
THE OTHER YOU ...?
URK !
DID I SAY "THE OTHER ME"? I MEANT... UH..."IT BOTHERED ME!"
UH-OH... GRANDPA HASN'T MET THE OTHER ME...!
...
YUGI ...
YOU'RE TALKING ABOUT THE PHARAOH'S SOUL, AREN'T YOU?
WHAT ?!
GRANDPA, HOW DID YOU...?!!
...

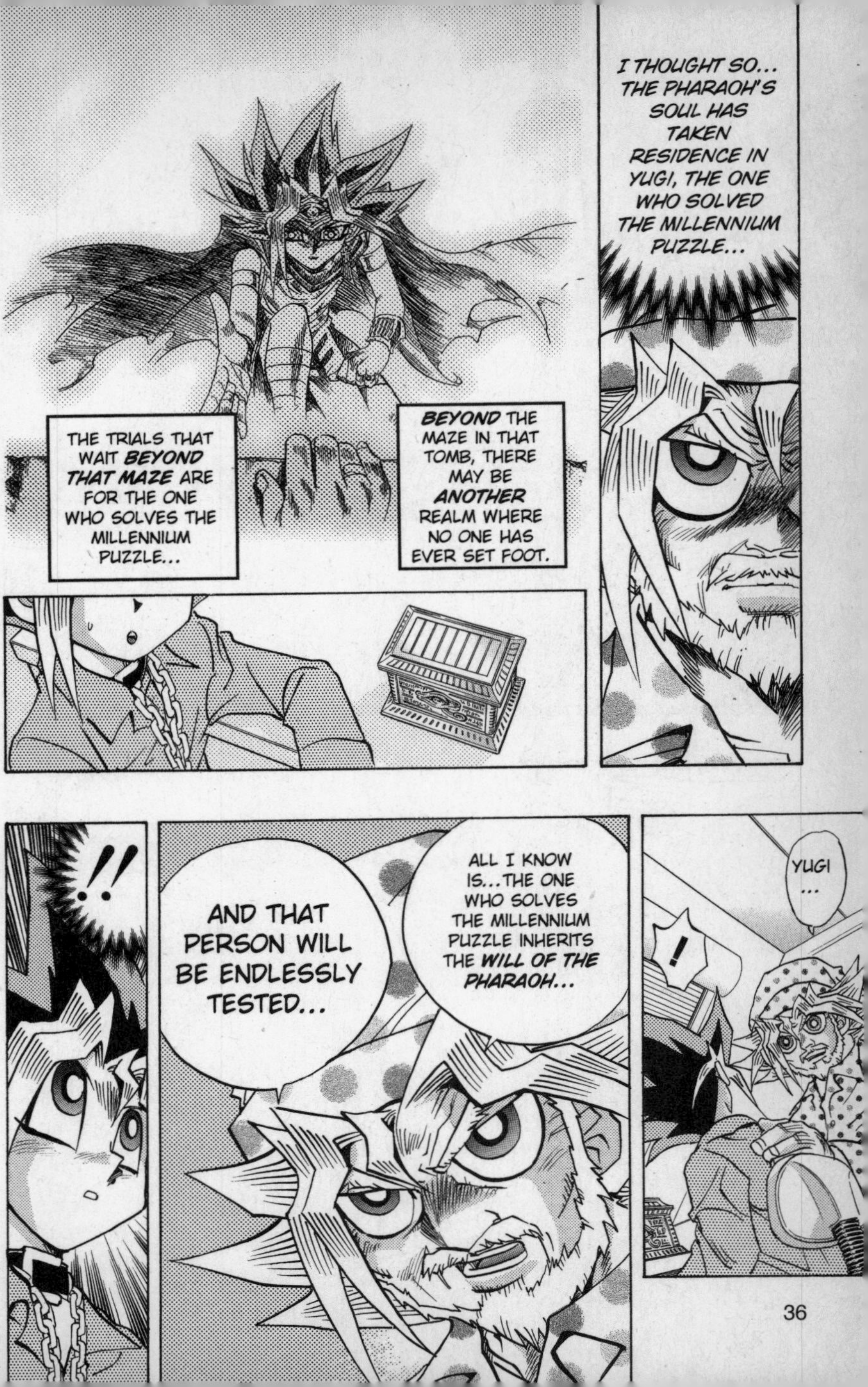
I THOUGHT SO... THE PHARAOH'S SOUL HAS TAKEN RESIDENCE IN YUGI, THE ONE WHO SOLVED THE MILLENNIUM PUZZLE...
BEYOND THE MAZE IN THAT TOMB, THERE MAY BE ANOTHER REALM WHERE NO ONE HAS EVER SET FOOT.
THE TRIALS THAT WAIT BEYOND THAT MAZE ARE FOR THE ONE WHO SOLVES THE MILLENNIUM PUZZLE...
YUGI ...
!
ALL I KNOW IS...THE ONE WHO SOLVES THE MILLENNIUM PUZZLE INHERITS THE WILL OF THE PHARAOH...
AND THAT PERSON WILL BE ENDLESSLY TESTED...
!!

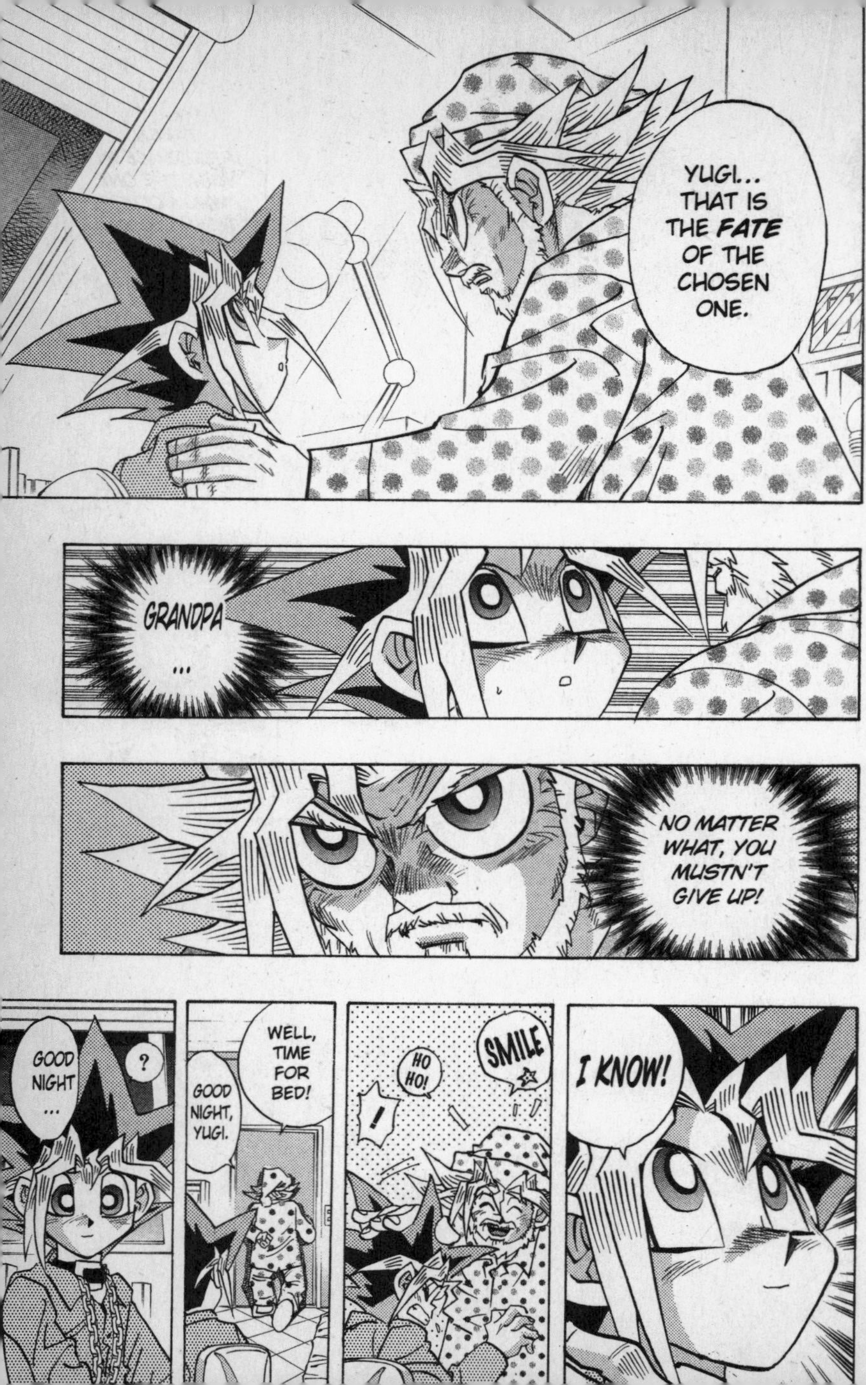
YUGI... THAT IS THE ***FATE*** OF THE CHOSEN ONE.
GRANDPA ...
NO MATTER WHAT, YOU MUSTN'T GIVE UP!
I KNOW!
SMILE
HO HO!
!
WELL, TIME FOR BED!
GOOD NIGHT, YUGI.
?
GOOD NIGHT ...

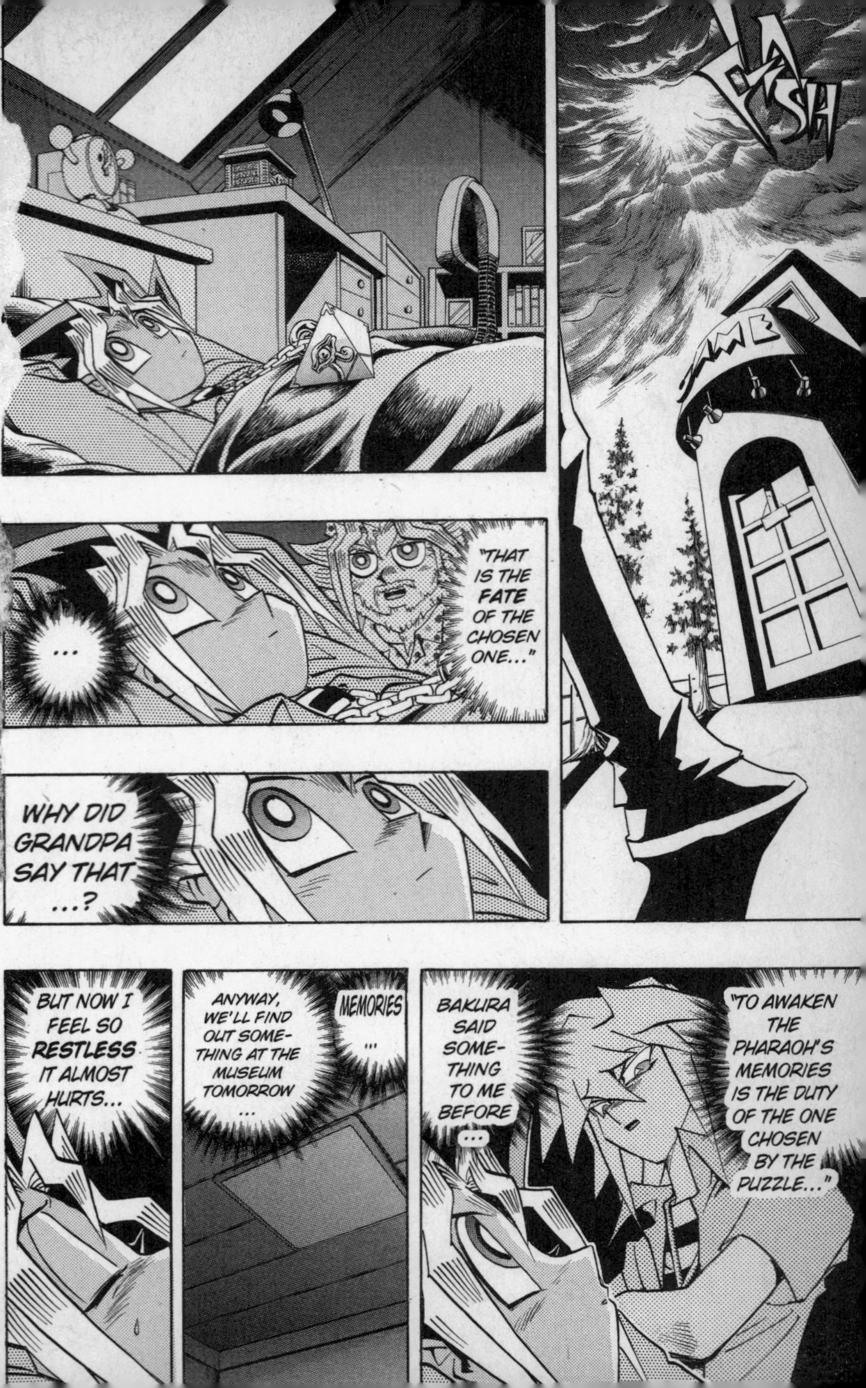
FLASH
"THAT IS THE FATE OF THE CHOSEN ONE..."
...
WHY DID GRANDPA SAY THAT ...?
"TO AWAKEN THE PHARAOH'S MEMORIES IS THE DUTY OF THE ONE CHOSEN BY THE PUZZLE..."
BAKURA SAID SOMETHING TO ME BEFORE ...
MEMORIES ...
ANYWAY, WE'LL FIND OUT SOMETHING AT THE MUSEUM TOMORROW ...
BUT NOW I FEEL SO RESTLESS IT ALMOST HURTS...

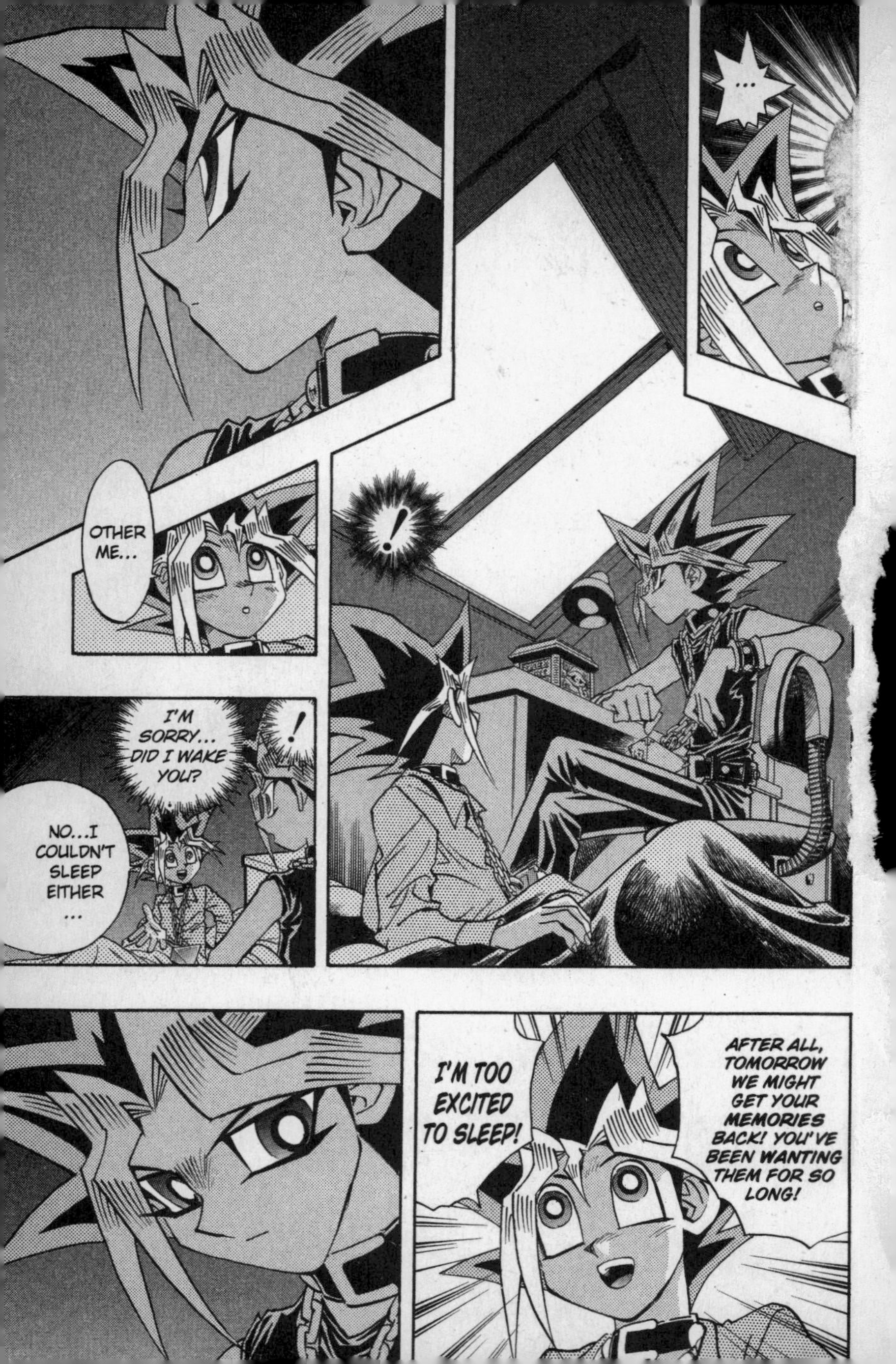
...
!
OTHER ME...
I'M SORRY... DID I WAKE YOU?
!
NO...I COULDN'T SLEEP EITHER...
AFTER ALL, TOMORROW WE MIGHT GET YOUR MEMORIES BACK! YOU'VE BEEN WANTING THEM FOR SO LONG!
I'M TOO EXCITED TO SLEEP!

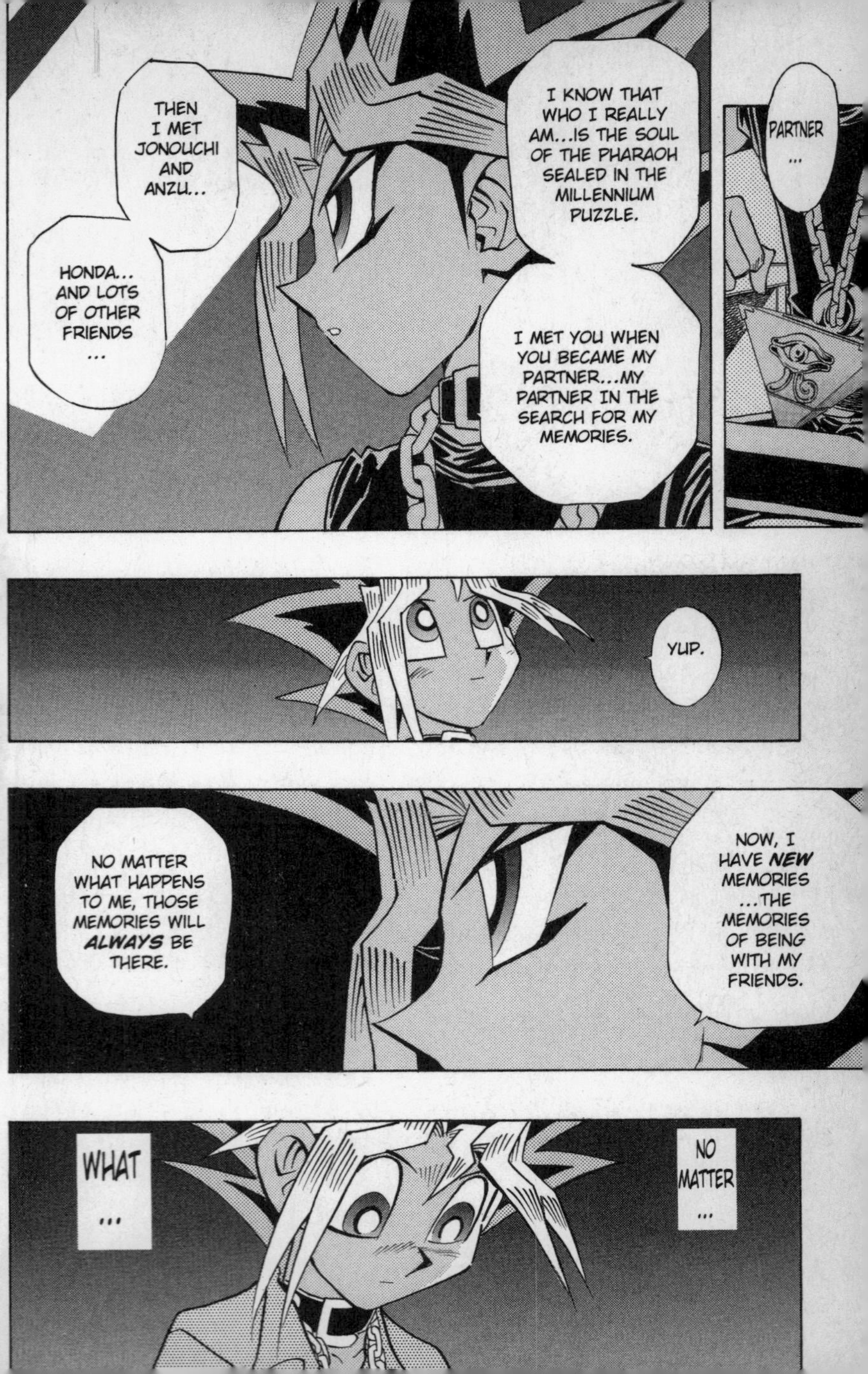
PARTNER ...
I KNOW THAT WHO I REALLY AM...IS THE SOUL OF THE PHARAOH SEALED IN THE MILLENNIUM PUZZLE.
I MET YOU WHEN YOU BECAME MY PARTNER...MY PARTNER IN THE SEARCH FOR MY MEMORIES.
THEN I MET JONOUCHI AND ANZU...
HONDA... AND LOTS OF OTHER FRIENDS ...
YUP.
NOW, I HAVE ***NEW*** MEMORIES ...THE MEMORIES OF BEING WITH MY FRIENDS.
NO MATTER WHAT HAPPENS TO ME, THOSE MEMORIES WILL ***ALWAYS*** BE THERE.
NO MATTER ...
WHAT ...

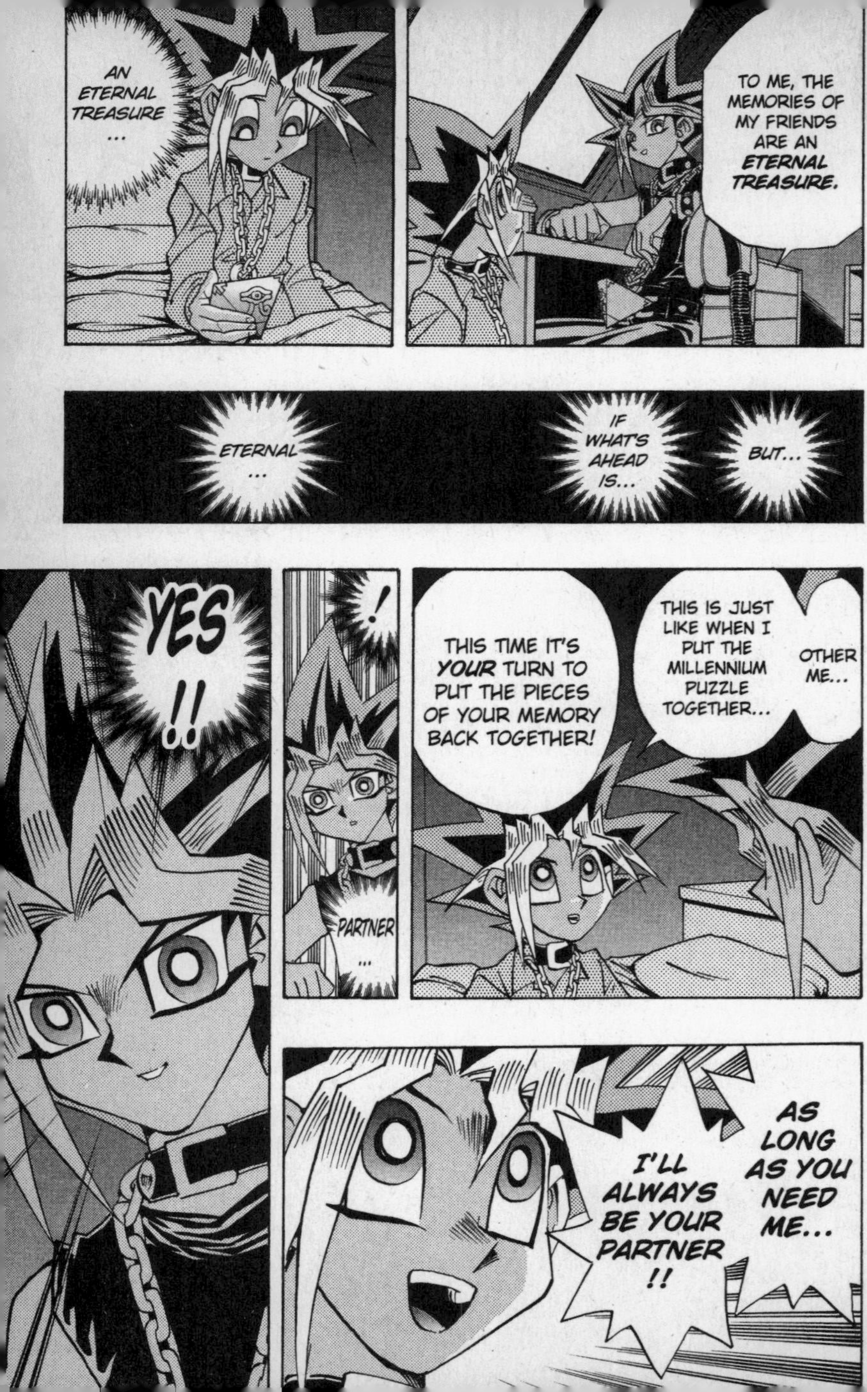
TO ME, THE MEMORIES OF MY FRIENDS ARE AN ETERNAL TREASURE.
AN ETERNAL TREASURE ...
BUT...
IF WHAT'S AHEAD IS...
ETERNAL ...
OTHER ME...
THIS IS JUST LIKE WHEN I PUT THE MILLENNIUM PUZZLE TOGETHER...
THIS TIME IT'S YOUR TURN TO PUT THE PIECES OF YOUR MEMORY BACK TOGETHER!
!
PARTNER ...
AS LONG AS YOU NEED ME...
I'LL ALWAYS BE YOUR PARTNER !!
YES !!

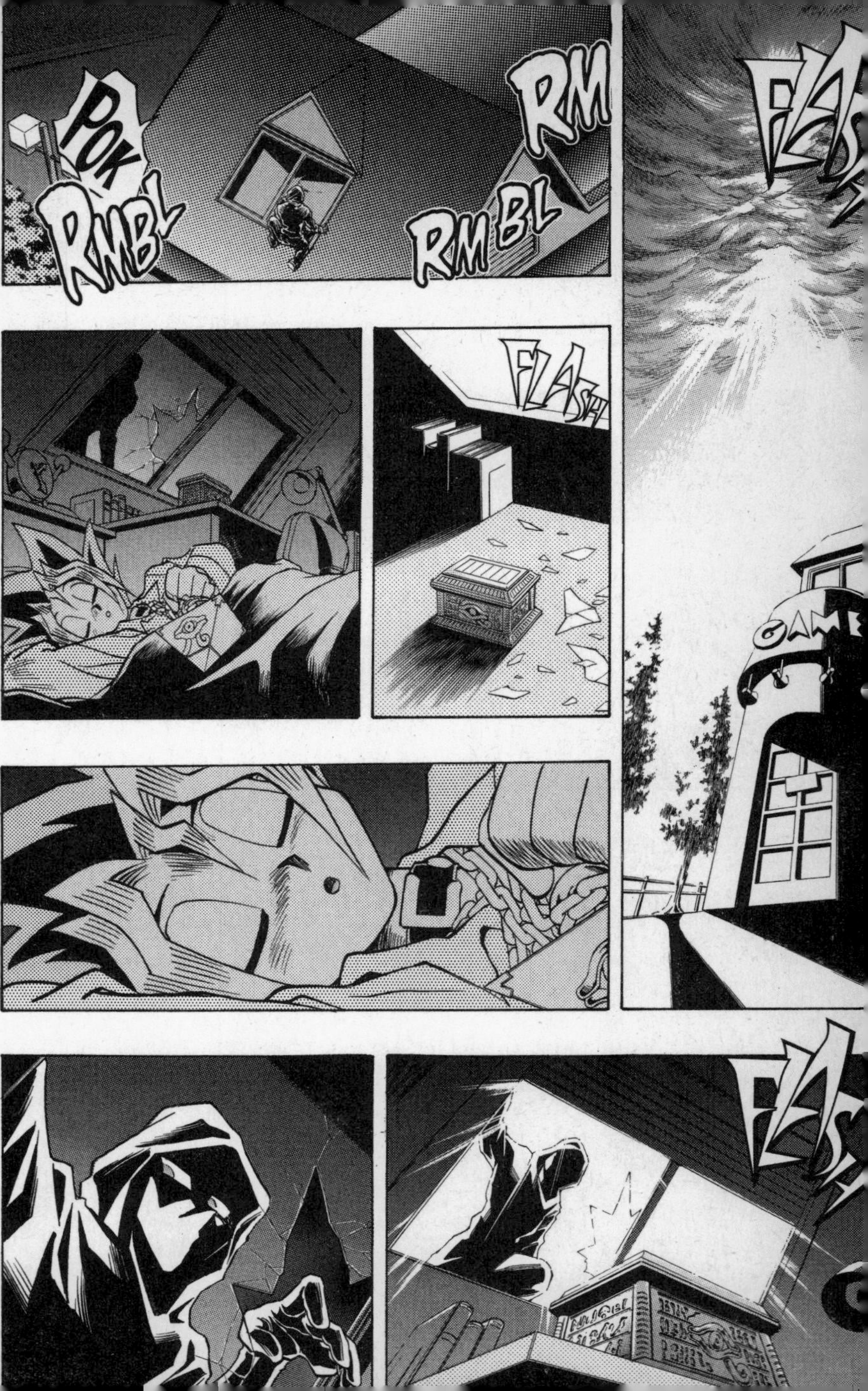
FLASH
RM
RMBL
POK
RMBL
FLASH
FLASH

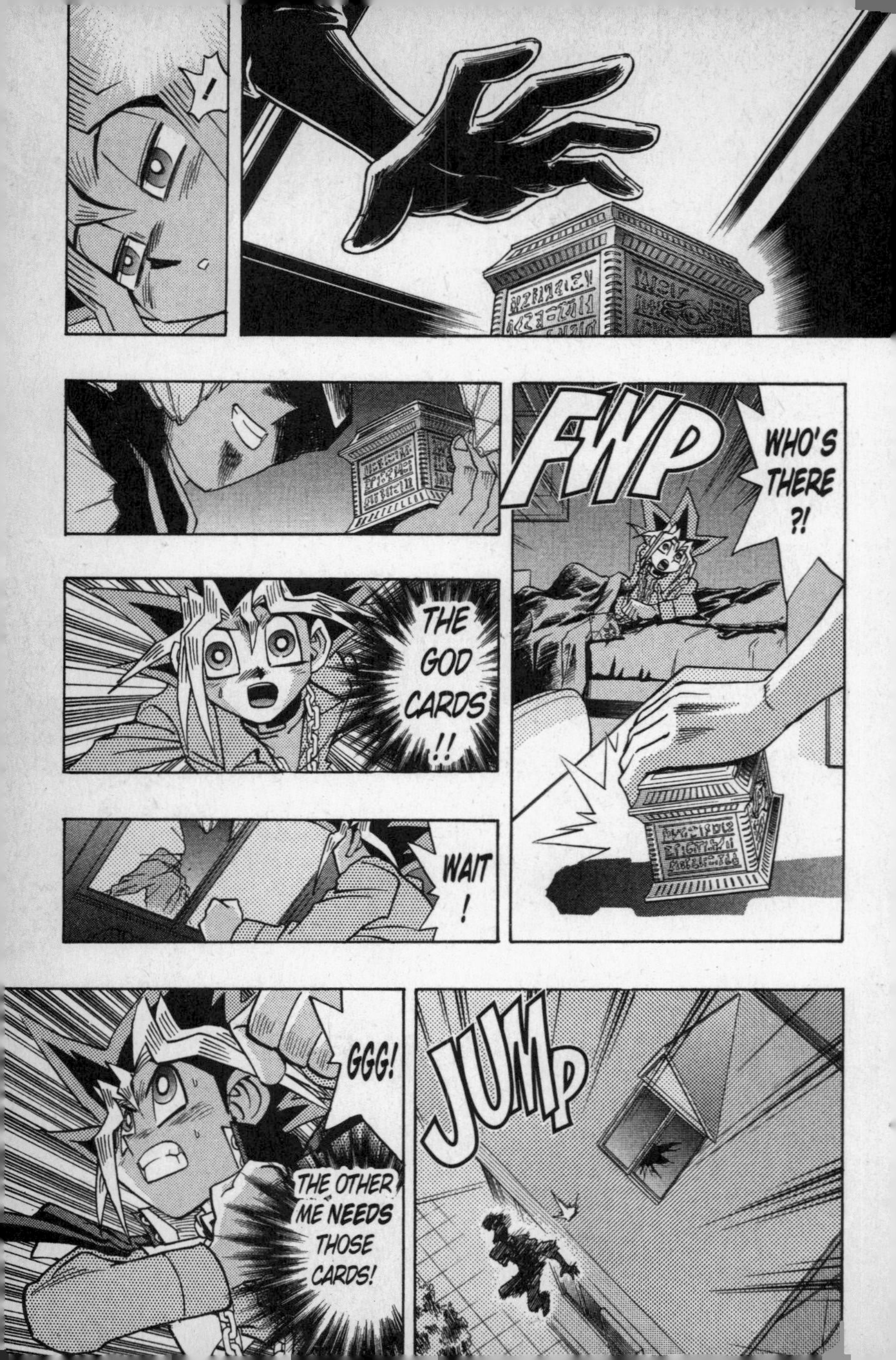
!
FWP
WHO'S THERE ?!
THE GOD CARDS !!
WAIT !
JUMP
GGG!
THE OTHER ME NEEDS THOSE CARDS!

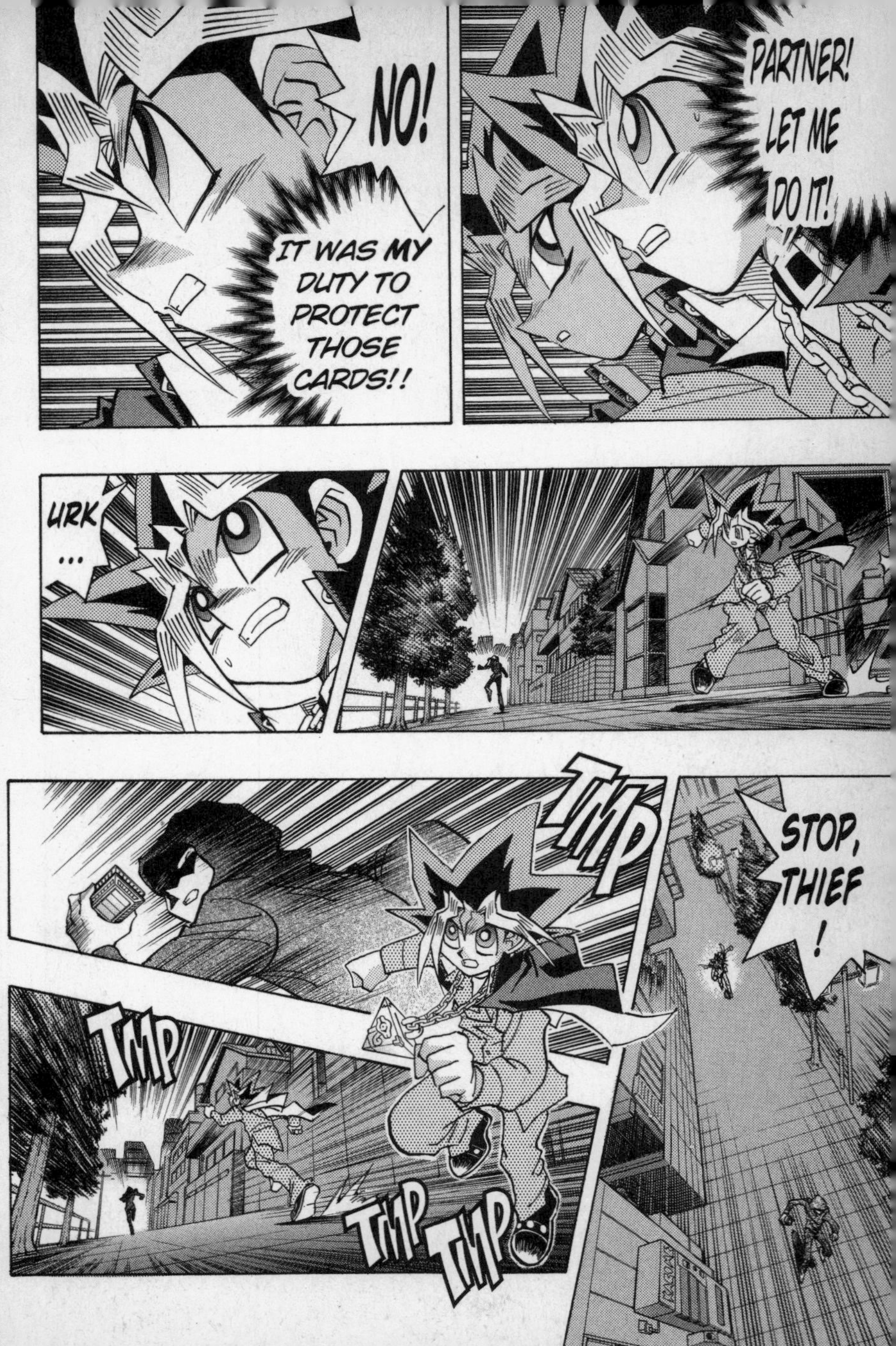
PARTNER! LET ME DO IT!
NO!
IT WAS MY DUTY TO PROTECT THOSE CARDS!!
URK ...
STOP, THIEF !
TMP
TMP
TMP TMP

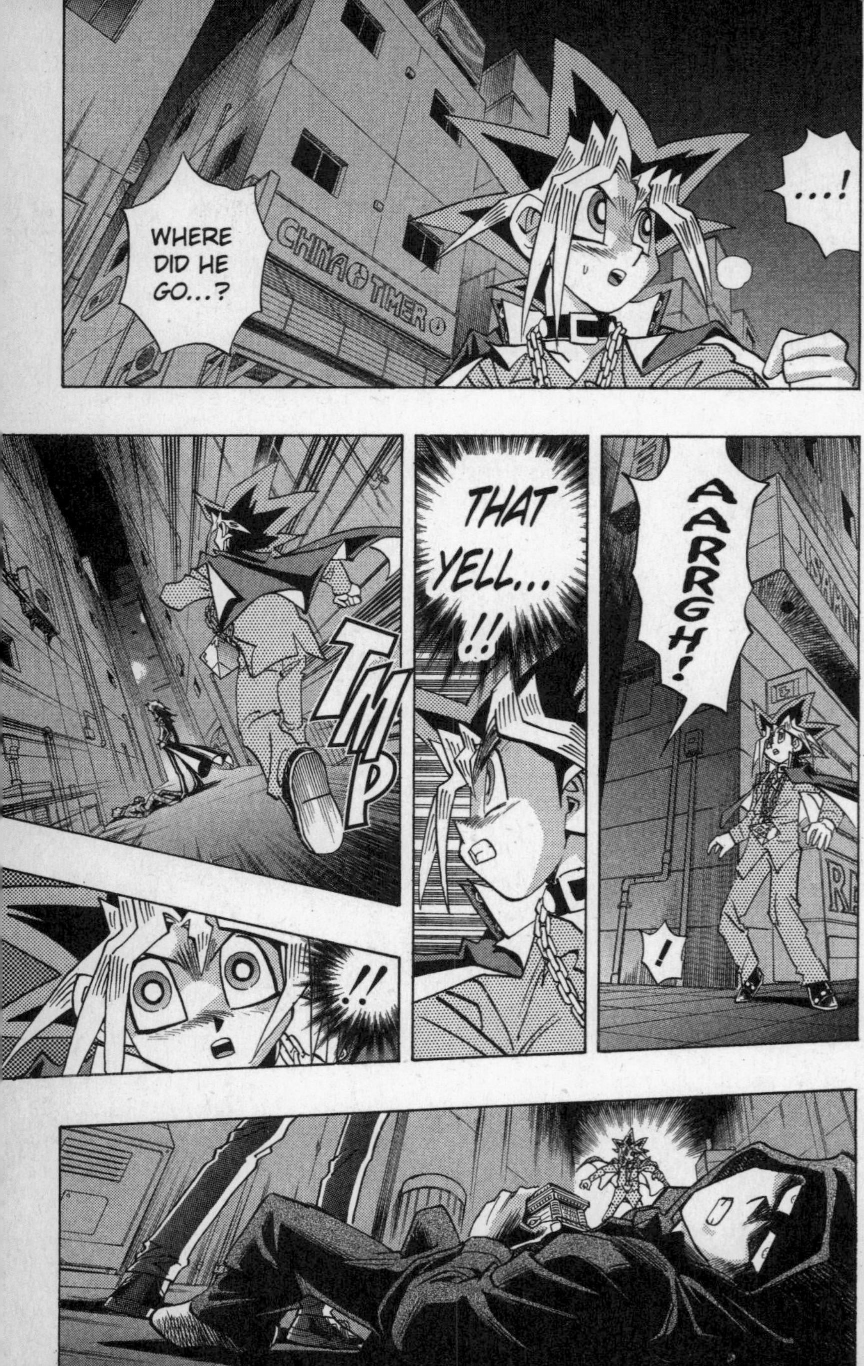
...!
WHERE DID HE GO...?
AARRGH!
!
THAT YELL...!!
TMP
!!

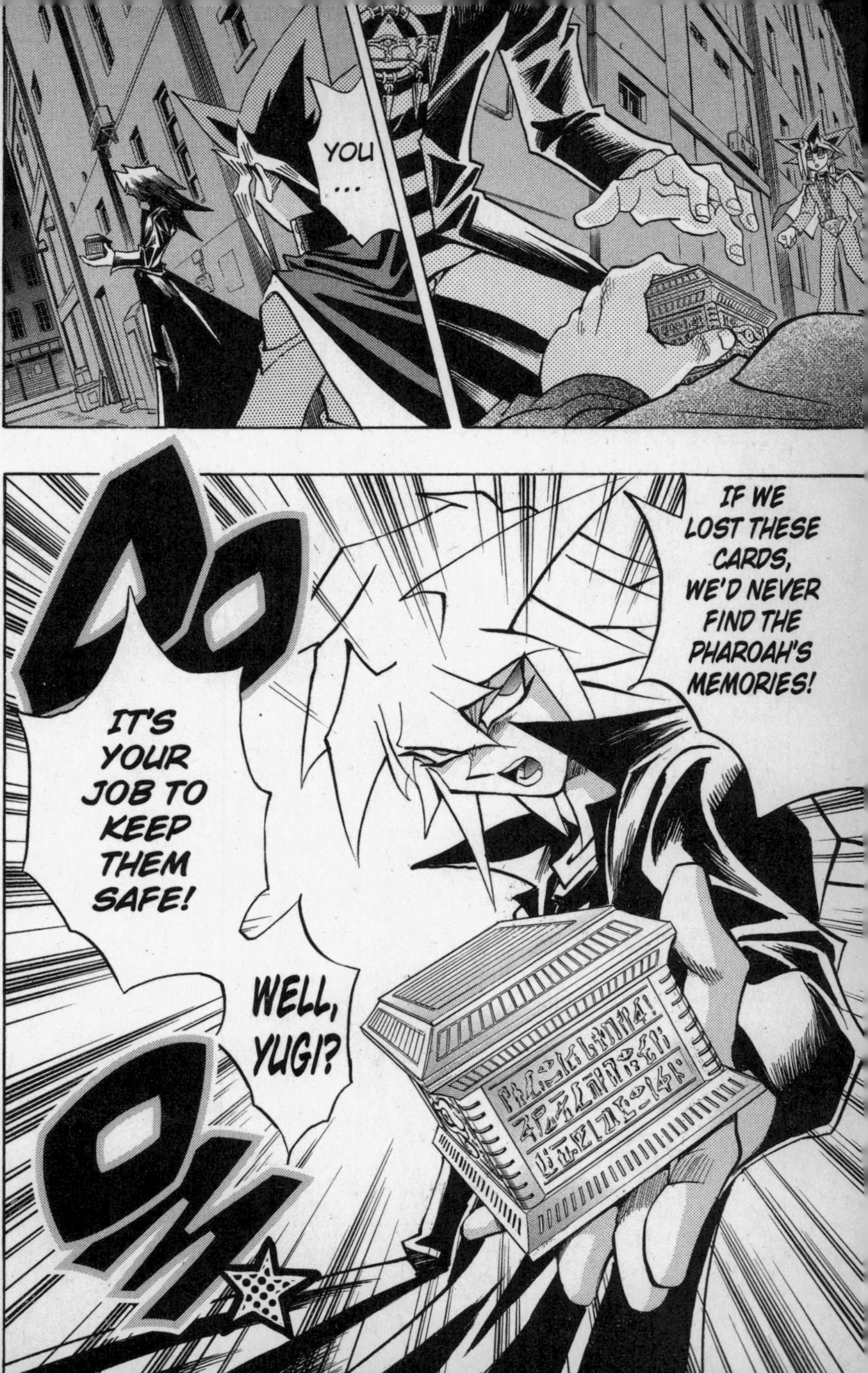
YOU ...
IF WE LOST THESE CARDS, WE'D NEVER FIND THE PHAROAH'S MEMORIES!
IT'S YOUR JOB TO KEEP THEM SAFE!
WELL, YUGI?

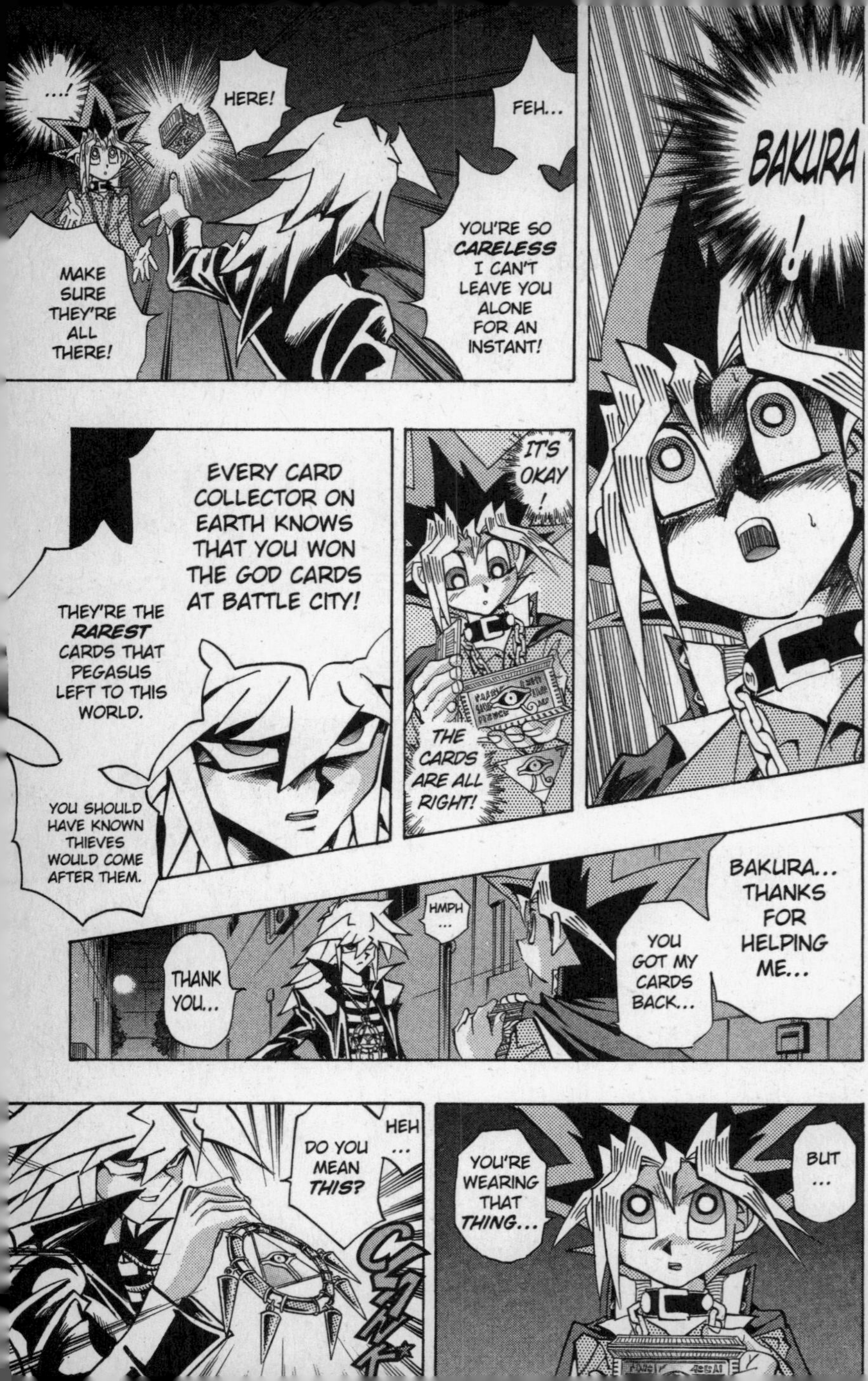
BAKURA!
FEH...
YOU'RE SO *CARELESS* I CAN'T LEAVE YOU ALONE FOR AN INSTANT!
HERE!
...!
MAKE SURE THEY'RE ALL THERE!
IT'S OKAY!
THE CARDS ARE ALL RIGHT!
EVERY CARD COLLECTOR ON EARTH KNOWS THAT YOU WON THE GOD CARDS AT BATTLE CITY!
THEY'RE THE *RAREST* CARDS THAT PEGASUS LEFT TO THIS WORLD.
YOU SHOULD HAVE KNOWN THIEVES WOULD COME AFTER THEM.
BAKURA... THANKS FOR HELPING ME...
YOU GOT MY CARDS BACK...
HMPH...
THANK YOU...
BUT...
YOU'RE WEARING THAT *THING*...
HEH...
DO YOU MEAN *THIS?*
CLINK

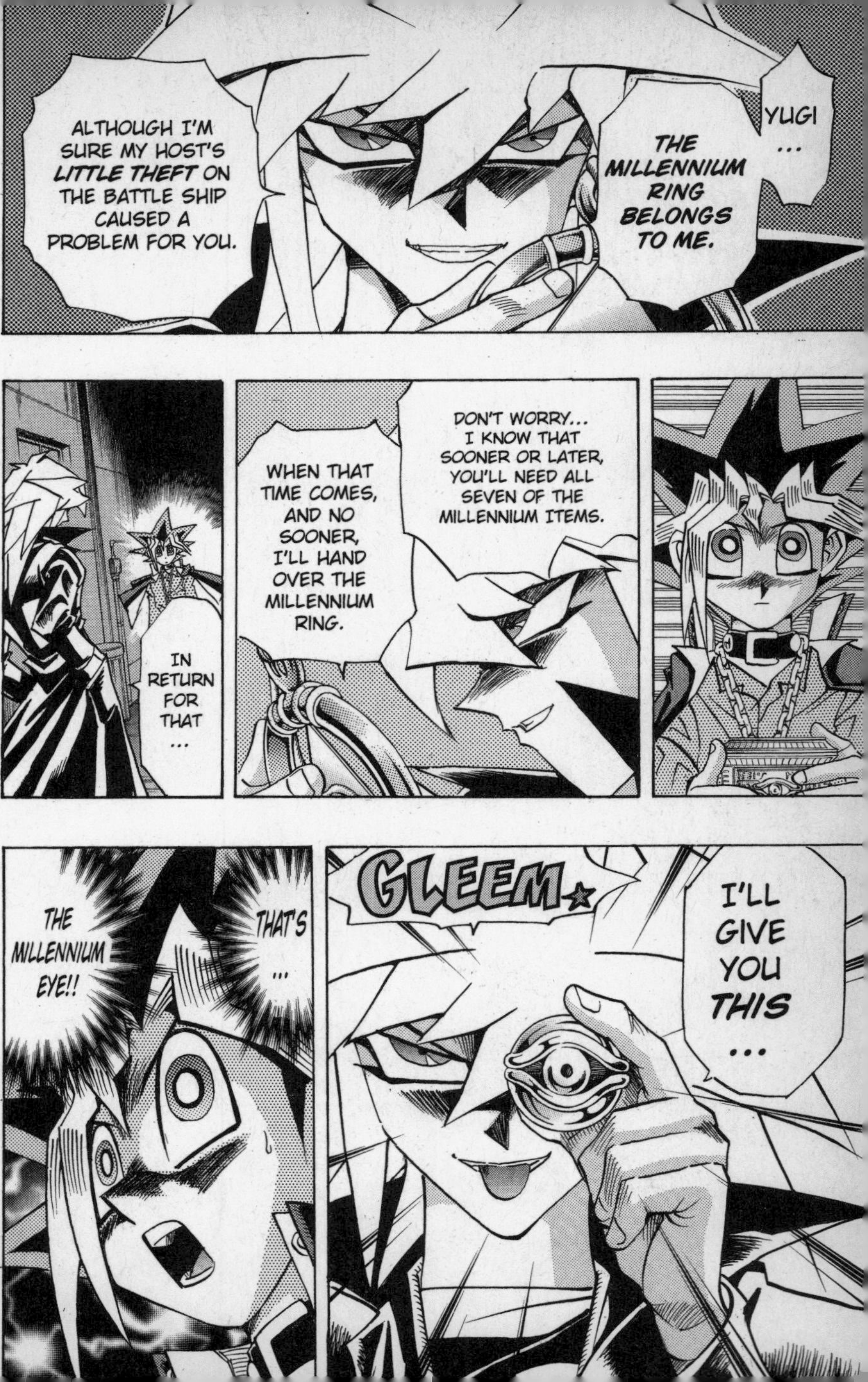
YUGI ...
THE MILLENNIUM RING BELONGS TO ME.
ALTHOUGH I'M SURE MY HOST'S LITTLE THEFT ON THE BATTLE SHIP CAUSED A PROBLEM FOR YOU.
DON'T WORRY... I KNOW THAT SOONER OR LATER, YOU'LL NEED ALL SEVEN OF THE MILLENNIUM ITEMS.
WHEN THAT TIME COMES, AND NO SOONER, I'LL HAND OVER THE MILLENNIUM RING.
IN RETURN FOR THAT ...
I'LL GIVE YOU THIS ...
GLEEM
THAT'S ...
THE MILLENNIUM EYE!!

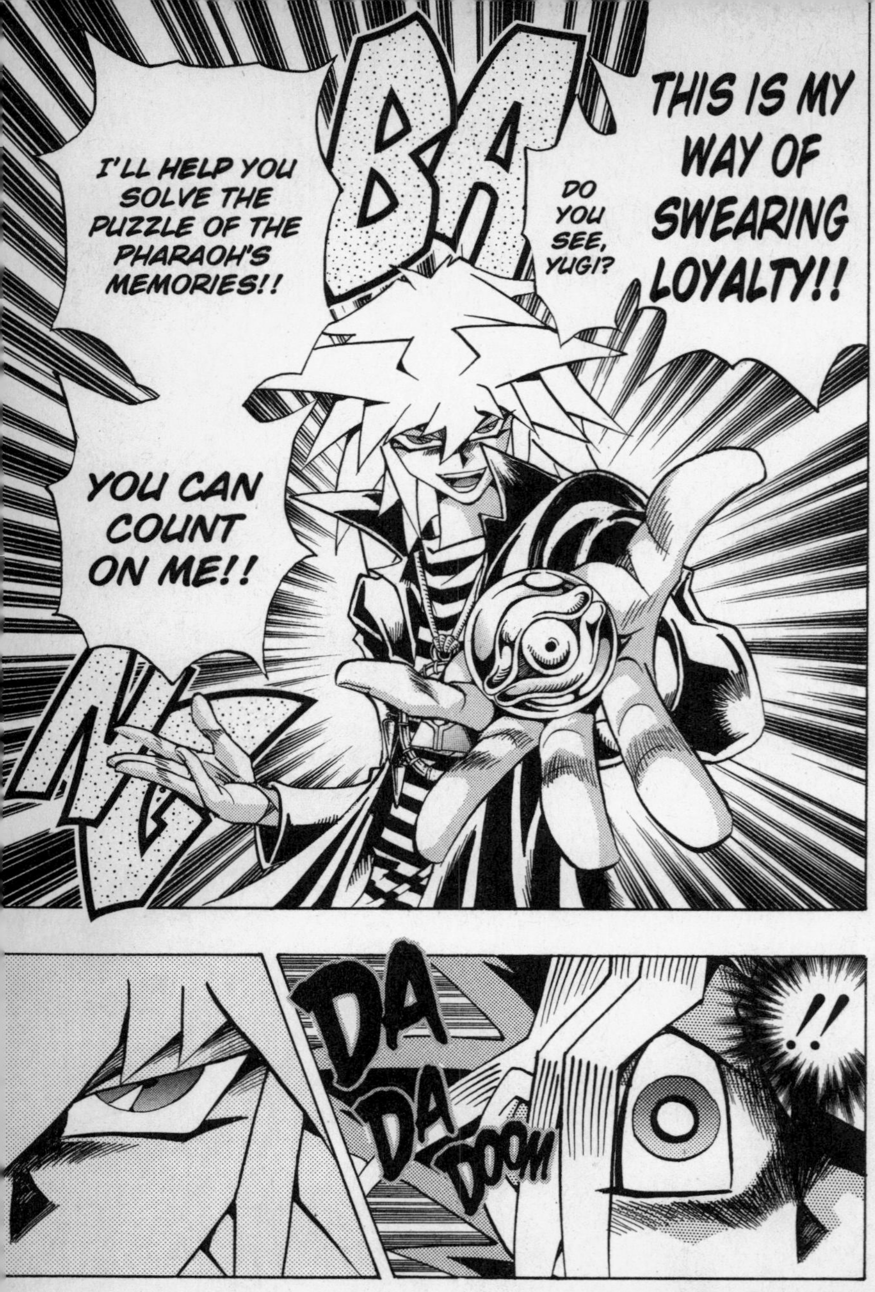
THIS IS MY WAY OF SWEARING LOYALTY!!
BA
DO YOU SEE, YUGI?
I'LL HELP YOU SOLVE THE PUZZLE OF THE PHARAOH'S MEMORIES!!
YOU CAN COUNT ON ME!!
N
!!
DA DA DOOM

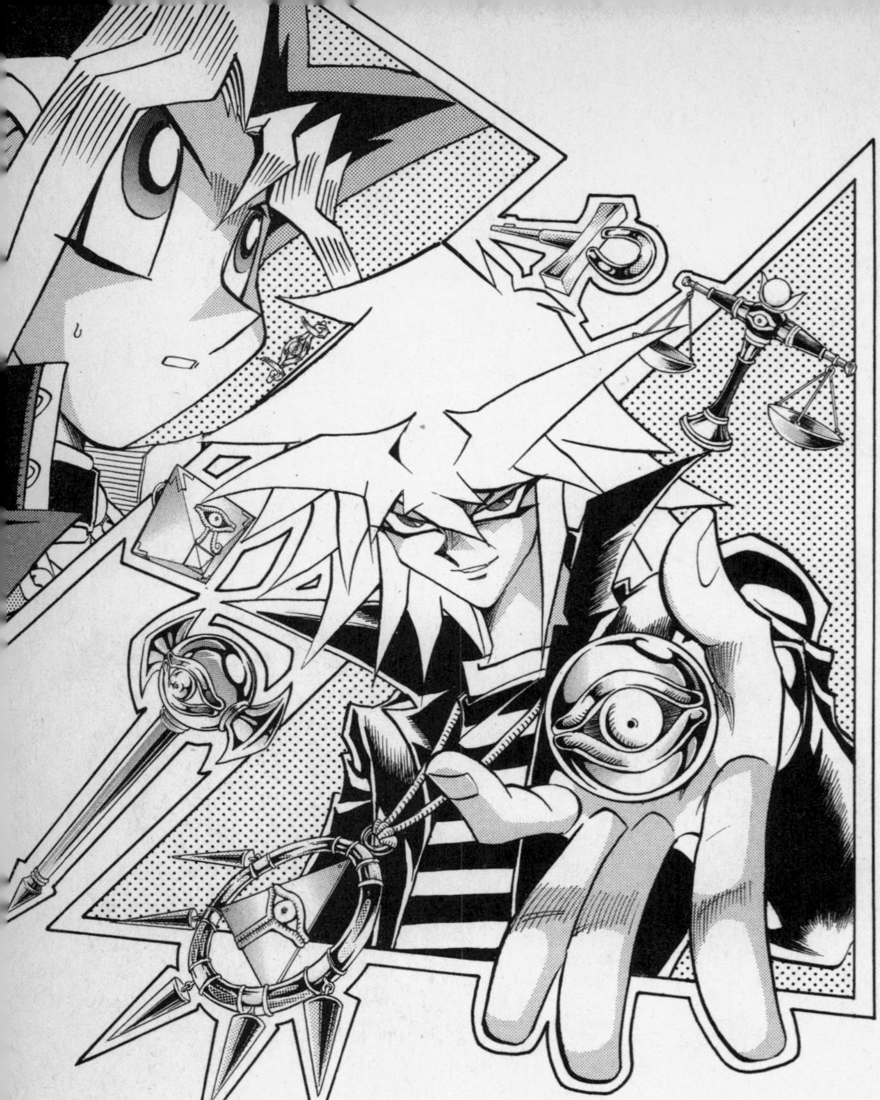

Duel 3: The Truth of the Artifact!!

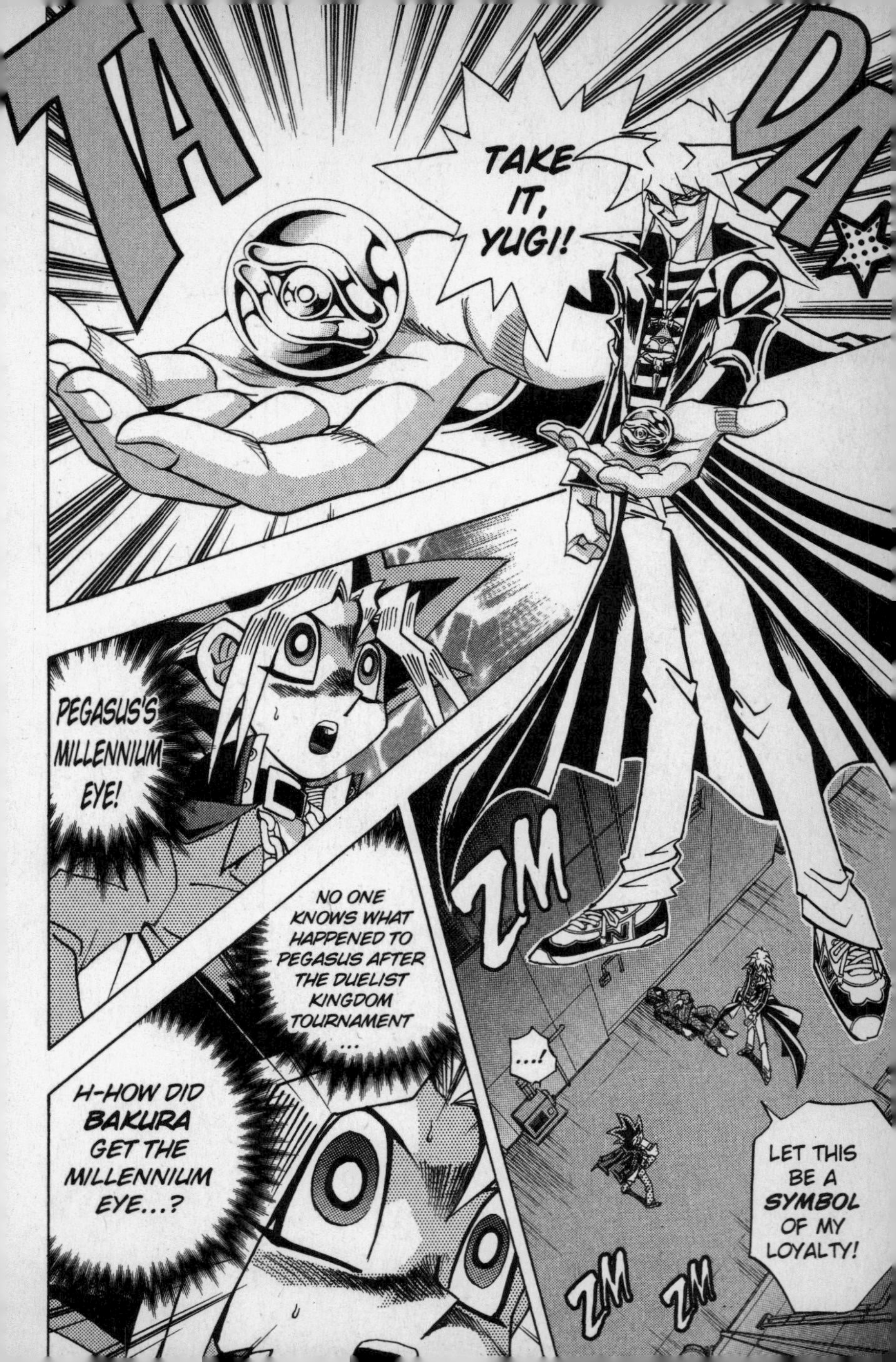
TA
DA
TAKE IT, YUGI!
ZM
...!
LET THIS BE A SYMBOL OF MY LOYALTY!
ZM
ZM
PEGASUS'S MILLENNIUM EYE!
NO ONE KNOWS WHAT HAPPENED TO PEGASUS AFTER THE DUELIST KINGDOM TOURNAMENT ...
H-HOW DID BAKURA GET THE MILLENNIUM EYE...?

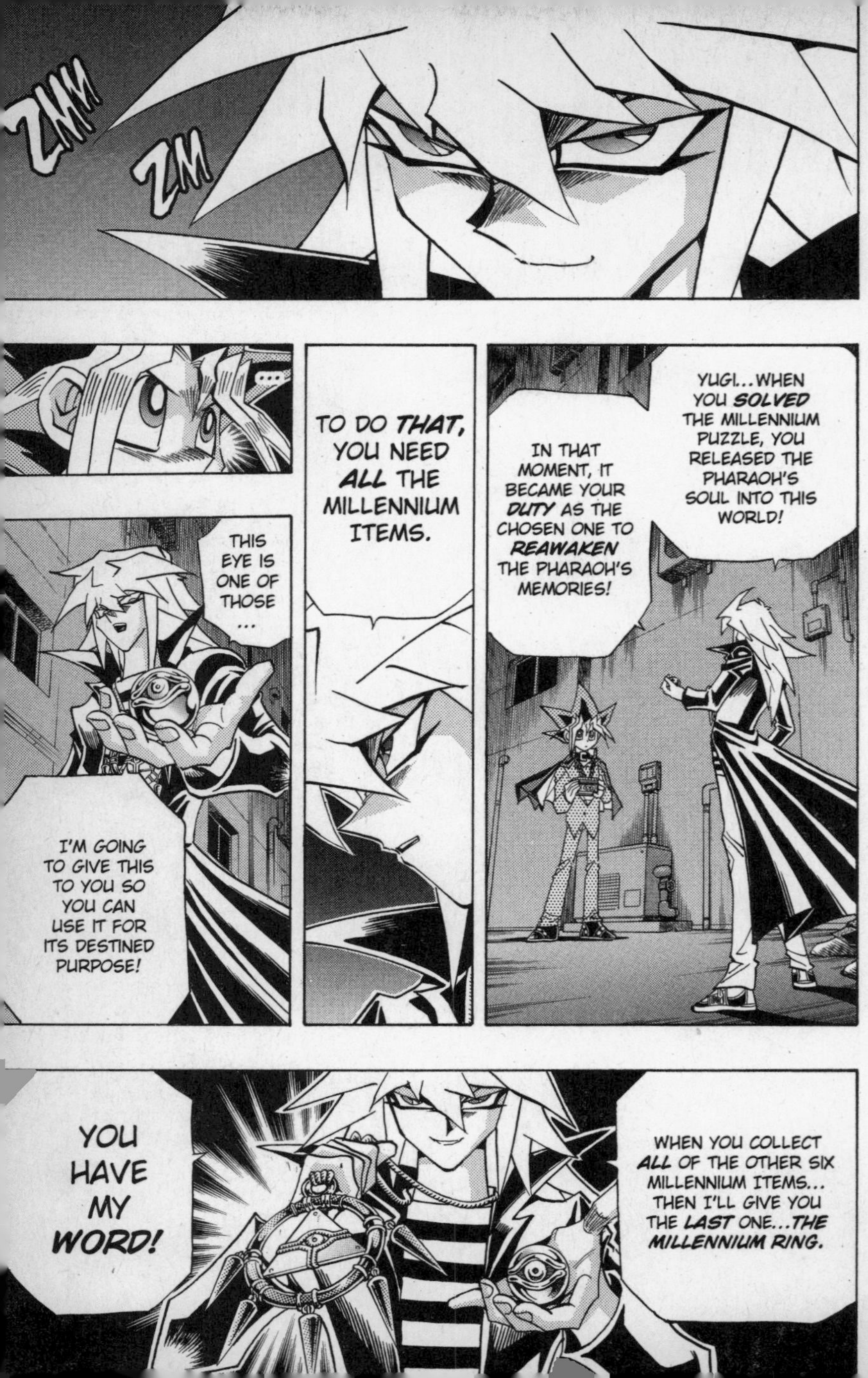
ZMM
ZM
YUGI...WHEN YOU SOLVED THE MILLENNIUM PUZZLE, YOU RELEASED THE PHARAOH'S SOUL INTO THIS WORLD!
IN THAT MOMENT, IT BECAME YOUR DUTY AS THE CHOSEN ONE TO REAWAKEN THE PHARAOH'S MEMORIES!
TO DO THAT, YOU NEED ALL THE MILLENNIUM ITEMS.
...
THIS EYE IS ONE OF THOSE ...
I'M GOING TO GIVE THIS TO YOU SO YOU CAN USE IT FOR ITS DESTINED PURPOSE!
WHEN YOU COLLECT ALL OF THE OTHER SIX MILLENNIUM ITEMS... THEN I'LL GIVE YOU THE LAST ONE...THE MILLENNIUM RING.
YOU HAVE MY WORD!

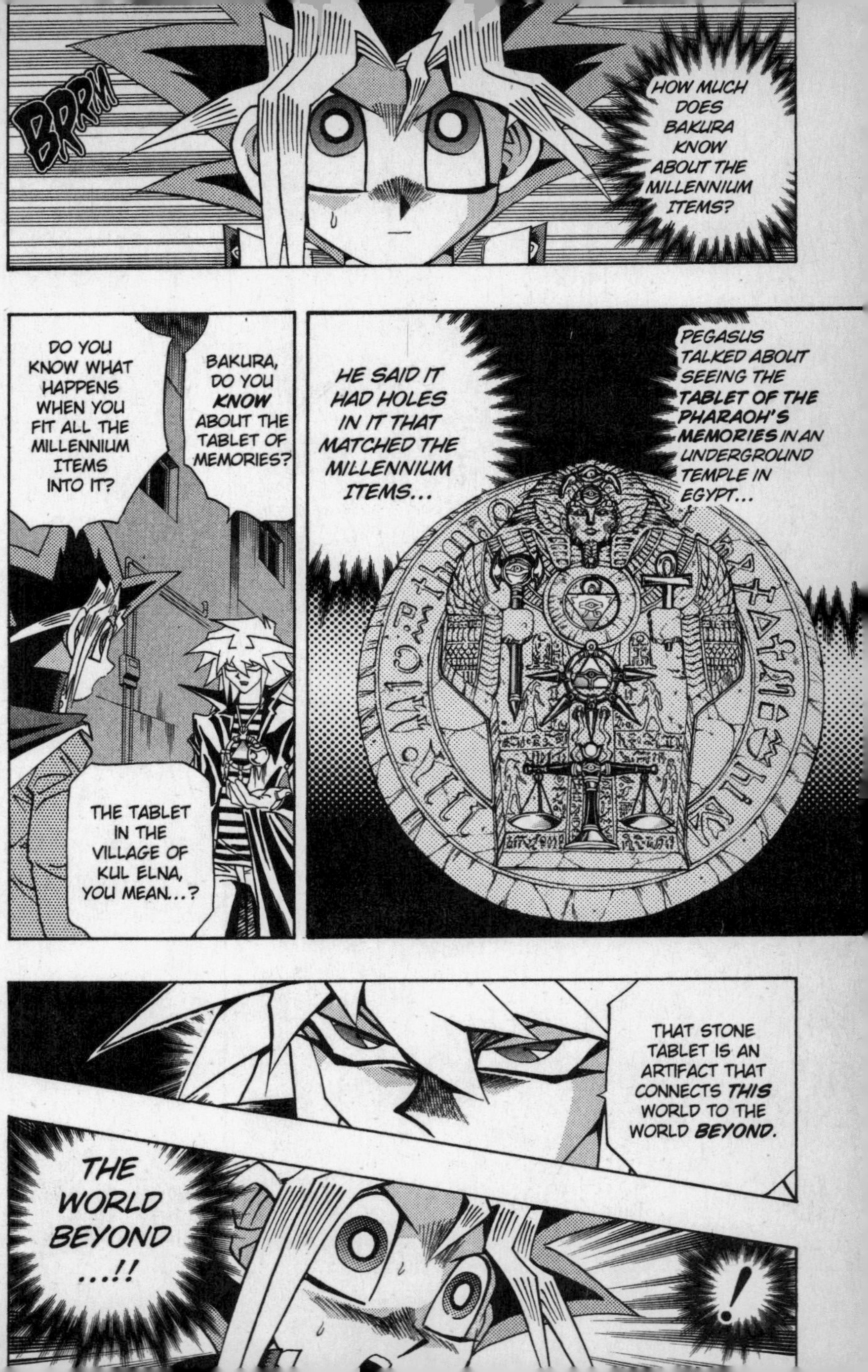
HOW MUCH DOES BAKURA KNOW ABOUT THE MILLENNIUM ITEMS?
BRRM
PEGASUS TALKED ABOUT SEEING THE TABLET OF THE PHARAOH'S MEMORIES IN AN UNDERGROUND TEMPLE IN EGYPT...
HE SAID IT HAD HOLES IN IT THAT MATCHED THE MILLENNIUM ITEMS...
BAKURA, DO YOU KNOW ABOUT THE TABLET OF MEMORIES?
DO YOU KNOW WHAT HAPPENS WHEN YOU FIT ALL THE MILLENNIUM ITEMS INTO IT?
THE TABLET IN THE VILLAGE OF KUL ELNA, YOU MEAN...?
THAT STONE TABLET IS AN ARTIFACT THAT CONNECTS THIS WORLD TO THE WORLD BEYOND.
!
THE WORLD BEYOND ...!!

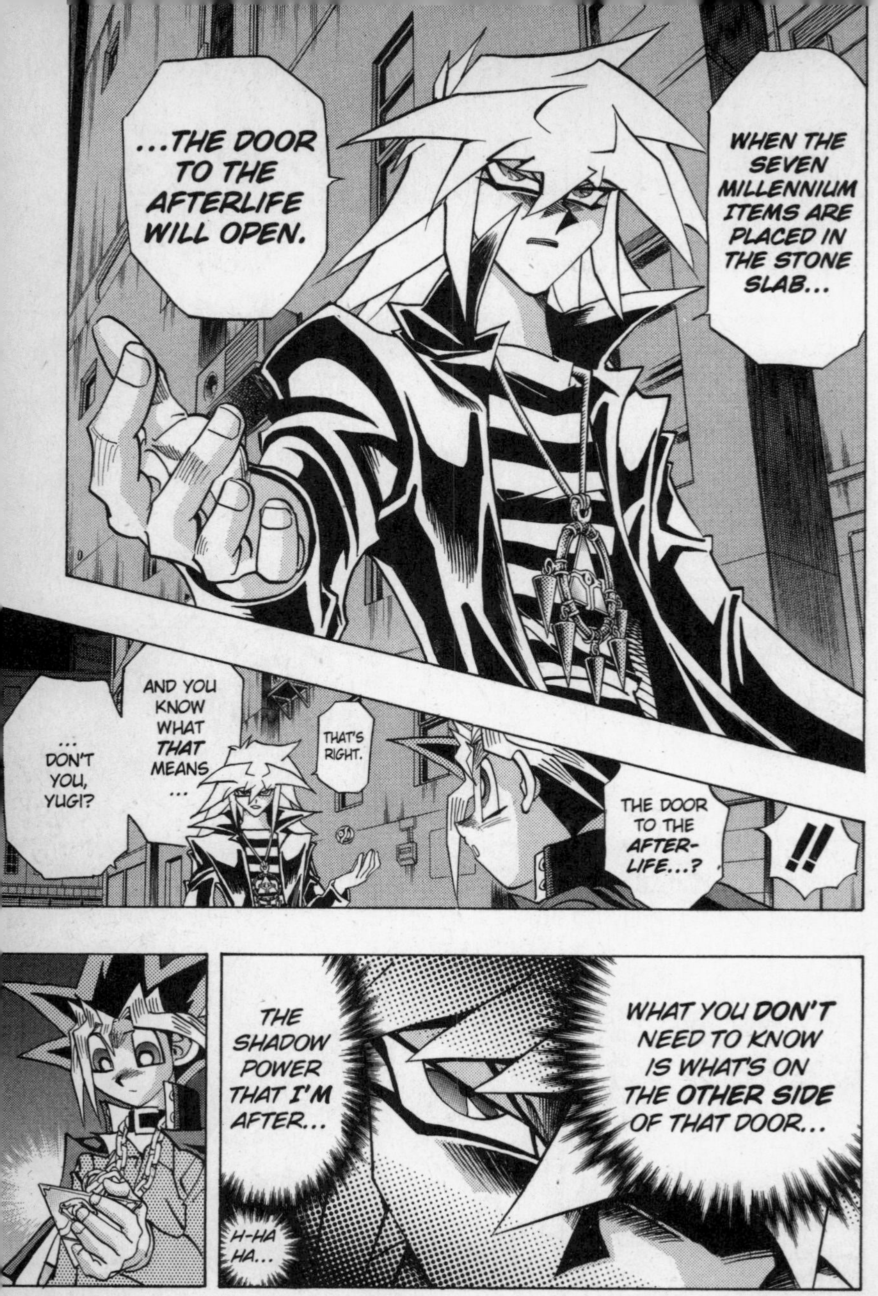
WHEN THE SEVEN MILLENNIUM ITEMS ARE PLACED IN THE STONE SLAB...
...THE DOOR TO THE AFTERLIFE WILL OPEN.
!!
THE DOOR TO THE AFTER-LIFE...?
THAT'S RIGHT.
AND YOU KNOW WHAT THAT MEANS...
...DON'T YOU, YUGI?
WHAT YOU DON'T NEED TO KNOW IS WHAT'S ON THE OTHER SIDE OF THAT DOOR...
THE SHADOW POWER THAT I'M AFTER...
H-HA HA...

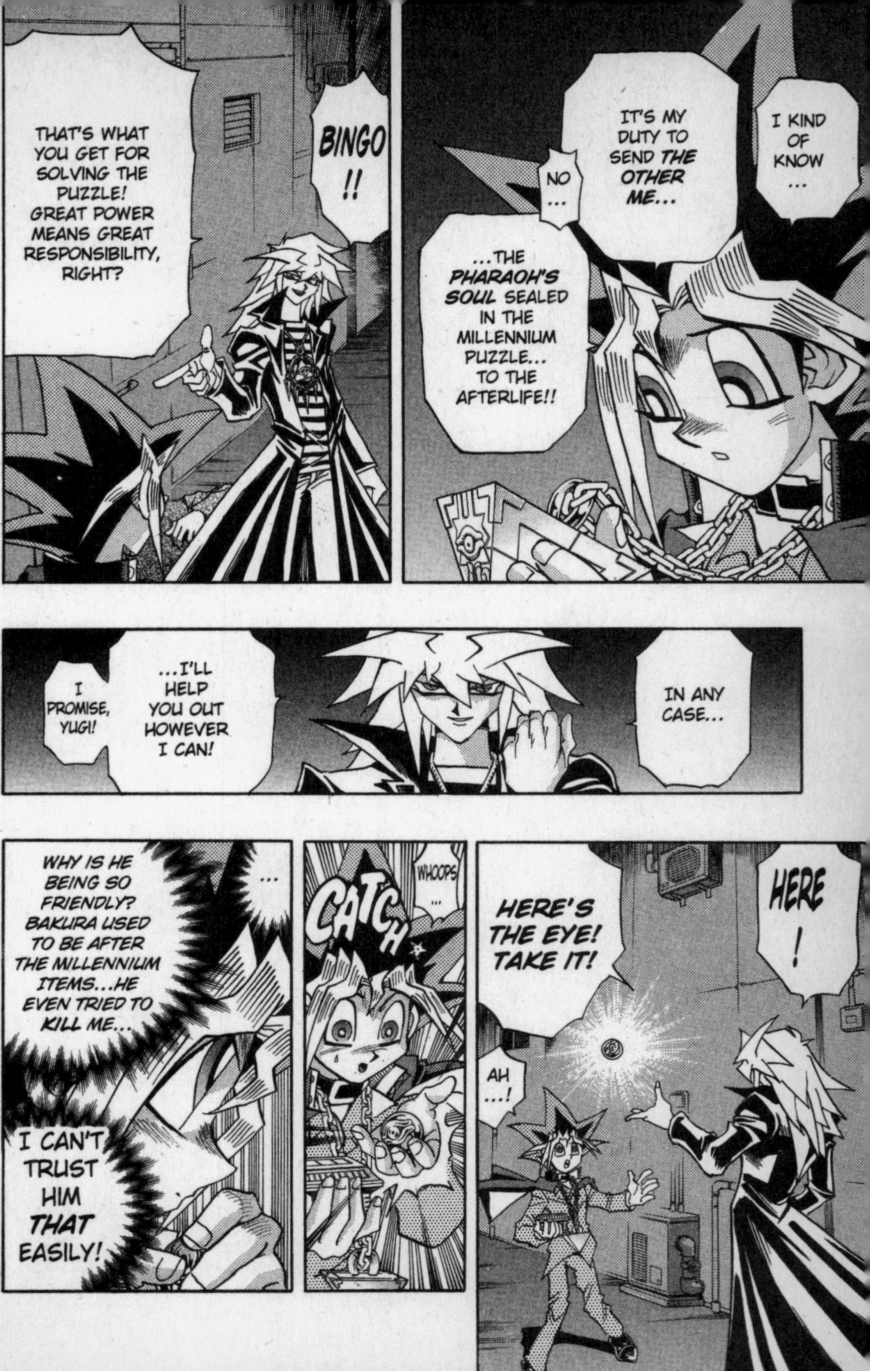
I KIND OF KNOW...
IT'S MY DUTY TO SEND THE OTHER ME...
NO...
...THE PHARAOH'S SOUL SEALED IN THE MILLENNIUM PUZZLE... TO THE AFTERLIFE!!
BINGO!!
THAT'S WHAT YOU GET FOR SOLVING THE PUZZLE! GREAT POWER MEANS GREAT RESPONSIBILITY, RIGHT?
IN ANY CASE...
...I'LL HELP YOU OUT HOWEVER I CAN!
I PROMISE, YUGI!
HERE!
HERE'S THE EYE! TAKE IT!
AH...!
WHOOPS...
CATCH
...
WHY IS HE BEING SO FRIENDLY? BAKURA USED TO BE AFTER THE MILLENNIUM ITEMS...HE EVEN TRIED TO KILL ME...
I CAN'T TRUST HIM THAT EASILY!

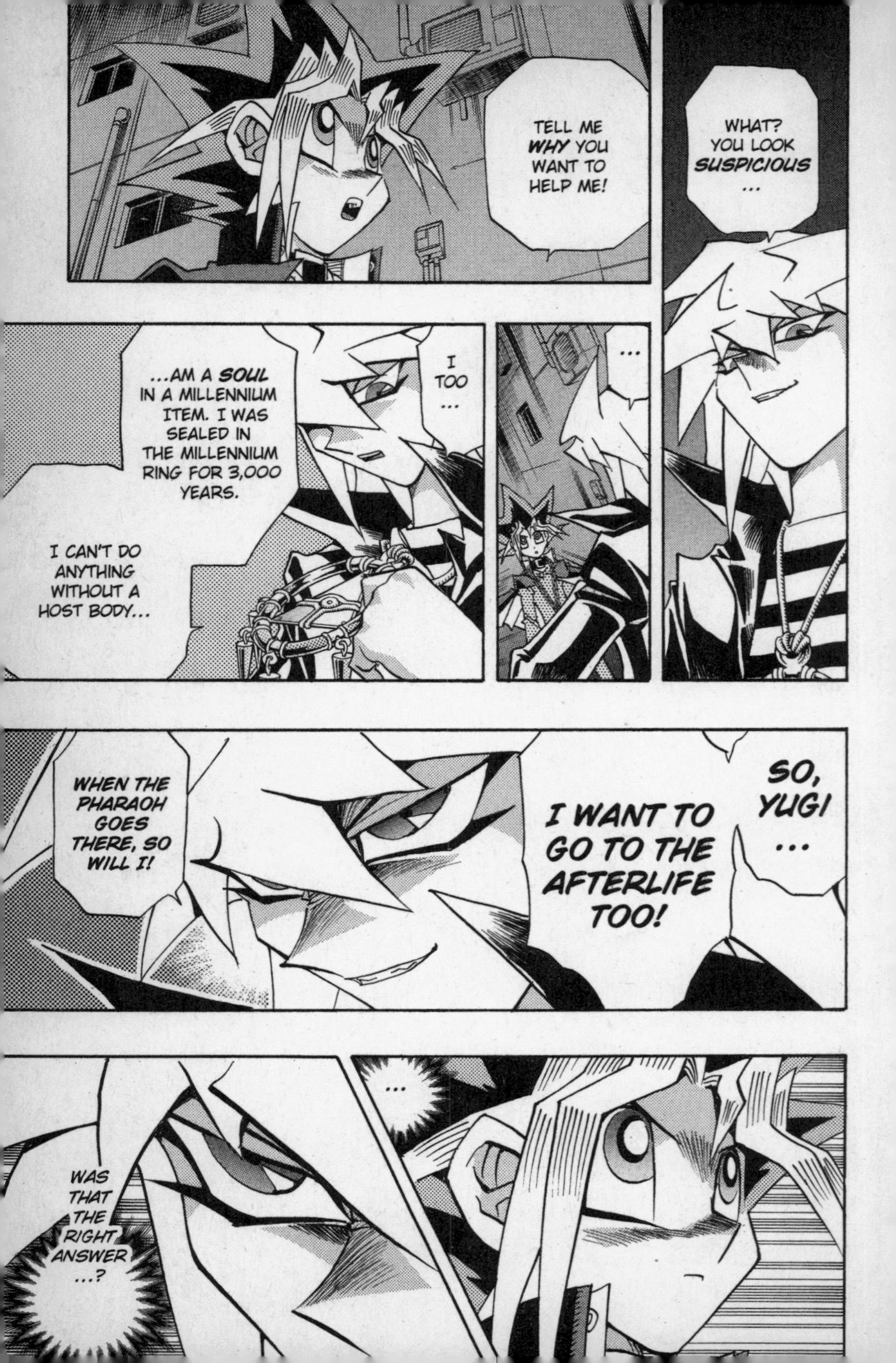
WHAT? YOU LOOK SUSPICIOUS ...
TELL ME WHY YOU WANT TO HELP ME!
...
I TOO ...
...AM A SOUL IN A MILLENNIUM ITEM. I WAS SEALED IN THE MILLENNIUM RING FOR 3,000 YEARS.
I CAN'T DO ANYTHING WITHOUT A HOST BODY...
SO, YUGI ...
I WANT TO GO TO THE AFTERLIFE TOO!
WHEN THE PHARAOH GOES THERE, SO WILL I!
...
WAS THAT THE RIGHT ANSWER ...?

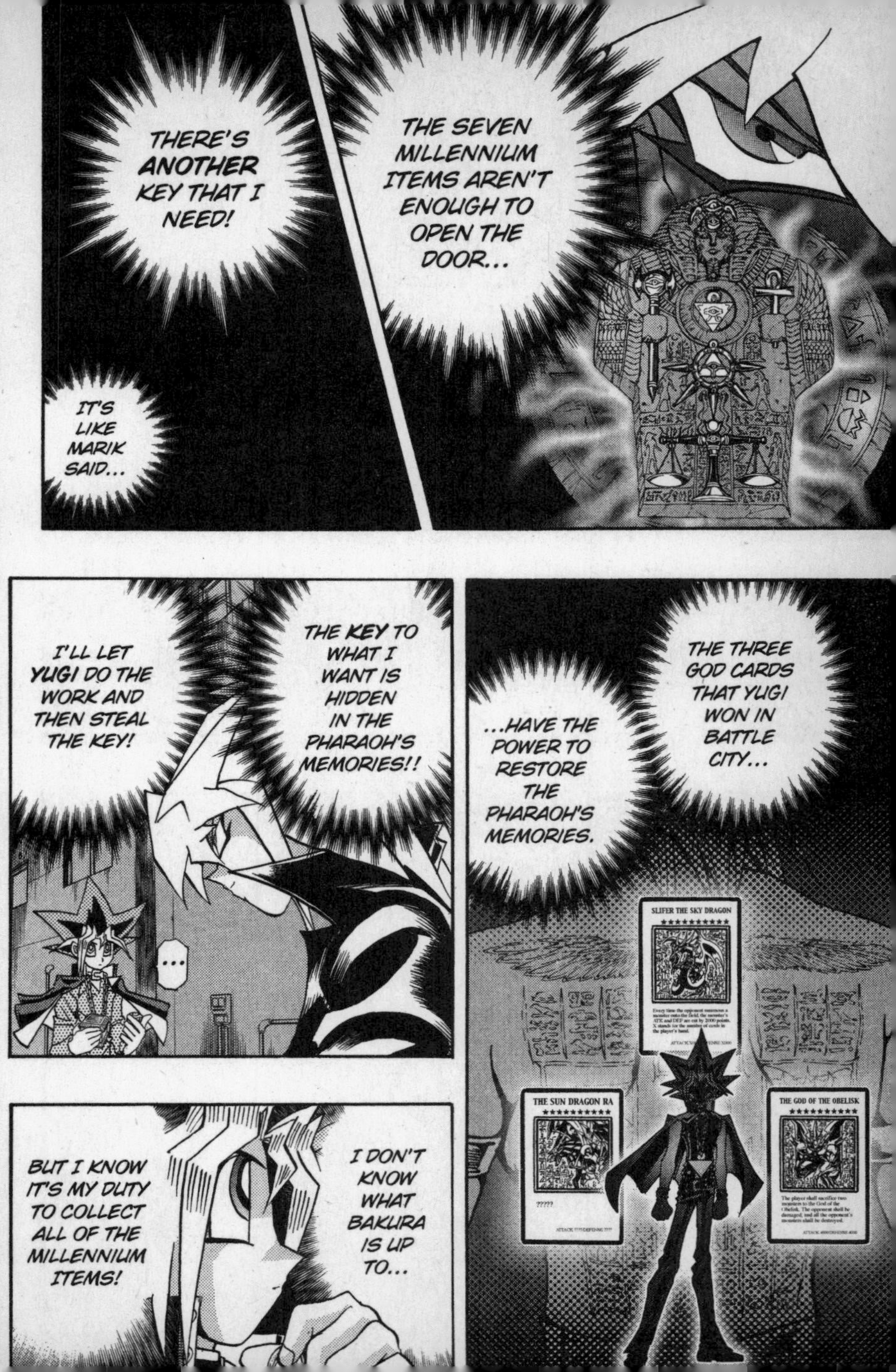
THE SEVEN MILLENNIUM ITEMS AREN'T ENOUGH TO OPEN THE DOOR...
THERE'S **ANOTHER** KEY THAT I NEED!
IT'S LIKE MARIK SAID...
THE THREE GOD CARDS THAT YUGI WON IN BATTLE CITY...
...HAVE THE POWER TO RESTORE THE PHARAOH'S MEMORIES.
SLIFER THE SKY DRAGON
THE SUN DRAGON RA
THE GOD OF THE OBELISK
THE **KEY** TO WHAT I WANT IS HIDDEN IN THE PHARAOH'S MEMORIES!!
I'LL LET **YUGI** DO THE WORK AND THEN STEAL THE KEY!
...
I DON'T KNOW WHAT BAKURA IS UP TO...
BUT I KNOW IT'S MY DUTY TO COLLECT ALL OF THE MILLENNIUM ITEMS!

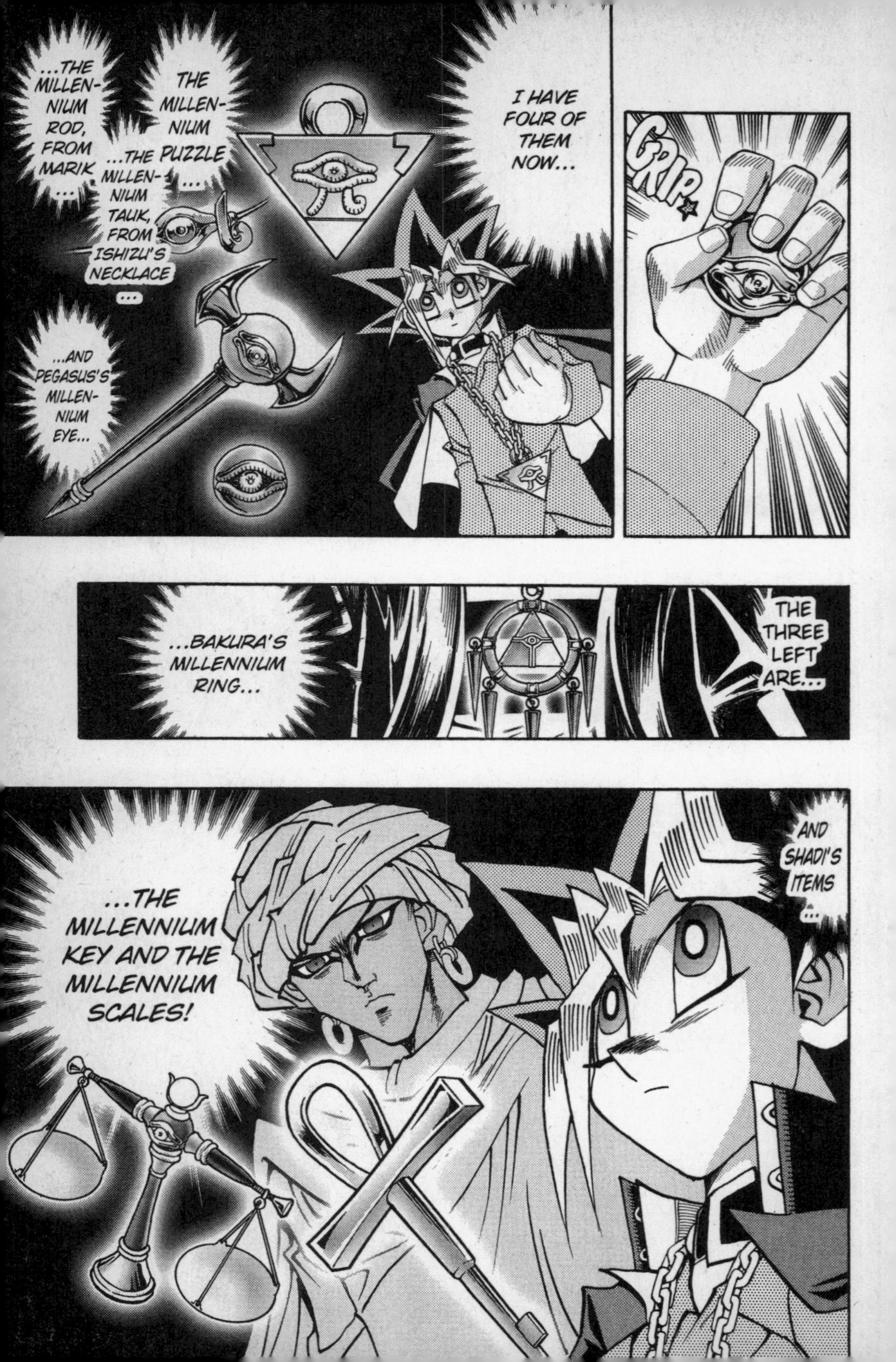
GRIP
I HAVE FOUR OF THEM NOW...
THE MILLENNIUM PUZZLE...
...THE MILLENNIUM ROD, FROM MARIK...
...THE MILLENNIUM TAUK, FROM ISHIZU'S NECKLACE...
...AND PEGASUS'S MILLENNIUM EYE...
THE THREE LEFT ARE...
...BAKURA'S MILLENNIUM RING...
AND SHADI'S ITEMS...
...THE MILLENNIUM KEY AND THE MILLENNIUM SCALES!

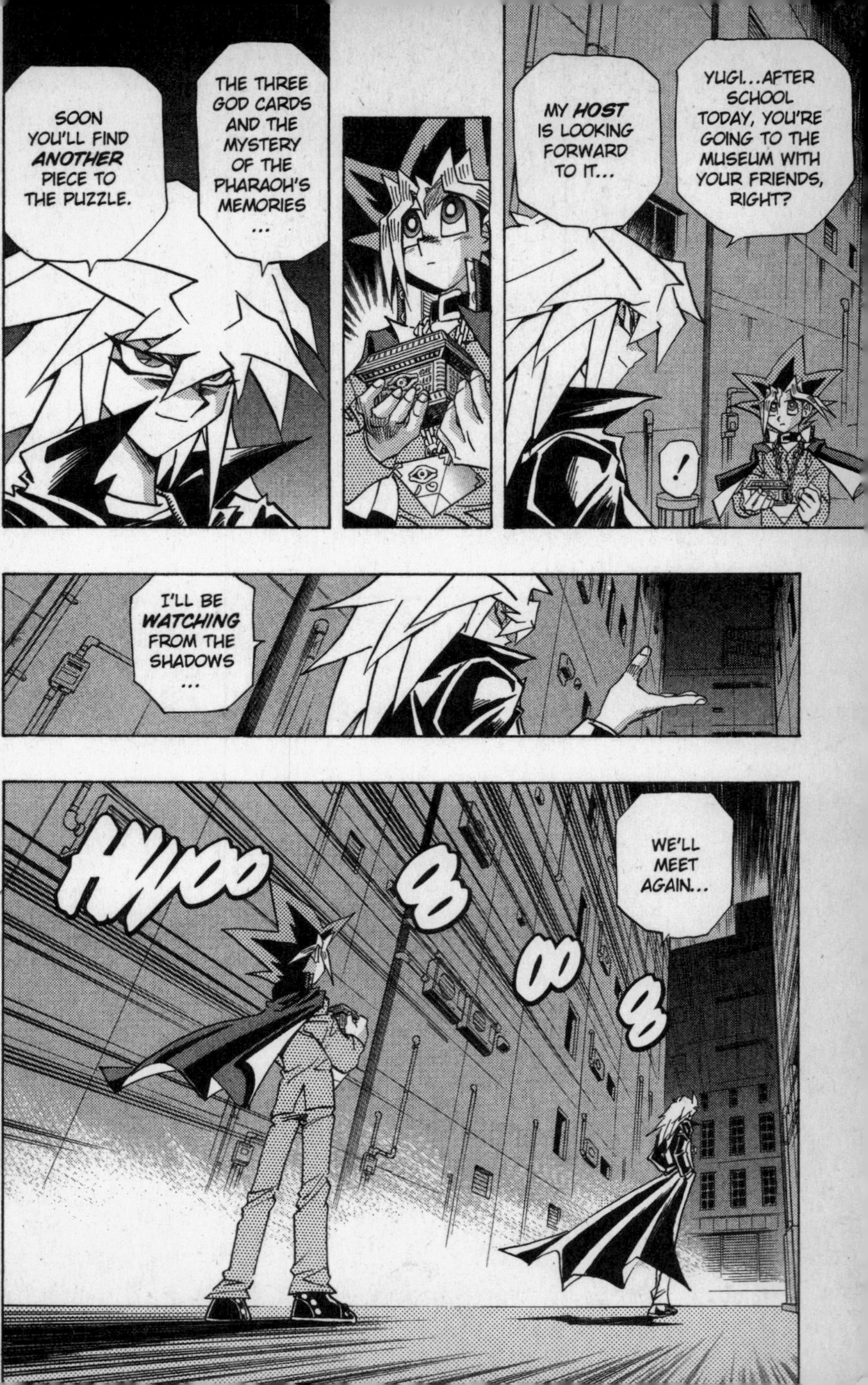

YUGI...AFTER SCHOOL TODAY, YOU'RE GOING TO THE MUSEUM WITH YOUR FRIENDS, RIGHT?
MY *HOST* IS LOOKING FORWARD TO IT...
!
THE THREE GOD CARDS AND THE MYSTERY OF THE PHARAOH'S MEMORIES ...
SOON YOU'LL FIND *ANOTHER* PIECE TO THE PUZZLE.
I'LL BE *WATCHING* FROM THE SHADOWS ...
WE'LL MEET AGAIN...
HYOOOOOO

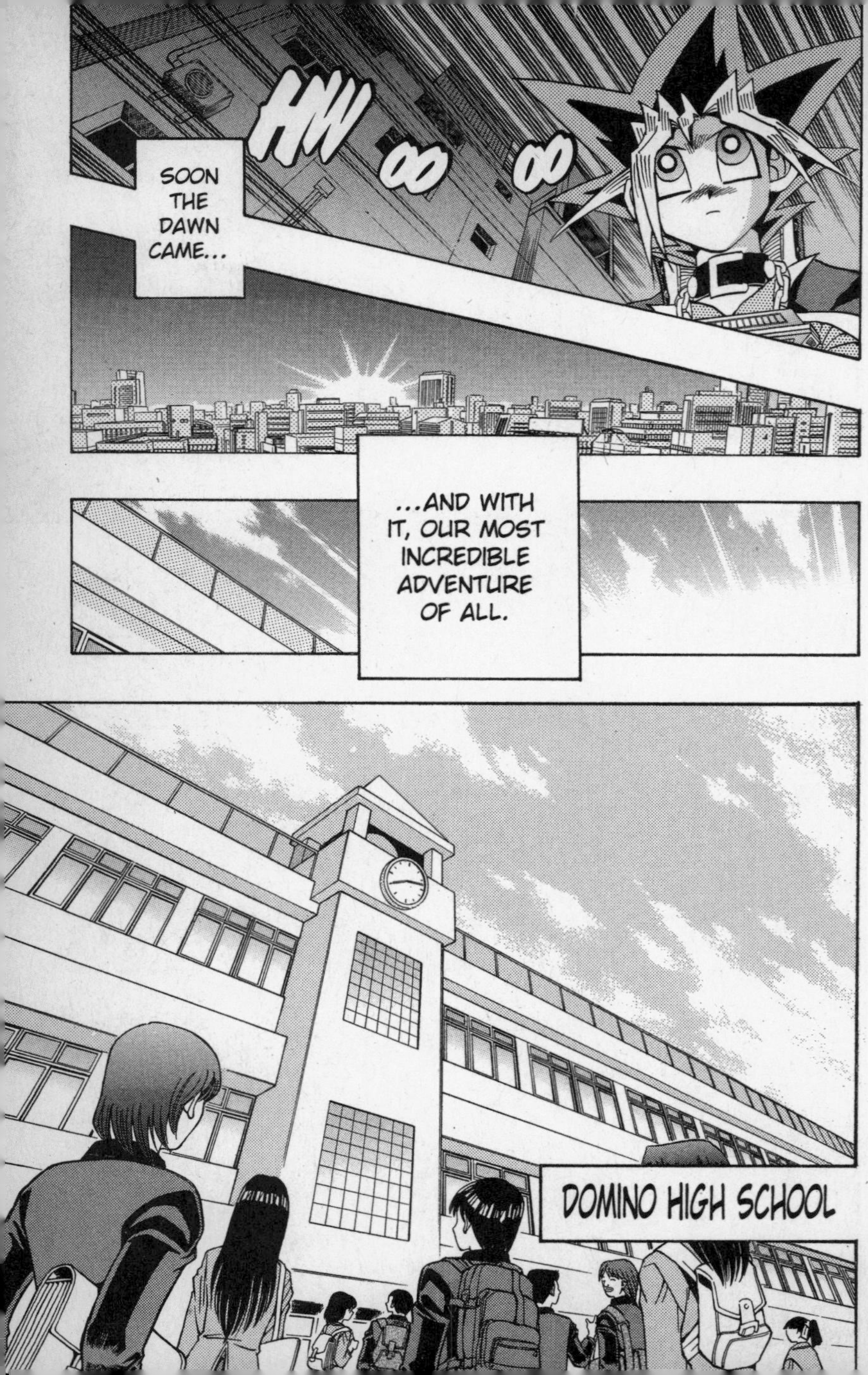
HWOOOO
SOON THE DAWN CAME...
...AND WITH IT, OUR MOST INCREDIBLE ADVENTURE OF ALL.
DOMINO HIGH SCHOOL

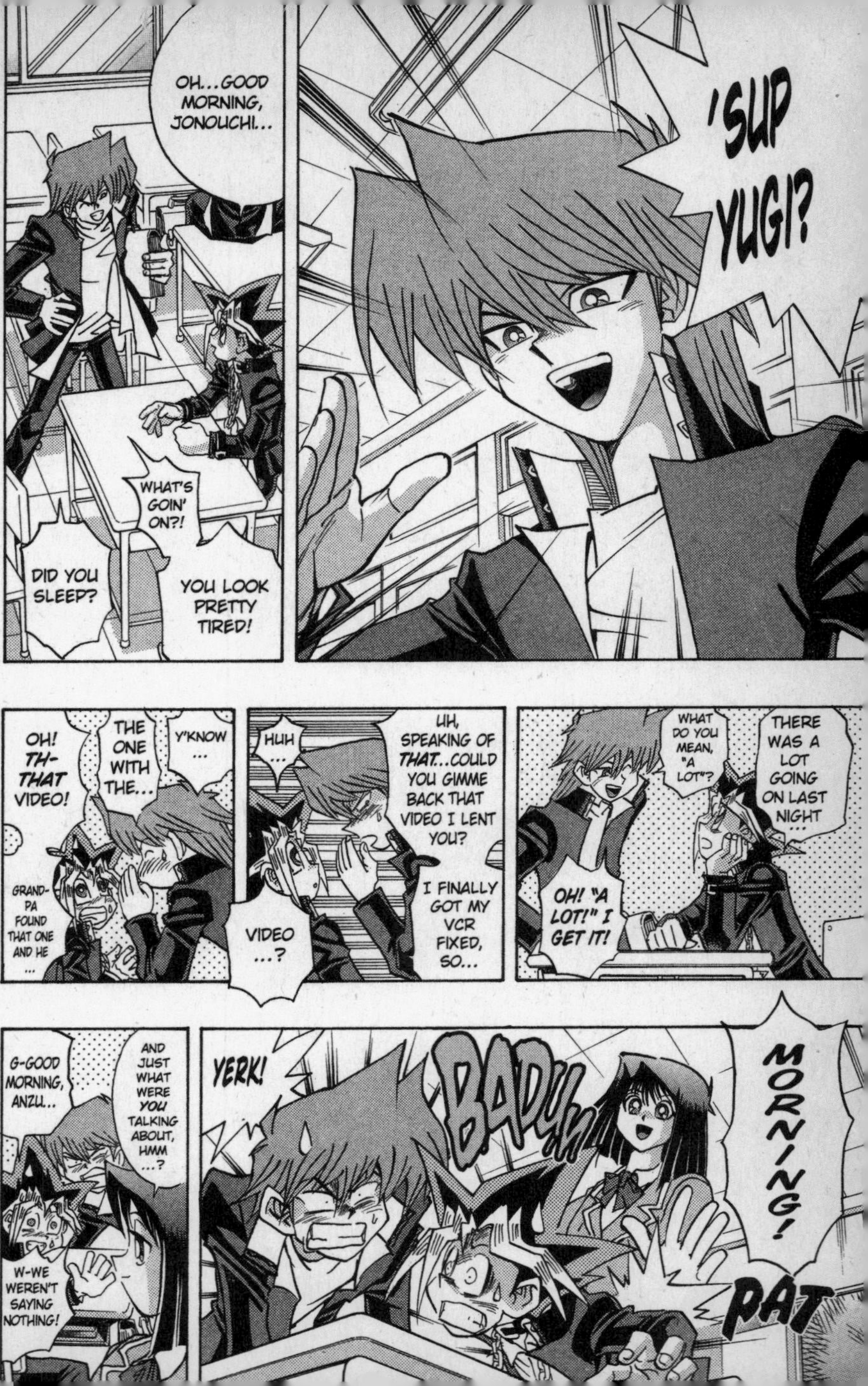
'SUP YUGI?
OH...GOOD MORNING, JONOUCHI...
WHAT'S GOIN' ON?!
YOU LOOK PRETTY TIRED!
DID YOU SLEEP?
THERE WAS A LOT GOING ON LAST NIGHT...
WHAT DO YOU MEAN, "A LOT"?
OH! "A LOT!" I GET IT!
UH, SPEAKING OF *THAT*...COULD YOU GIMME BACK THAT VIDEO I LENT YOU?
HUH...
I FINALLY GOT MY VCR FIXED, SO...
VIDEO...?
Y'KNOW...
THE ONE WITH THE...
OH! *TH-THAT* VIDEO!
GRANDPA FOUND THAT ONE AND HE...
MORNING!
BADUM
YERK!
PAT
AND JUST WHAT WERE *YOU* TALKING ABOUT, HMM...?
G-GOOD MORNING, ANZU...
W-WE WEREN'T SAYING NOTHING!

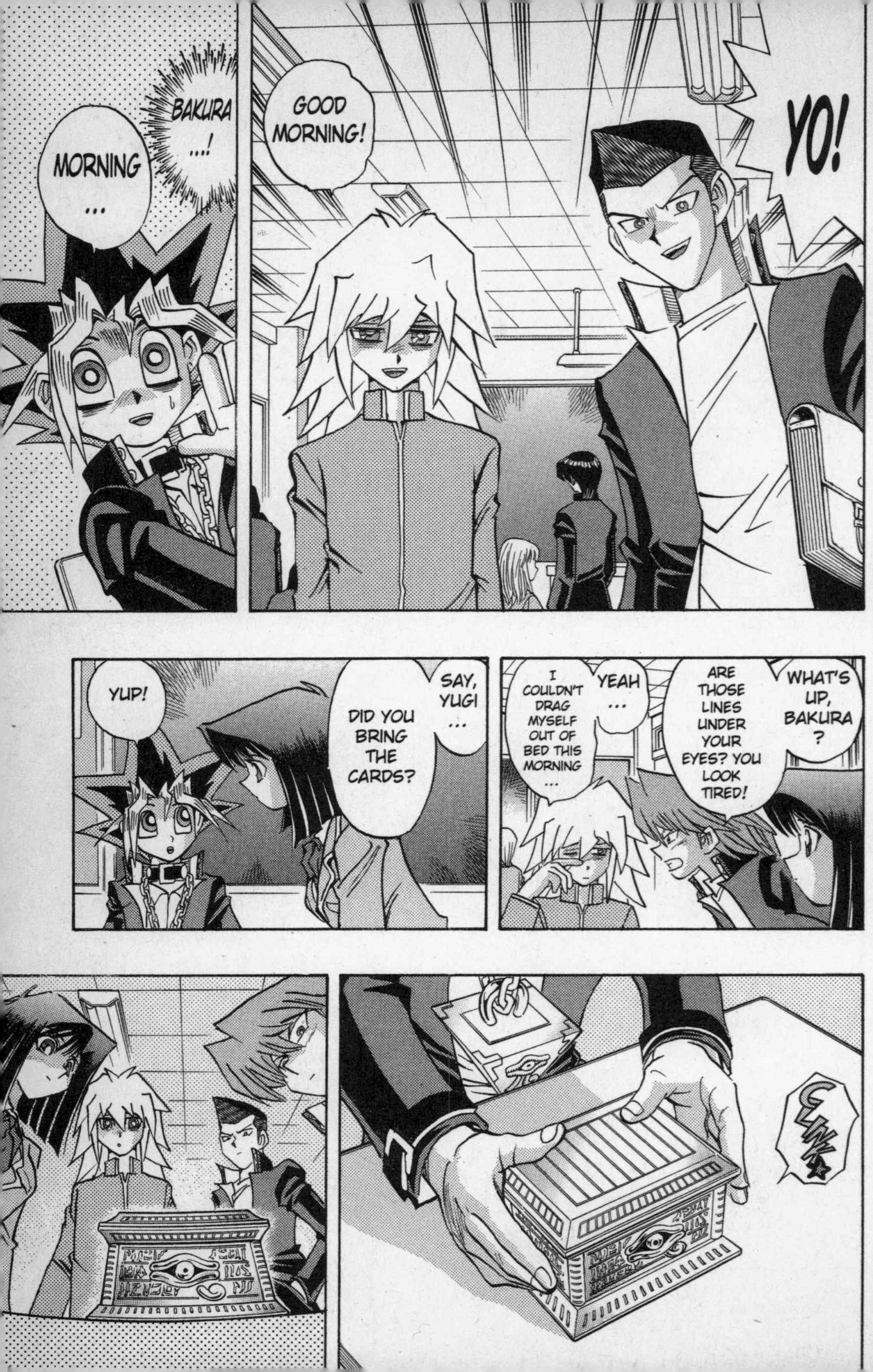
YO!
GOOD MORNING!
BAKURA ...!
MORNING ...
WHAT'S UP, BAKURA?
ARE THOSE LINES UNDER YOUR EYES? YOU LOOK TIRED!
YEAH ...
I COULDN'T DRAG MYSELF OUT OF BED THIS MORNING ...
SAY, YUGI ...
DID YOU BRING THE CARDS?
YUP!
CLINK

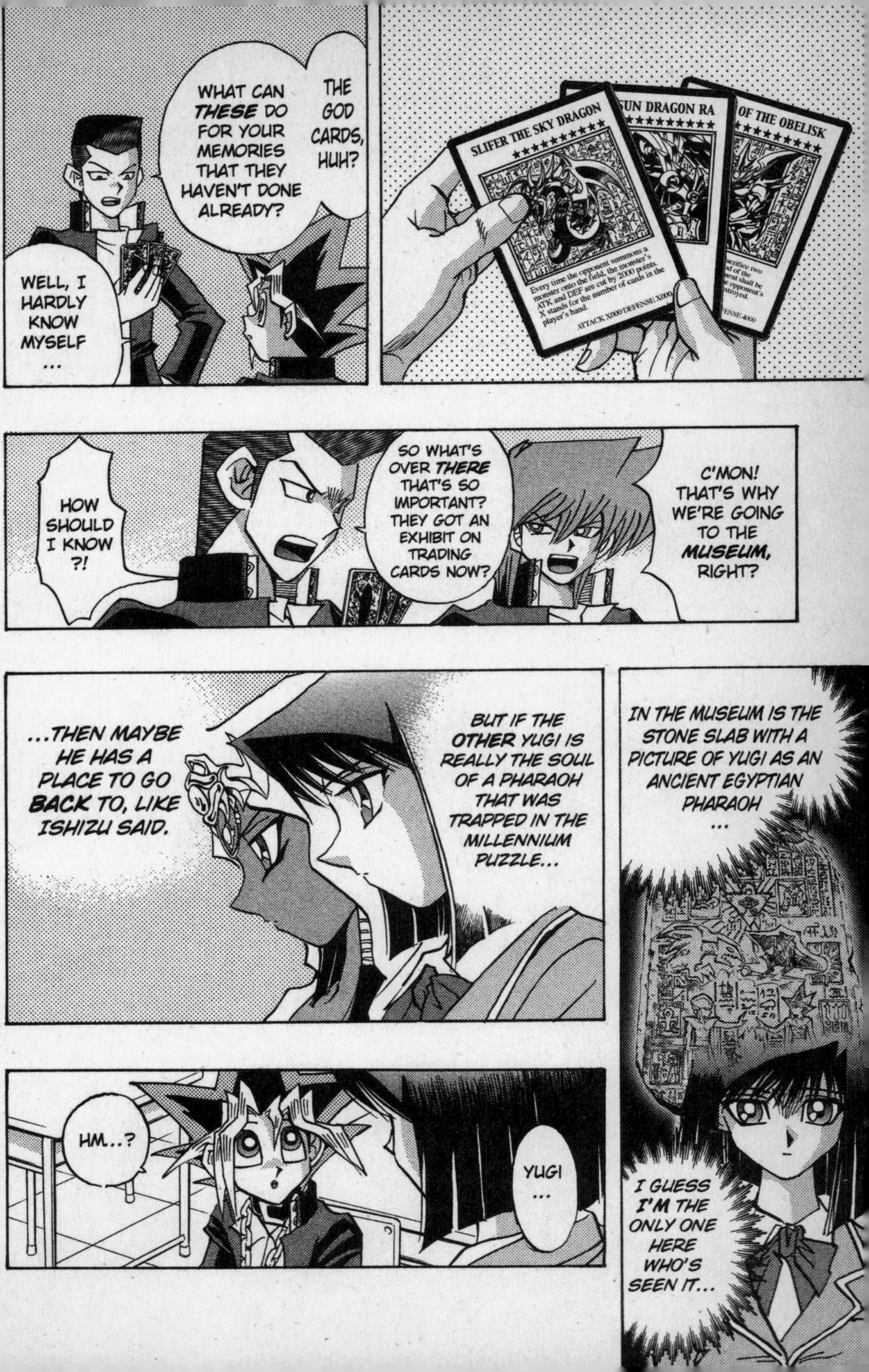
SLIFER THE SKY DRAGON
SUN DRAGON RA
OF THE OBELISK
Every time the opponent summons a monster onto the field, the monster's ATK and DEF are cut by 2000 points. X stands for the number of cards in the player's hand.
ATTACK X000/DEFENSE X000
THE GOD CARDS, HUH?
WHAT CAN THESE DO FOR YOUR MEMORIES THAT THEY HAVEN'T DONE ALREADY?
WELL, I HARDLY KNOW MYSELF ...
C'MON! THAT'S WHY WE'RE GOING TO THE MUSEUM, RIGHT?
SO WHAT'S OVER THERE THAT'S SO IMPORTANT? THEY GOT AN EXHIBIT ON TRADING CARDS NOW?
HOW SHOULD I KNOW ?!
IN THE MUSEUM IS THE STONE SLAB WITH A PICTURE OF YUGI AS AN ANCIENT EGYPTIAN PHARAOH ...
I GUESS I'M THE ONLY ONE HERE WHO'S SEEN IT...
BUT IF THE OTHER YUGI IS REALLY THE SOUL OF A PHARAOH THAT WAS TRAPPED IN THE MILLENNIUM PUZZLE...
...THEN MAYBE HE HAS A PLACE TO GO BACK TO, LIKE ISHIZU SAID.
YUGI ...
HM...?

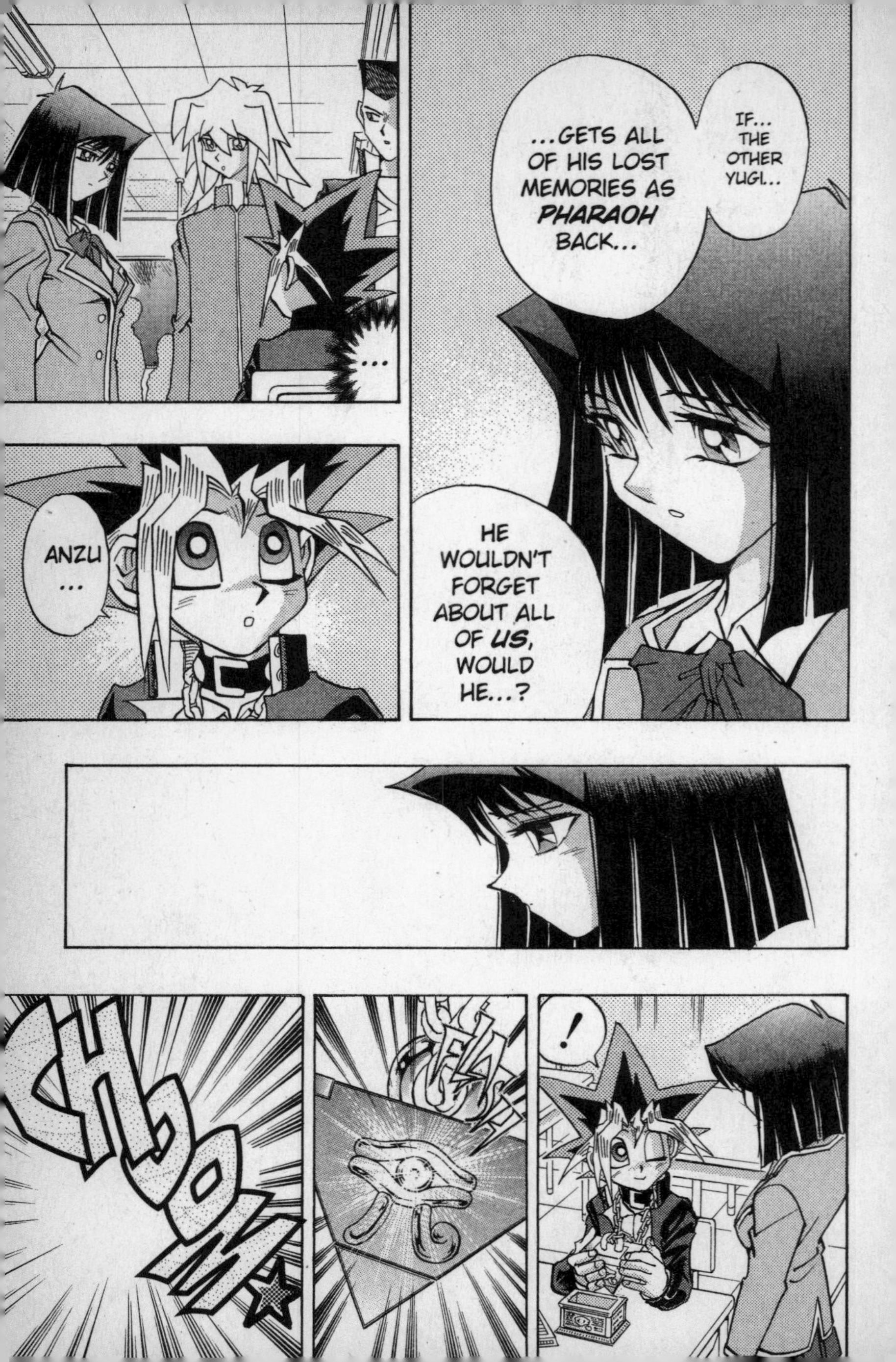
IF... THE OTHER YUGI...
...GETS ALL OF HIS LOST MEMORIES AS PHARAOH BACK...
HE WOULDN'T FORGET ABOUT ALL OF US, WOULD HE...?
...
ANZU ...
!
CHOOM

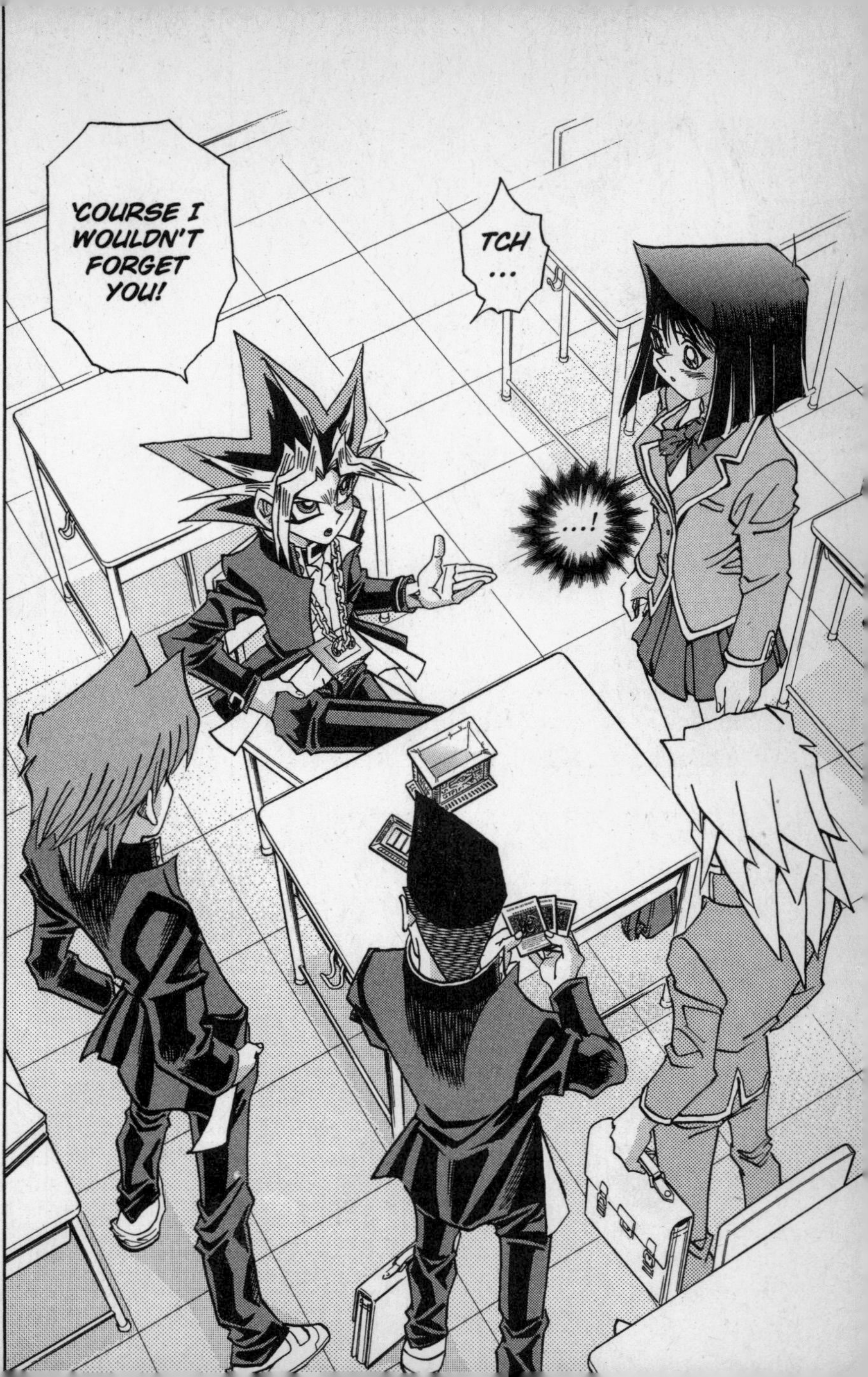
TCH ...
'COURSE I WOULDN'T FORGET YOU!
...!

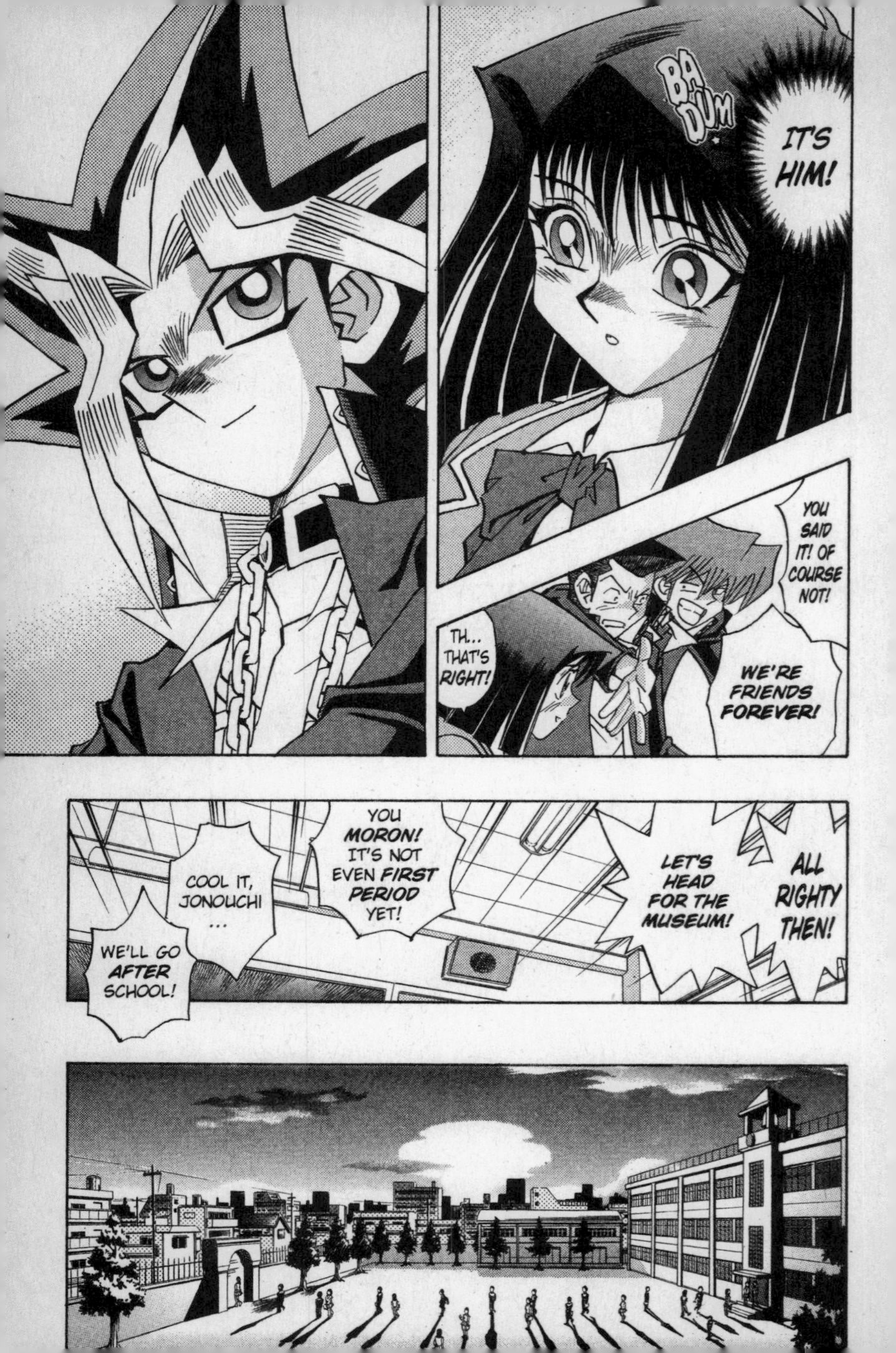
BA DUM
IT'S HIM!
YOU SAID IT! OF COURSE NOT!
WE'RE FRIENDS FOREVER!
TH... THAT'S RIGHT!
ALL RIGHTY THEN!
LET'S HEAD FOR THE MUSEUM!
YOU MORON! IT'S NOT EVEN FIRST PERIOD YET!
COOL IT, JONOUCHI ...
WE'LL GO AFTER SCHOOL!

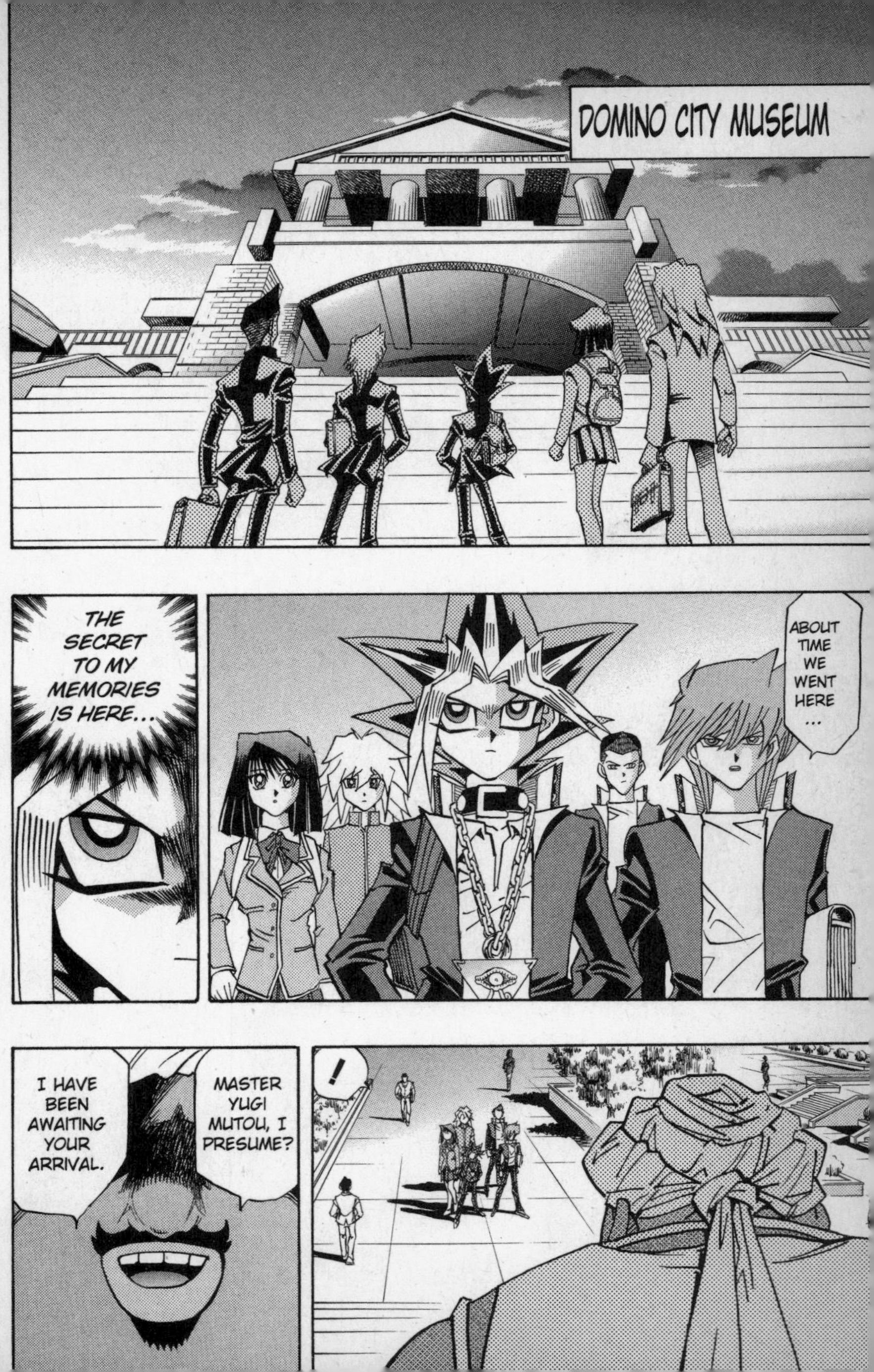
DOMINO CITY MUSEUM
ABOUT TIME WE WENT HERE ...
THE SECRET TO MY MEMORIES IS HERE...
!
MASTER YUGI MUTOU, I PRESUME?
I HAVE BEEN AWAITING YOUR ARRIVAL.

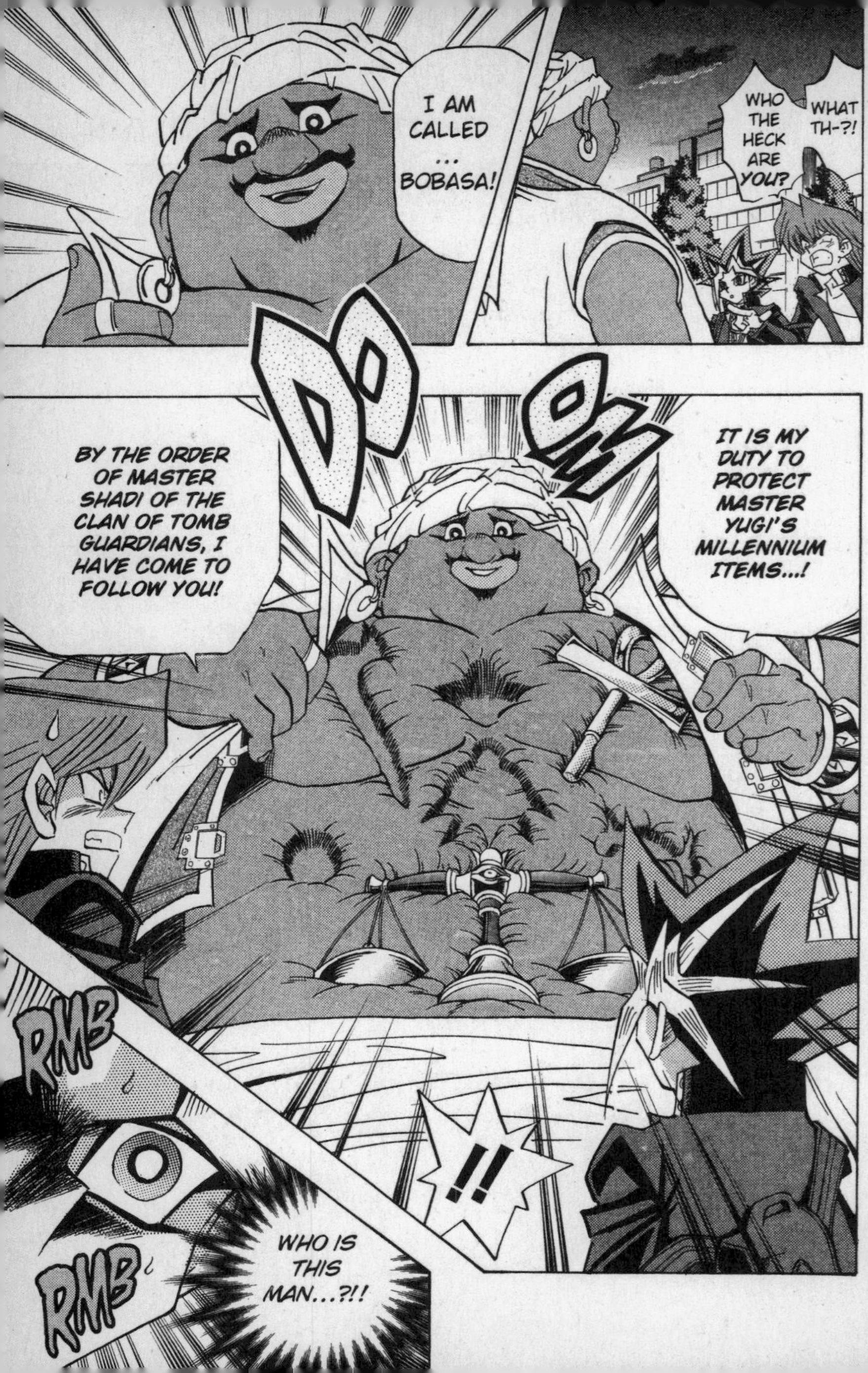
WHAT TH-?!
WHO THE HECK ARE YOU?
I AM CALLED ... BOBASA!
DOOM
IT IS MY DUTY TO PROTECT MASTER YUGI'S MILLENNIUM ITEMS...!
BY THE ORDER OF MASTER SHADI OF THE CLAN OF TOMB GUARDIANS, I HAVE COME TO FOLLOW YOU!
!!
RMB
RMB
WHO IS THIS MAN...?!!

Duel 4: Voyage into Memories

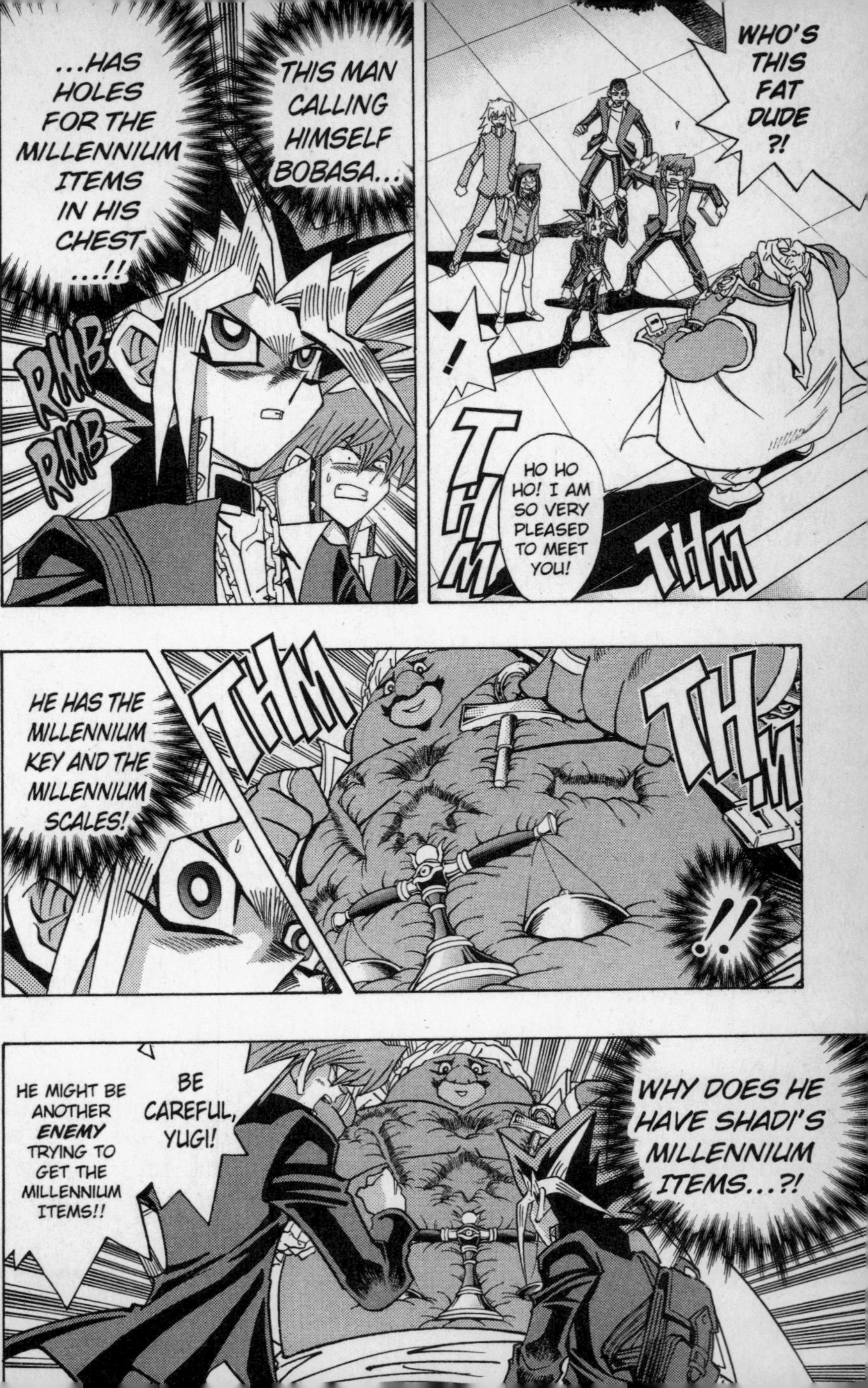
WHO'S THIS FAT DUDE ?!
!
THM
HO HO HO! I AM SO VERY PLEASED TO MEET YOU!
THM
THIS MAN CALLING HIMSELF BOBASA...
...HAS HOLES FOR THE MILLENNIUM ITEMS IN HIS CHEST ...!!
RMB RMB
THM
THM
HE HAS THE MILLENNIUM KEY AND THE MILLENNIUM SCALES!
!!
WHY DOES HE HAVE SHADI'S MILLENNIUM ITEMS...?!
BE CAREFUL, YUGI!
HE MIGHT BE ANOTHER ENEMY TRYING TO GET THE MILLENNIUM ITEMS!!

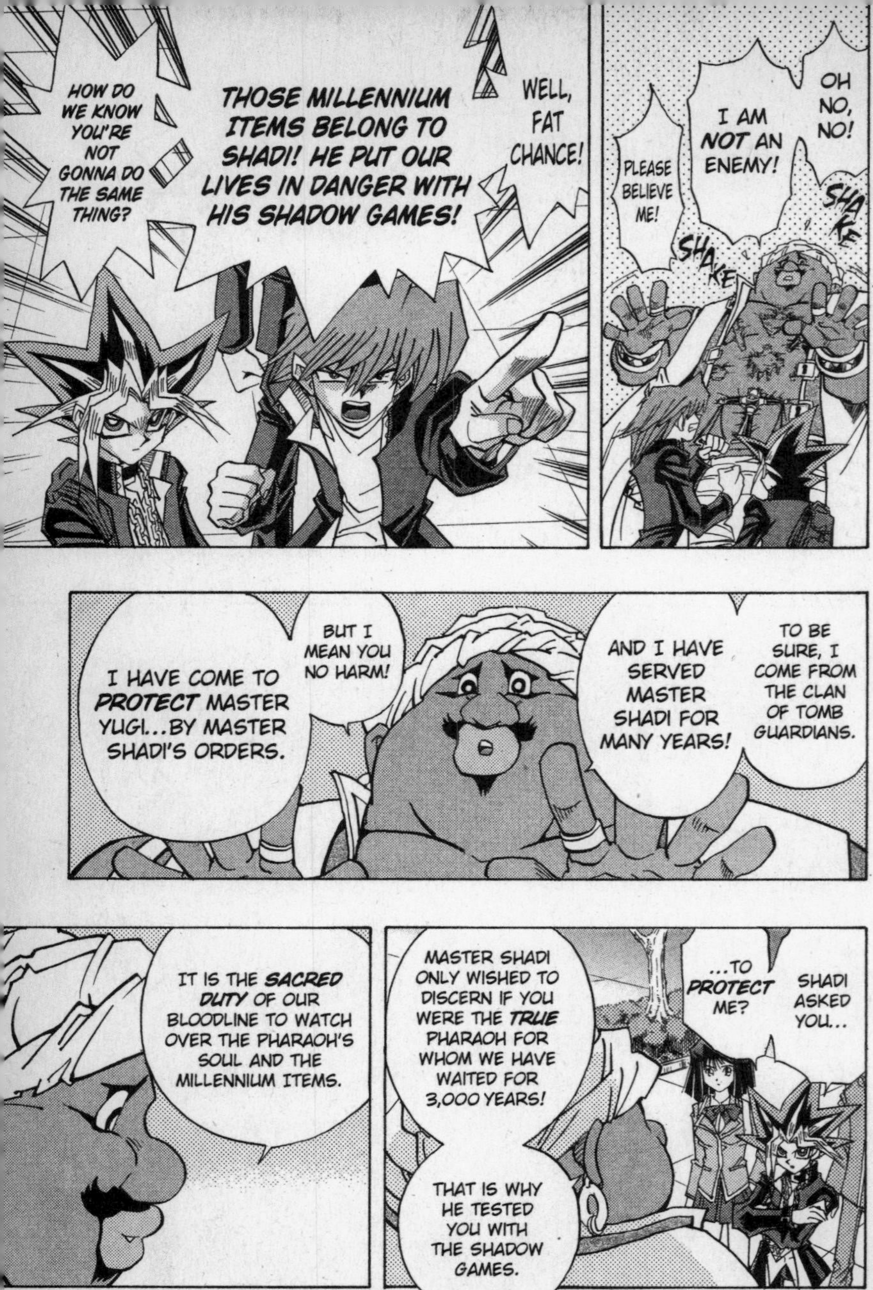
OH NO, NO!
I AM NOT AN ENEMY!
PLEASE BELIEVE ME!
SHAKE
SHAKE
WELL, FAT CHANCE!
THOSE MILLENNIUM ITEMS BELONG TO SHADI! HE PUT OUR LIVES IN DANGER WITH HIS SHADOW GAMES!
HOW DO WE KNOW YOU'RE NOT GONNA DO THE SAME THING?
TO BE SURE, I COME FROM THE CLAN OF TOMB GUARDIANS.
AND I HAVE SERVED MASTER SHADI FOR MANY YEARS!
BUT I MEAN YOU NO HARM!
I HAVE COME TO PROTECT MASTER YUGI...BY MASTER SHADI'S ORDERS.
SHADI ASKED YOU...
...TO PROTECT ME?
MASTER SHADI ONLY WISHED TO DISCERN IF YOU WERE THE TRUE PHARAOH FOR WHOM WE HAVE WAITED FOR 3,000 YEARS!
THAT IS WHY HE TESTED YOU WITH THE SHADOW GAMES.
IT IS THE SACRED DUTY OF OUR BLOODLINE TO WATCH OVER THE PHARAOH'S SOUL AND THE MILLENNIUM ITEMS.

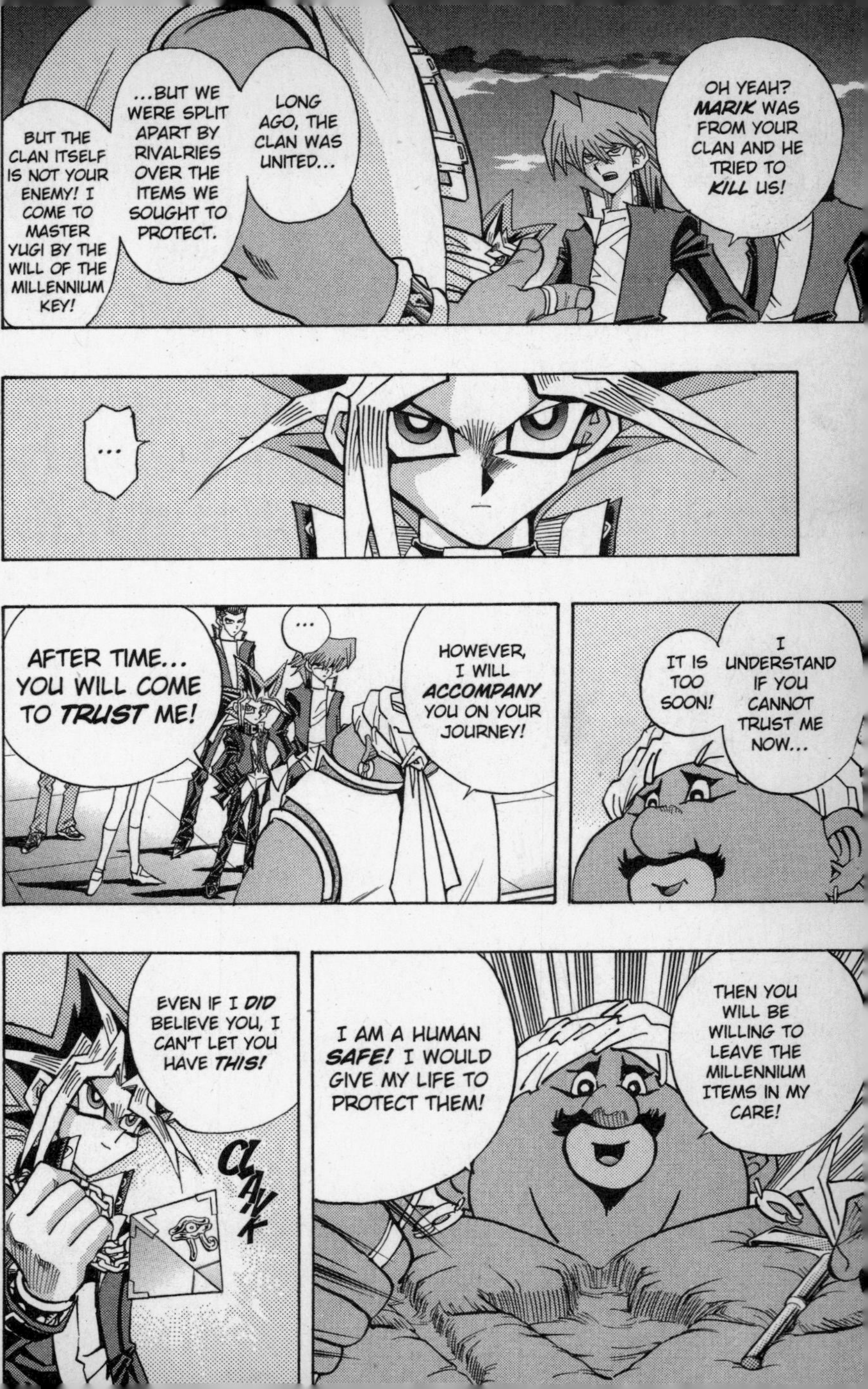

OH YEAH? MARIK WAS FROM YOUR CLAN AND HE TRIED TO KILL US!
LONG AGO, THE CLAN WAS UNITED...
...BUT WE WERE SPLIT APART BY RIVALRIES OVER THE ITEMS WE SOUGHT TO PROTECT.
BUT THE CLAN ITSELF IS NOT YOUR ENEMY! I COME TO MASTER YUGI BY THE WILL OF THE MILLENNIUM KEY!
...
I UNDERSTAND IF YOU CANNOT TRUST ME NOW...
IT IS TOO SOON!
HOWEVER, I WILL ACCOMPANY YOU ON YOUR JOURNEY!
...
AFTER TIME... YOU WILL COME TO TRUST ME!
THEN YOU WILL BE WILLING TO LEAVE THE MILLENNIUM ITEMS IN MY CARE!
I AM A HUMAN SAFE! I WOULD GIVE MY LIFE TO PROTECT THEM!
EVEN IF I DID BELIEVE YOU, I CAN'T LET YOU HAVE THIS!
CLANK

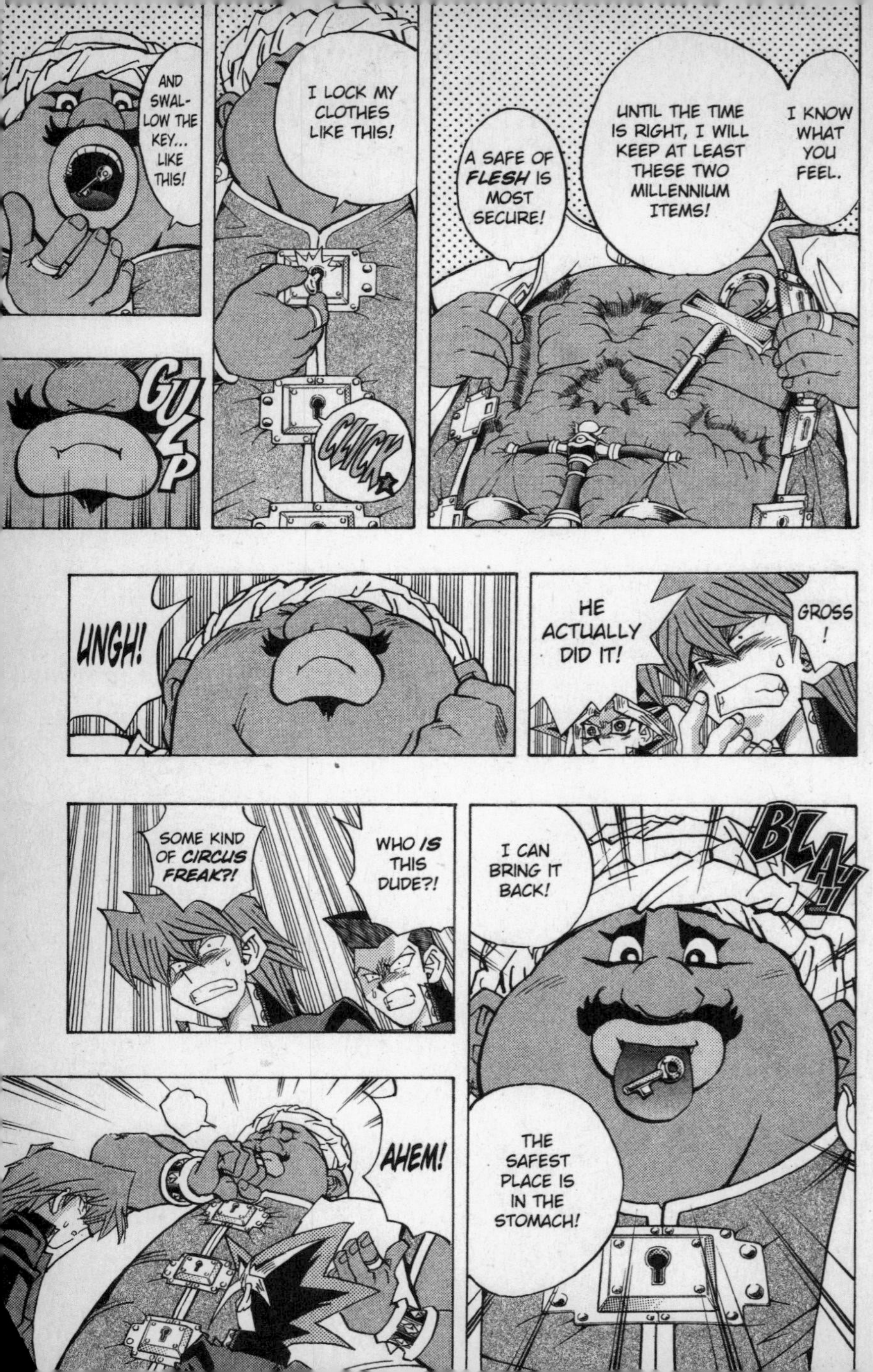

I KNOW WHAT YOU FEEL.
UNTIL THE TIME IS RIGHT, I WILL KEEP AT LEAST THESE TWO MILLENNIUM ITEMS!
A SAFE OF *FLESH* IS MOST SECURE!
I LOCK MY CLOTHES LIKE THIS!
CLICK
AND SWAL-LOW THE KEY... LIKE THIS!
GULP
GROSS!
HE ACTUALLY DID IT!
UNGH!
BLAH!!
I CAN BRING IT BACK!
THE SAFEST PLACE IS IN THE STOMACH!
WHO *IS* THIS DUDE?!
SOME KIND OF *CIRCUS FREAK?!*
AHEM!

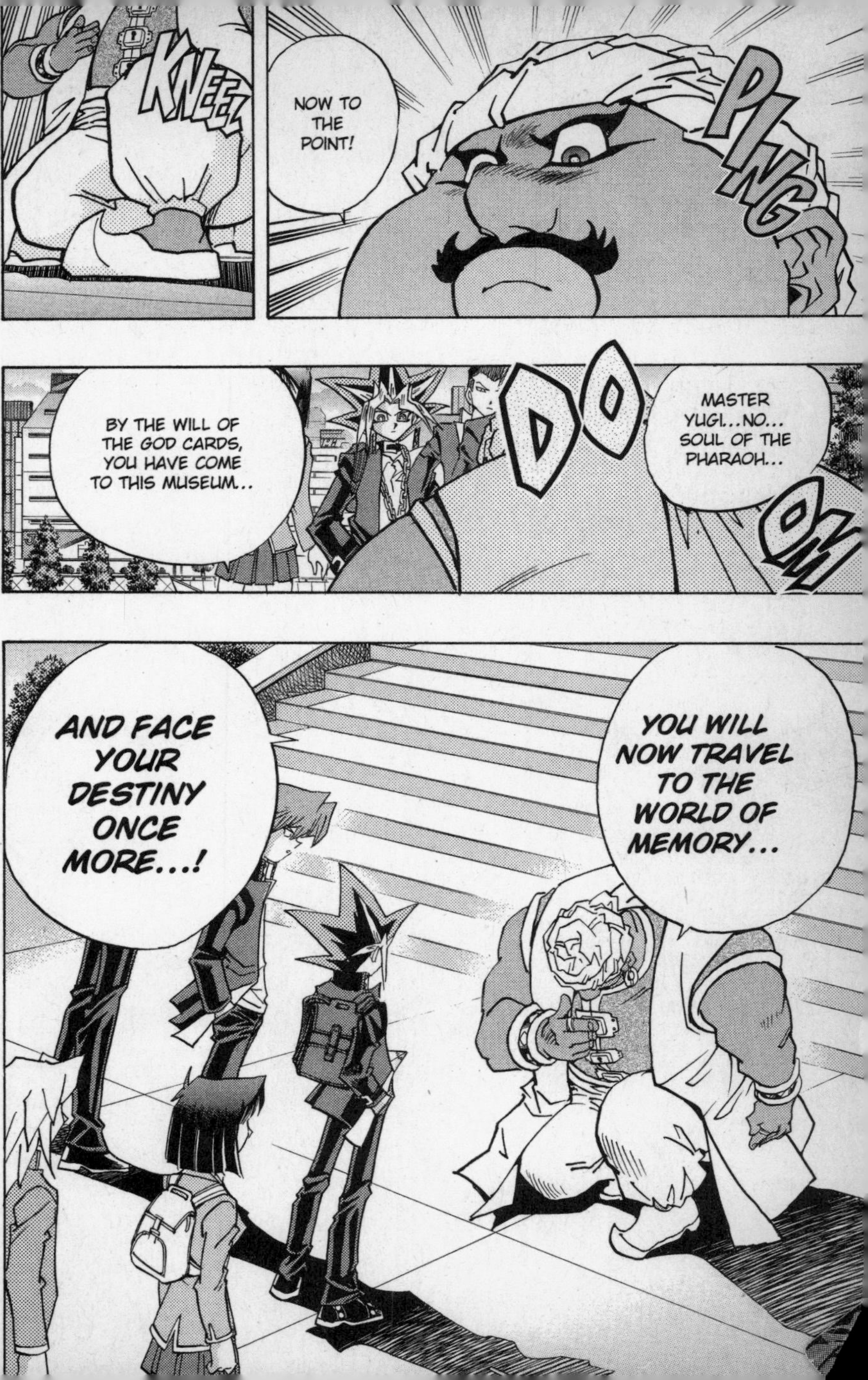
PING
NOW TO THE POINT!
KNEEL
MASTER YUGI...NO... SOUL OF THE PHARAOH...
DOOM
BY THE WILL OF THE GOD CARDS, YOU HAVE COME TO THIS MUSEUM...
YOU WILL NOW TRAVEL TO THE WORLD OF MEMORY...
AND FACE YOUR DESTINY ONCE MORE...!

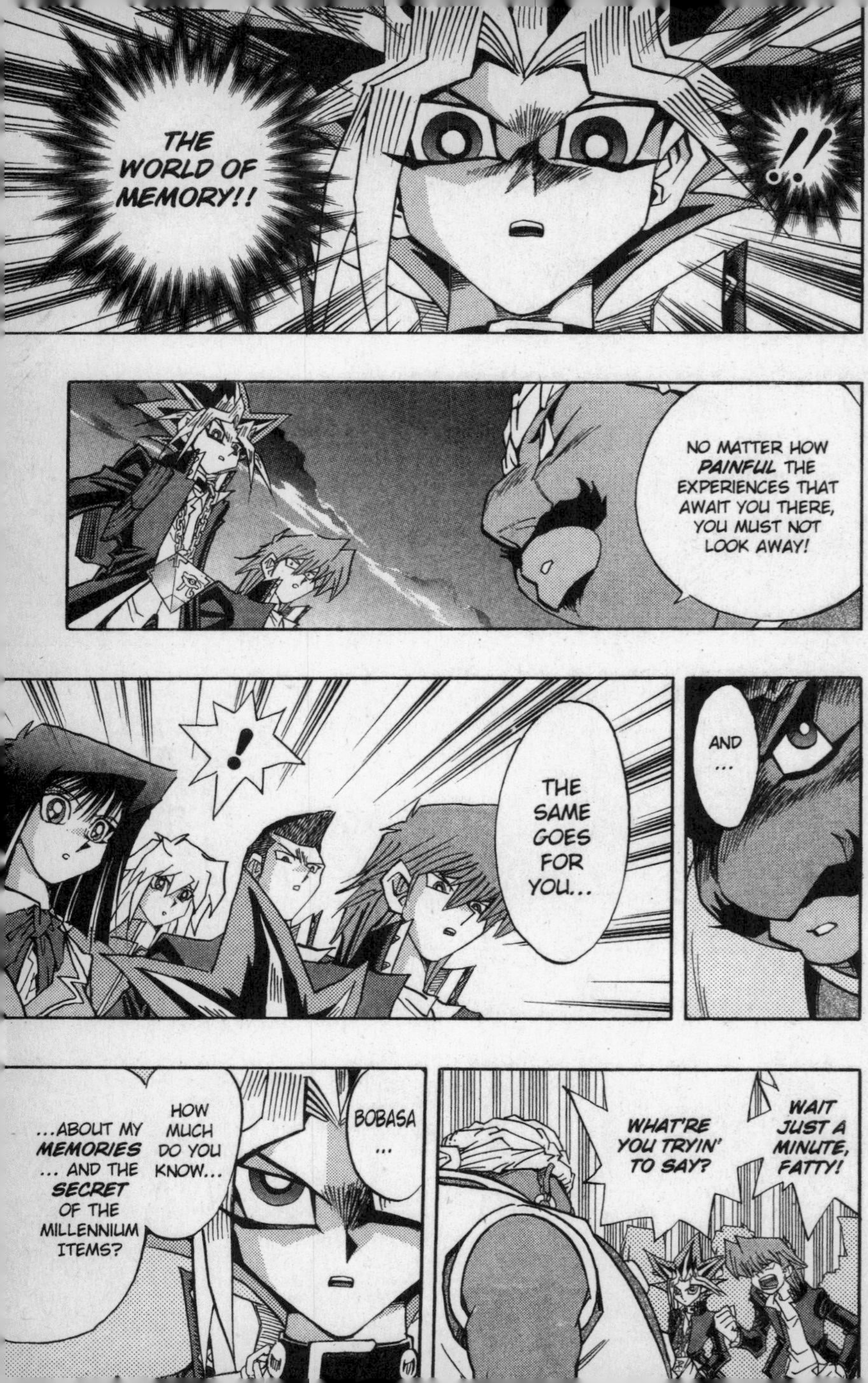
!!
THE WORLD OF MEMORY!!
NO MATTER HOW PAINFUL THE EXPERIENCES THAT AWAIT YOU THERE, YOU MUST NOT LOOK AWAY!
AND ...
THE SAME GOES FOR YOU...
!
WAIT JUST A MINUTE, FATTY!
WHAT'RE YOU TRYIN' TO SAY?
BOBASA ...
HOW MUCH DO YOU KNOW...
...ABOUT MY MEMORIES ... AND THE SECRET OF THE MILLENNIUM ITEMS?

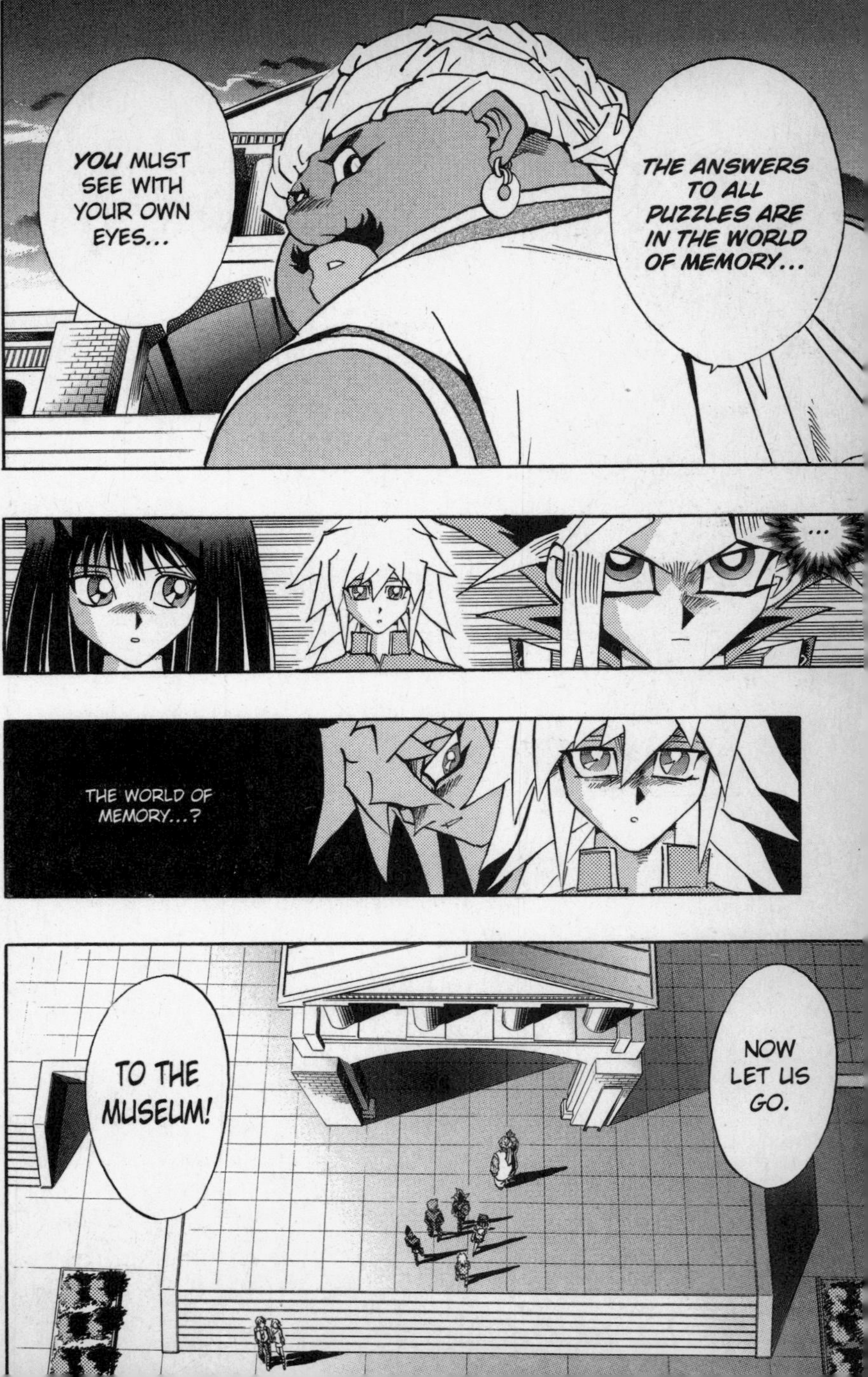
THE ANSWERS TO ALL PUZZLES ARE IN THE WORLD OF MEMORY...
YOU MUST SEE WITH YOUR OWN EYES...
...
THE WORLD OF MEMORY...?
NOW LET US GO.
TO THE MUSEUM!

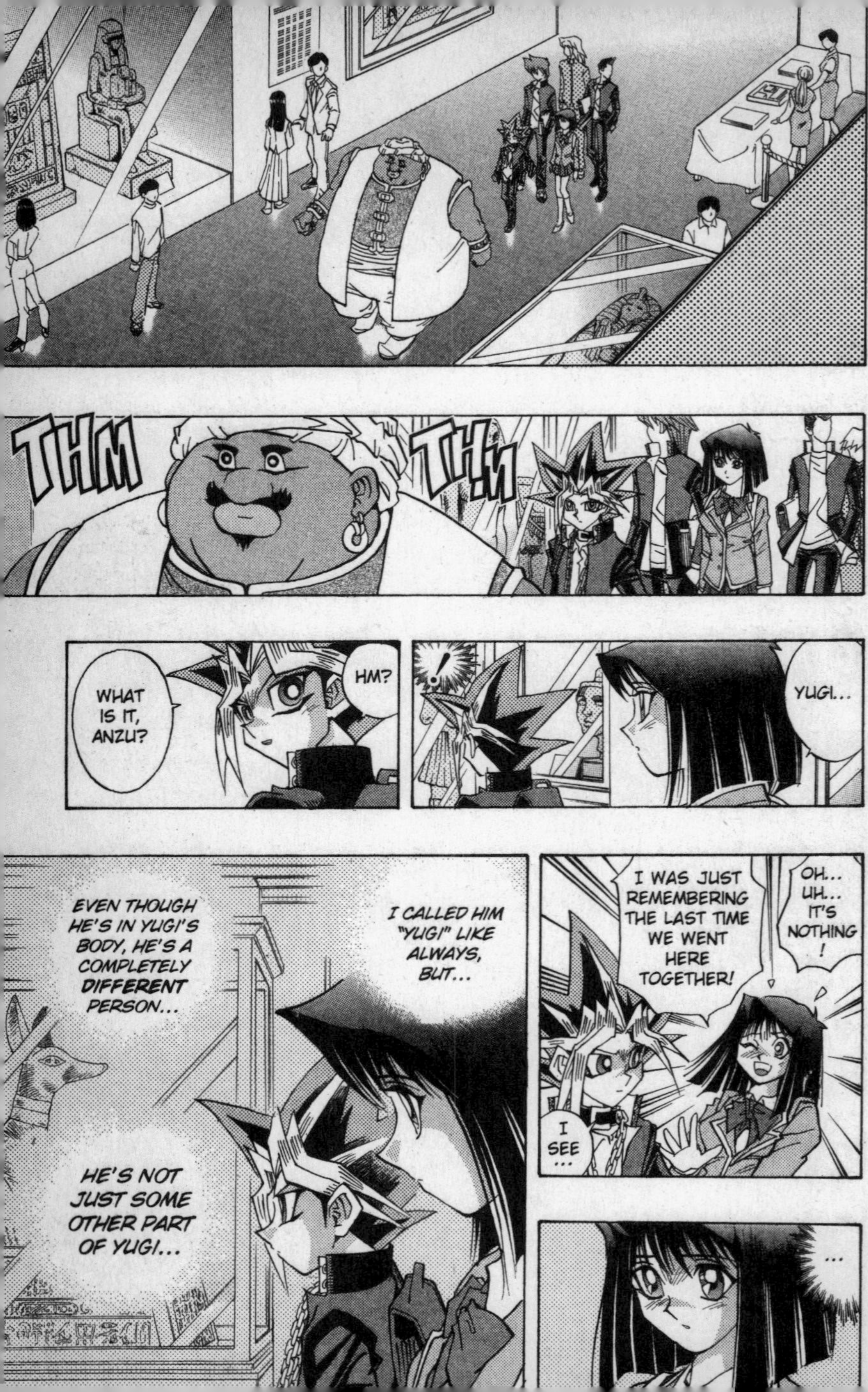
THM
THM
YUGI...
!
HM?
WHAT IS IT, ANZU?
OH... UH... IT'S NOTHING!
I WAS JUST REMEMBERING THE LAST TIME WE WENT HERE TOGETHER!
I SEE...
...
I CALLED HIM "YUGI" LIKE ALWAYS, BUT...
EVEN THOUGH HE'S IN YUGI'S BODY, HE'S A COMPLETELY DIFFERENT PERSON...
HE'S NOT JUST SOME OTHER PART OF YUGI...

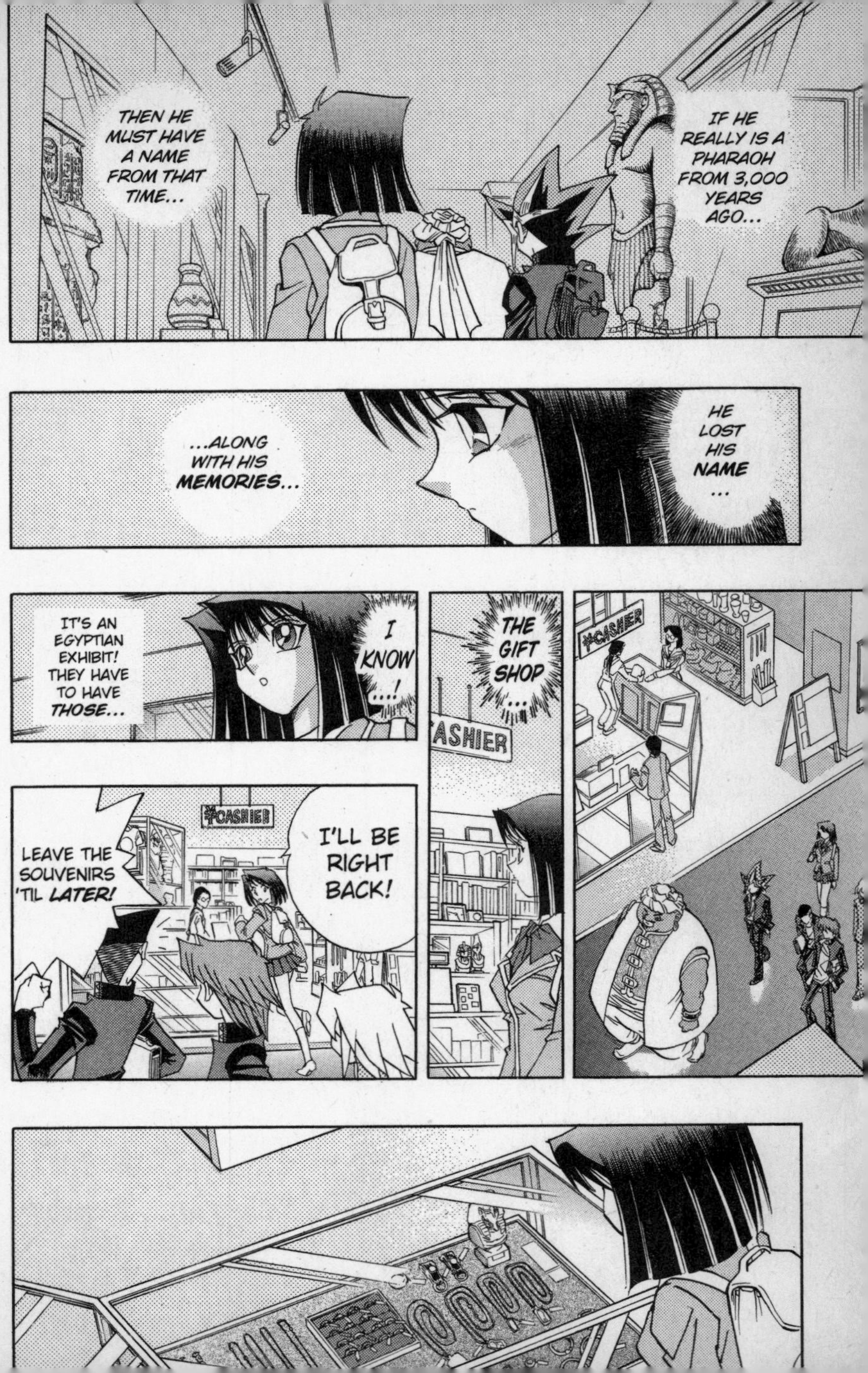
IF HE REALLY IS A PHARAOH FROM 3,000 YEARS AGO...
THEN HE MUST HAVE A NAME FROM THAT TIME...
HE LOST HIS NAME ...
...ALONG WITH HIS MEMORIES...
¥CASHIER
THE GIFT SHOP ...
CASHIER
I KNOW ...!
IT'S AN EGYPTIAN EXHIBIT! THEY HAVE TO HAVE THOSE...
I'LL BE RIGHT BACK!
¥CASHIER
LEAVE THE SOUVENIRS 'TIL LATER!

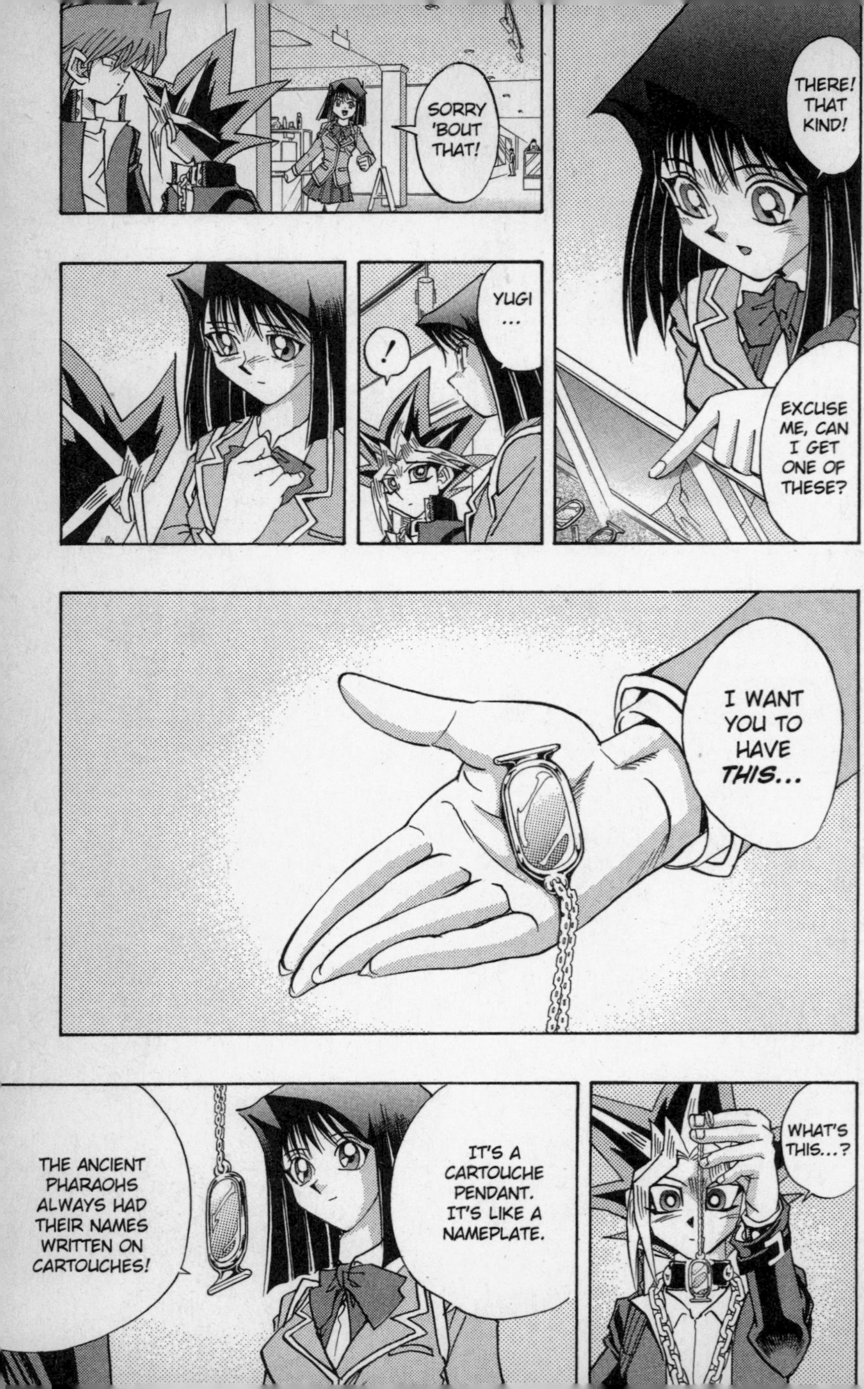
THERE! THAT KIND!
EXCUSE ME, CAN I GET ONE OF THESE?
SORRY 'BOUT THAT!
YUGI ...
!
I WANT YOU TO HAVE *THIS...*
WHAT'S THIS...?
IT'S A CARTOUCHE PENDANT. IT'S LIKE A NAMEPLATE.
THE ANCIENT PHARAOHS ALWAYS HAD THEIR NAMES WRITTEN ON CARTOUCHES!

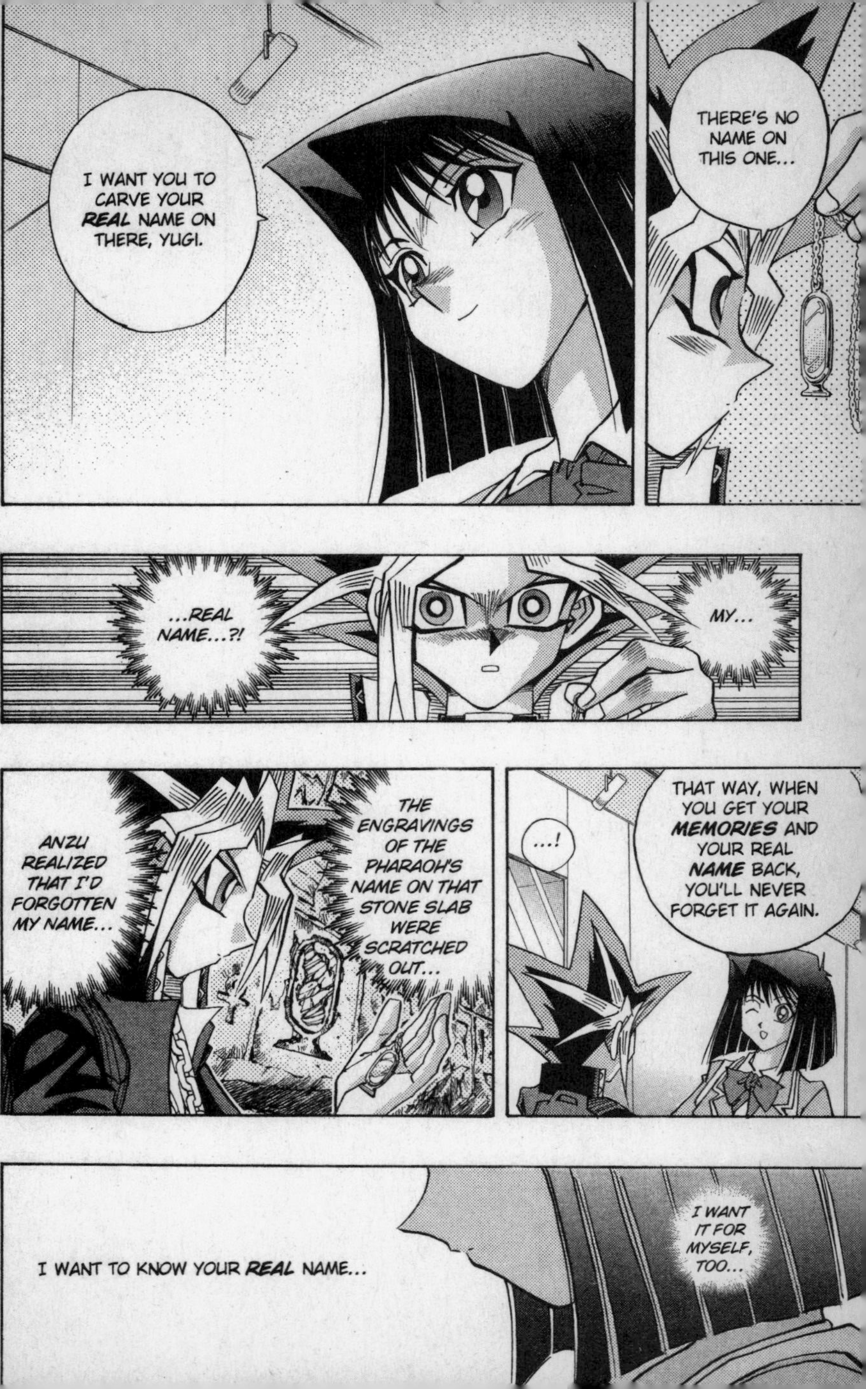
THERE'S NO NAME ON THIS ONE...
I WANT YOU TO CARVE YOUR REAL NAME ON THERE, YUGI.
MY...
...REAL NAME...?!
THAT WAY, WHEN YOU GET YOUR MEMORIES AND YOUR REAL NAME BACK, YOU'LL NEVER FORGET IT AGAIN.
...!
THE ENGRAVINGS OF THE PHARAOH'S NAME ON THAT STONE SLAB WERE SCRATCHED OUT...
ANZU REALIZED THAT I'D FORGOTTEN MY NAME...
I WANT IT FOR MYSELF, TOO...
I WANT TO KNOW YOUR REAL NAME...

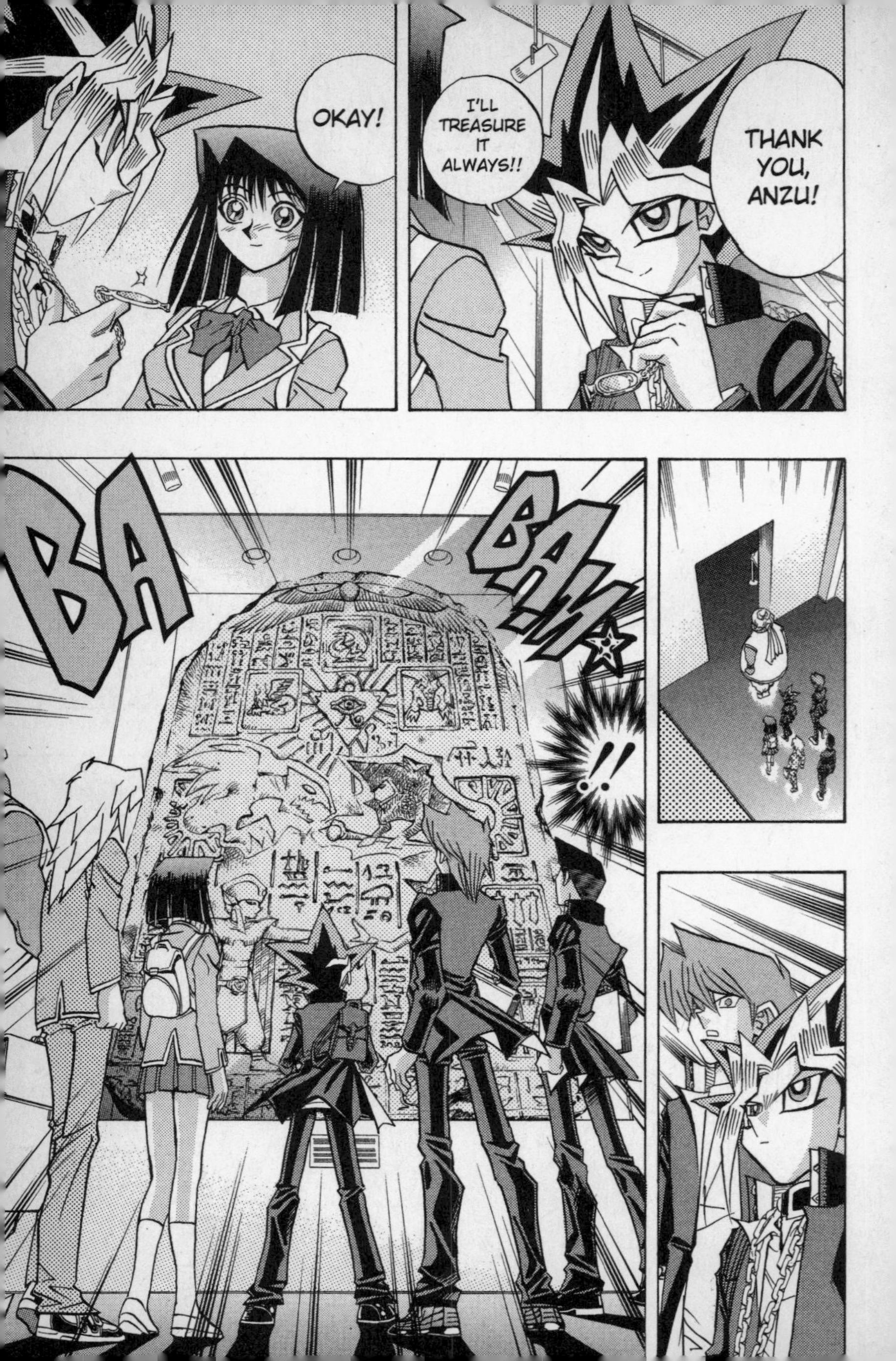
THANK YOU, ANZU!
I'LL TREASURE IT ALWAYS!!
OKAY!
BA
BA
!!

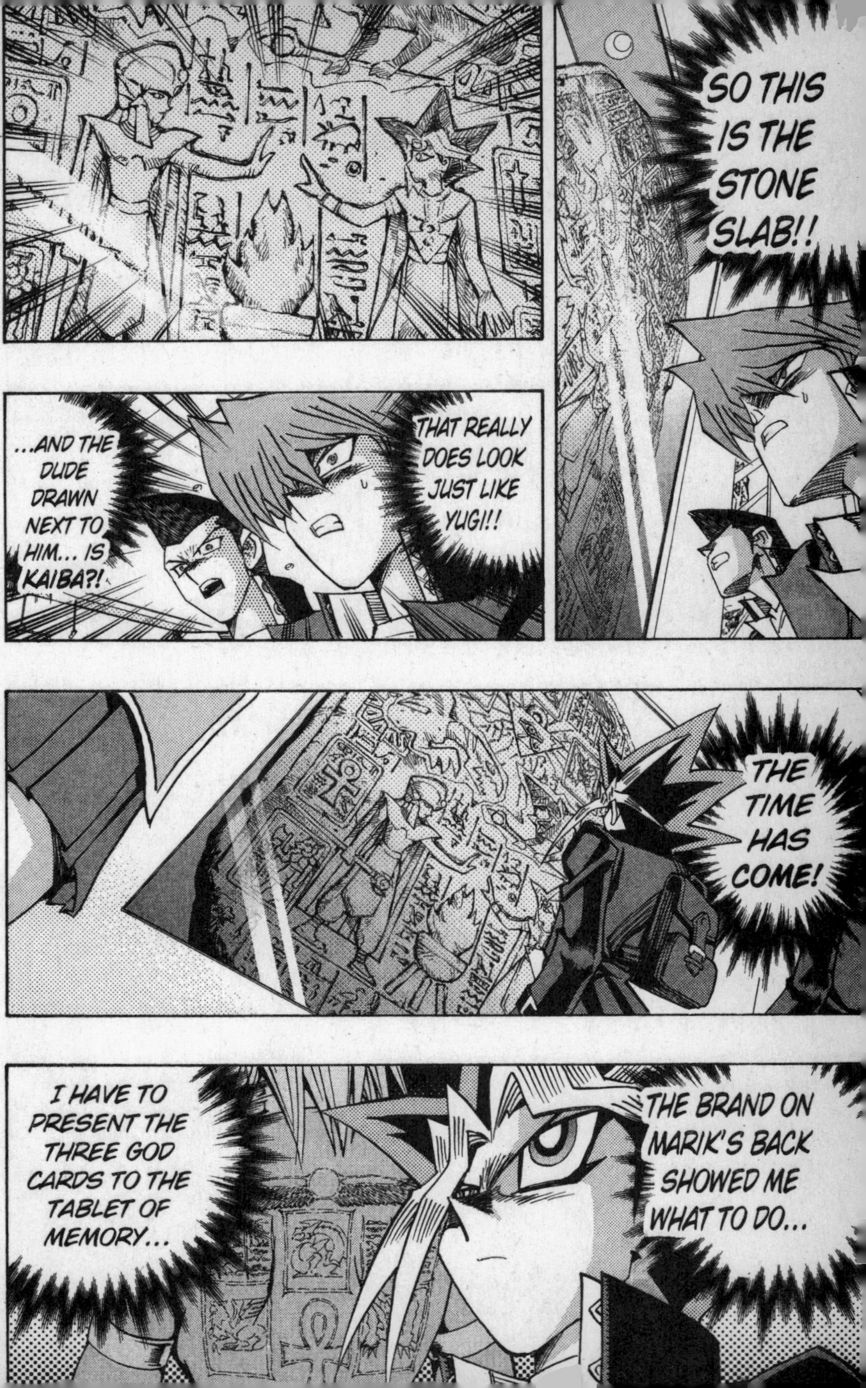
SO THIS IS THE STONE SLAB!!
THAT REALLY DOES LOOK JUST LIKE YUGI!!
...AND THE DUDE DRAWN NEXT TO HIM... IS KAIBA?!
THE TIME HAS COME!
THE BRAND ON MARIK'S BACK SHOWED ME WHAT TO DO...
I HAVE TO PRESENT THE THREE GOD CARDS TO THE TABLET OF MEMORY...

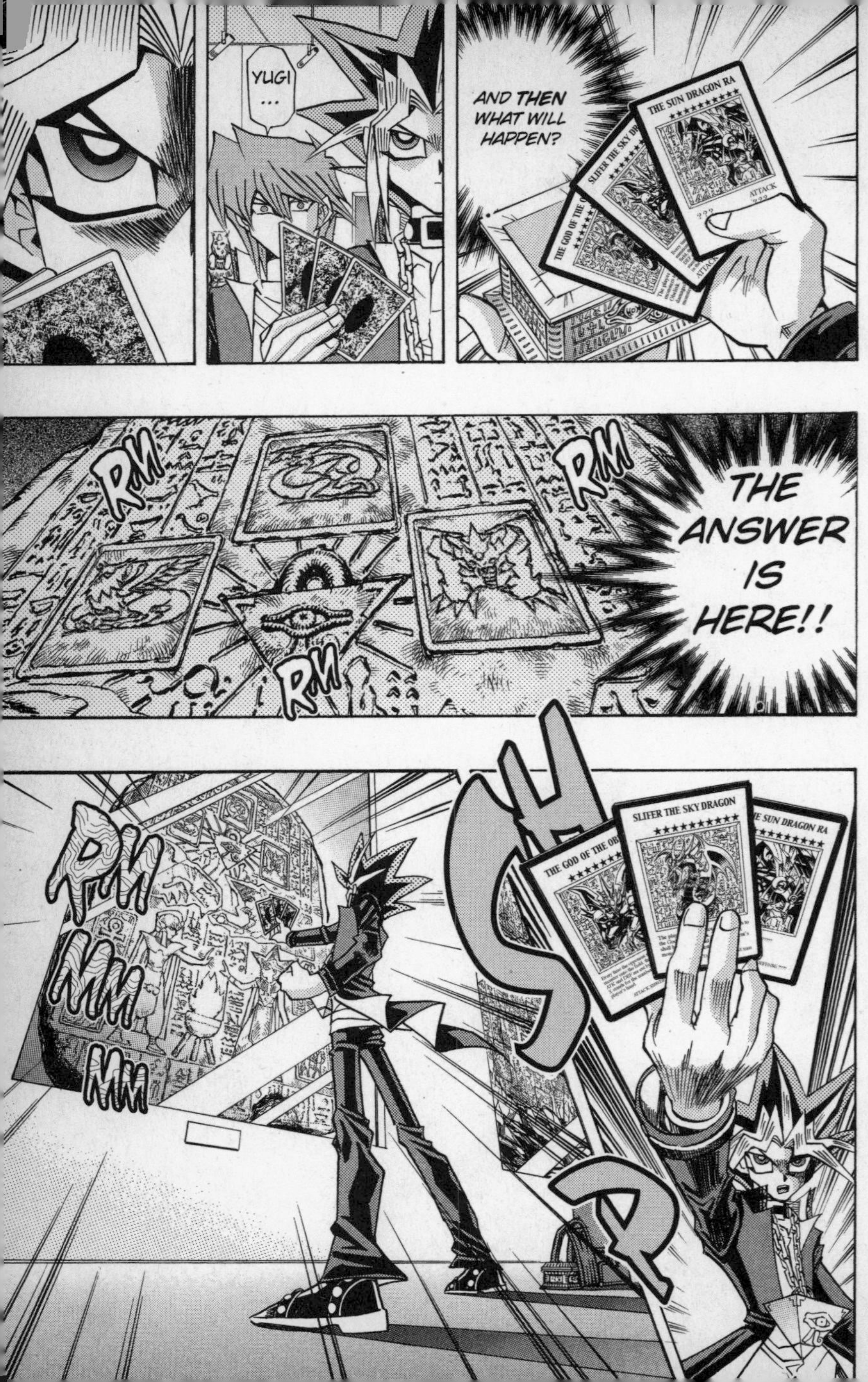
AND THEN WHAT WILL HAPPEN?
THE SUN DRAGON RA
YUGI ...
RM
RM
THE ANSWER IS HERE!!
RM
SLIFER THE SKY DRAGON
THE SUN DRAGON RA

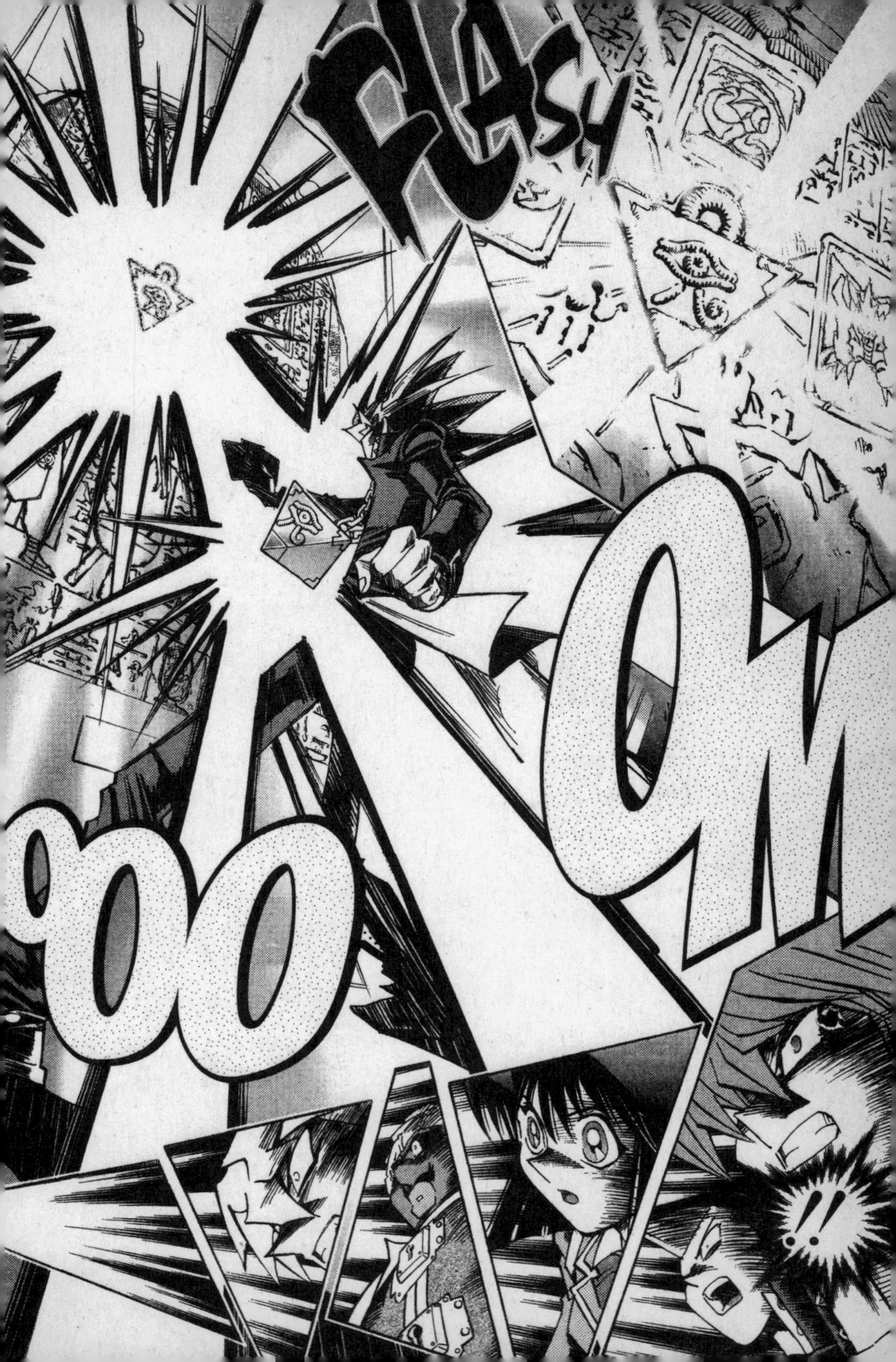
FLASH
!!

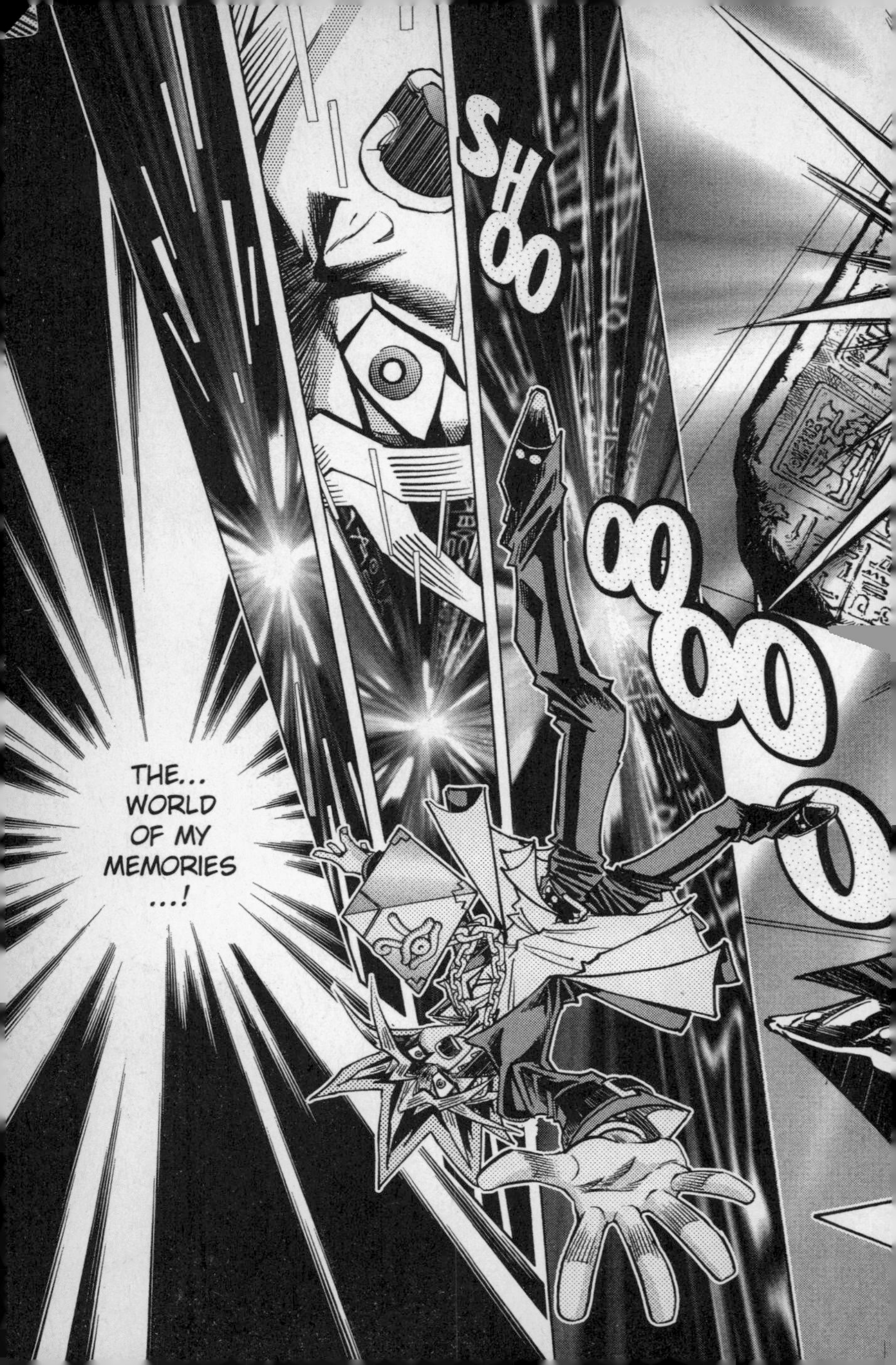
SHOO
OOOOO
THE... WORLD OF MY MEMORIES ...!

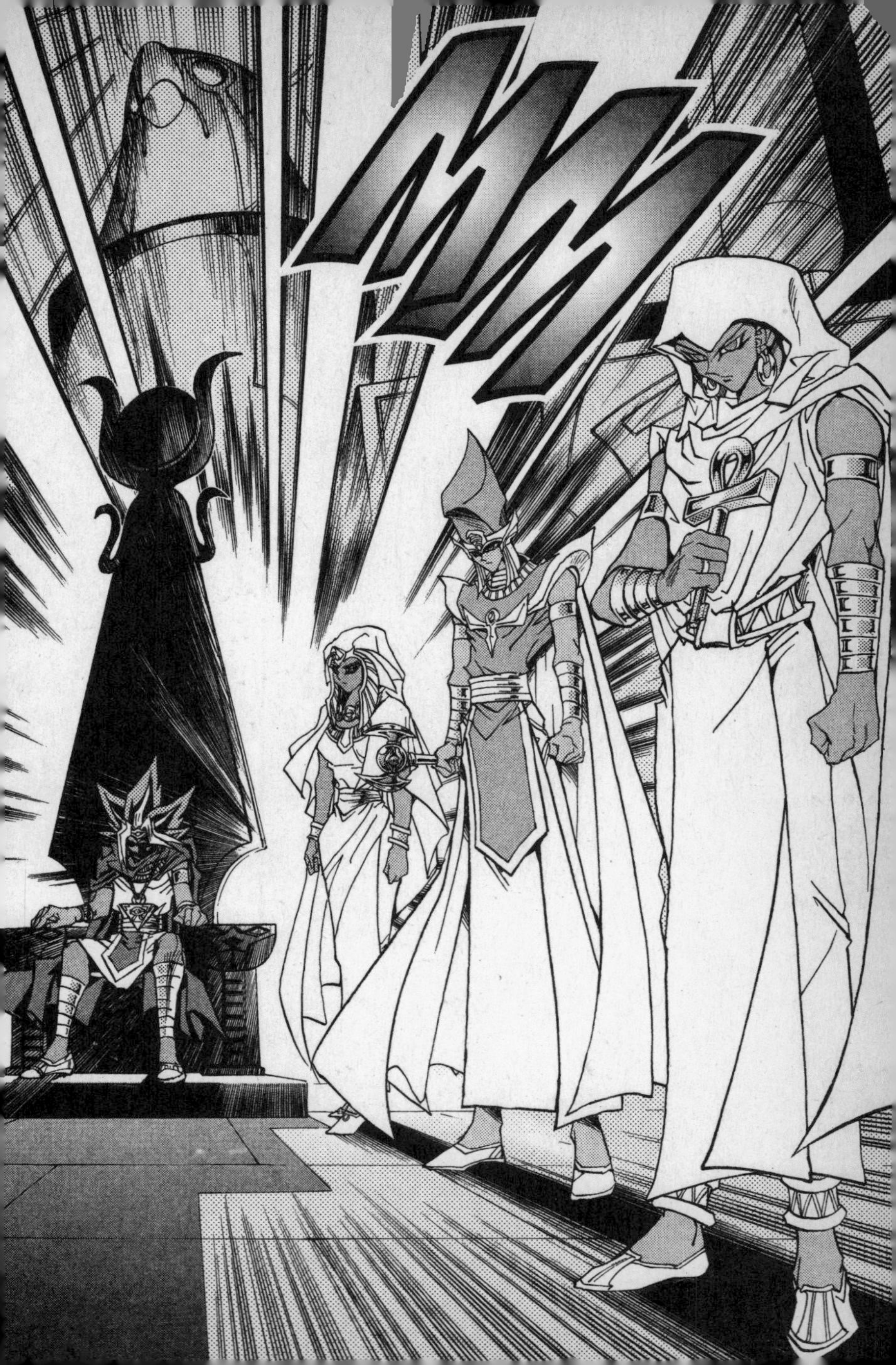

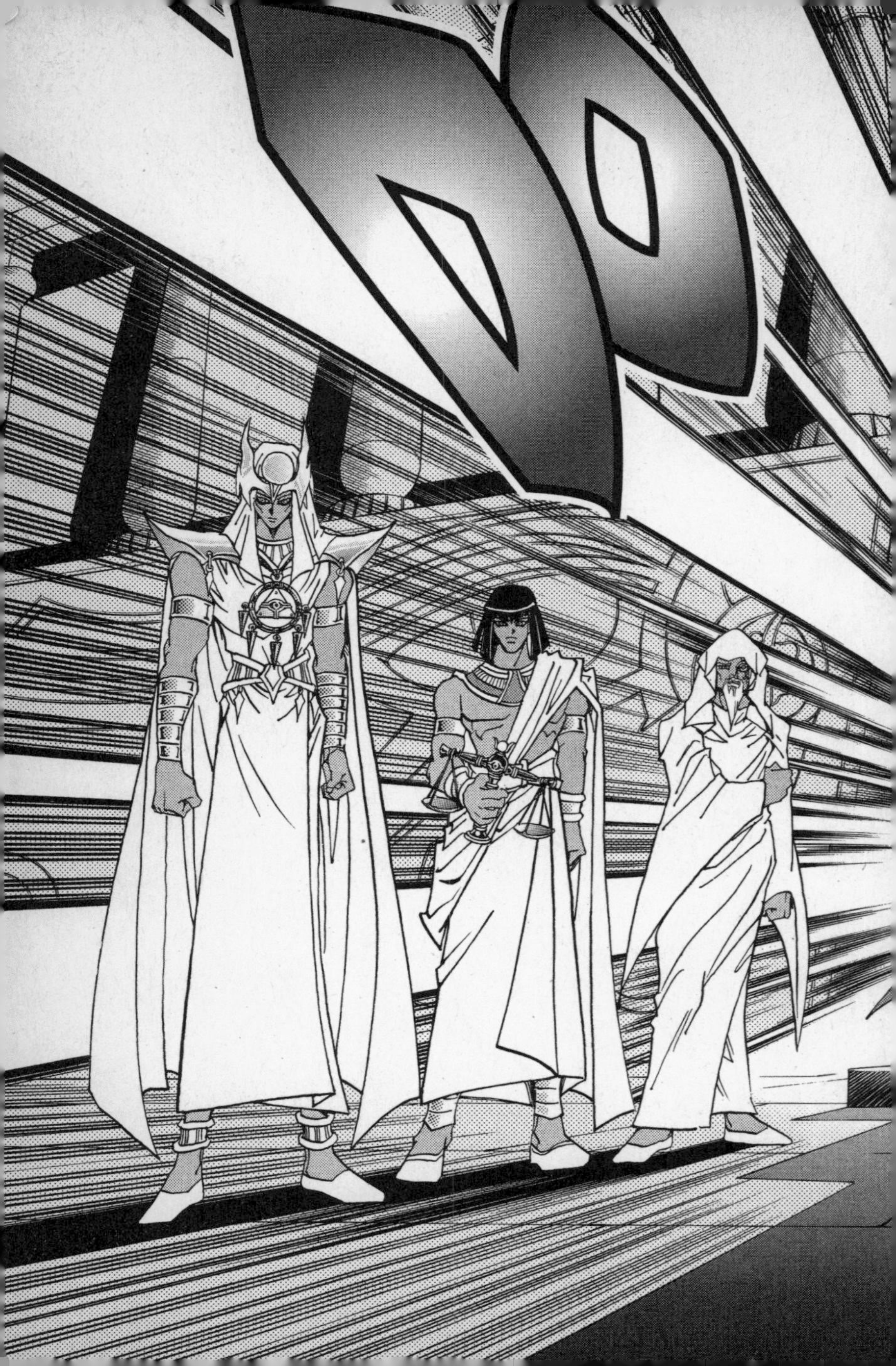

Duel 5: The Six Chosen Priests

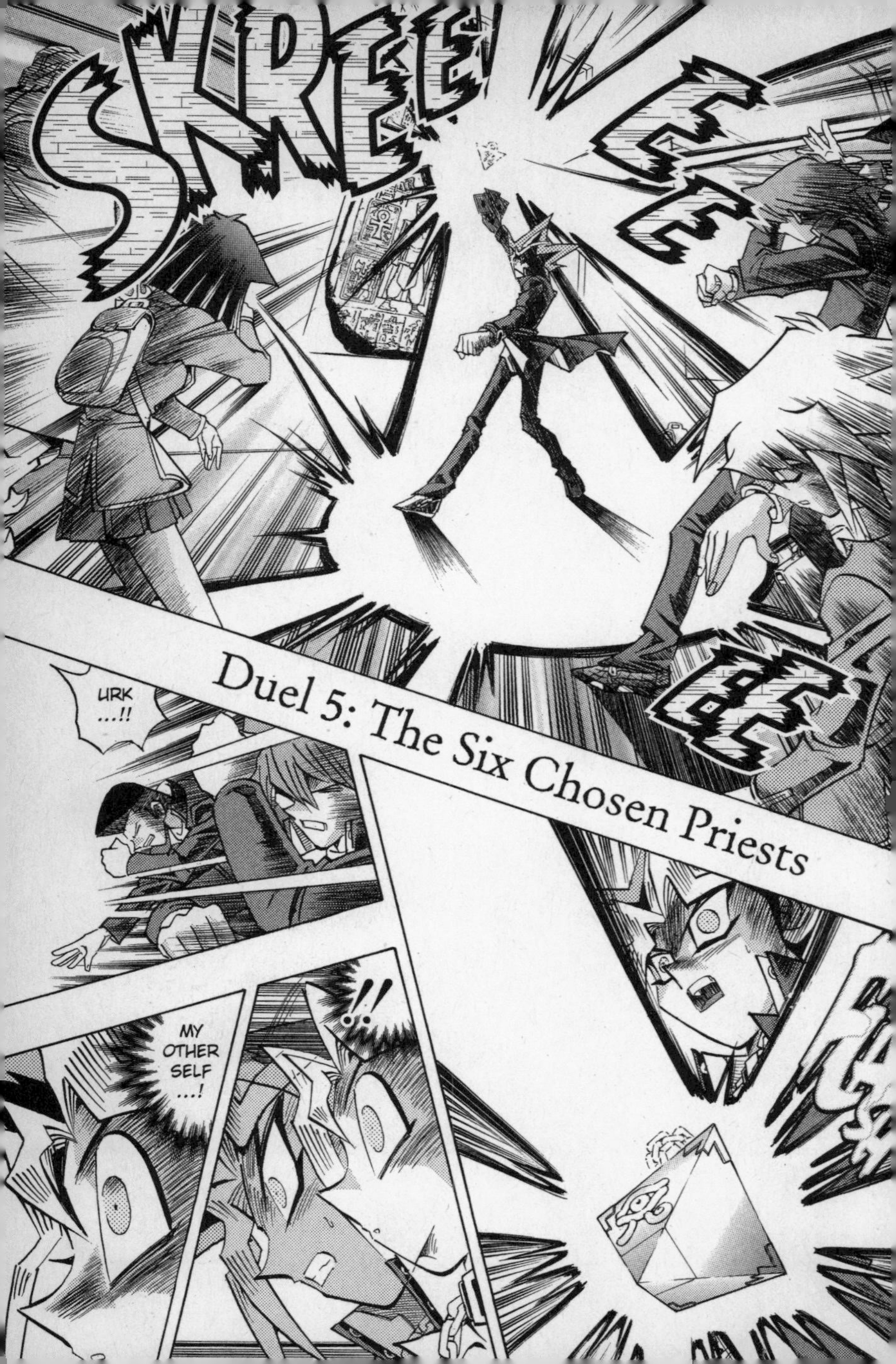
URK ...!!
!!
MY OTHER SELF ...!

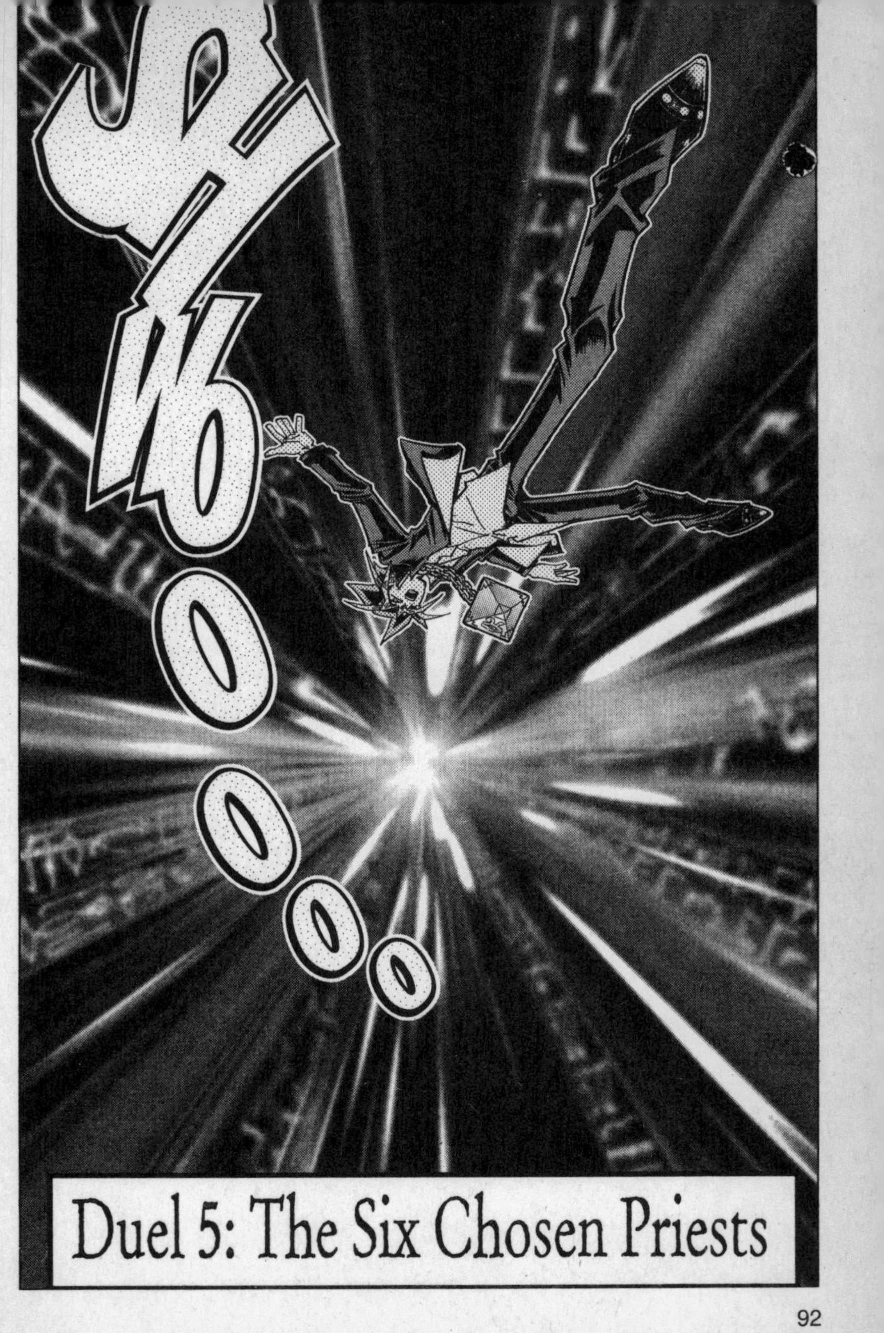

Duel 5: The Six Chosen Priests

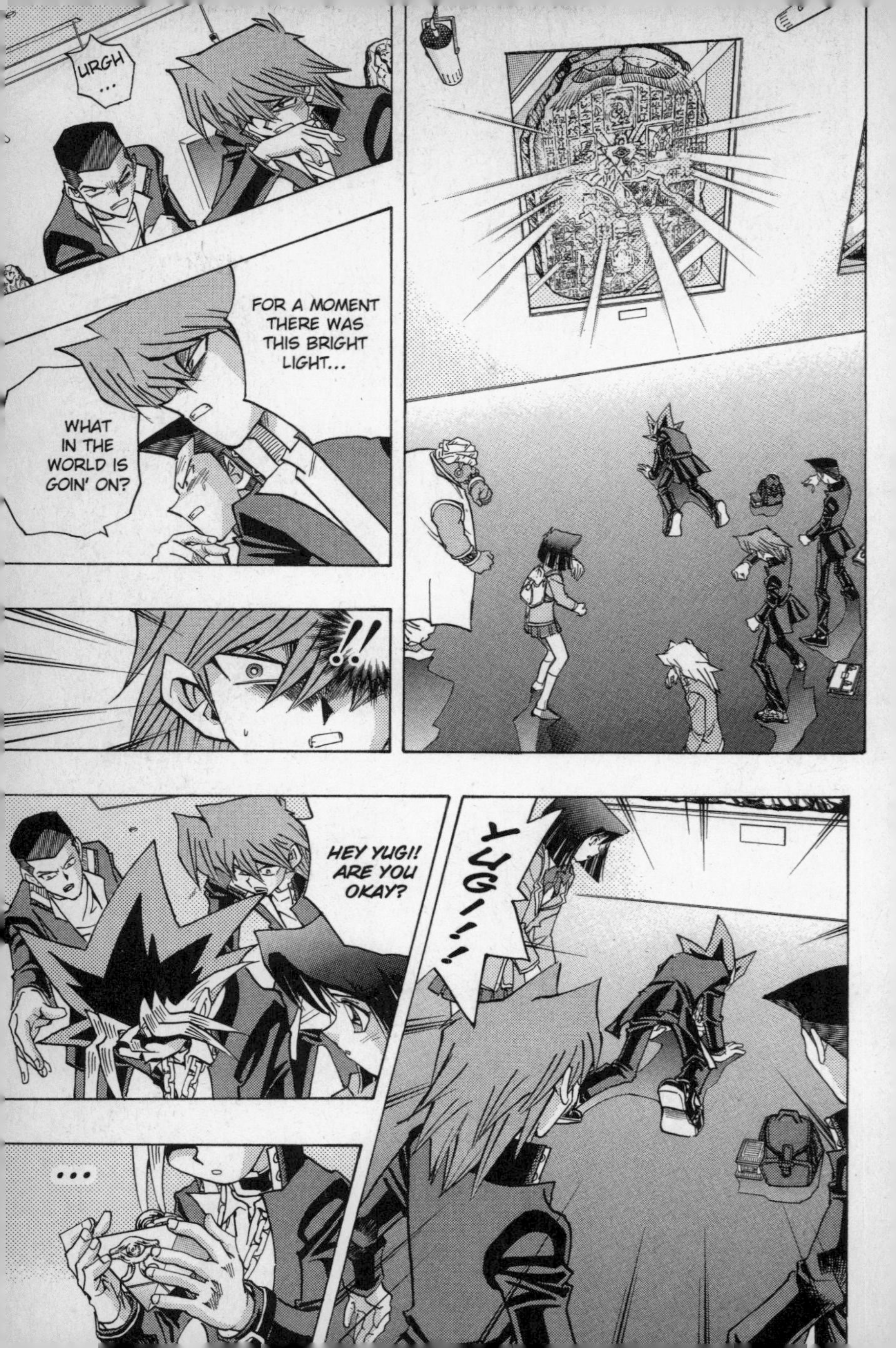
URGH ...
FOR A MOMENT THERE WAS THIS BRIGHT LIGHT...
WHAT IN THE WORLD IS GOIN' ON?
!!
YUGI!!!
HEY YUGI! ARE YOU OKAY?
...

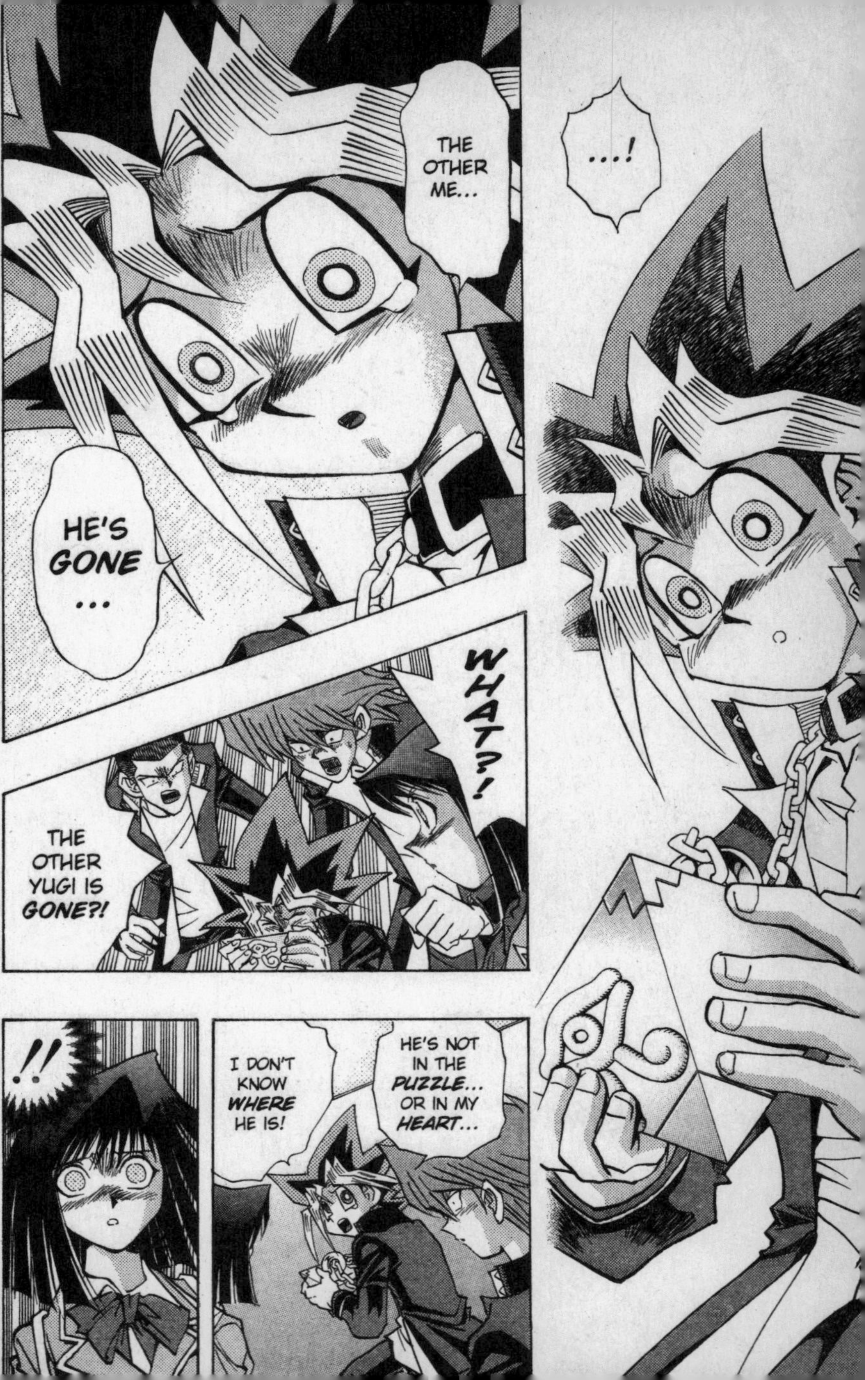
...!
THE OTHER ME...
HE'S GONE...
WHAT?!
THE OTHER YUGI IS GONE?!
HE'S NOT IN THE PUZZLE... OR IN MY HEART...
I DON'T KNOW WHERE HE IS!
!!

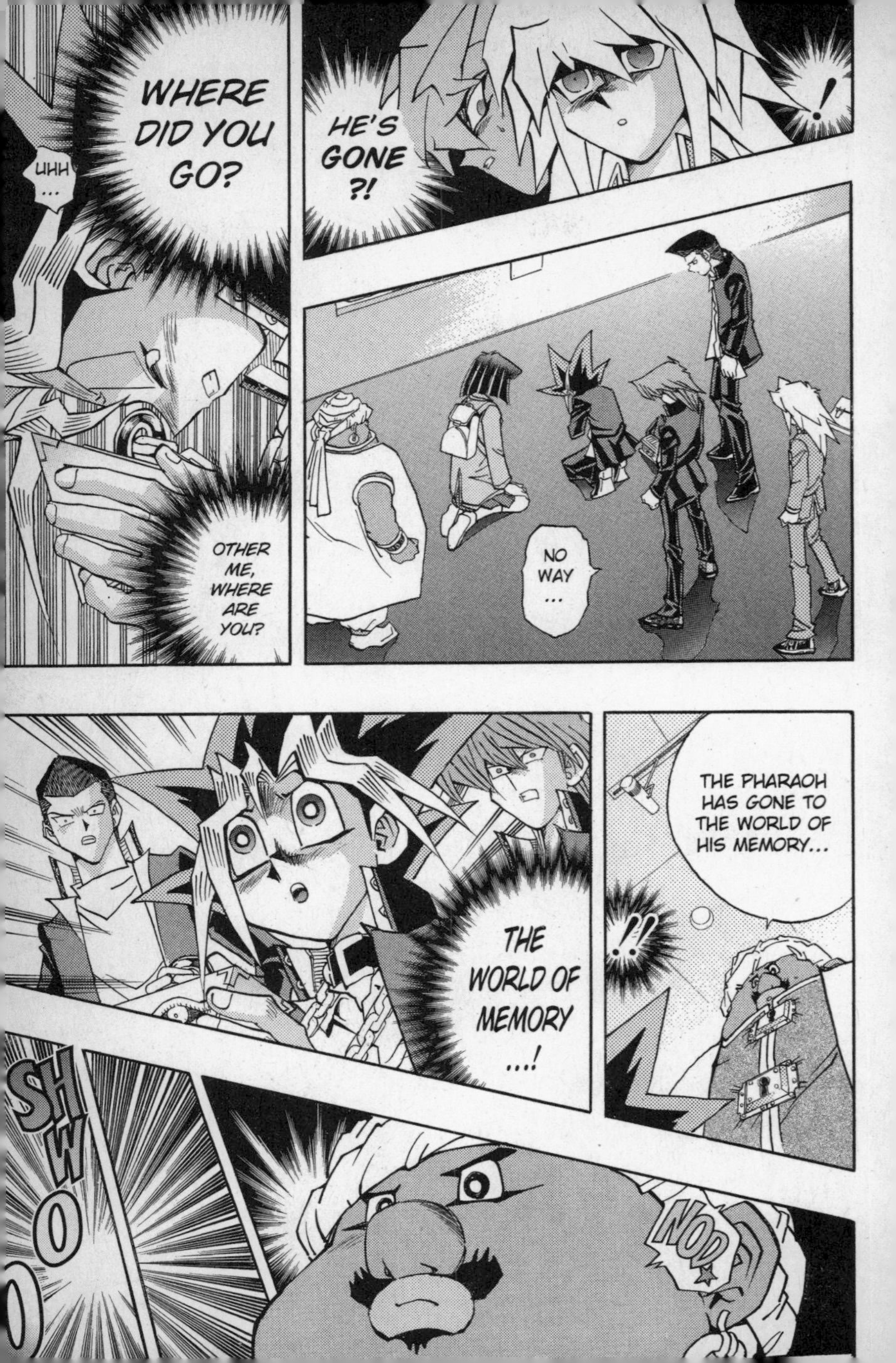
!
HE'S GONE ?!
NO WAY ...
WHERE DID YOU GO?
UHH ...
OTHER ME, WHERE ARE YOU?
THE PHARAOH HAS GONE TO THE WORLD OF HIS MEMORY...
!!
THE WORLD OF MEMORY ...!
NOD
SHWOO

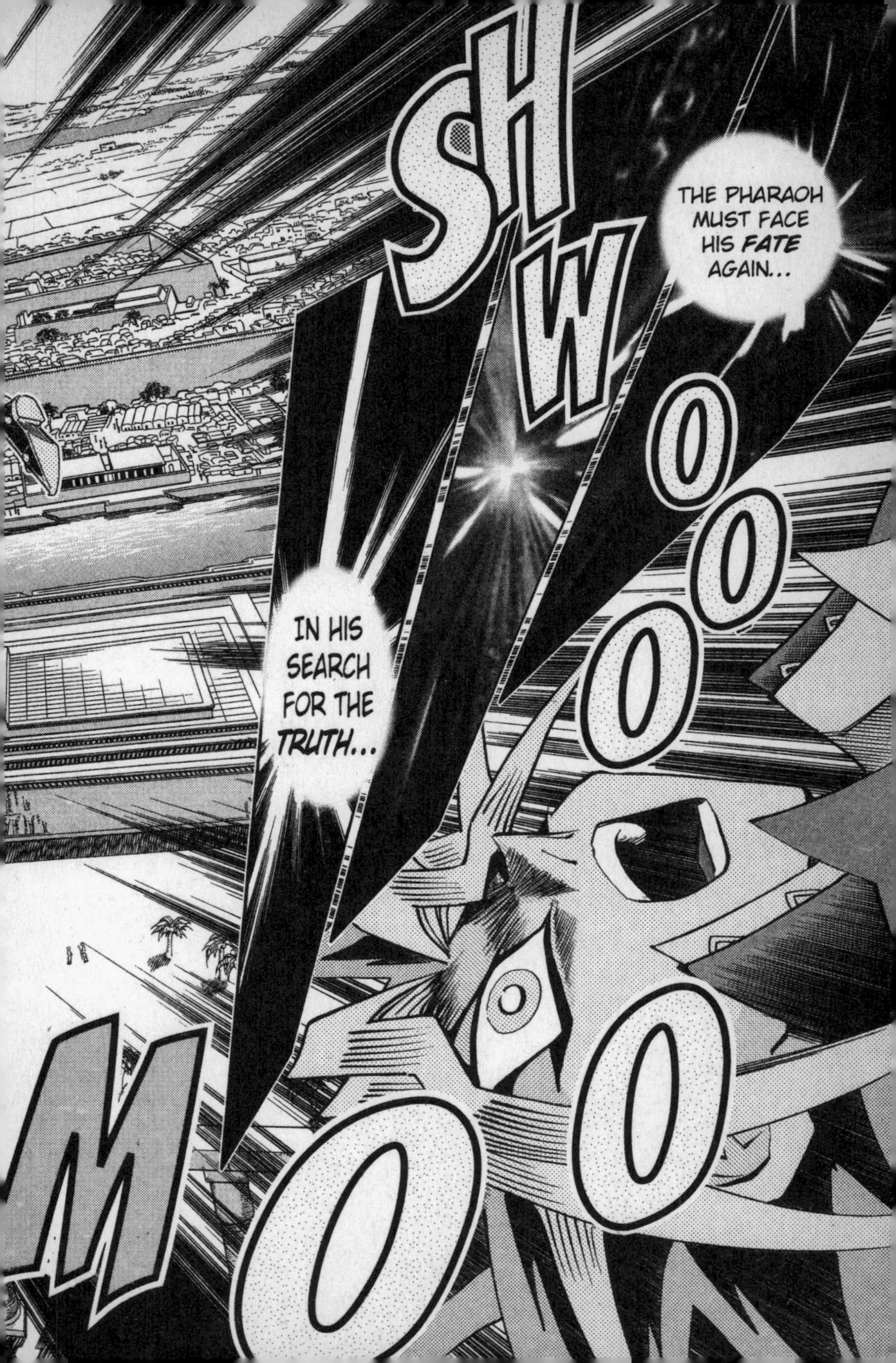

THE PHARAOH MUST FACE HIS *FATE* AGAIN...
SHWOOOOOOOM
IN HIS SEARCH FOR THE *TRUTH*...

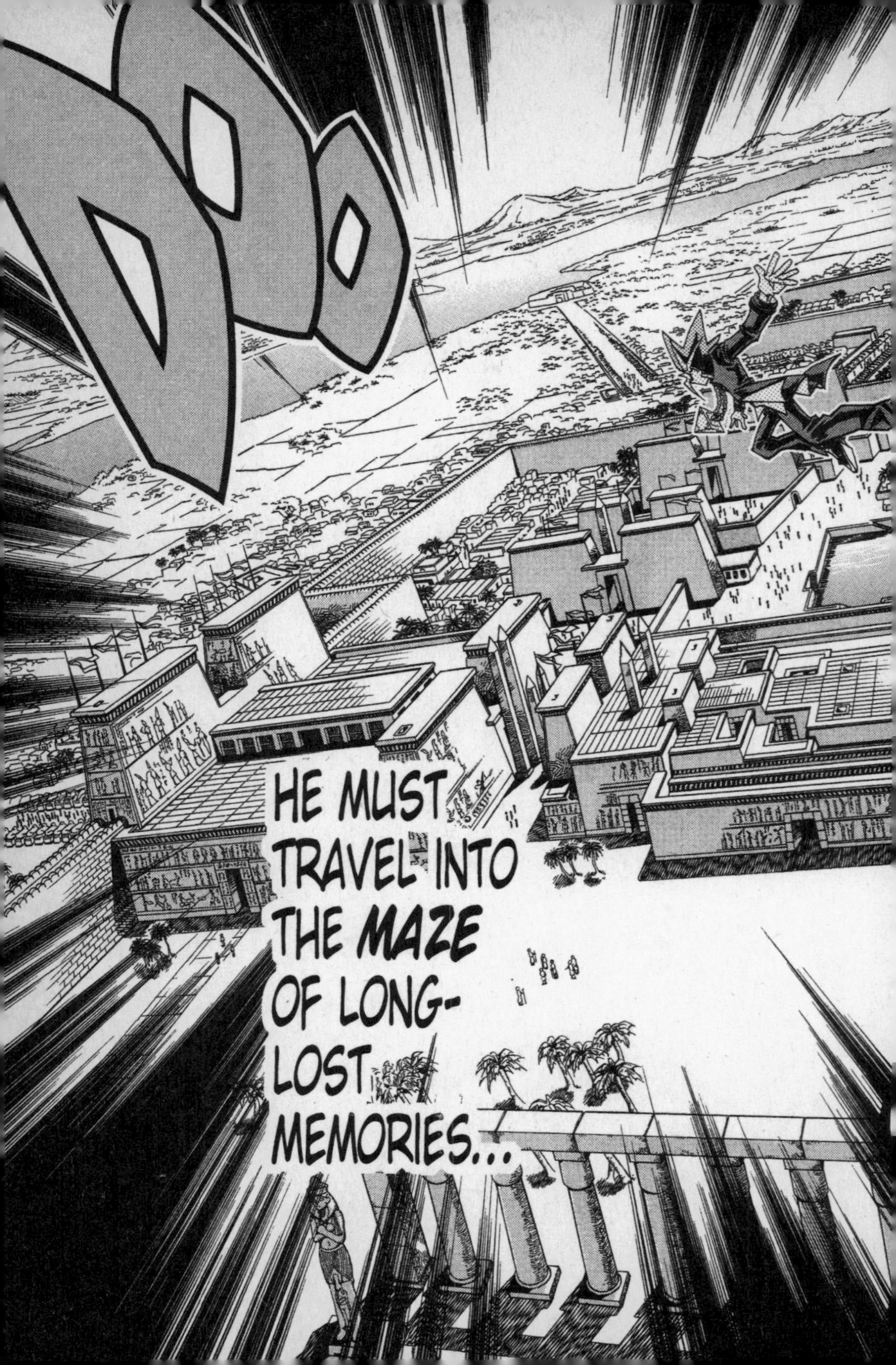
HE MUST TRAVEL INTO THE *MAZE* OF LONG-LOST MEMORIES...

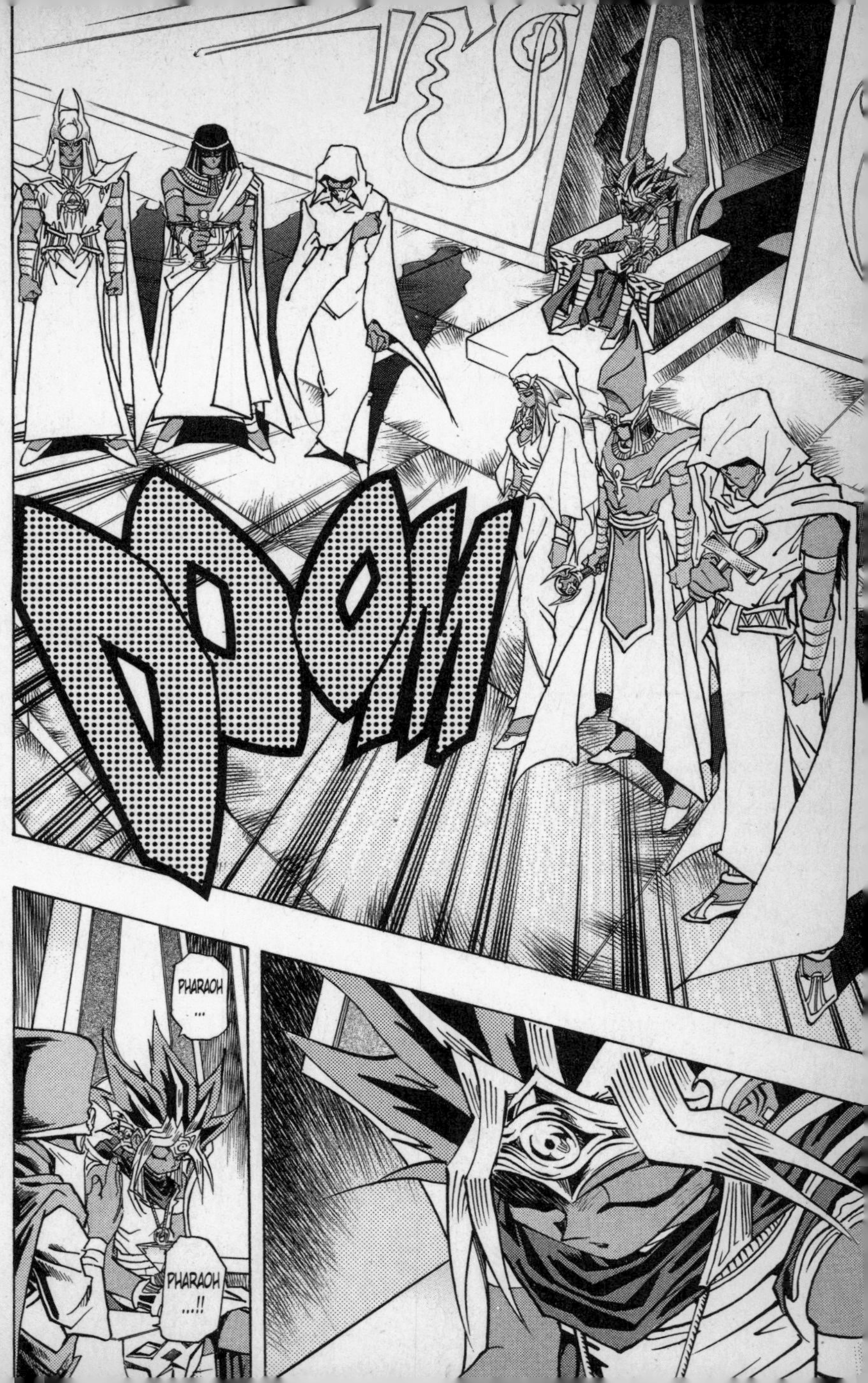
DOOM
PHARAOH ...
PHARAOH ...!!

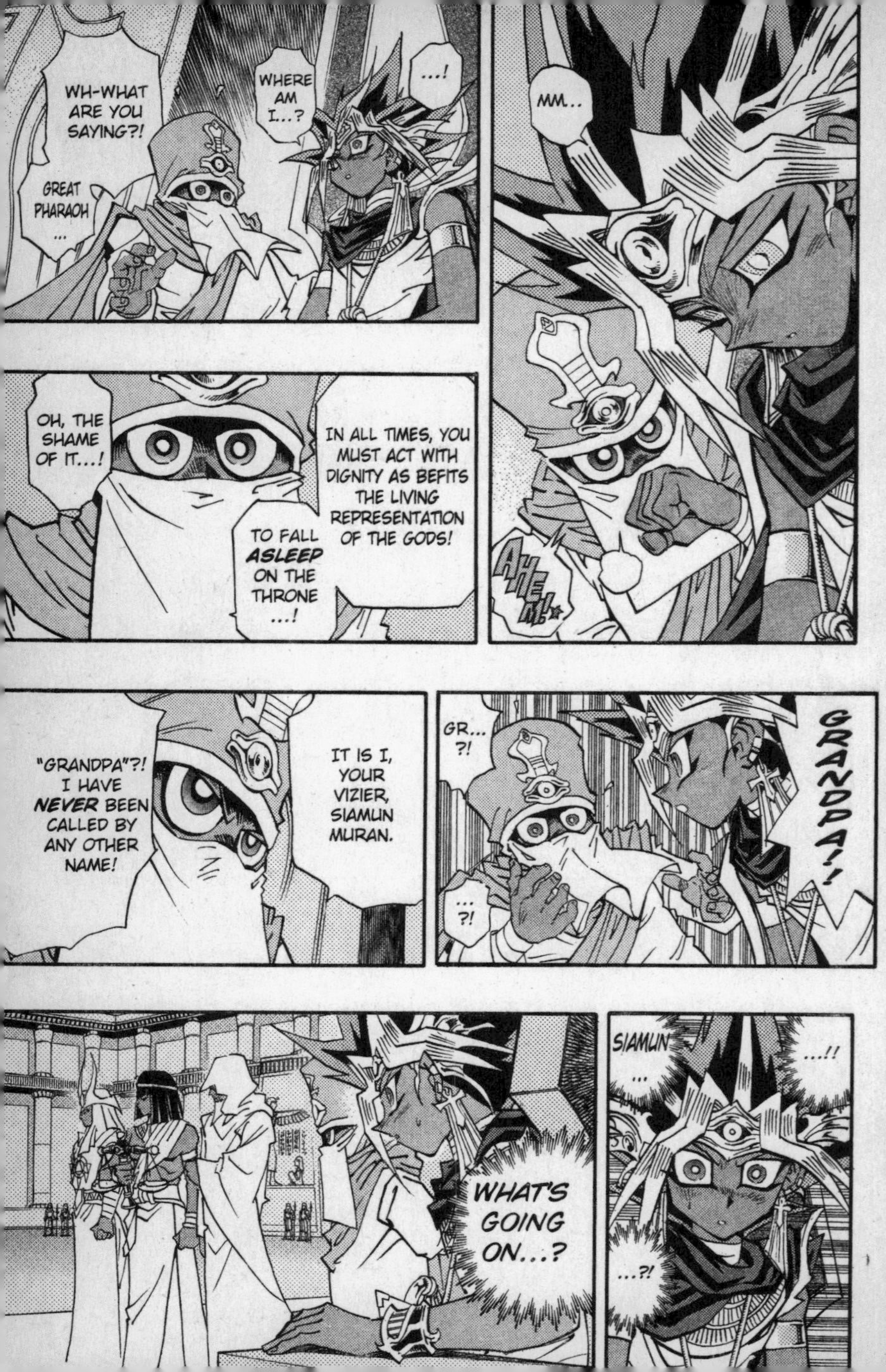
MM...
AHEM!
...!
WHERE AM I...?
WH-WHAT ARE YOU SAYING?!
GREAT PHARAOH ...
IN ALL TIMES, YOU MUST ACT WITH DIGNITY AS BEFITS THE LIVING REPRESENTATION OF THE GODS!
OH, THE SHAME OF IT...!
TO FALL **ASLEEP** ON THE THRONE ...!
GRANDPA!!
GR... ?!
... ?!
IT IS I, YOUR VIZIER, SIAMUN MURAN.
"GRANDPA"?! I HAVE **NEVER** BEEN CALLED BY ANY OTHER NAME!
...!!
SIAMUN ...
...?!
WHAT'S GOING ON...?

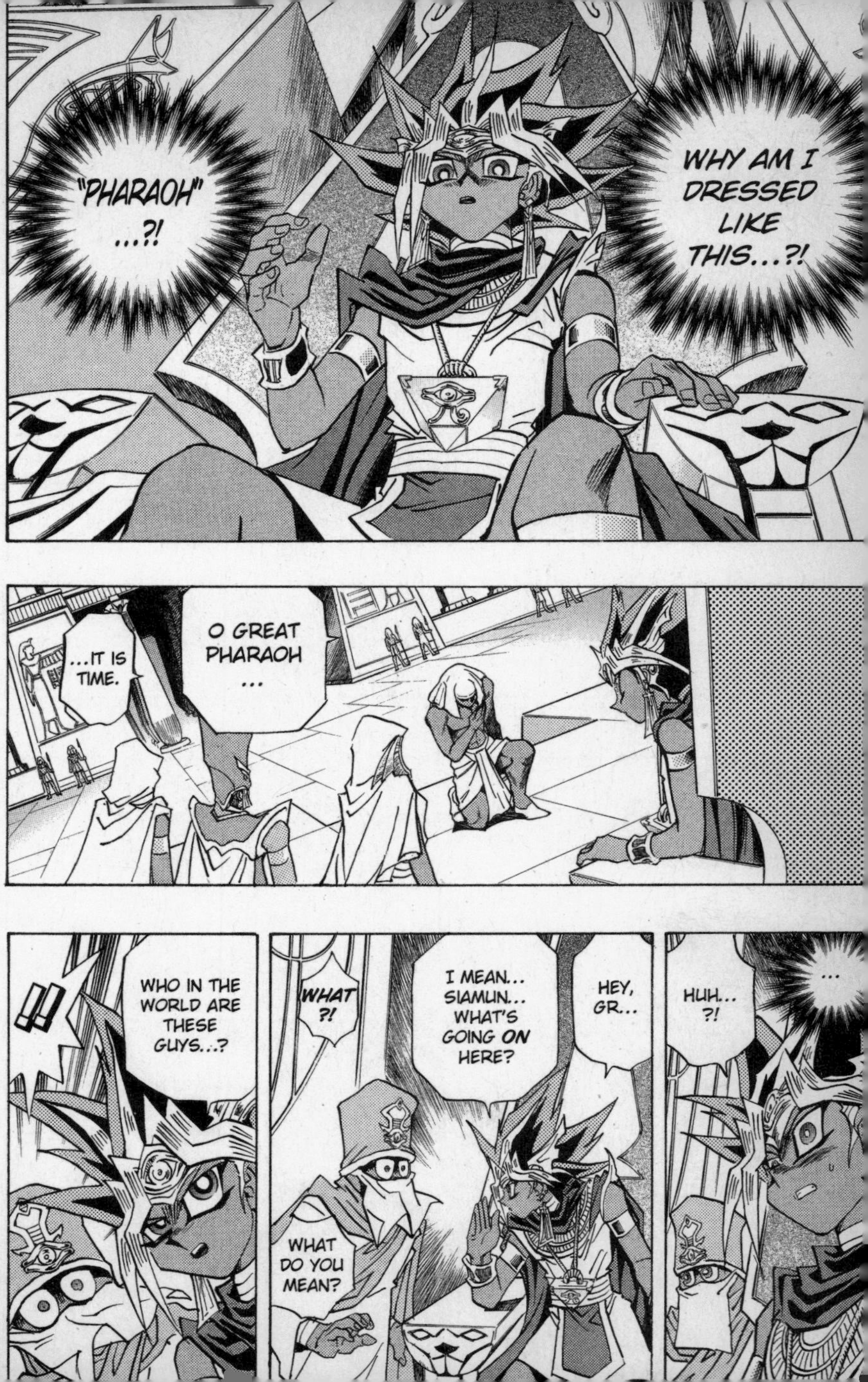

WHY AM I DRESSED LIKE THIS...?!
"PHARAOH" ...?!
O GREAT PHARAOH ...
...IT IS TIME.
...
HUH...?!
HEY, GR...
I MEAN... SIAMUN... WHAT'S GOING ON HERE?
WHAT?!
WHAT DO YOU MEAN?
WHO IN THE WORLD ARE THESE GUYS...?
!!

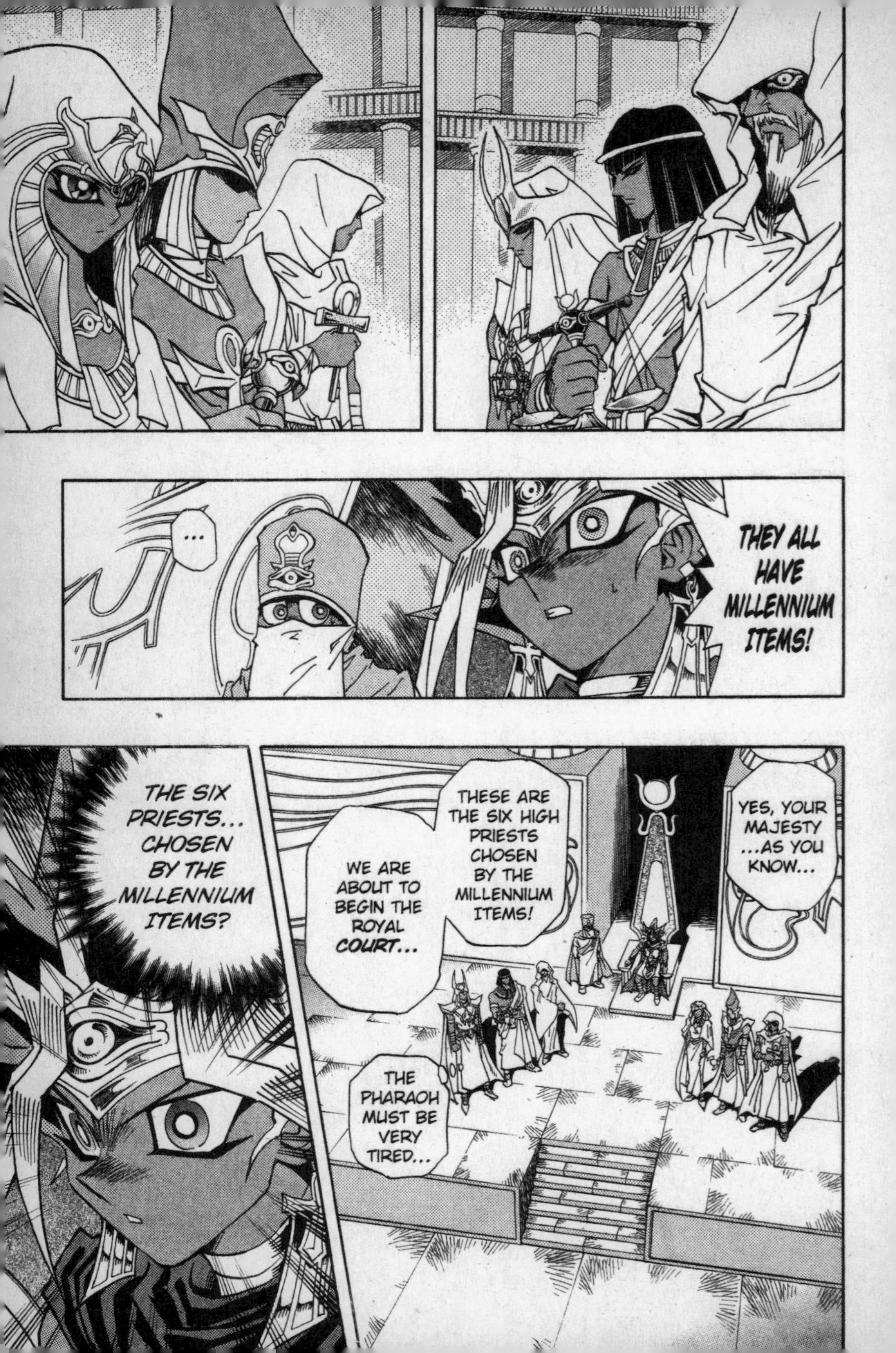
THEY ALL HAVE MILLENNIUM ITEMS!
...
YES, YOUR MAJESTY ...AS YOU KNOW...
THESE ARE THE SIX HIGH PRIESTS CHOSEN BY THE MILLENNIUM ITEMS!
WE ARE ABOUT TO BEGIN THE ROYAL COURT...
THE PHARAOH MUST BE VERY TIRED...
THE SIX PRIESTS... CHOSEN BY THE MILLENNIUM ITEMS?

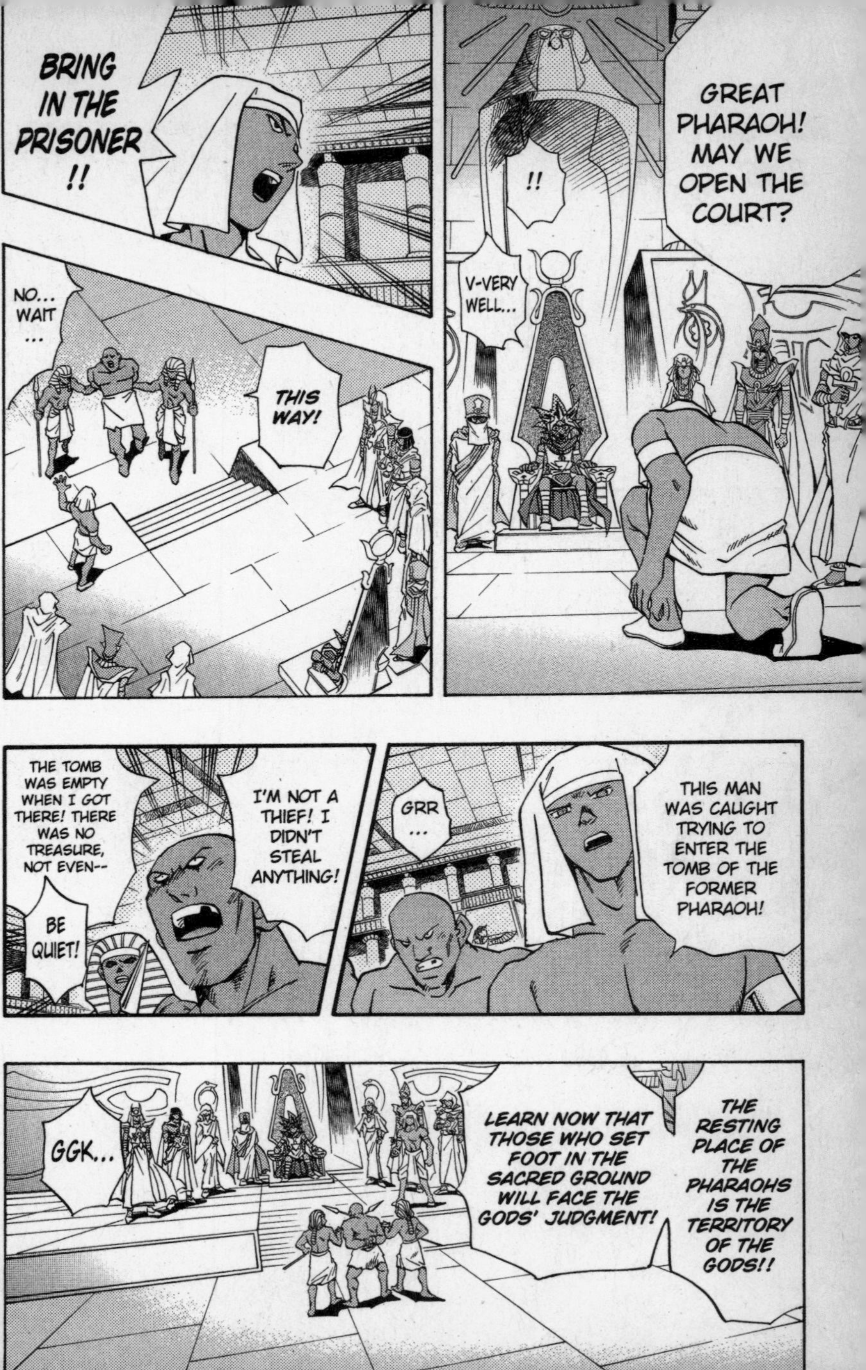
GREAT PHARAOH! MAY WE OPEN THE COURT?
!!
V-VERY WELL...
BRING IN THE PRISONER !!
THIS WAY!
NO... WAIT ...
THIS MAN WAS CAUGHT TRYING TO ENTER THE TOMB OF THE FORMER PHARAOH!
GRR ...
I'M NOT A THIEF! I DIDN'T STEAL ANYTHING!
THE TOMB WAS EMPTY WHEN I GOT THERE! THERE WAS NO TREASURE, NOT EVEN--
BE QUIET!
THE RESTING PLACE OF THE PHARAOHS IS THE TERRITORY OF THE GODS!!
LEARN NOW THAT THOSE WHO SET FOOT IN THE SACRED GROUND WILL FACE THE GODS' JUDGMENT!
GGK...

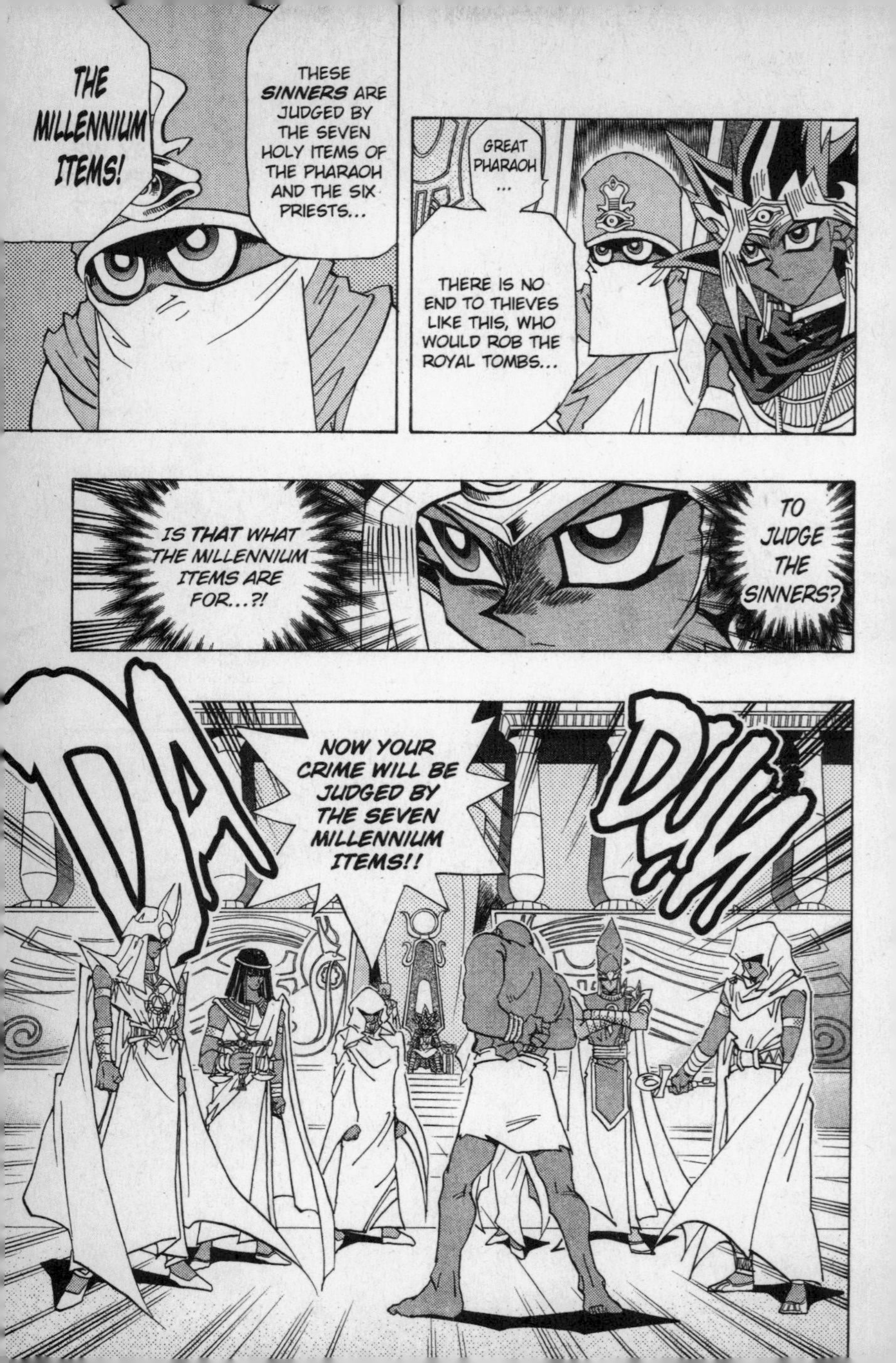
GREAT PHARAOH ...
THERE IS NO END TO THIEVES LIKE THIS, WHO WOULD ROB THE ROYAL TOMBS...
THESE *SINNERS* ARE JUDGED BY THE SEVEN HOLY ITEMS OF THE PHARAOH AND THE SIX PRIESTS...
THE MILLENNIUM ITEMS!
TO JUDGE THE SINNERS?
IS THAT WHAT THE MILLENNIUM ITEMS ARE FOR...?!
DA
DUM
NOW YOUR CRIME WILL BE JUDGED BY THE SEVEN MILLENNIUM ITEMS!!

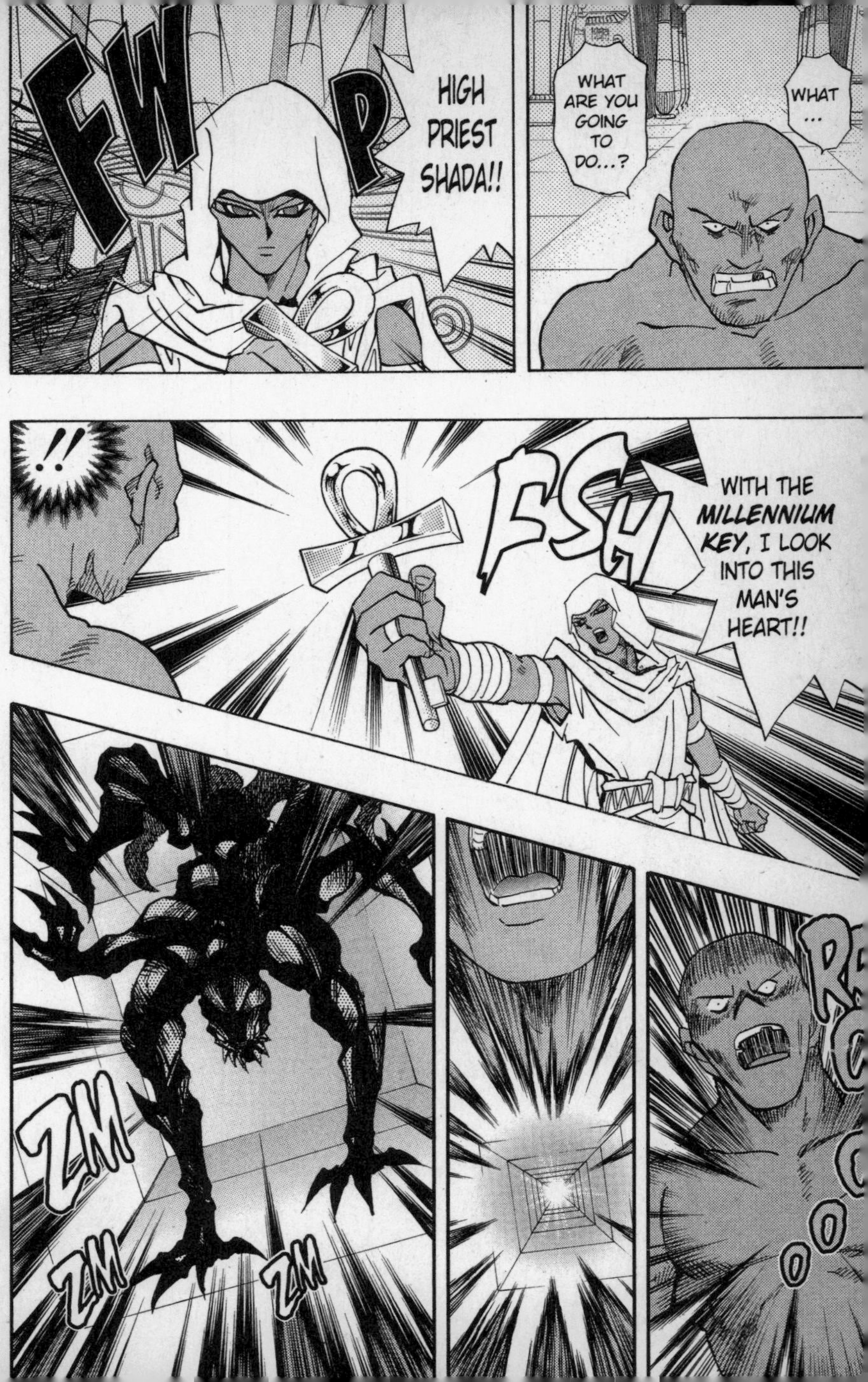
WHAT ...
WHAT ARE YOU GOING TO DO...?
HIGH PRIEST SHADA!!
FWP
WITH THE *MILLENNIUM KEY*, I LOOK INTO THIS MAN'S HEART!!
FSH
!!
ROOOOO
ZM
ZM
ZM

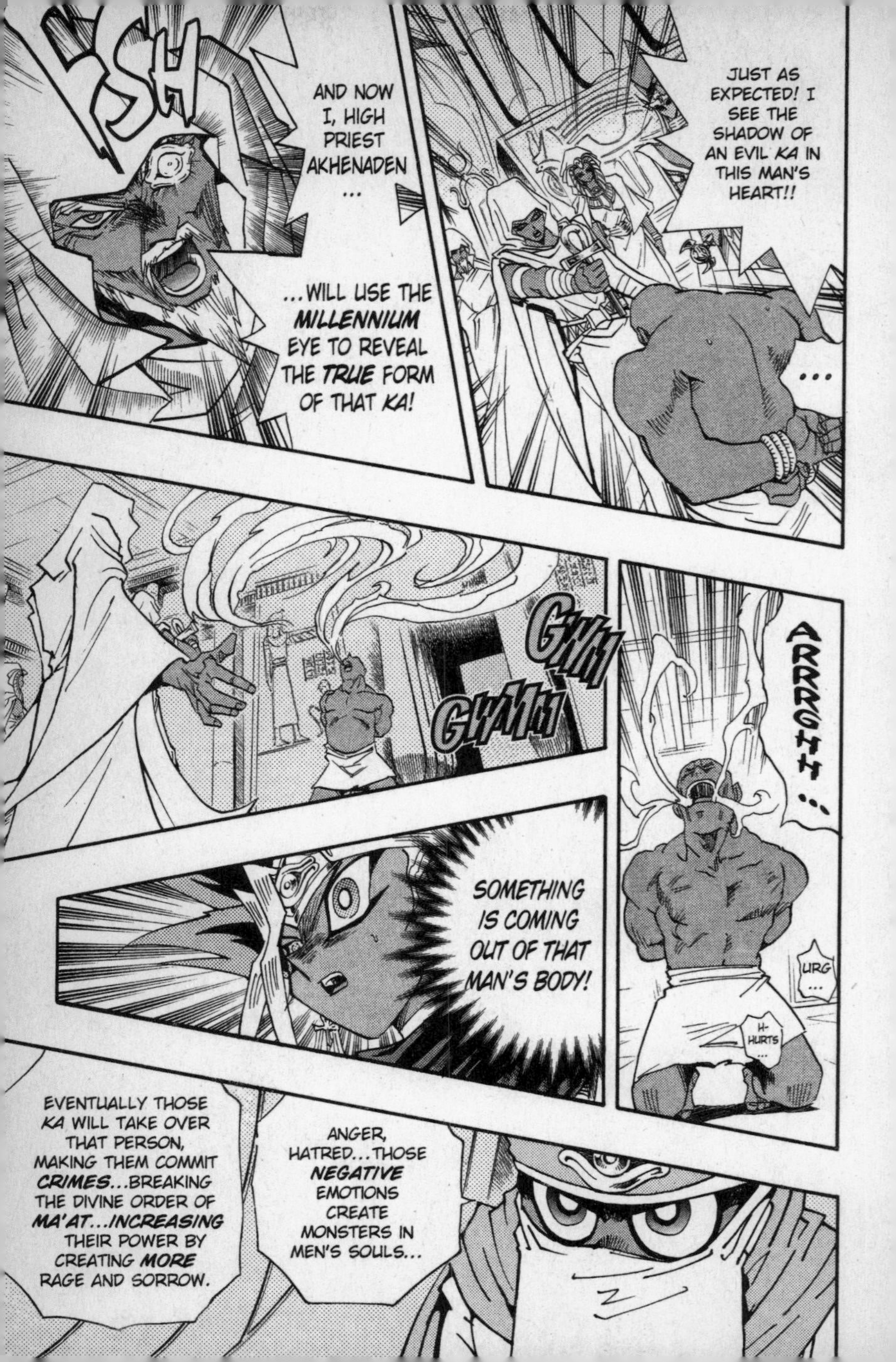
JUST AS EXPECTED! I SEE THE SHADOW OF AN EVIL KA IN THIS MAN'S HEART!!
...
SH
AND NOW I, HIGH PRIEST AKHENADEN ...
...WILL USE THE MILLENNIUM EYE TO REVEAL THE TRUE FORM OF THAT KA!
ARRRGHH...
URG ...
H-HURTS ...
SOMETHING IS COMING OUT OF THAT MAN'S BODY!
ANGER, HATRED...THOSE NEGATIVE EMOTIONS CREATE MONSTERS IN MEN'S SOULS...
EVENTUALLY THOSE KA WILL TAKE OVER THAT PERSON, MAKING THEM COMMIT CRIMES...BREAKING THE DIVINE ORDER OF MA'AT...INCREASING THEIR POWER BY CREATING MORE RAGE AND SORROW.

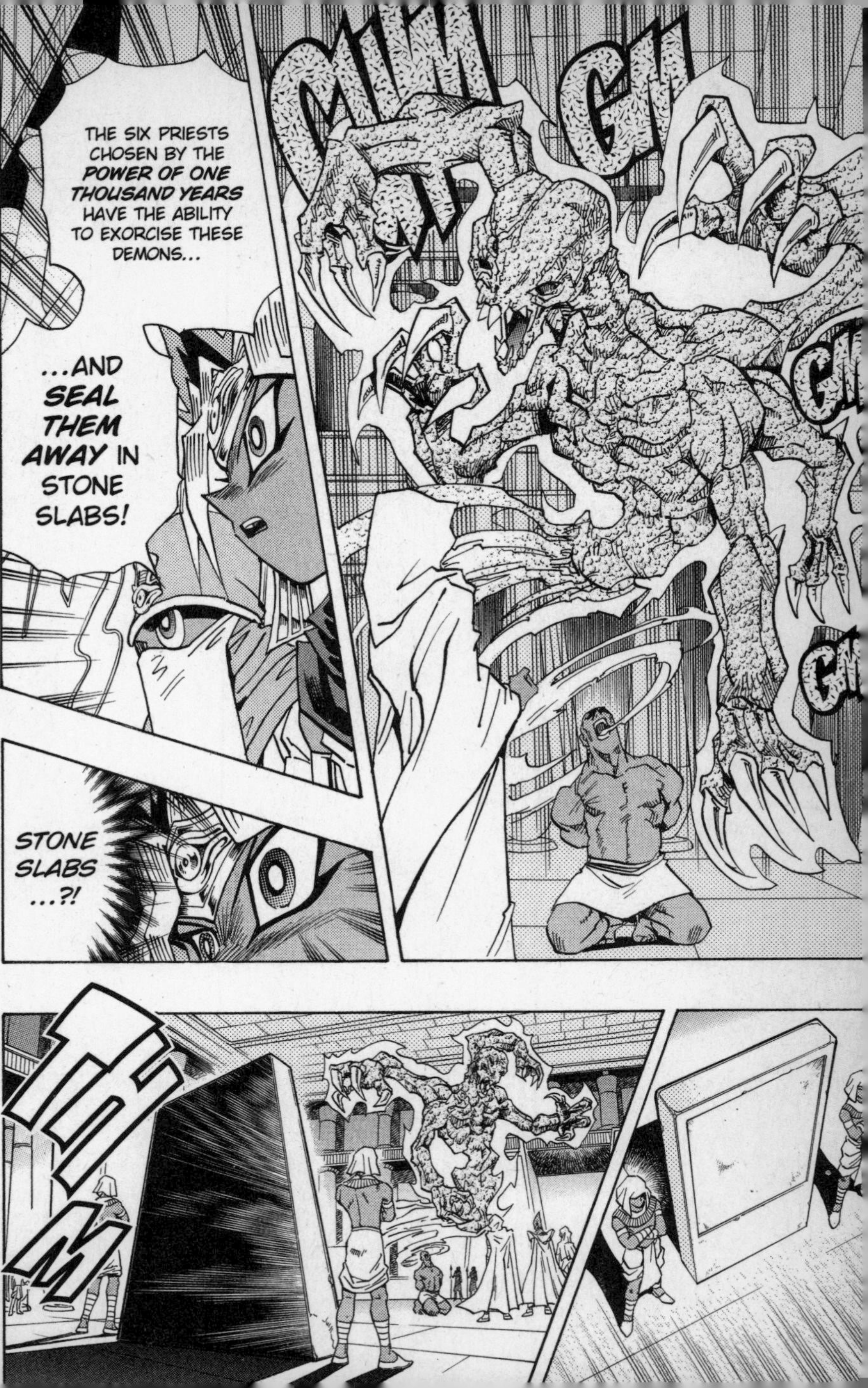

GMM
GM
THE SIX PRIESTS CHOSEN BY THE POWER OF ONE THOUSAND YEARS HAVE THE ABILITY TO EXORCISE THESE DEMONS...
...AND SEAL THEM AWAY IN STONE SLABS!
STONE SLABS ...?!
THM

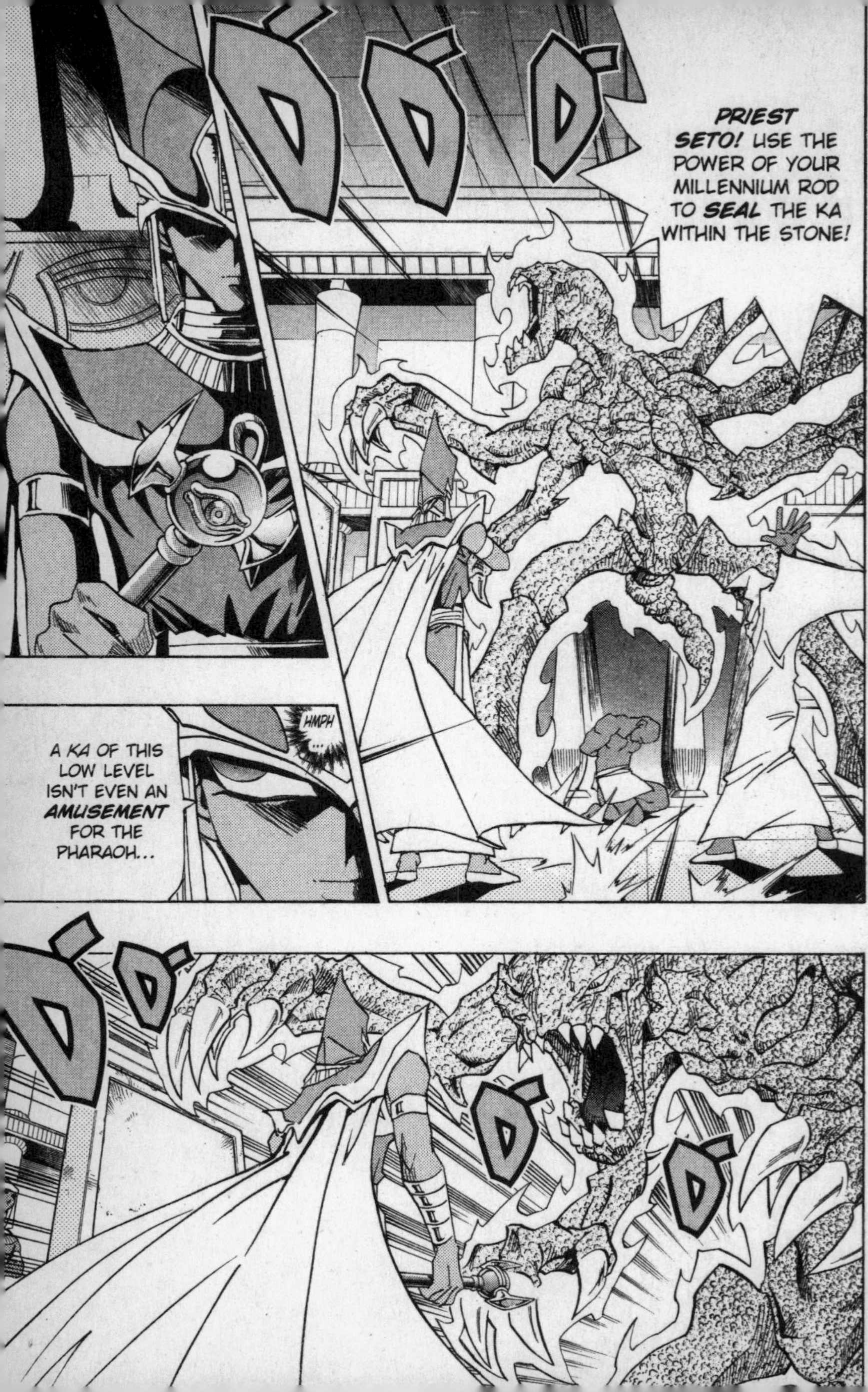
PRIEST SETO! USE THE POWER OF YOUR MILLENNIUM ROD TO SEAL THE KA WITHIN THE STONE!
HMPH...
A KA OF THIS LOW LEVEL ISN'T EVEN AN AMUSEMENT FOR THE PHARAOH...

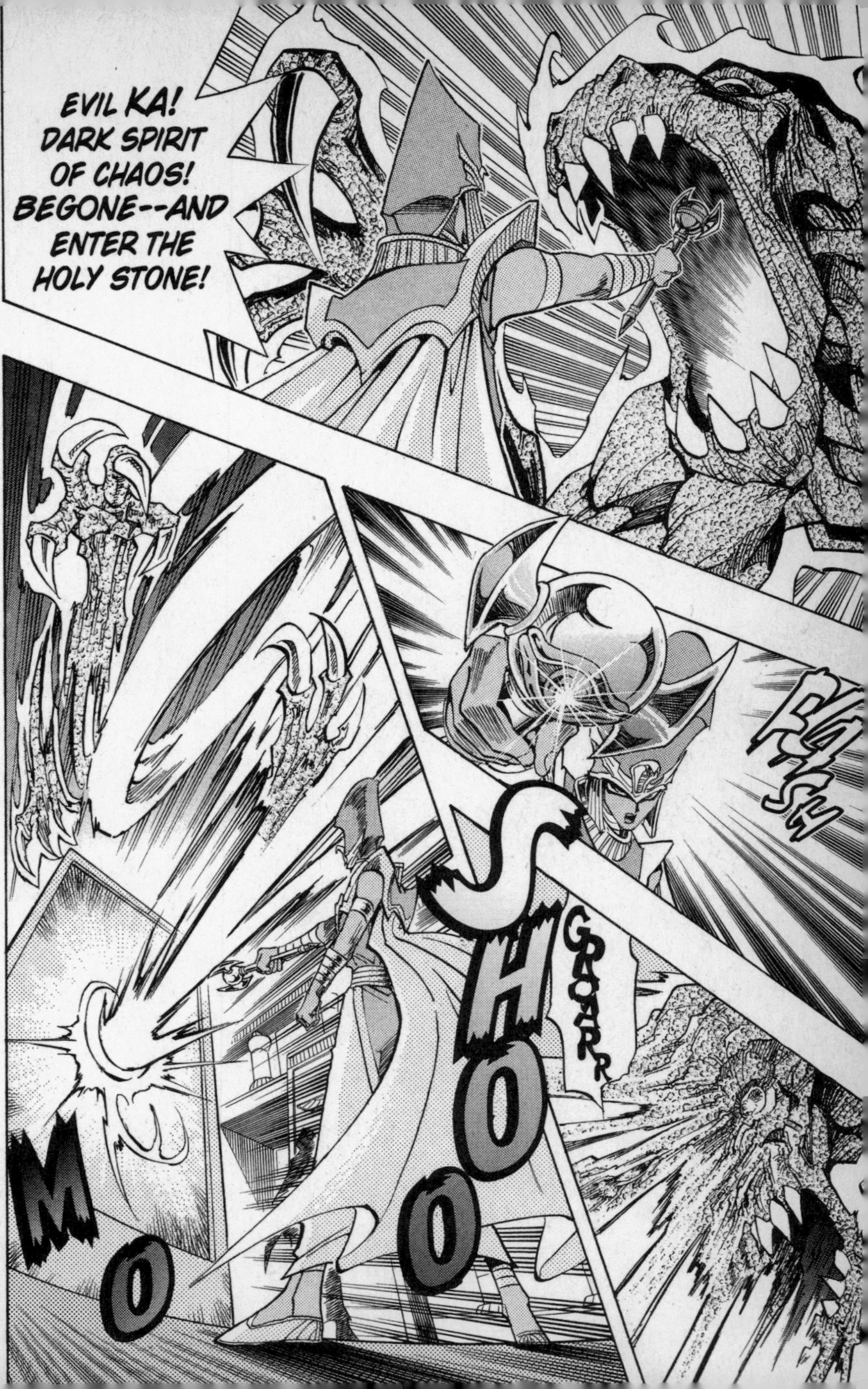
EVIL KA! DARK SPIRIT OF CHAOS! BEGONE--AND ENTER THE HOLY STONE!
FLASH
GRAORRR
SHOOOOM

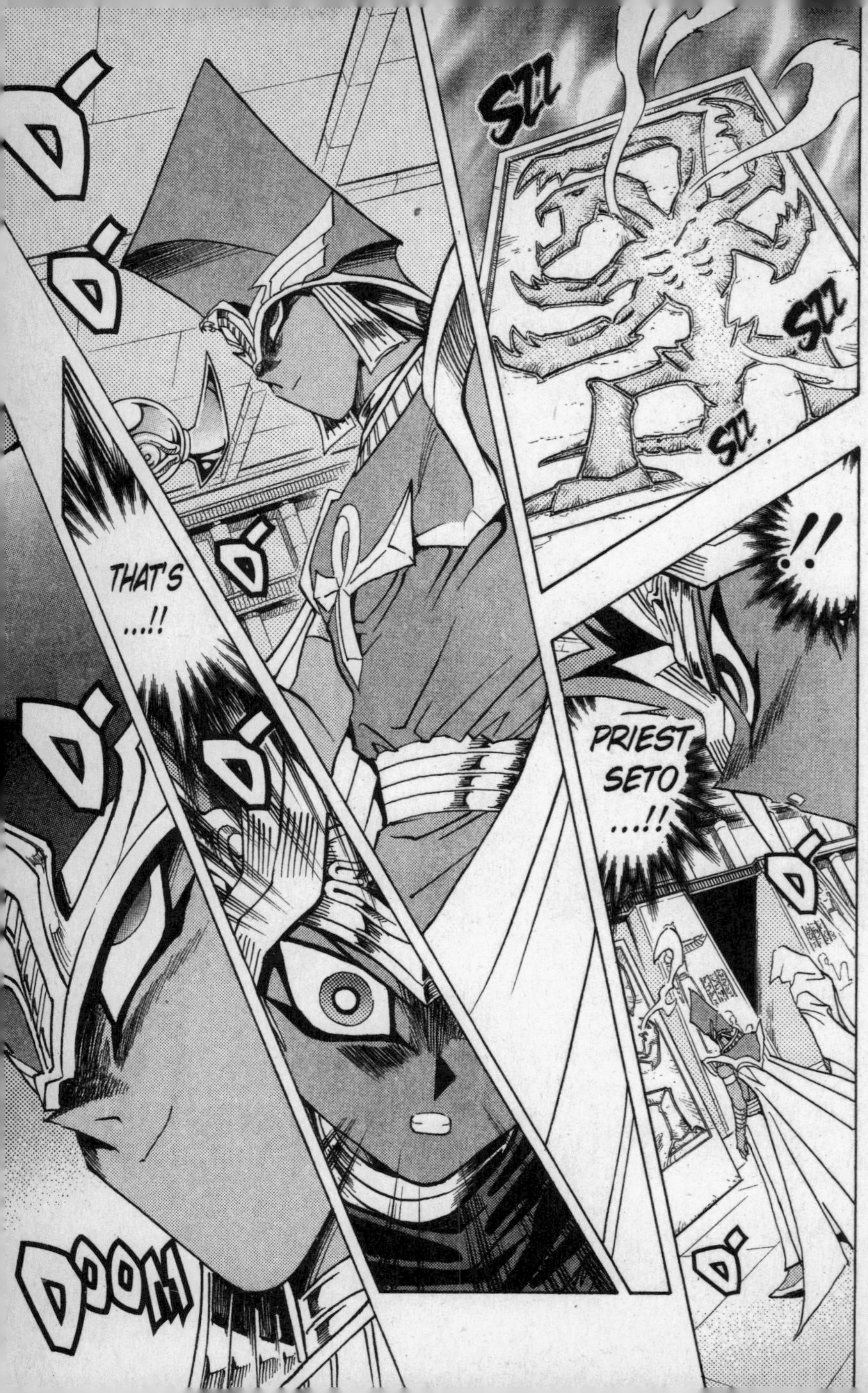
SZZ
SZZ
SZZ
!!
PRIEST SETO ...!!
THAT'S ...!!
DOOM

Duel 6: The Evil Shadow

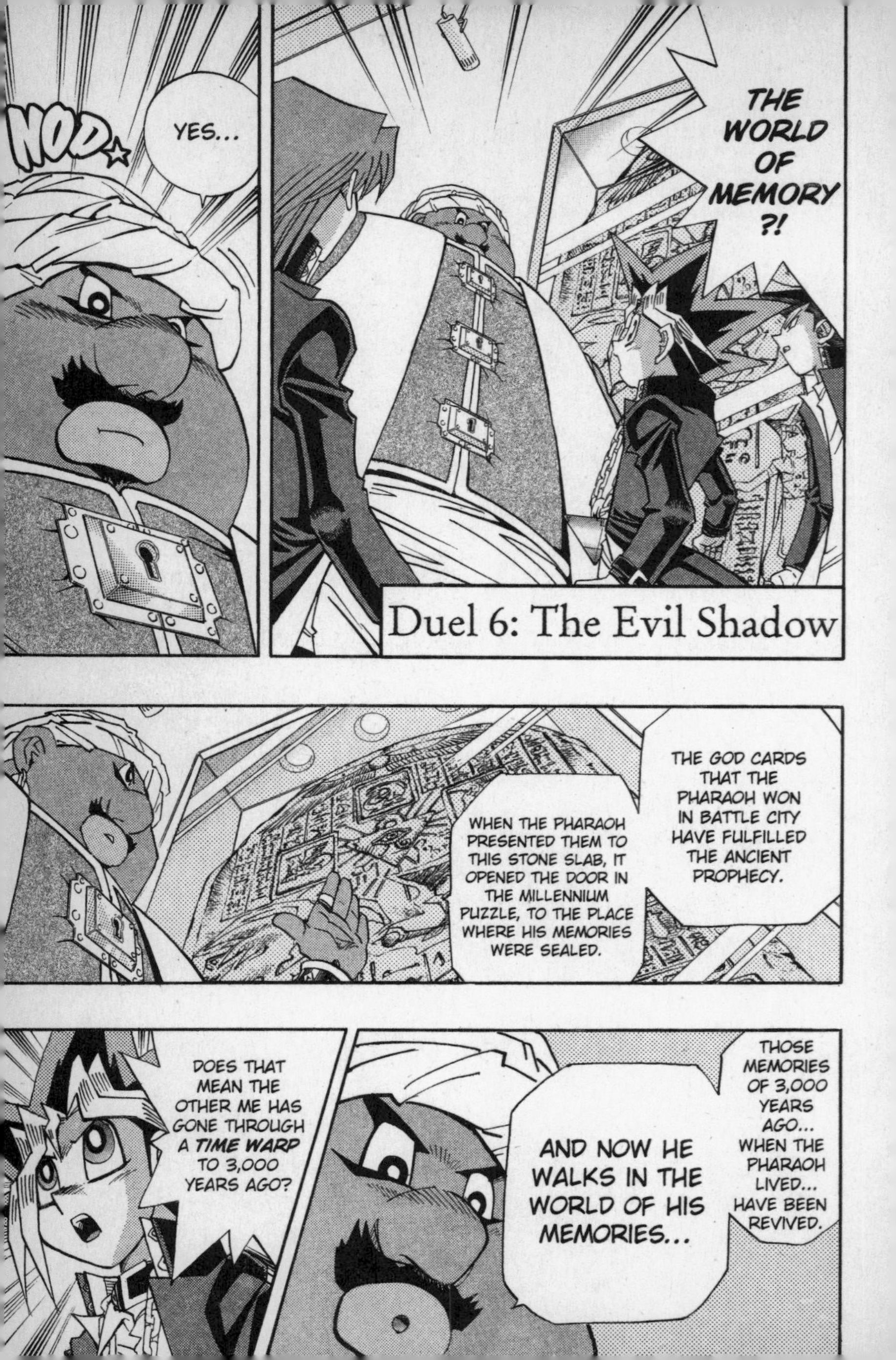

THE WORLD OF MEMORY ?!
NOD☆
YES...
THE GOD CARDS THAT THE PHARAOH WON IN BATTLE CITY HAVE FULFILLED THE ANCIENT PROPHECY.
WHEN THE PHARAOH PRESENTED THEM TO THIS STONE SLAB, IT OPENED THE DOOR IN THE MILLENNIUM PUZZLE, TO THE PLACE WHERE HIS MEMORIES WERE SEALED.
THOSE MEMORIES OF 3,000 YEARS AGO... WHEN THE PHARAOH LIVED... HAVE BEEN REVIVED.
AND NOW HE WALKS IN THE WORLD OF HIS MEMORIES...
DOES THAT MEAN THE OTHER ME HAS GONE THROUGH A *TIME WARP* TO 3,000 YEARS AGO?

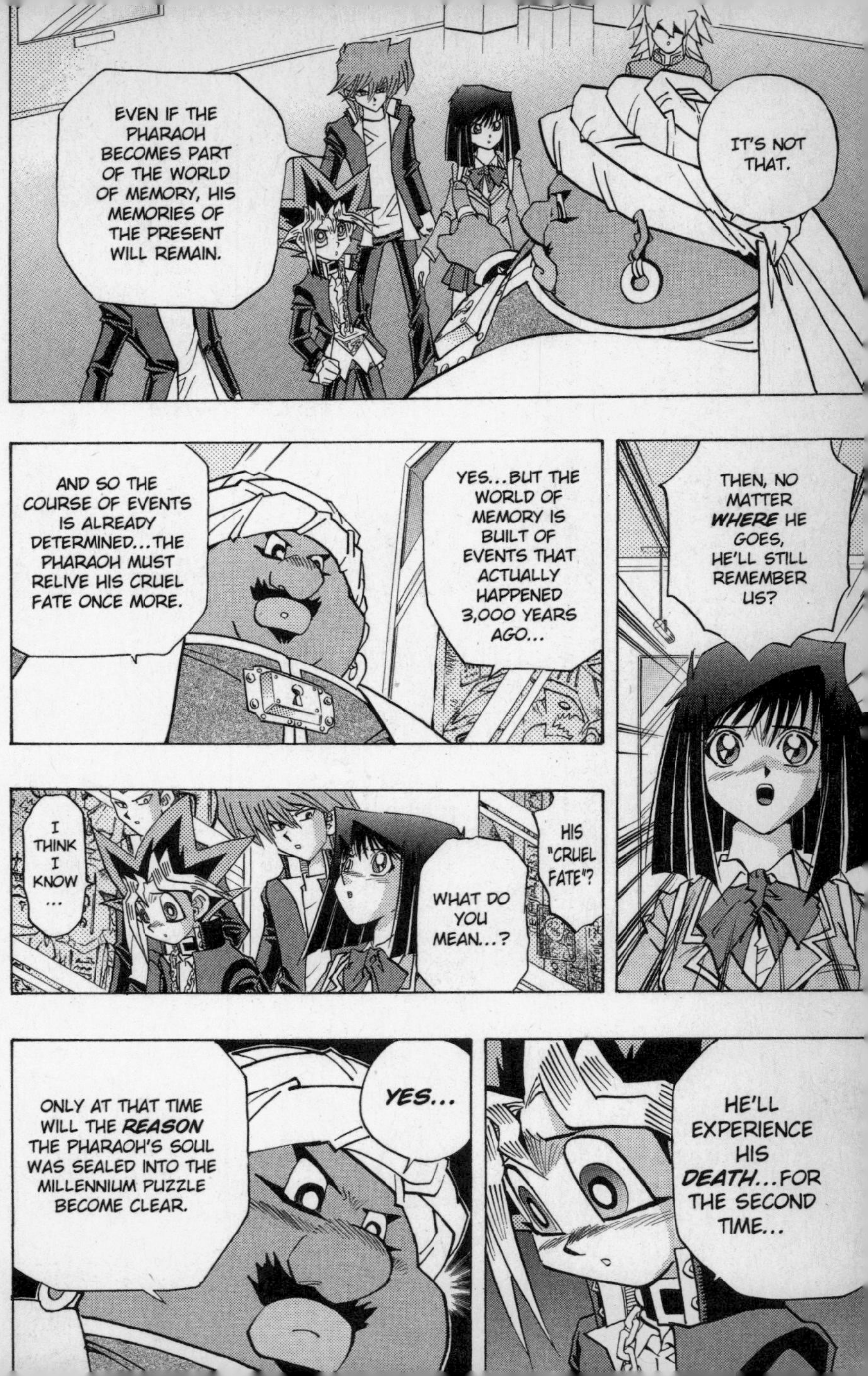

IT'S NOT THAT.
EVEN IF THE PHARAOH BECOMES PART OF THE WORLD OF MEMORY, HIS MEMORIES OF THE PRESENT WILL REMAIN.
THEN, NO MATTER *WHERE* HE GOES, HE'LL STILL REMEMBER US?
YES...BUT THE WORLD OF MEMORY IS BUILT OF EVENTS THAT ACTUALLY HAPPENED 3,000 YEARS AGO...
AND SO THE COURSE OF EVENTS IS ALREADY DETERMINED...THE PHARAOH MUST RELIVE HIS CRUEL FATE ONCE MORE.
HIS "CRUEL FATE"?
WHAT DO YOU MEAN...?
I THINK I KNOW...
HE'LL EXPERIENCE HIS *DEATH*...FOR THE SECOND TIME...
YES...
ONLY AT THAT TIME WILL THE *REASON* THE PHARAOH'S SOUL WAS SEALED INTO THE MILLENNIUM PUZZLE BECOME CLEAR.

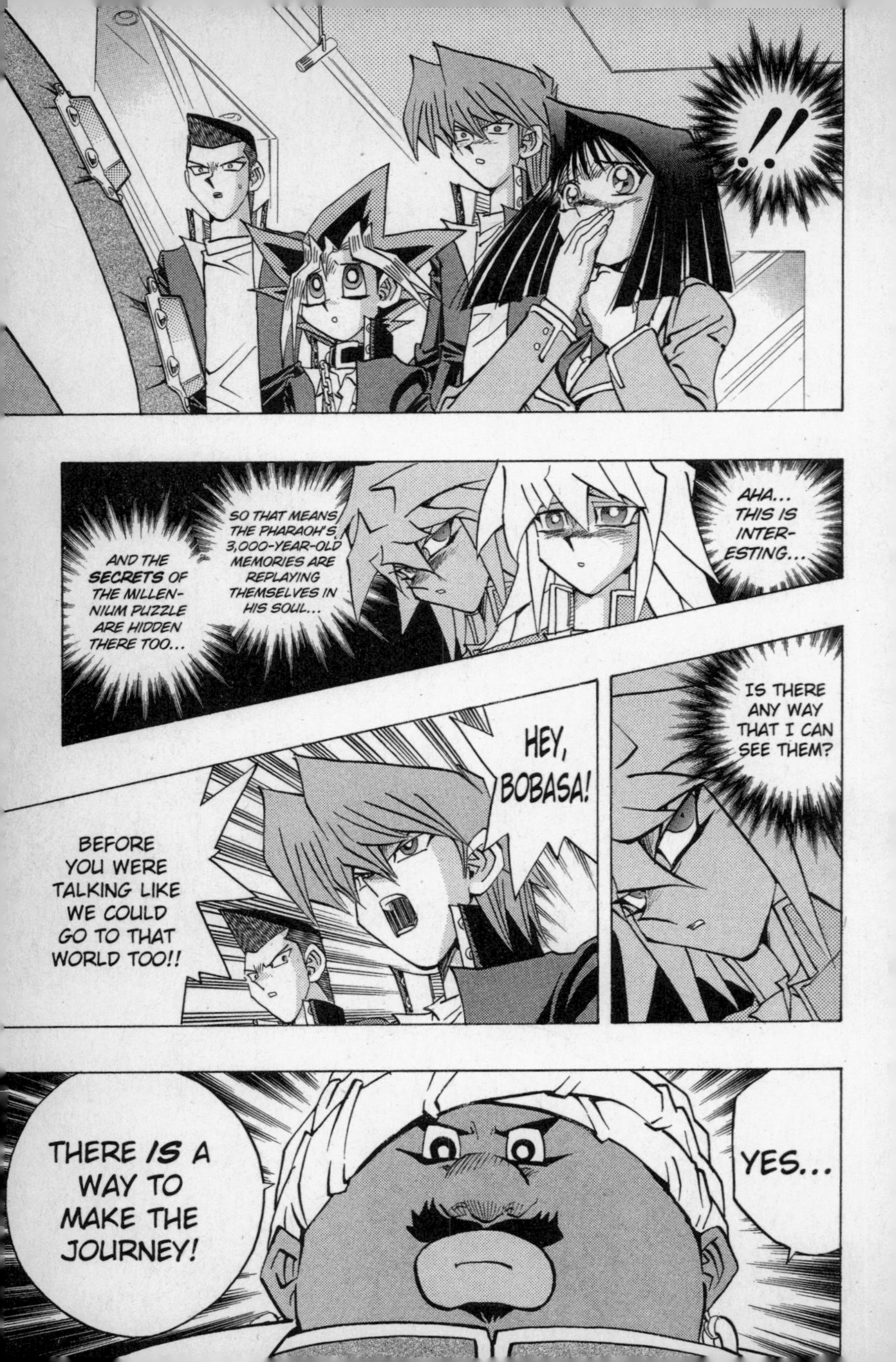
!!
AHA... THIS IS INTER-ESTING...
SO THAT MEANS THE PHARAOH'S 3,000-YEAR-OLD MEMORIES ARE REPLAYING THEMSELVES IN HIS SOUL...
AND THE SECRETS OF THE MILLEN-NIUM PUZZLE ARE HIDDEN THERE TOO...
IS THERE ANY WAY THAT I CAN SEE THEM?
HEY, BOBASA!
BEFORE YOU WERE TALKING LIKE WE COULD GO TO THAT WORLD TOO!!
YES...
THERE IS A WAY TO MAKE THE JOURNEY!

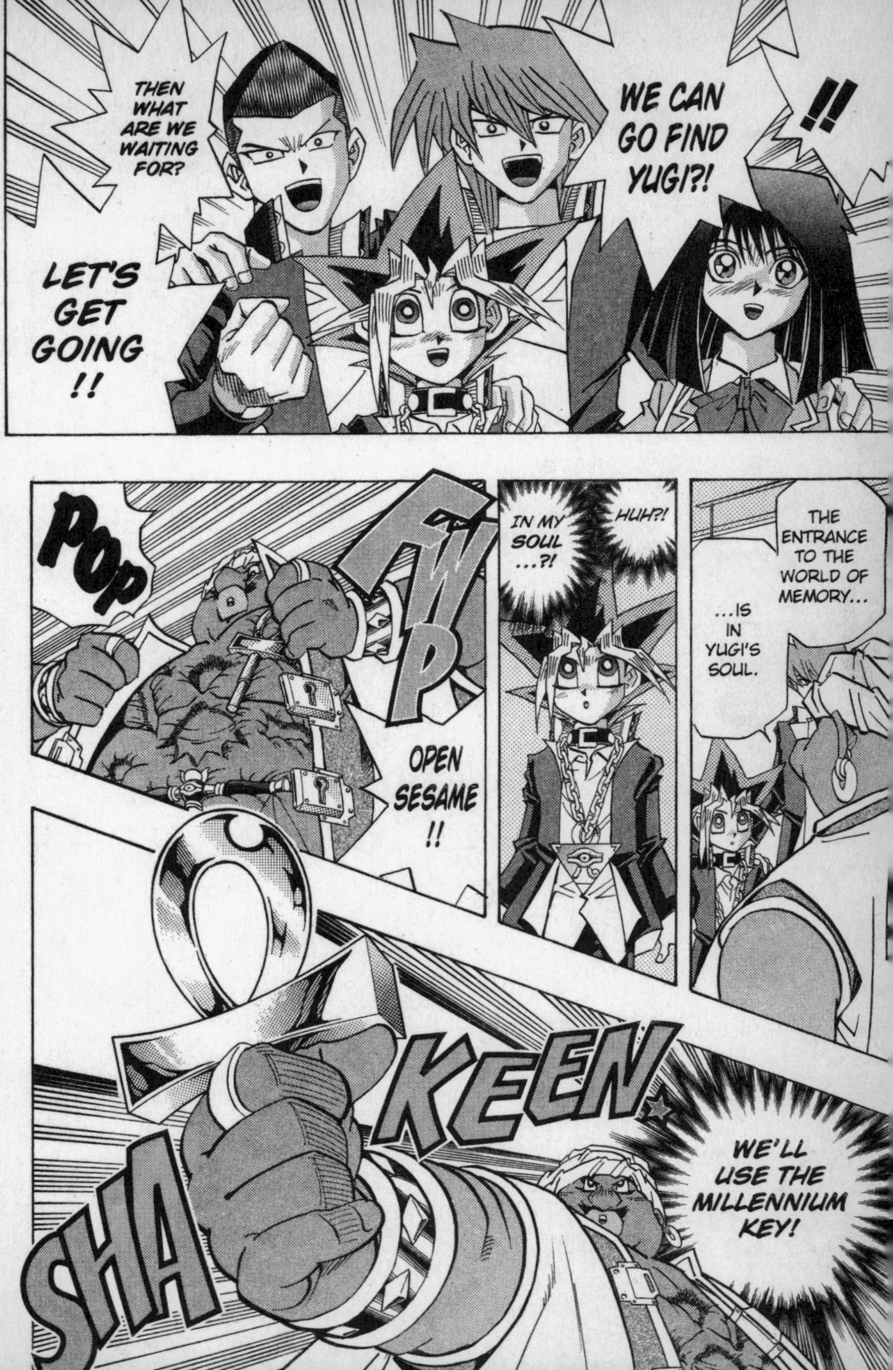
!!
WE CAN GO FIND YUGI?!
THEN WHAT ARE WE WAITING FOR?
LET'S GET GOING !!
THE ENTRANCE TO THE WORLD OF MEMORY...
...IS IN YUGI'S SOUL.
HUH?!
IN MY SOUL ...?!
FWP
POP
OPEN SESAME !!
SHA KEEN
WE'LL USE THE MILLENNIUM KEY!

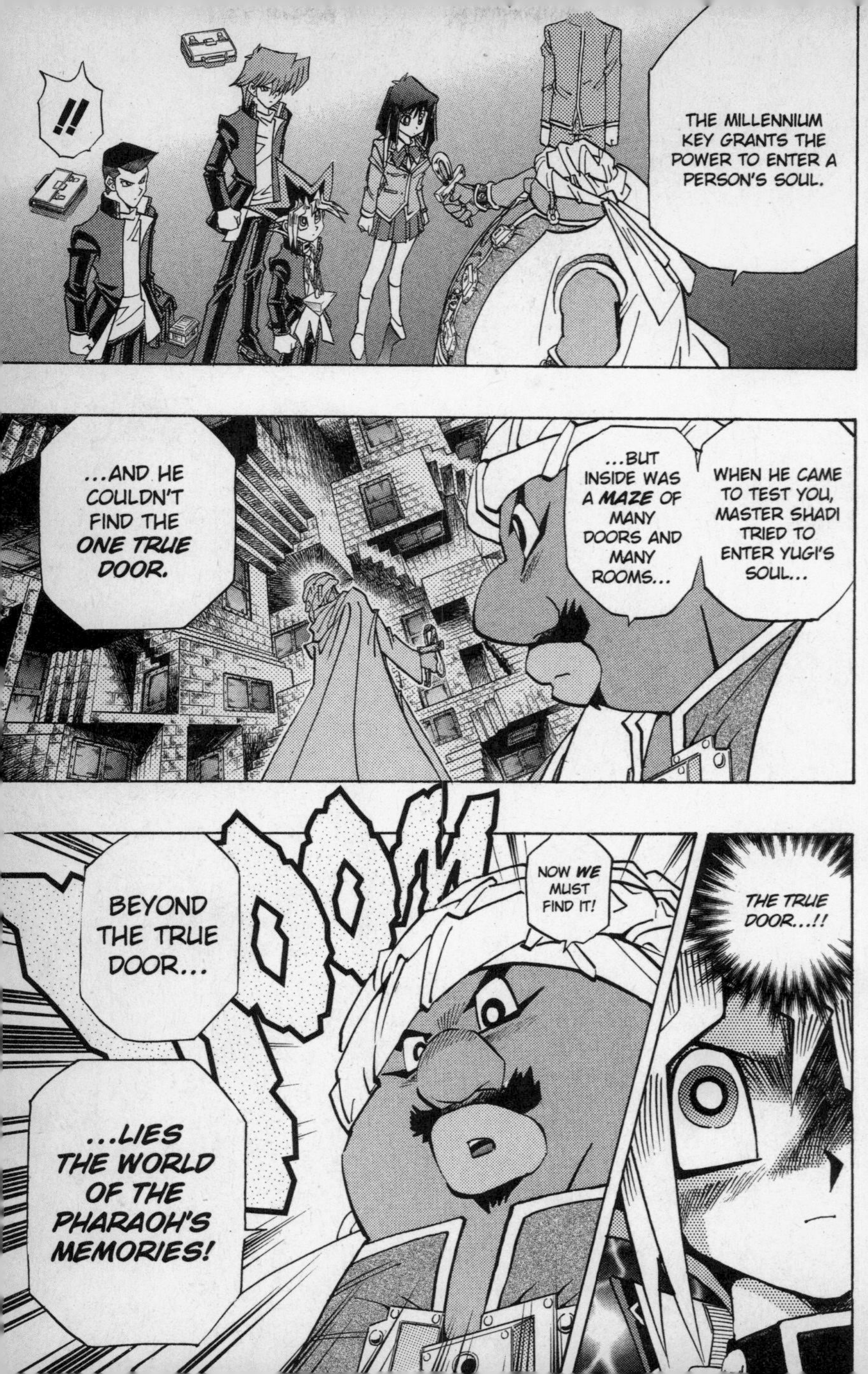
THE MILLENNIUM KEY GRANTS THE POWER TO ENTER A PERSON'S SOUL.
!!
WHEN HE CAME TO TEST YOU, MASTER SHADI TRIED TO ENTER YUGI'S SOUL...
...BUT INSIDE WAS A *MAZE* OF MANY DOORS AND MANY ROOMS...
...AND HE COULDN'T FIND THE *ONE TRUE DOOR.*
THE TRUE DOOR...!!
NOW *WE* MUST FIND IT!
DOOM
BEYOND THE TRUE DOOR...
...LIES THE WORLD OF THE PHARAOH'S MEMORIES!

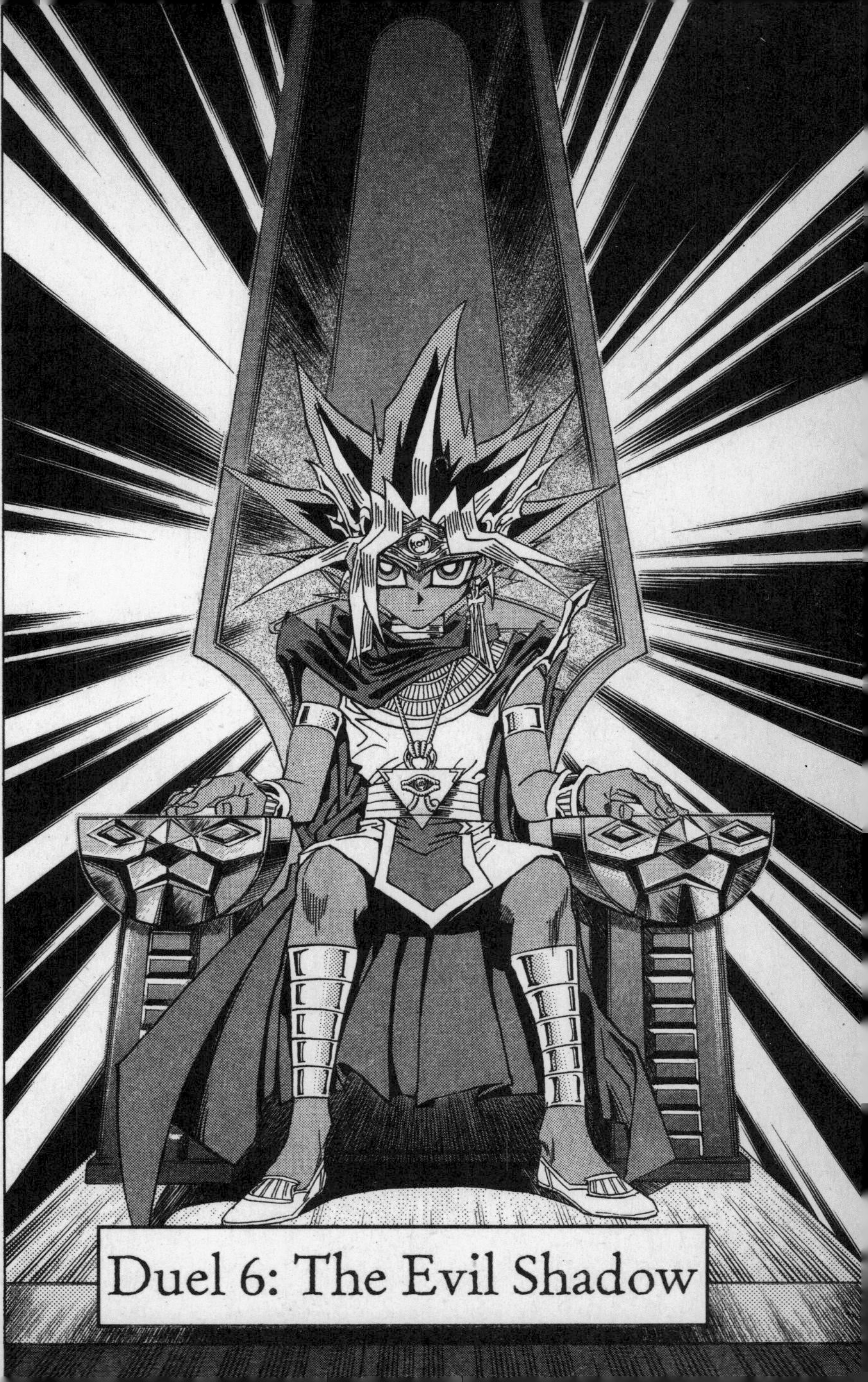

Duel 6: The Evil Shadow

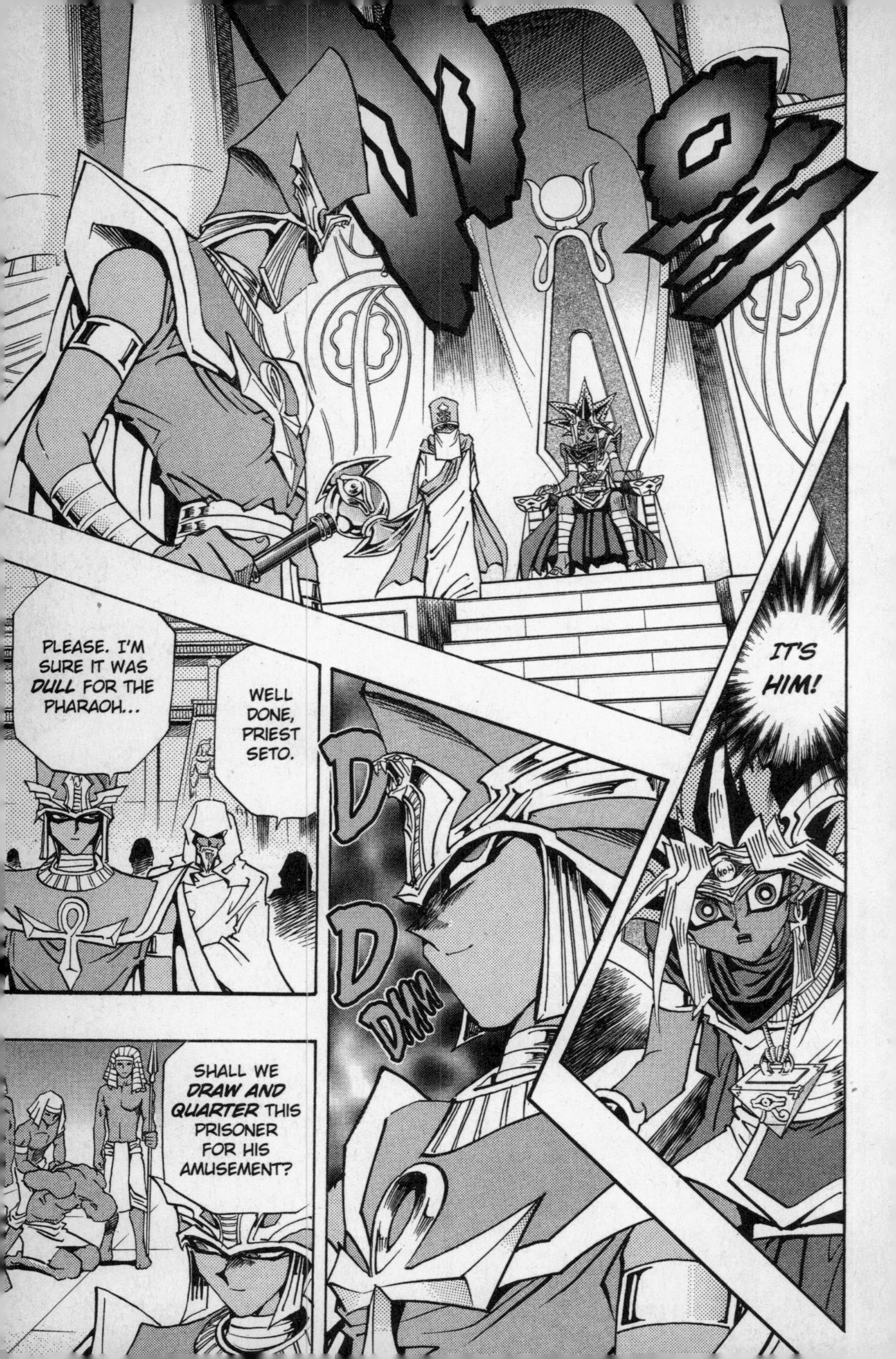
IT'S HIM!
WELL DONE, PRIEST SETO.
PLEASE. I'M SURE IT WAS DULL FOR THE PHARAOH...
SHALL WE DRAW AND QUARTER THIS PRISONER FOR HIS AMUSEMENT?

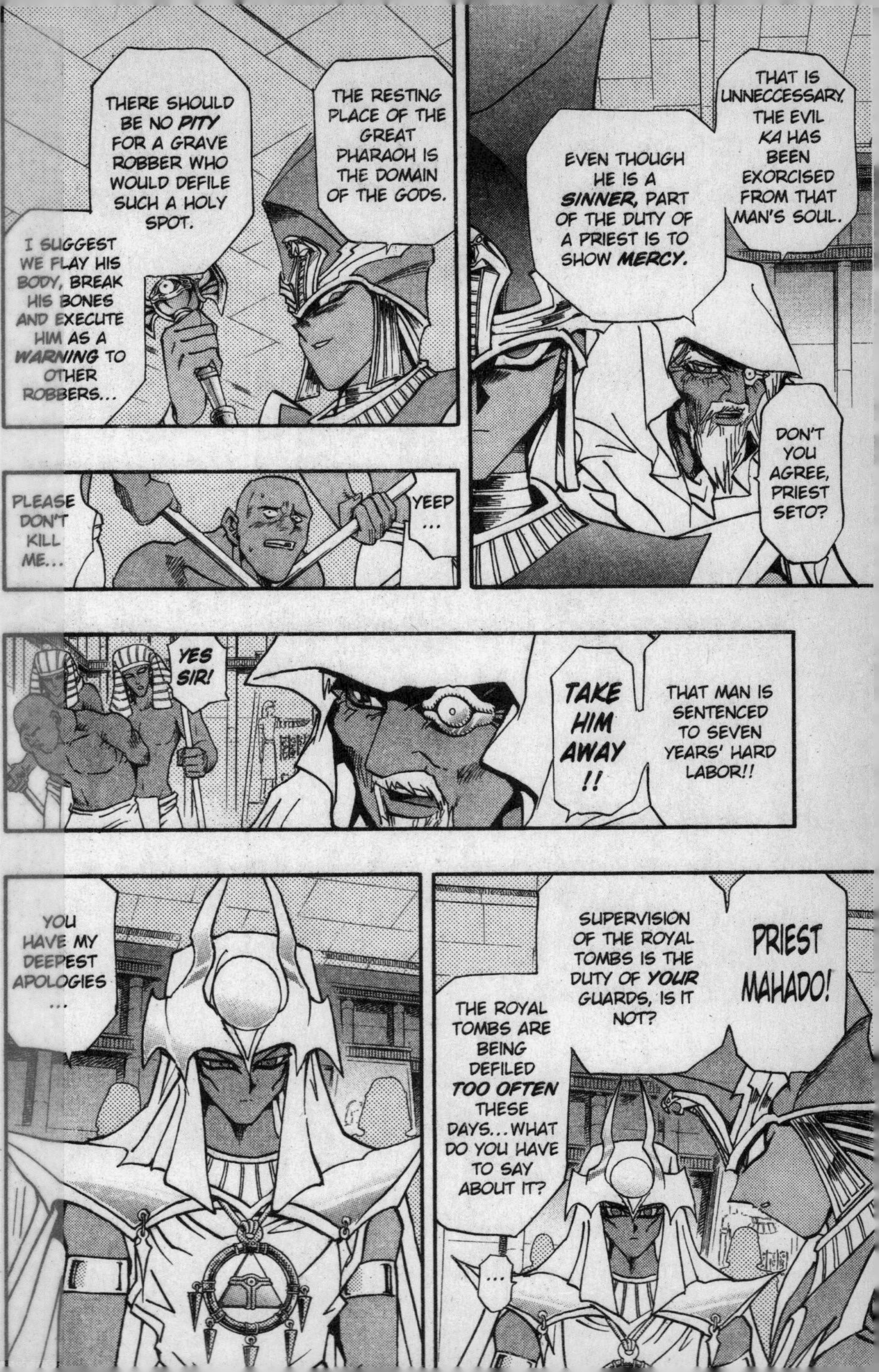
THE RESTING PLACE OF THE GREAT PHARAOH IS THE DOMAIN OF THE GODS.
THERE SHOULD BE NO PITY FOR A GRAVE ROBBER WHO WOULD DEFILE SUCH A HOLY SPOT.
I SUGGEST WE FLAY HIS BODY, BREAK HIS BONES AND EXECUTE HIM AS A WARNING TO OTHER ROBBERS...
YEEP...
PLEASE DON'T KILL ME...
THAT IS UNNECCESSARY. THE EVIL KA HAS BEEN EXORCISED FROM THAT MAN'S SOUL.
EVEN THOUGH HE IS A SINNER, PART OF THE DUTY OF A PRIEST IS TO SHOW MERCY.
DON'T YOU AGREE, PRIEST SETO?
THAT MAN IS SENTENCED TO SEVEN YEARS' HARD LABOR!!
TAKE HIM AWAY!!
YES SIR!
PRIEST MAHADO!
SUPERVISION OF THE ROYAL TOMBS IS THE DUTY OF YOUR GUARDS, IS IT NOT?
THE ROYAL TOMBS ARE BEING DEFILED TOO OFTEN THESE DAYS...WHAT DO YOU HAVE TO SAY ABOUT IT?
...
YOU HAVE MY DEEPEST APOLOGIES...

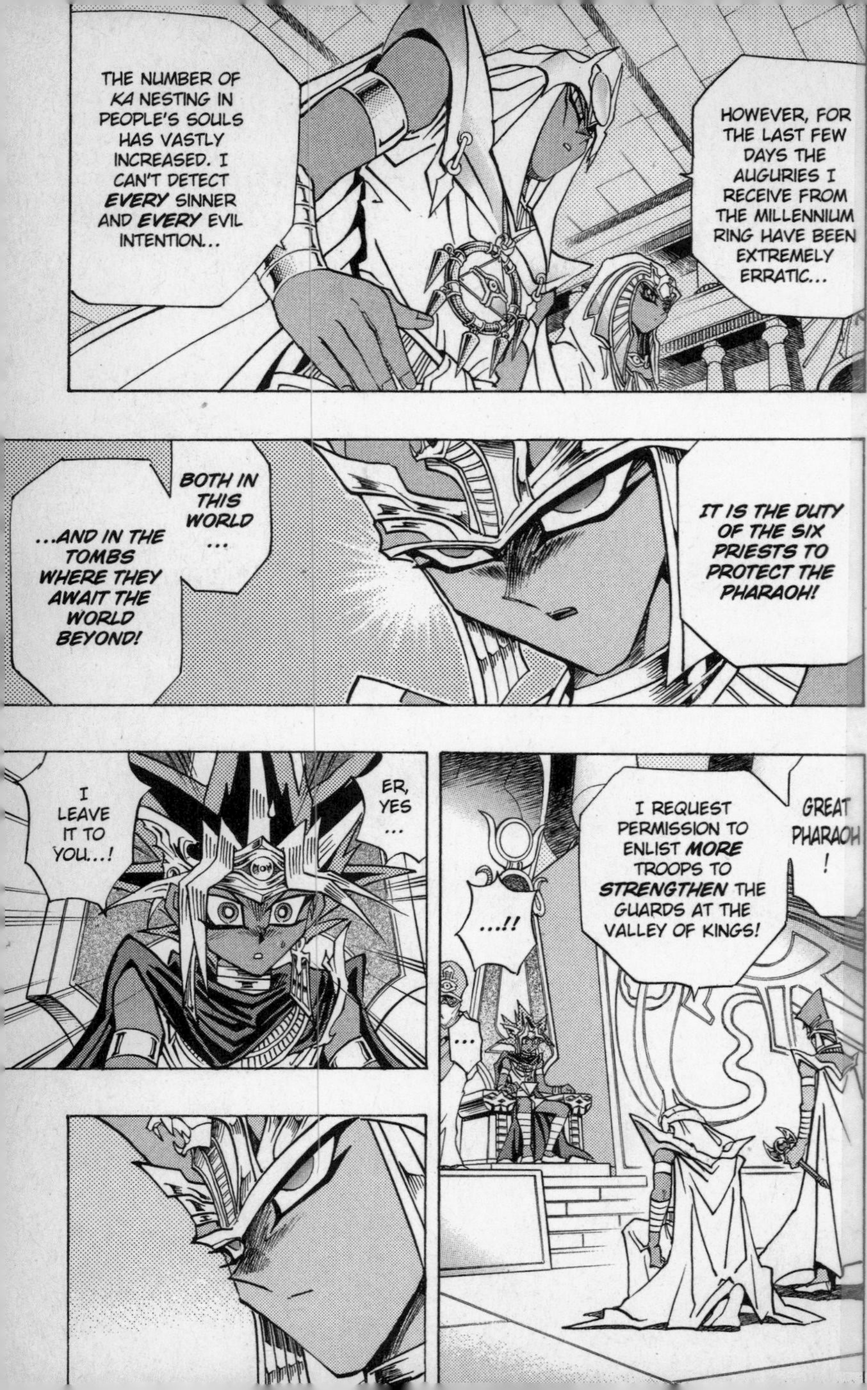
HOWEVER, FOR THE LAST FEW DAYS THE AUGURIES I RECEIVE FROM THE MILLENNIUM RING HAVE BEEN EXTREMELY ERRATIC...
THE NUMBER OF KA NESTING IN PEOPLE'S SOULS HAS VASTLY INCREASED. I CAN'T DETECT EVERY SINNER AND EVERY EVIL INTENTION...
IT IS THE DUTY OF THE SIX PRIESTS TO PROTECT THE PHARAOH!
BOTH IN THIS WORLD ...
...AND IN THE TOMBS WHERE THEY AWAIT THE WORLD BEYOND!
GREAT PHARAOH!
I REQUEST PERMISSION TO ENLIST MORE TROOPS TO STRENGTHEN THE GUARDS AT THE VALLEY OF KINGS!
...!!
...
ER, YES ...
I LEAVE IT TO YOU...!

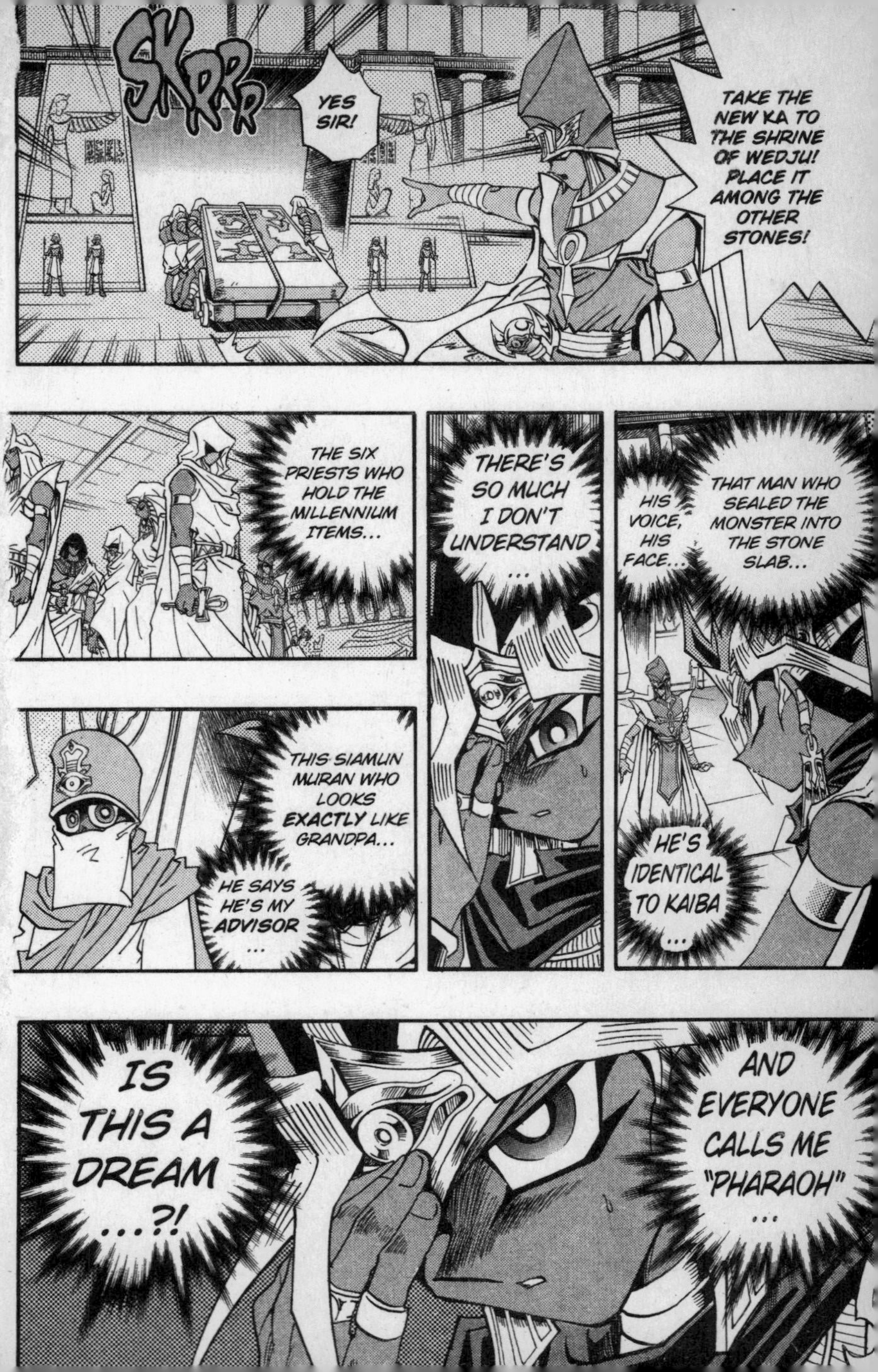

TAKE THE NEW KA TO THE SHRINE OF WEDJU! PLACE IT AMONG THE OTHER STONES!
YES SIR!
SKRRR
THAT MAN WHO SEALED THE MONSTER INTO THE STONE SLAB...
HIS VOICE, HIS FACE...
HE'S IDENTICAL TO KAIBA ...
THERE'S SO MUCH I DON'T UNDERSTAND ...
THE SIX PRIESTS WHO HOLD THE MILLENNIUM ITEMS...
THIS SIAMUN MURAN WHO LOOKS EXACTLY LIKE GRANDPA...
HE SAYS HE'S MY ADVISOR ...
AND EVERYONE CALLS ME "PHARAOH" ...
IS THIS A DREAM ...?!

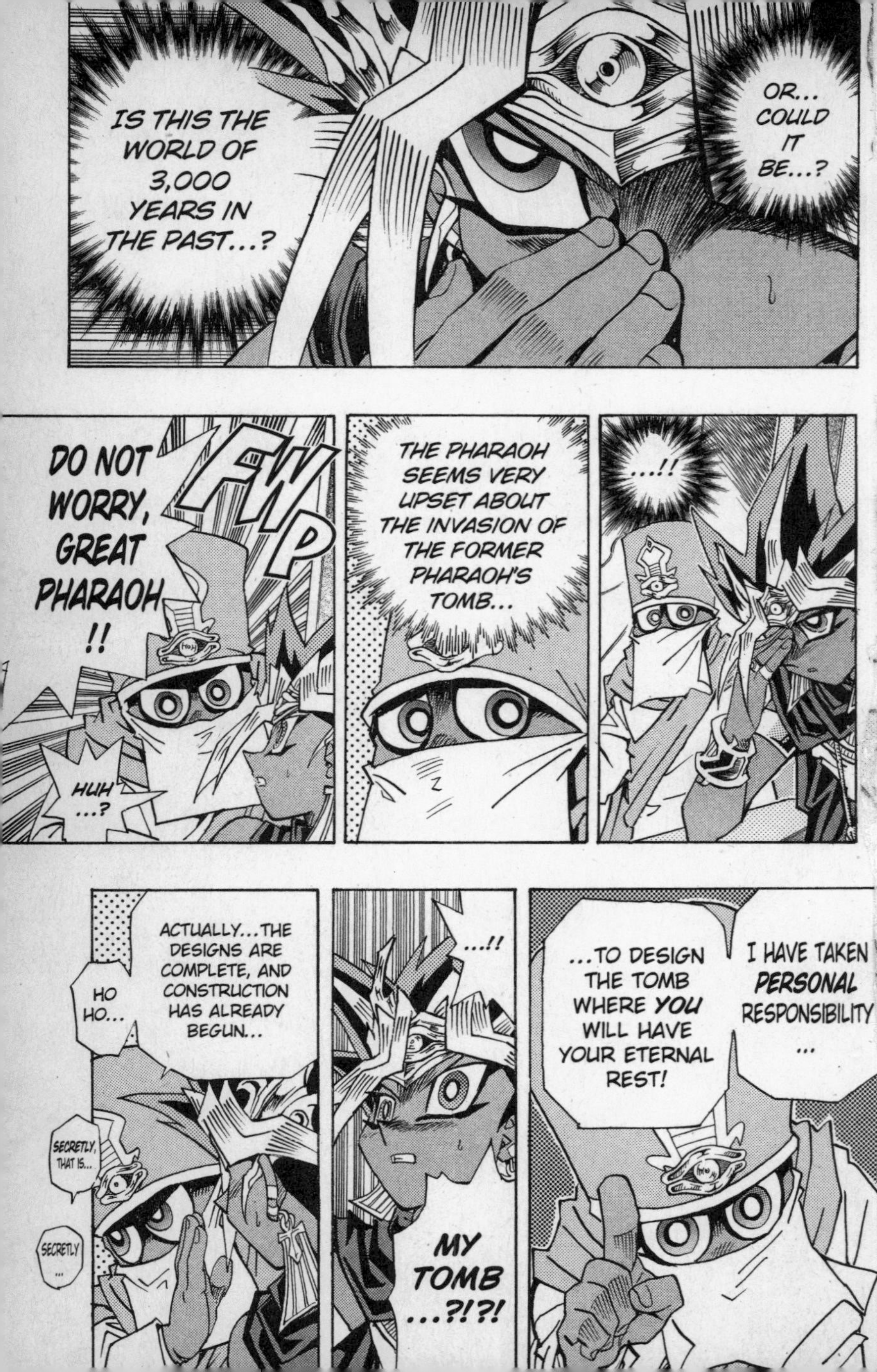
OR... COULD IT BE...?
IS THIS THE WORLD OF 3,000 YEARS IN THE PAST...?
...!!
THE PHARAOH SEEMS VERY UPSET ABOUT THE INVASION OF THE FORMER PHARAOH'S TOMB...
FWP
DO NOT WORRY, GREAT PHARAOH!!
HUH...?
I HAVE TAKEN PERSONAL RESPONSIBILITY...
...TO DESIGN THE TOMB WHERE YOU WILL HAVE YOUR ETERNAL REST!
...!!
MY TOMB...?!?!
ACTUALLY...THE DESIGNS ARE COMPLETE, AND CONSTRUCTION HAS ALREADY BEGUN...
HO HO...
SECRETLY, THAT IS...
SECRETLY...

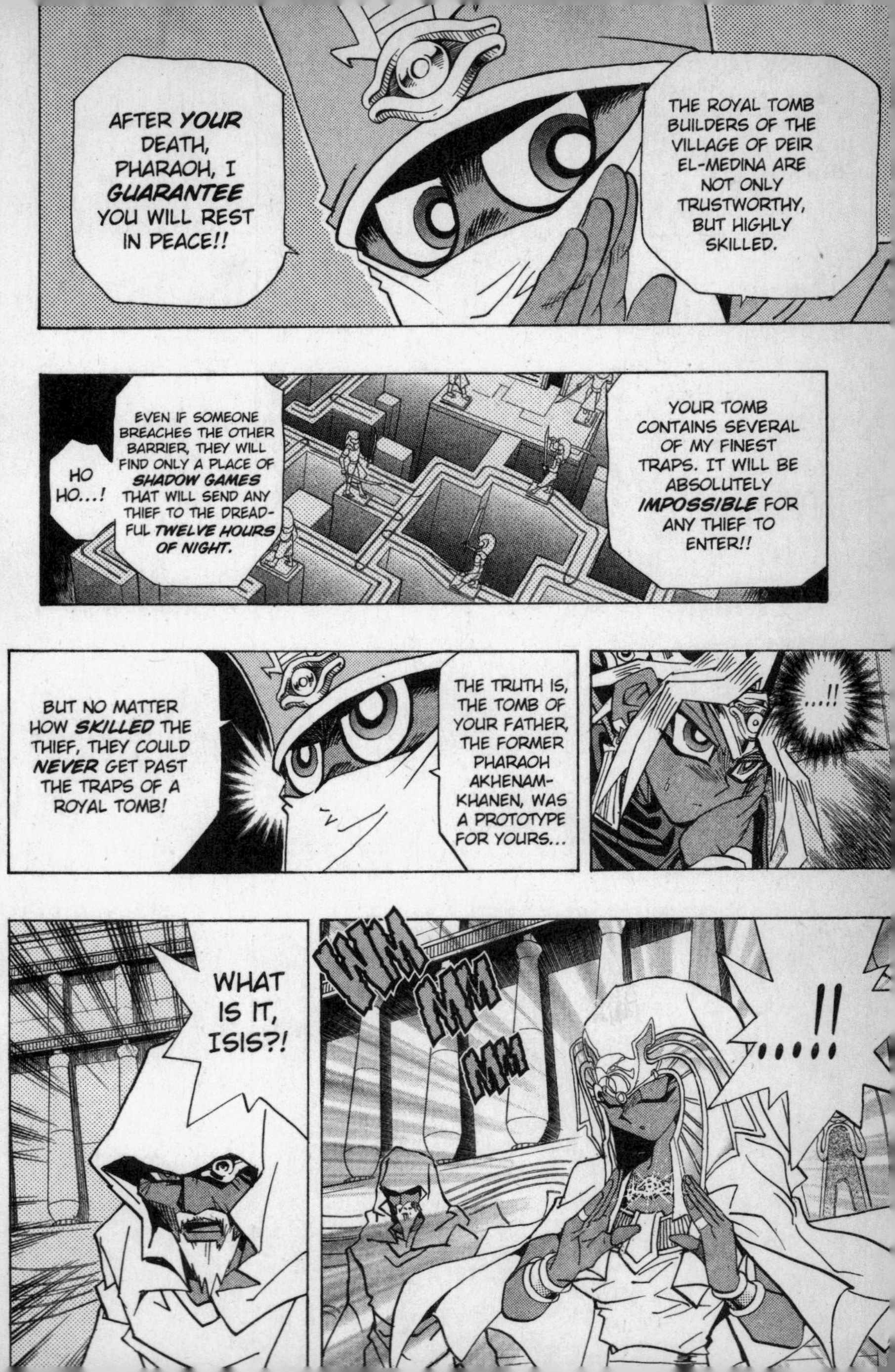
THE ROYAL TOMB BUILDERS OF THE VILLAGE OF DEIR EL-MEDINA ARE NOT ONLY TRUSTWORTHY, BUT HIGHLY SKILLED.
AFTER *YOUR* DEATH, PHARAOH, I *GUARANTEE* YOU WILL REST IN PEACE!!
YOUR TOMB CONTAINS SEVERAL OF MY FINEST TRAPS. IT WILL BE ABSOLUTELY *IMPOSSIBLE* FOR ANY THIEF TO ENTER!!
EVEN IF SOMEONE BREACHES THE OTHER BARRIER, THEY WILL FIND ONLY A PLACE OF *SHADOW GAMES* THAT WILL SEND ANY THIEF TO THE DREAD-FUL *TWELVE HOURS OF NIGHT.*
HO HO...!
...!!
THE TRUTH IS, THE TOMB OF YOUR FATHER, THE FORMER PHARAOH AKHENAM-KHANEN, WAS A PROTOTYPE FOR YOURS...
BUT NO MATTER HOW *SKILLED* THE THIEF, THEY COULD *NEVER* GET PAST THE TRAPS OF A ROYAL TOMB!
WMMMMMM
....!!
WHAT IS IT, ISIS?!

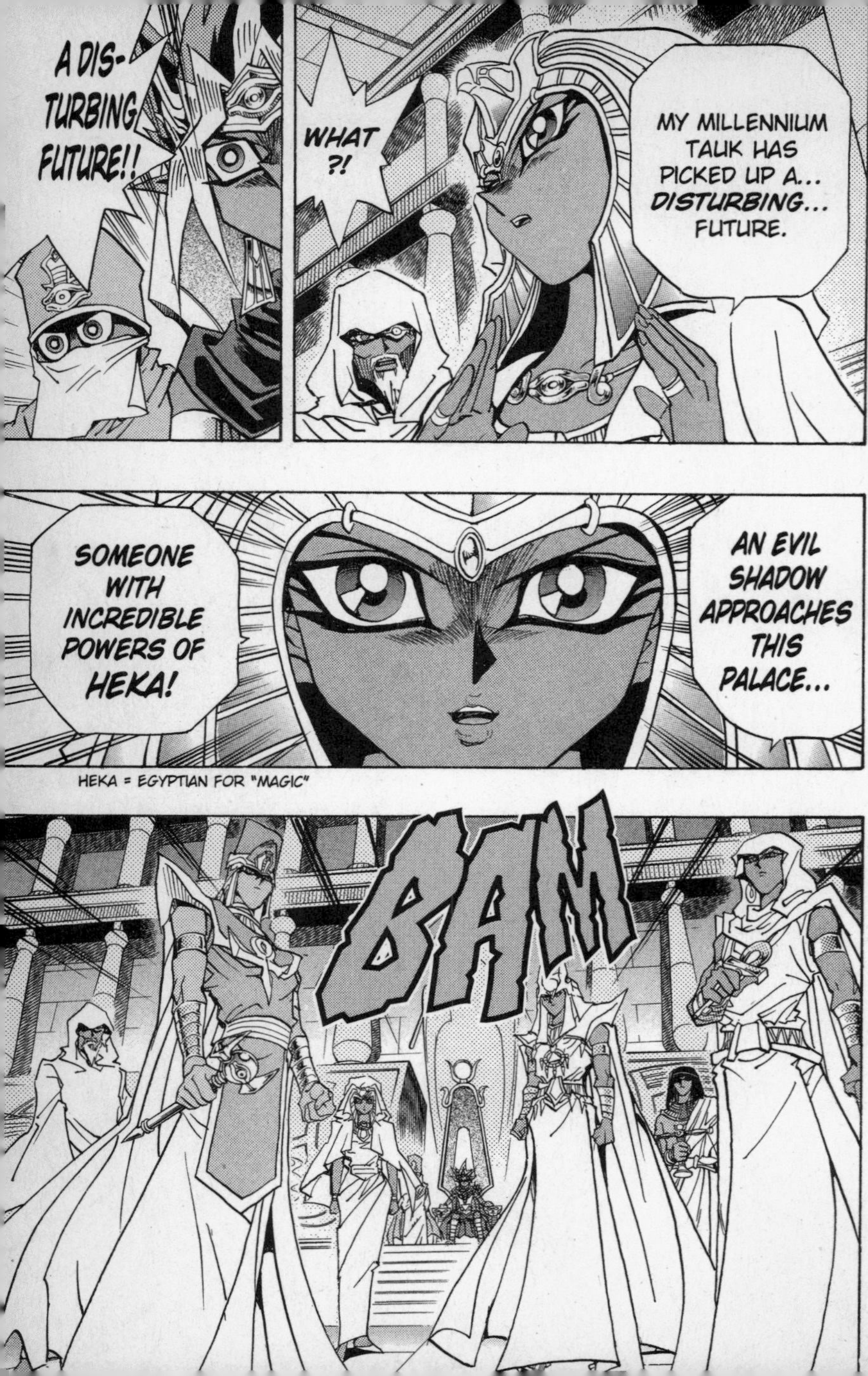
MY MILLENNIUM TAUK HAS PICKED UP A... DISTURBING... FUTURE.
WHAT ?!
A DIS-TURBING FUTURE!!
AN EVIL SHADOW APPROACHES THIS PALACE...
SOMEONE WITH INCREDIBLE POWERS OF HEKA!
BAM
HEKA = EGYPTIAN FOR "MAGIC"

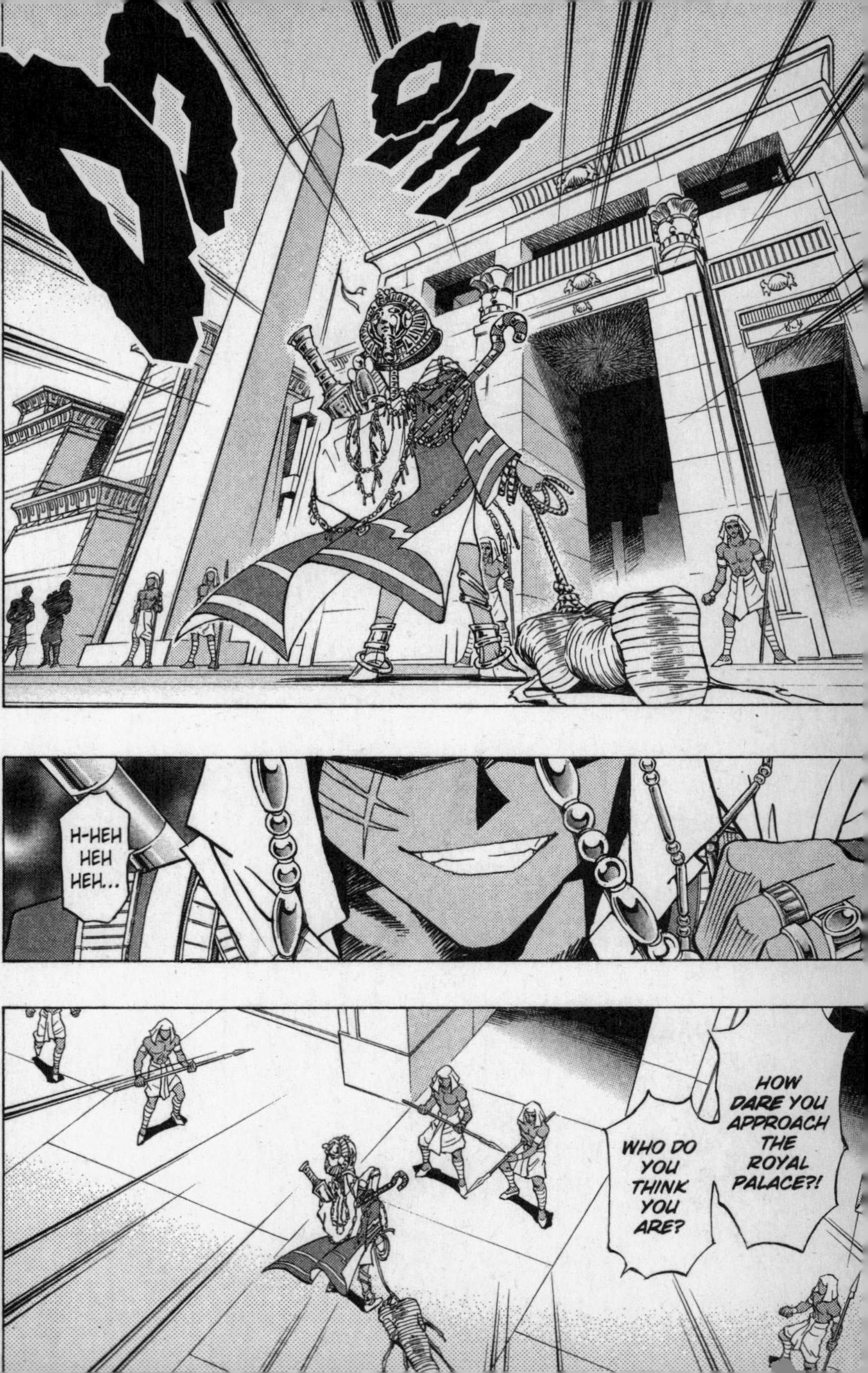
DOOM
H-HEH HEH HEH...
HOW DARE YOU APPROACH THE ROYAL PALACE?!
WHO DO YOU THINK YOU ARE?

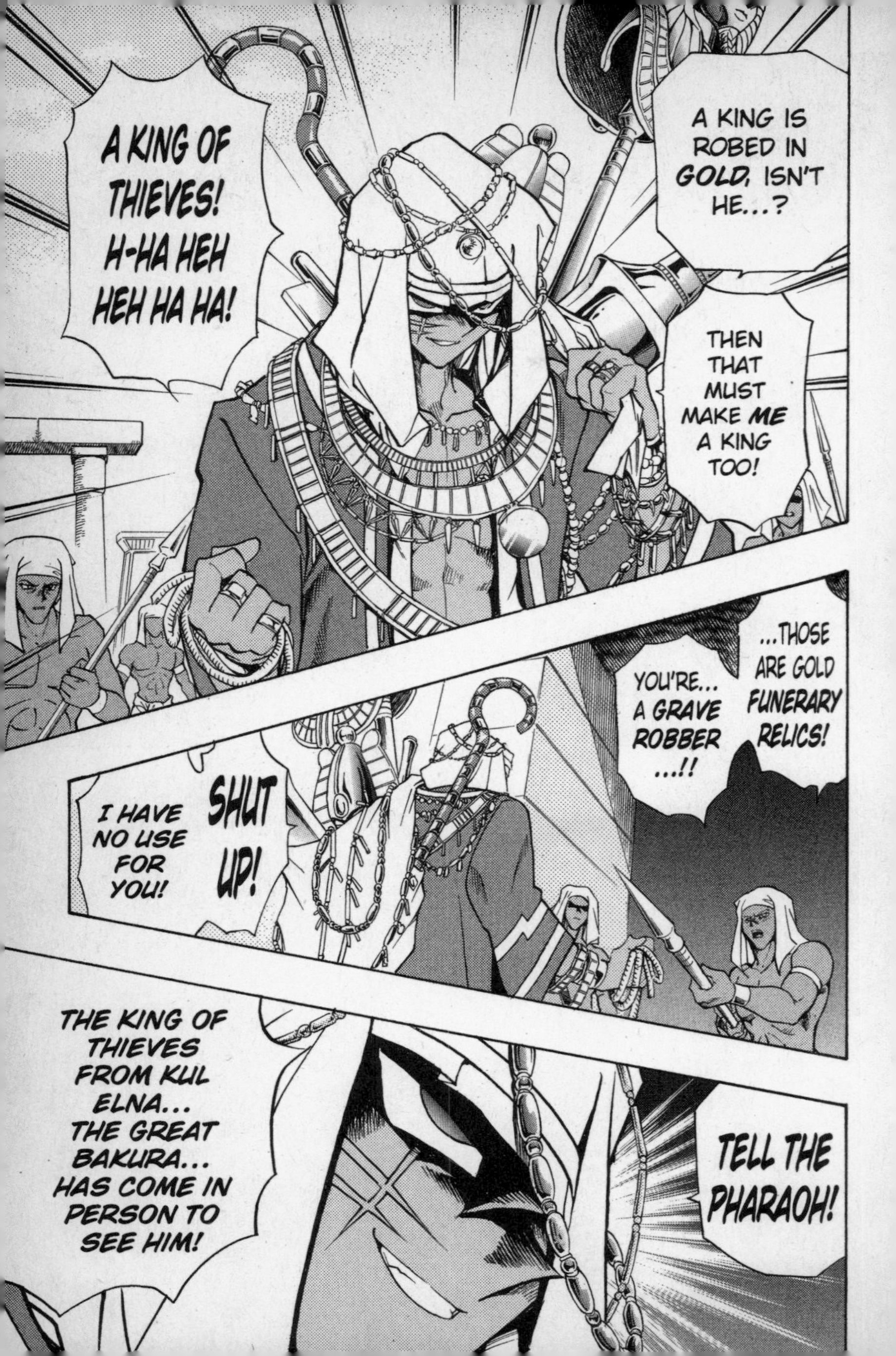
A KING IS ROBED IN GOLD, ISN'T HE...?
THEN THAT MUST MAKE ME A KING TOO!
A KING OF THIEVES! H-HA HEH HEH HA HA!
...THOSE ARE GOLD FUNERARY RELICS!
YOU'RE... A GRAVE ROBBER ...!!
SHUT UP!
I HAVE NO USE FOR YOU!
TELL THE PHARAOH!
THE KING OF THIEVES FROM KUL ELNA... THE GREAT BAKURA... HAS COME IN PERSON TO SEE HIM!

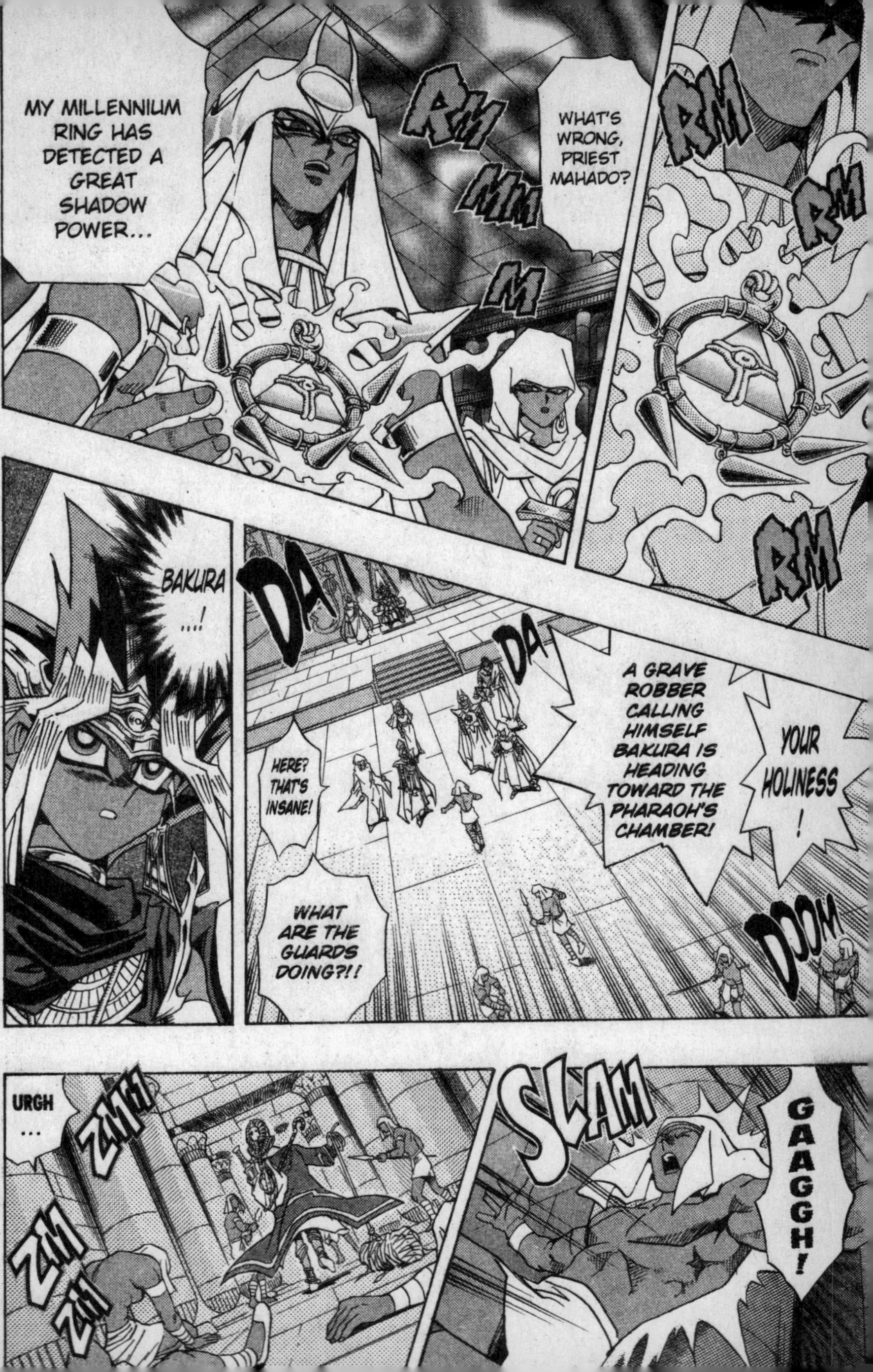
RM
RM
RM
WHAT'S WRONG, PRIEST MAHADO?
RMMMM
MY MILLENNIUM RING HAS DETECTED A GREAT SHADOW POWER...
YOUR HOLINESS!
A GRAVE ROBBER CALLING HIMSELF BAKURA IS HEADING TOWARD THE PHARAOH'S CHAMBER!
DA
DA
HERE? THAT'S INSANE!
WHAT ARE THE GUARDS DOING?!!
DOOM
BAKURA...!
GAAGGH!
SLAM
URGH...

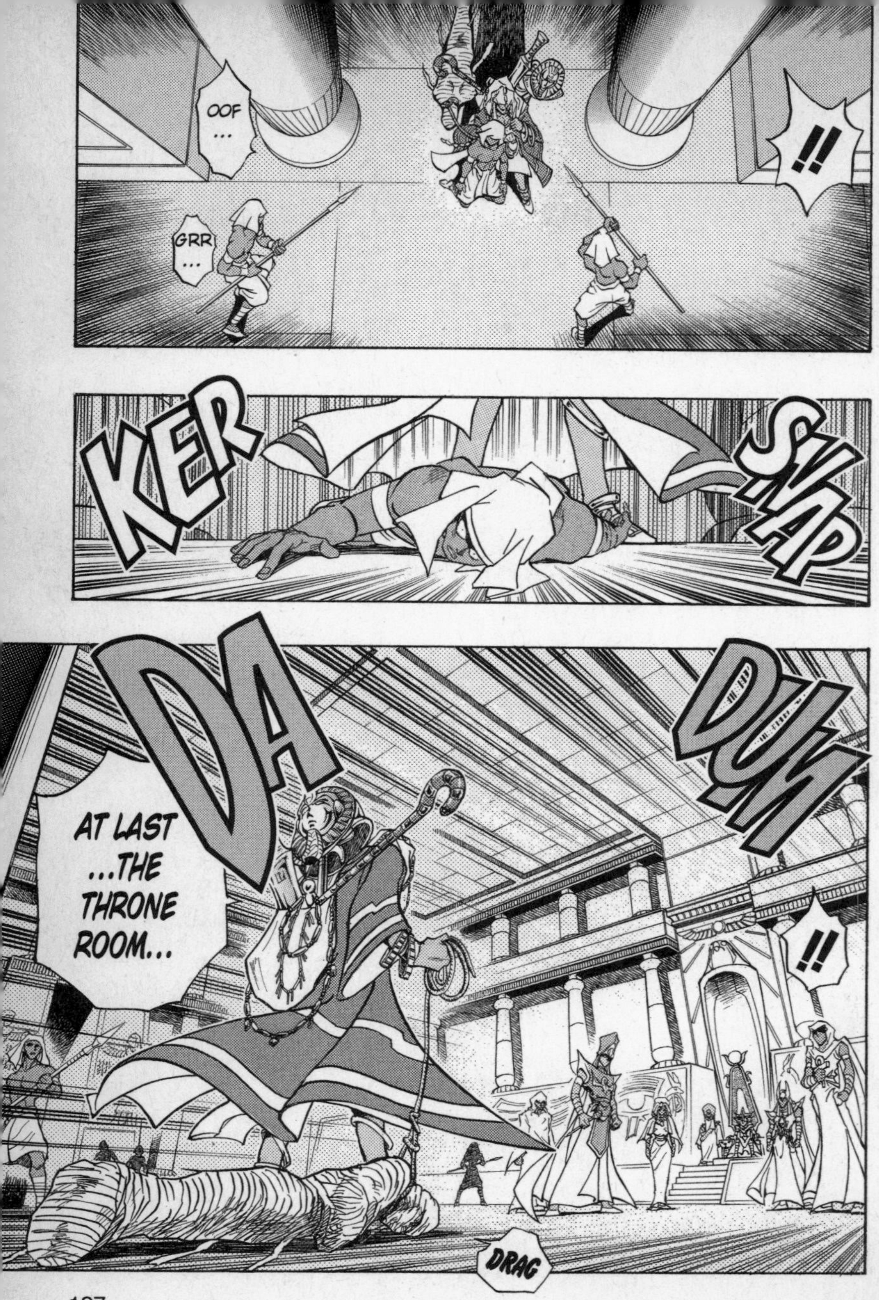
!!
OOF ...
GRR ...
KER SNAP
DA DUM
!!
AT LAST ...THE THRONE ROOM...
DRAG

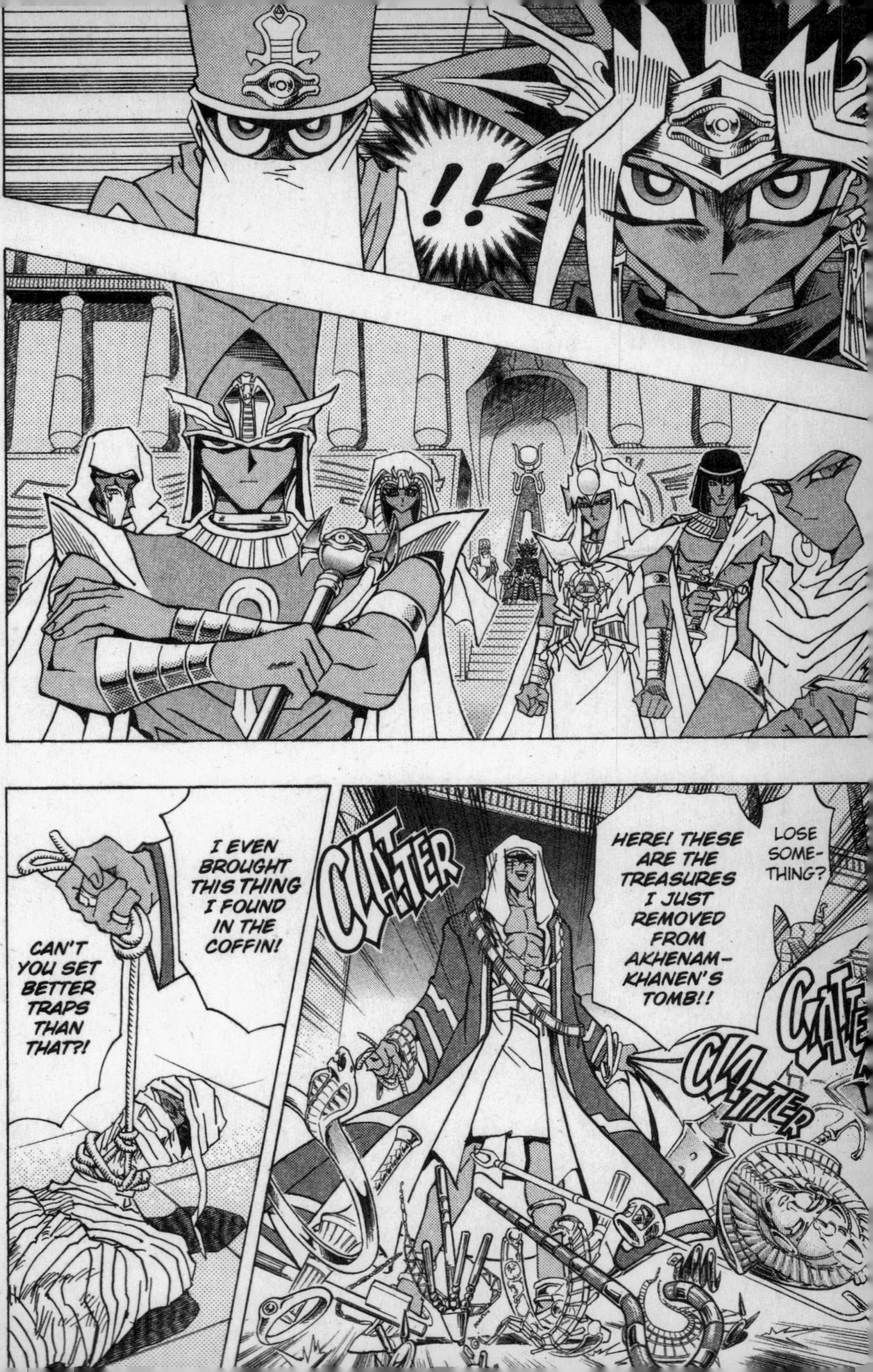
!!
LOSE SOME-THING?
HERE! THESE ARE THE TREASURES I JUST REMOVED FROM AKHENAM-KHANEN'S TOMB!!
CLATTER
CLATTER
CLATTER
I EVEN BROUGHT THIS THING I FOUND IN THE COFFIN!
CAN'T YOU SET BETTER TRAPS THAN THAT?!

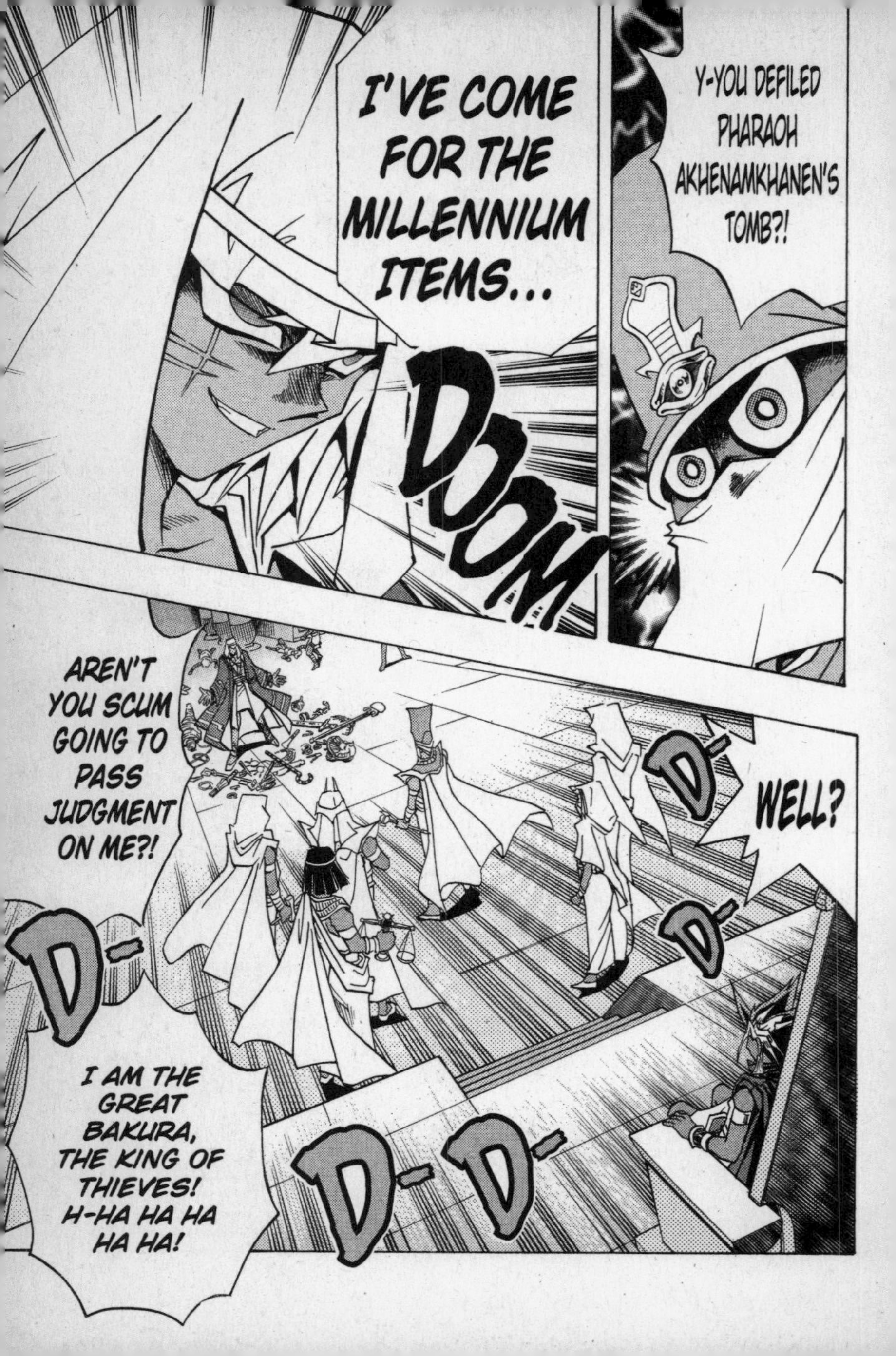
Y-YOU DEFILED PHARAOH AKHENAMKHANEN'S TOMB?!
I'VE COME FOR THE MILLENNIUM ITEMS...
DOOM
D-
WELL?
D-
AREN'T YOU SCUM GOING TO PASS JUDGMENT ON ME?!
D-
D-D-
I AM THE GREAT BAKURA, THE KING OF THIEVES! H-HA HA HA HA HA!

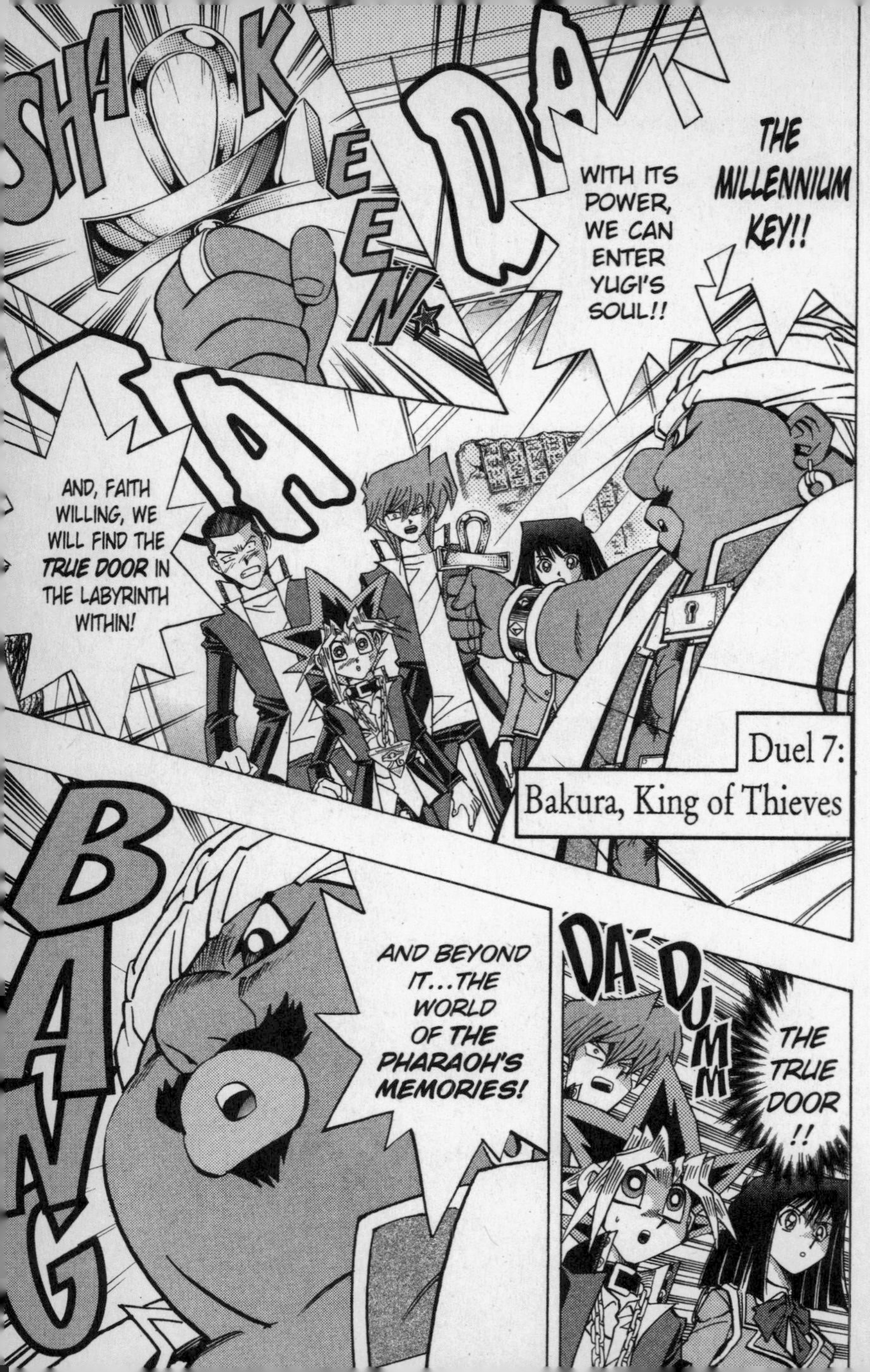
THE MILLENNIUM KEY!!
WITH ITS POWER, WE CAN ENTER YUGI'S SOUL!!
DA
SHAKEEN☆
AND, FAITH WILLING, WE WILL FIND THE TRUE DOOR IN THE LABYRINTH WITHIN!
Duel 7:
Bakura, King of Thieves
DA-DUMM
THE TRUE DOOR!!
AND BEYOND IT...THE WORLD OF THE PHARAOH'S MEMORIES!
BANG

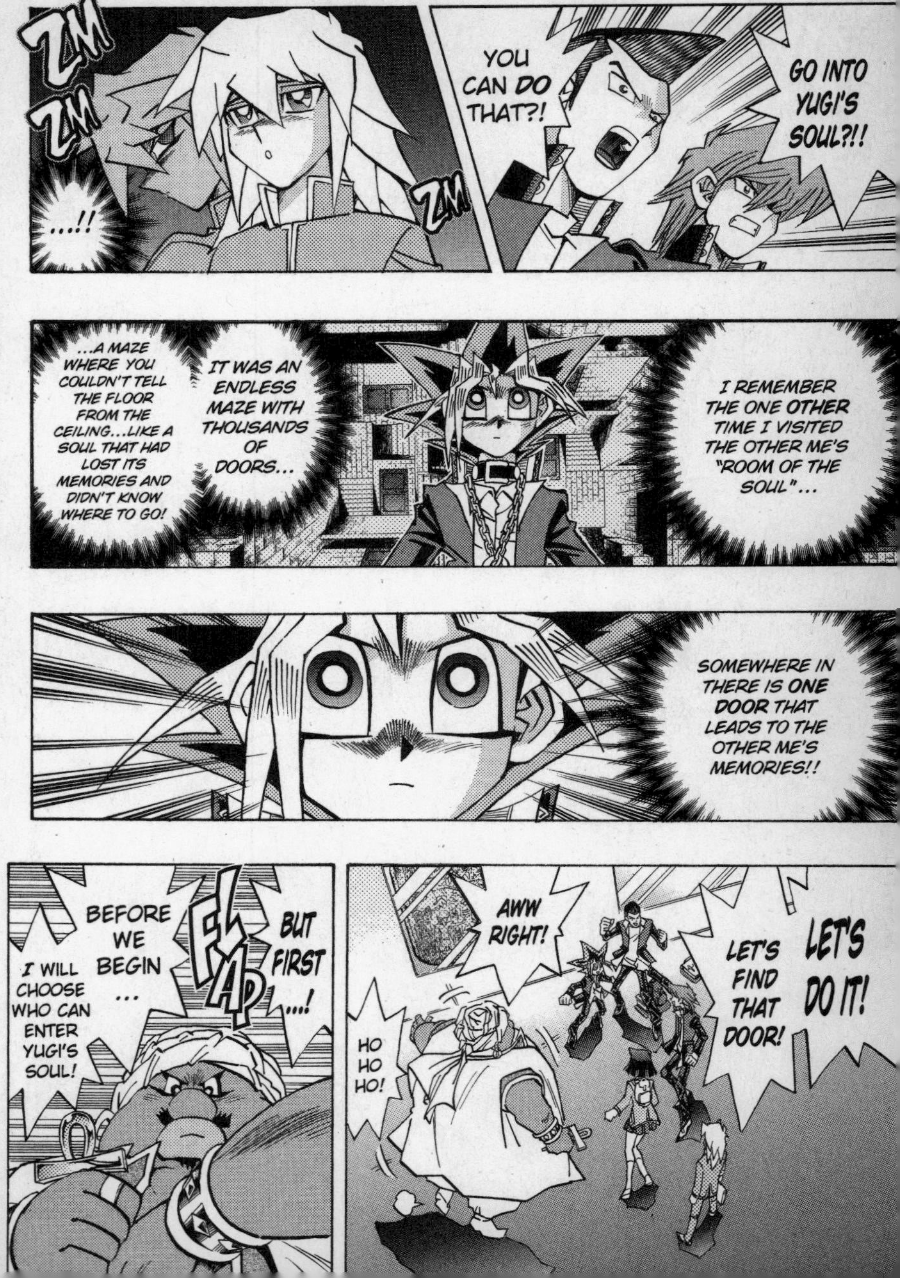
GO INTO YUGI'S SOUL?!!
YOU CAN DO THAT?!
ZM
ZM
ZM
....!!
I REMEMBER THE ONE OTHER TIME I VISITED THE OTHER ME'S "ROOM OF THE SOUL"...
IT WAS AN ENDLESS MAZE WITH THOUSANDS OF DOORS...
...A MAZE WHERE YOU COULDN'T TELL THE FLOOR FROM THE CEILING...LIKE A SOUL THAT HAD LOST ITS MEMORIES AND DIDN'T KNOW WHERE TO GO!
SOMEWHERE IN THERE IS ONE DOOR THAT LEADS TO THE OTHER ME'S MEMORIES!!
LET'S DO IT!
LET'S FIND THAT DOOR!
AWW RIGHT!
HO HO HO!
BUT FIRST ....!
FLAP
BEFORE WE BEGIN ...
I WILL CHOOSE WHO CAN ENTER YUGI'S SOUL!

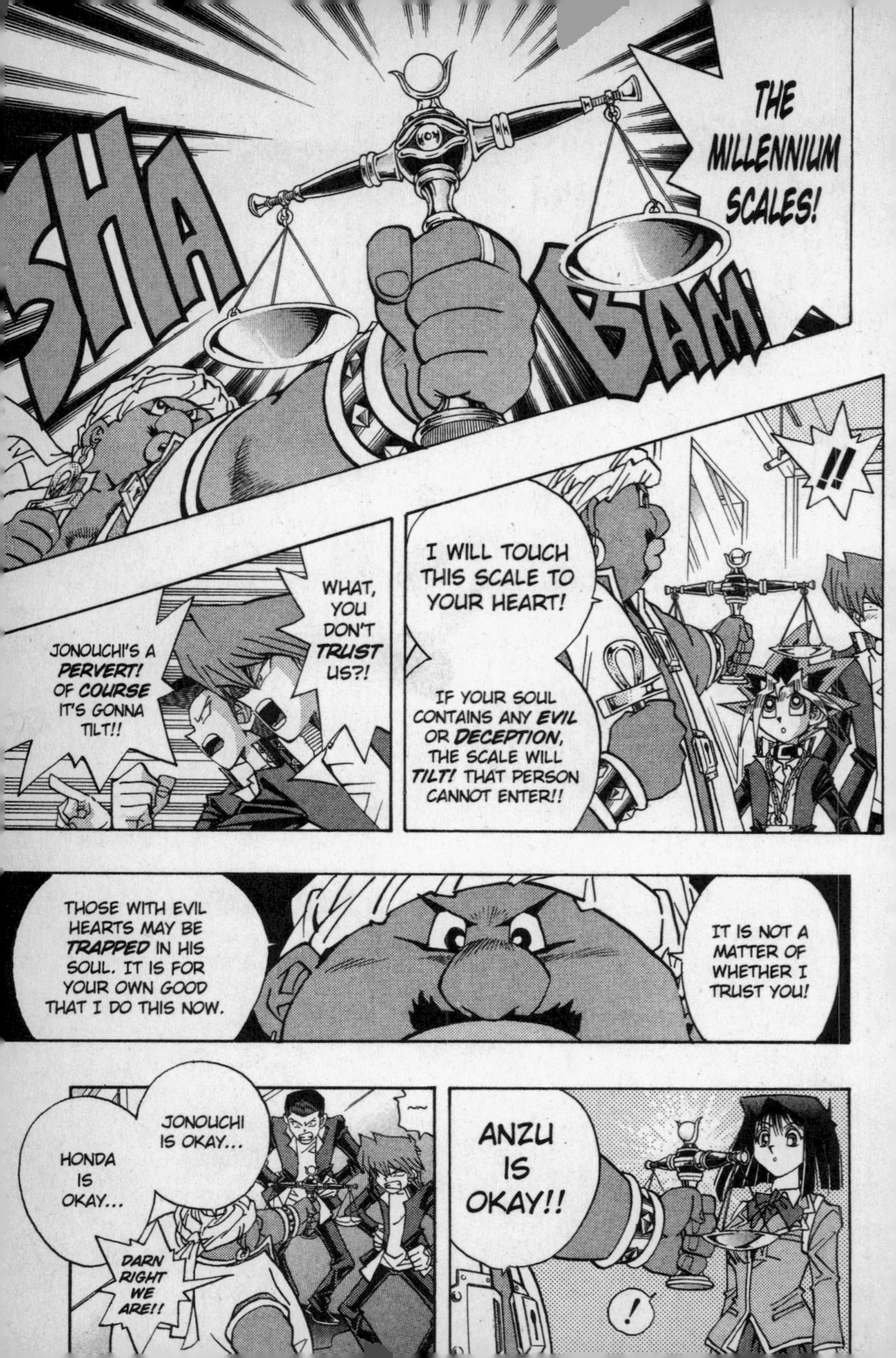
THE MILLENNIUM SCALES!
BAM
SHA
!!
I WILL TOUCH THIS SCALE TO YOUR HEART!
IF YOUR SOUL CONTAINS ANY *EVIL* OR *DECEPTION*, THE SCALE WILL *TILT!* THAT PERSON CANNOT ENTER!!
WHAT, YOU DON'T *TRUST* US?!
JONOUCHI'S A *PERVERT!* OF *COURSE* IT'S GONNA TILT!!
IT IS NOT A MATTER OF WHETHER I TRUST YOU!
THOSE WITH EVIL HEARTS MAY BE *TRAPPED* IN HIS SOUL. IT IS FOR YOUR OWN GOOD THAT I DO THIS NOW.
ANZU IS OKAY!!
!
JONOUCHI IS OKAY...
HONDA IS OKAY...
DARN RIGHT WE ARE!!

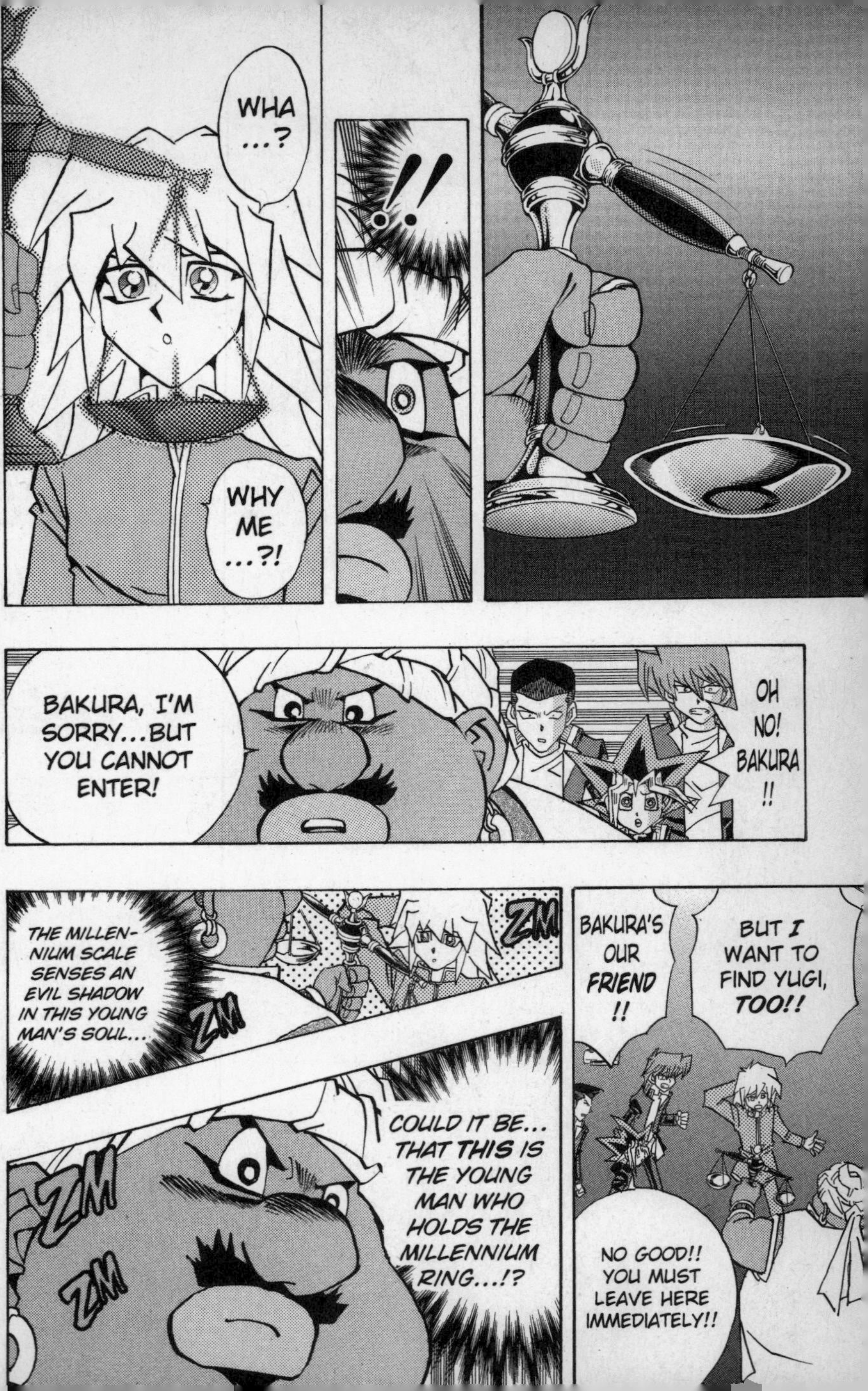
!!
WHA ...?
WHY ME ...?!
OH NO! BAKURA !!
BAKURA, I'M SORRY...BUT YOU CANNOT ENTER!
BUT I WANT TO FIND YUGI, TOO!!
BAKURA'S OUR FRIEND !!
NO GOOD!! YOU MUST LEAVE HERE IMMEDIATELY!!
ZM
THE MILLENNIUM SCALE SENSES AN EVIL SHADOW IN THIS YOUNG MAN'S SOUL...
ZM
COULD IT BE... THAT THIS IS THE YOUNG MAN WHO HOLDS THE MILLENNIUM RING...!?
ZM
ZM

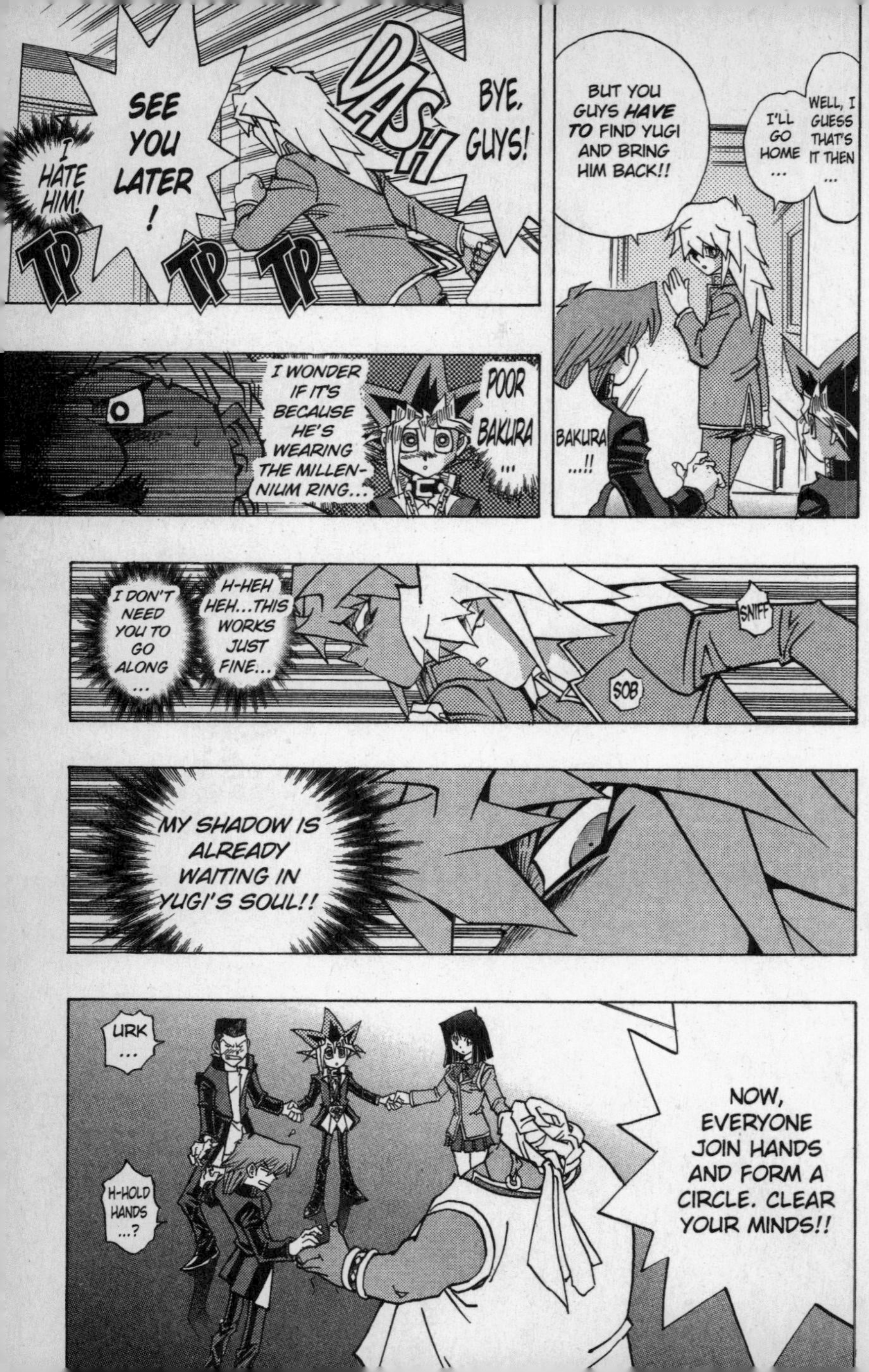

WELL, I GUESS THAT'S IT THEN...
I'LL GO HOME...
BUT YOU GUYS HAVE TO FIND YUGI AND BRING HIM BACK!!
BAKURA...!!
BYE, GUYS!
DASH
SEE YOU LATER!
I HATE HIM!
TP TP TP
POOR BAKURA...
I WONDER IF IT'S BECAUSE HE'S WEARING THE MILLENNIUM RING...
SNIFF
SOB
H-HEH HEH...THIS WORKS JUST FINE...
I DON'T NEED YOU TO GO ALONG...
MY SHADOW IS ALREADY WAITING IN YUGI'S SOUL!!
NOW, EVERYONE JOIN HANDS AND FORM A CIRCLE. CLEAR YOUR MINDS!!
URK...
H-HOLD HANDS...?

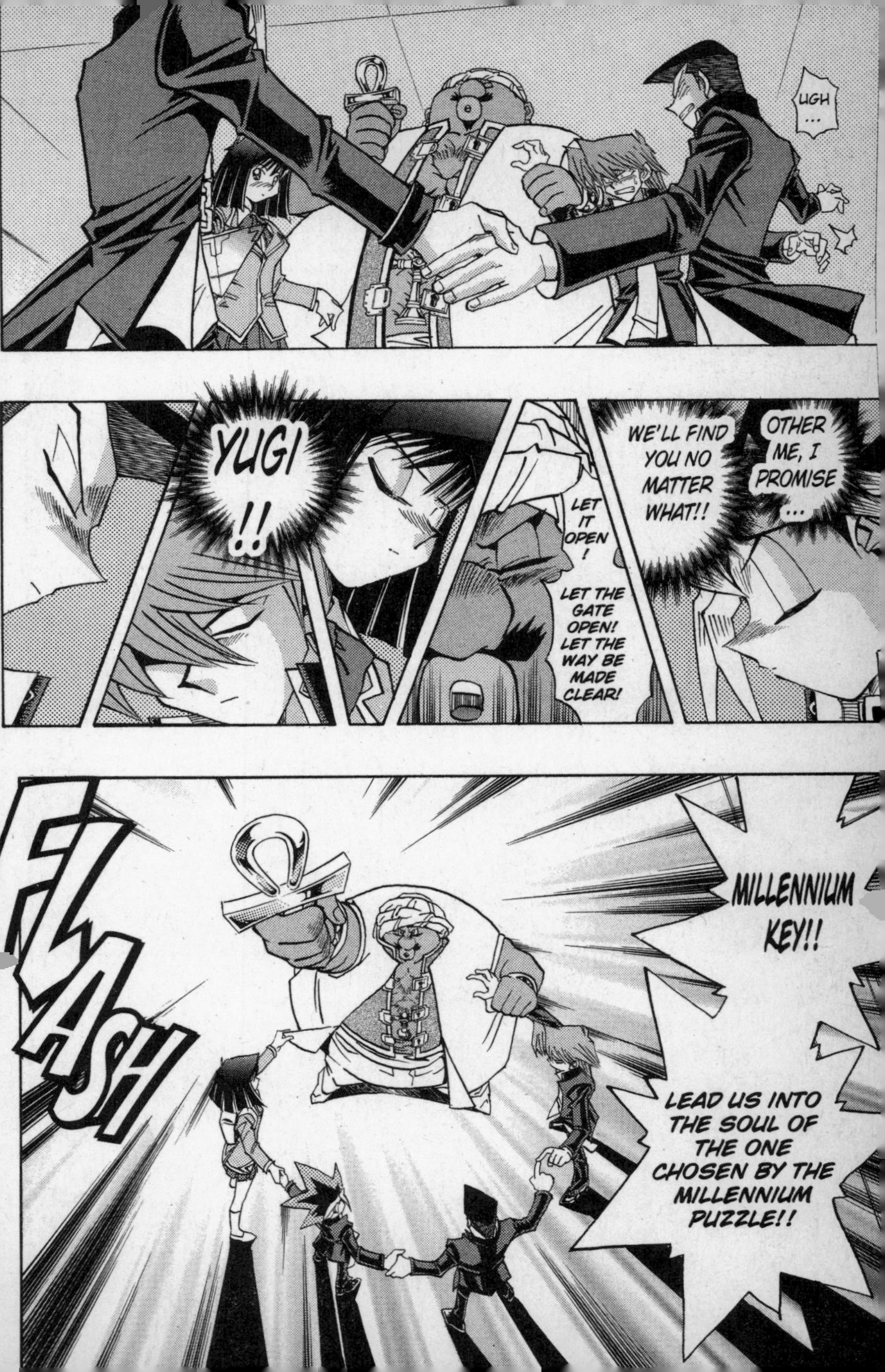
UGH ...
OTHER ME, I PROMISE ...
WE'LL FIND YOU NO MATTER WHAT!!
LET IT OPEN!
LET THE GATE OPEN! LET THE WAY BE MADE CLEAR!
YUGI!!
MILLENNIUM KEY!!
LEAD US INTO THE SOUL OF THE ONE CHOSEN BY THE MILLENNIUM PUZZLE!!
FLASH

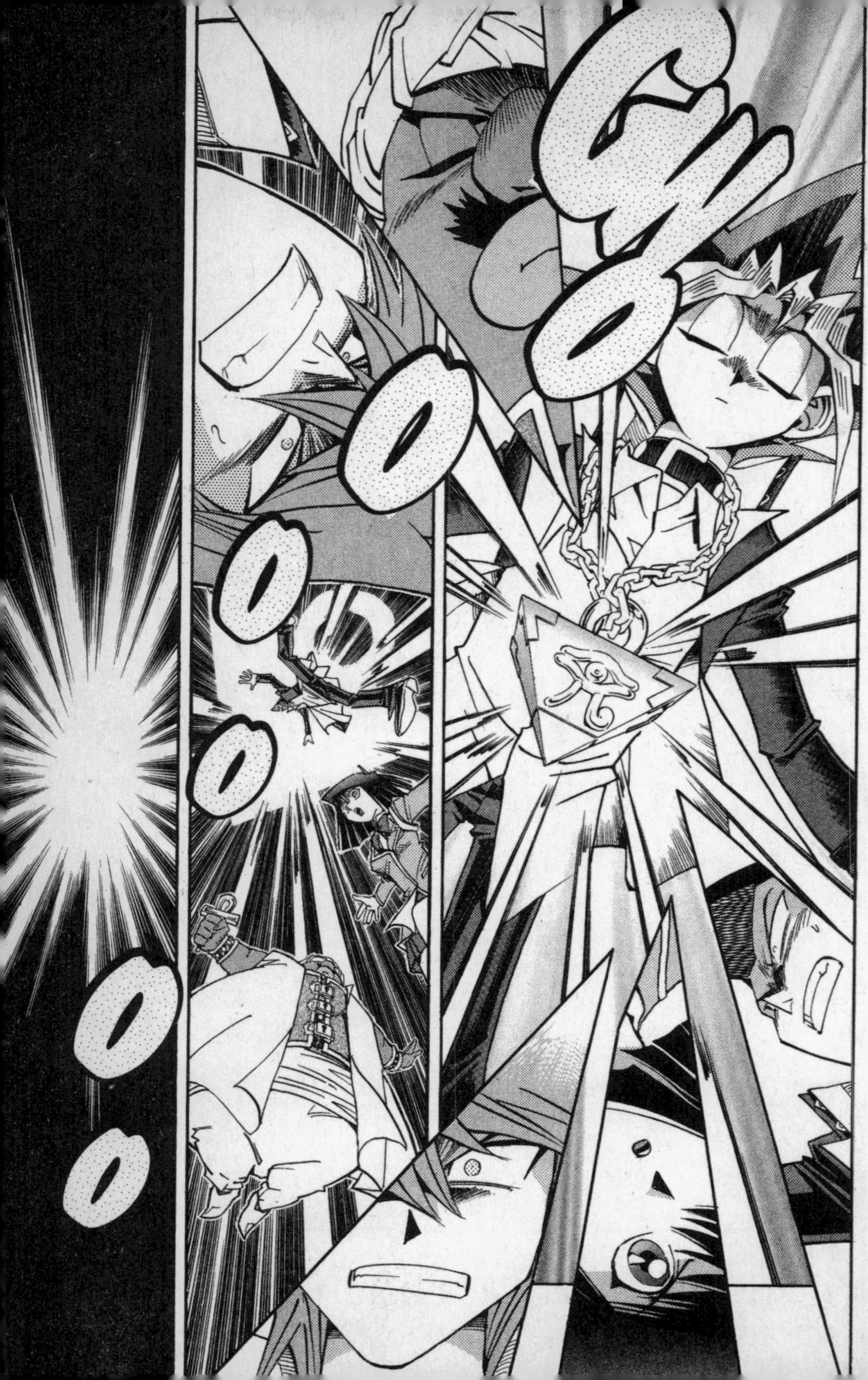
GWOOOOOO

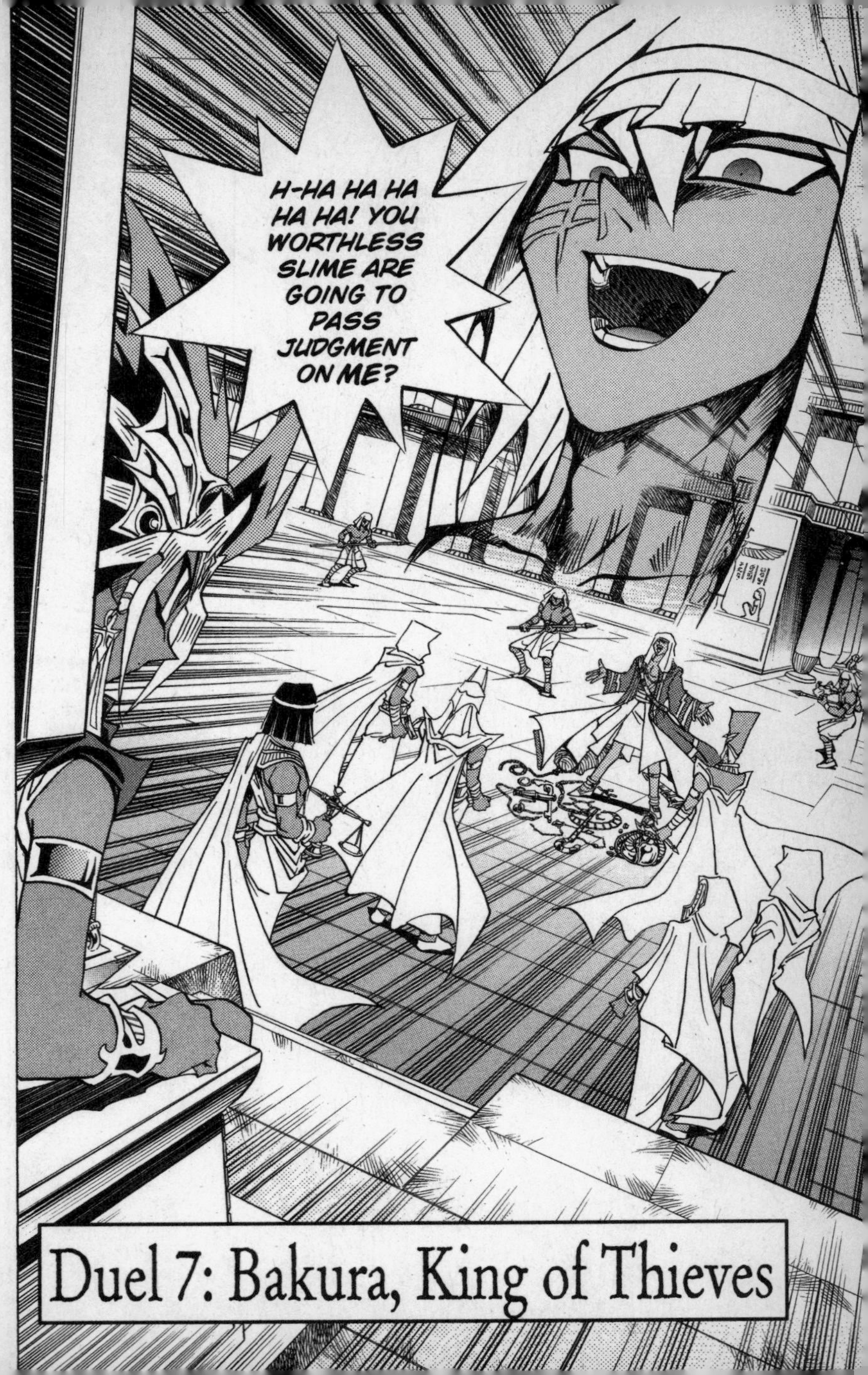
H-HA HA HA HA HA! YOU WORTHLESS SLIME ARE GOING TO PASS JUDGMENT ON ME?
Duel 7: Bakura, King of Thieves

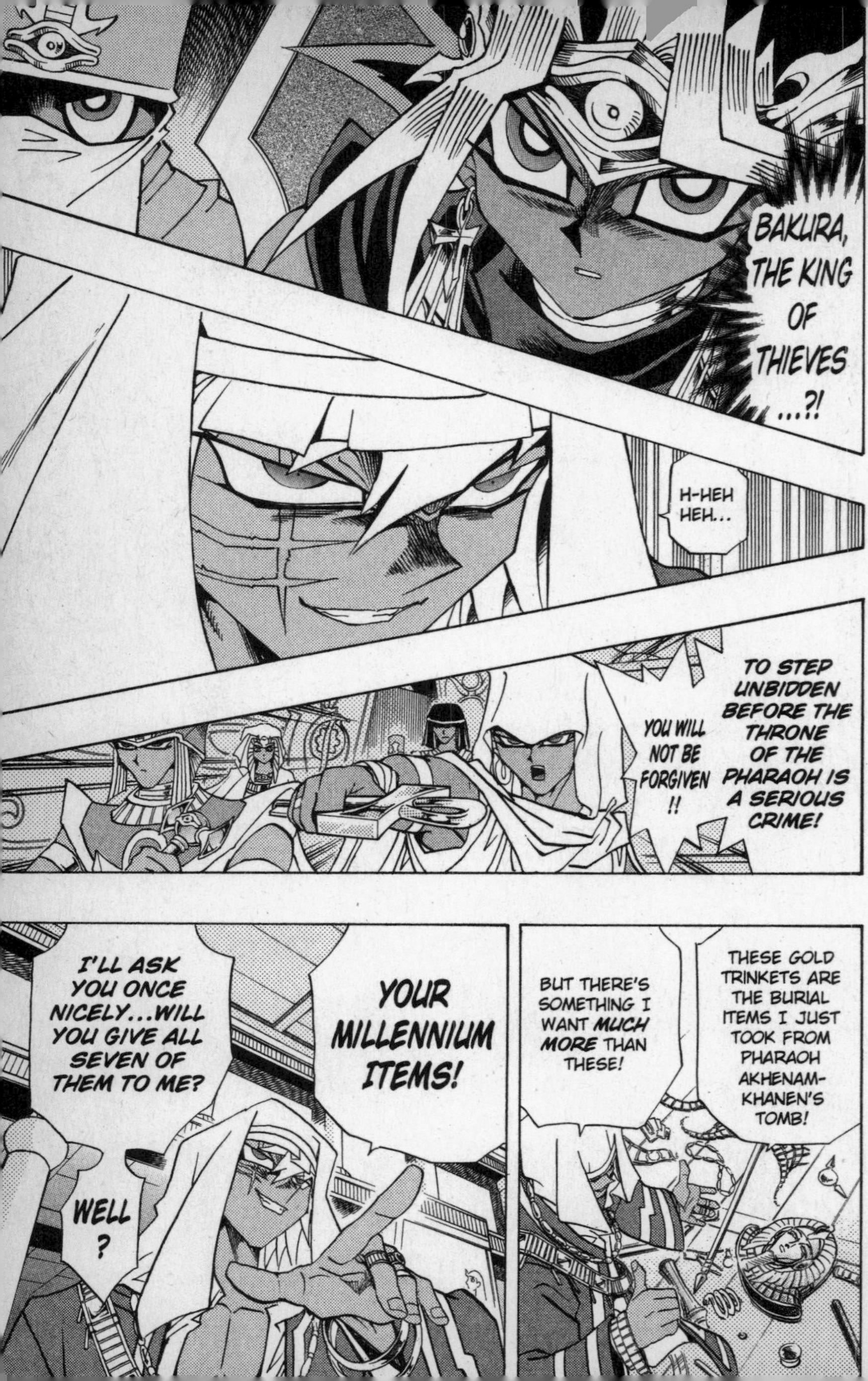
BAKURA, THE KING OF THIEVES ...?!
H-HEH HEH...
TO STEP UNBIDDEN BEFORE THE THRONE OF THE PHARAOH IS A SERIOUS CRIME!
YOU WILL NOT BE FORGIVEN !!
THESE GOLD TRINKETS ARE THE BURIAL ITEMS I JUST TOOK FROM PHARAOH AKHENAM-KHANEN'S TOMB!
BUT THERE'S SOMETHING I WANT *MUCH MORE* THAN THESE!
YOUR MILLENNIUM ITEMS!
I'LL ASK YOU ONCE NICELY...WILL YOU GIVE ALL SEVEN OF THEM TO ME?
WELL ?

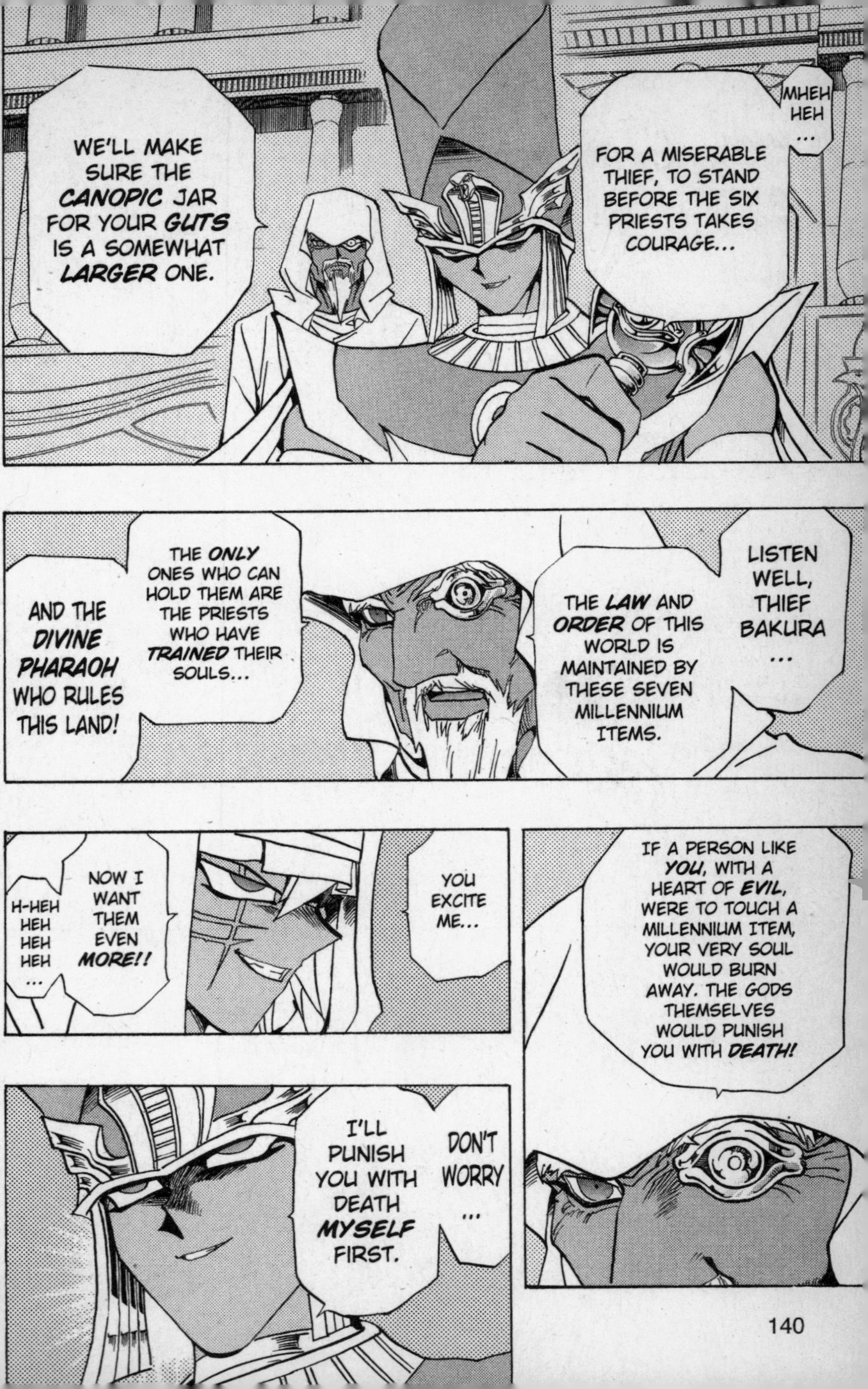
MHEH HEH ...
FOR A MISERABLE THIEF, TO STAND BEFORE THE SIX PRIESTS TAKES COURAGE...
WE'LL MAKE SURE THE CANOPIC JAR FOR YOUR GUTS IS A SOMEWHAT LARGER ONE.
LISTEN WELL, THIEF BAKURA ...
THE LAW AND ORDER OF THIS WORLD IS MAINTAINED BY THESE SEVEN MILLENNIUM ITEMS.
THE ONLY ONES WHO CAN HOLD THEM ARE THE PRIESTS WHO HAVE TRAINED THEIR SOULS...
AND THE DIVINE PHARAOH WHO RULES THIS LAND!
IF A PERSON LIKE YOU, WITH A HEART OF EVIL, WERE TO TOUCH A MILLENNIUM ITEM, YOUR VERY SOUL WOULD BURN AWAY. THE GODS THEMSELVES WOULD PUNISH YOU WITH DEATH!
YOU EXCITE ME...
NOW I WANT THEM EVEN MORE!!
H-HEH HEH HEH HEH ...
DON'T WORRY ...
I'LL PUNISH YOU WITH DEATH MYSELF FIRST.

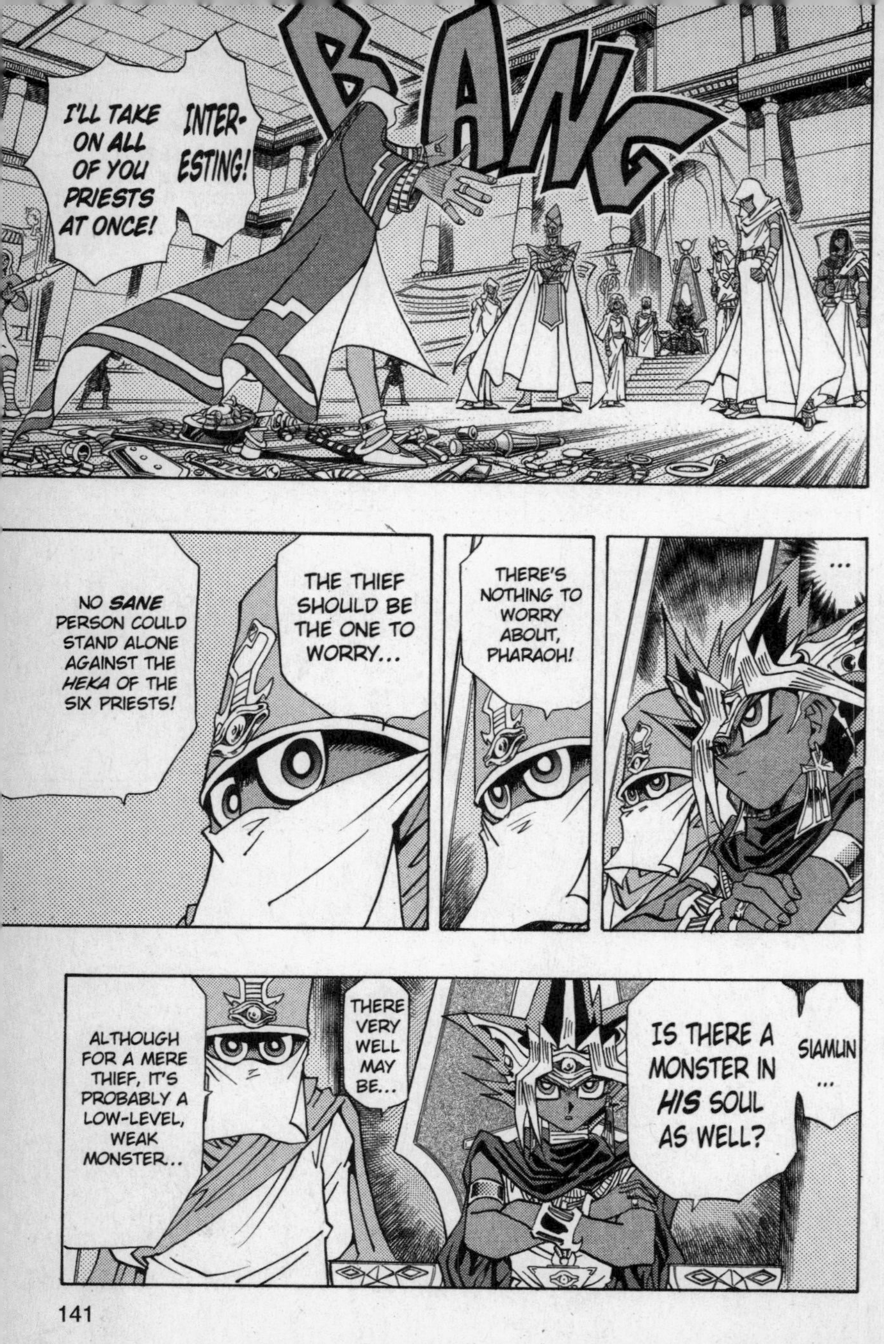
BANG
INTER-ESTING!
I'LL TAKE ON ALL OF YOU PRIESTS AT ONCE!
...
THERE'S NOTHING TO WORRY ABOUT, PHARAOH!
THE THIEF SHOULD BE THE ONE TO WORRY...
NO *SANE* PERSON COULD STAND ALONE AGAINST THE *HEKA* OF THE SIX PRIESTS!
SIAMUN ...
IS THERE A MONSTER IN *HIS* SOUL AS WELL?
THERE VERY WELL MAY BE...
ALTHOUGH FOR A MERE THIEF, IT'S PROBABLY A LOW-LEVEL, WEAK MONSTER...

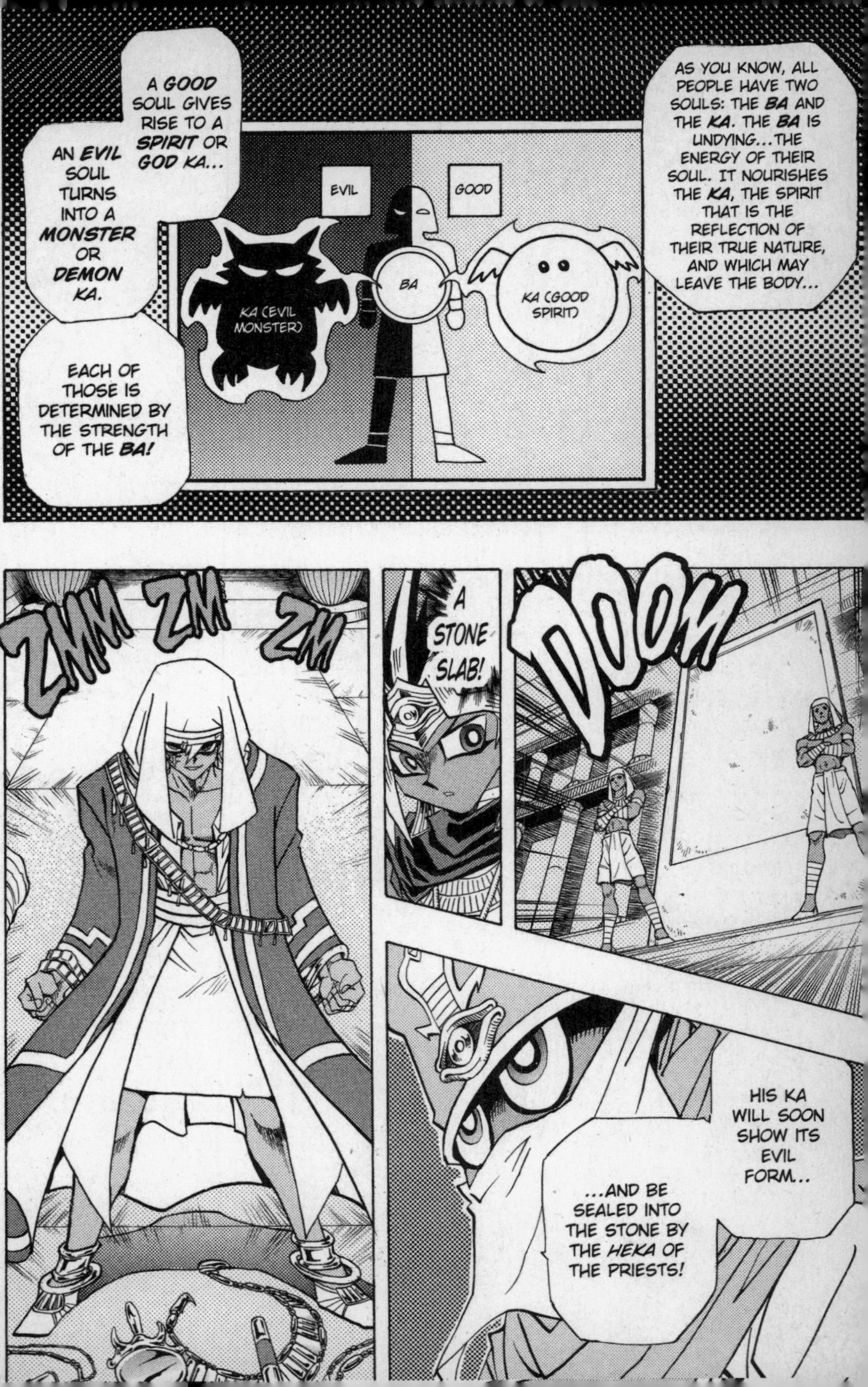
AS YOU KNOW, ALL PEOPLE HAVE TWO SOULS: THE BA AND THE KA. THE BA IS UNDYING...THE ENERGY OF THEIR SOUL. IT NOURISHES THE KA, THE SPIRIT THAT IS THE REFLECTION OF THEIR TRUE NATURE, AND WHICH MAY LEAVE THE BODY...
A GOOD SOUL GIVES RISE TO A SPIRIT OR GOD KA...
AN EVIL SOUL TURNS INTO A MONSTER OR DEMON KA.
GOOD
EVIL
KA (GOOD SPIRIT)
BA
KA (EVIL MONSTER)
EACH OF THOSE IS DETERMINED BY THE STRENGTH OF THE BA!
DOOM
A STONE SLAB!
HIS KA WILL SOON SHOW ITS EVIL FORM...
...AND BE SEALED INTO THE STONE BY THE HEKA OF THE PRIESTS!
ZMM ZM ZM

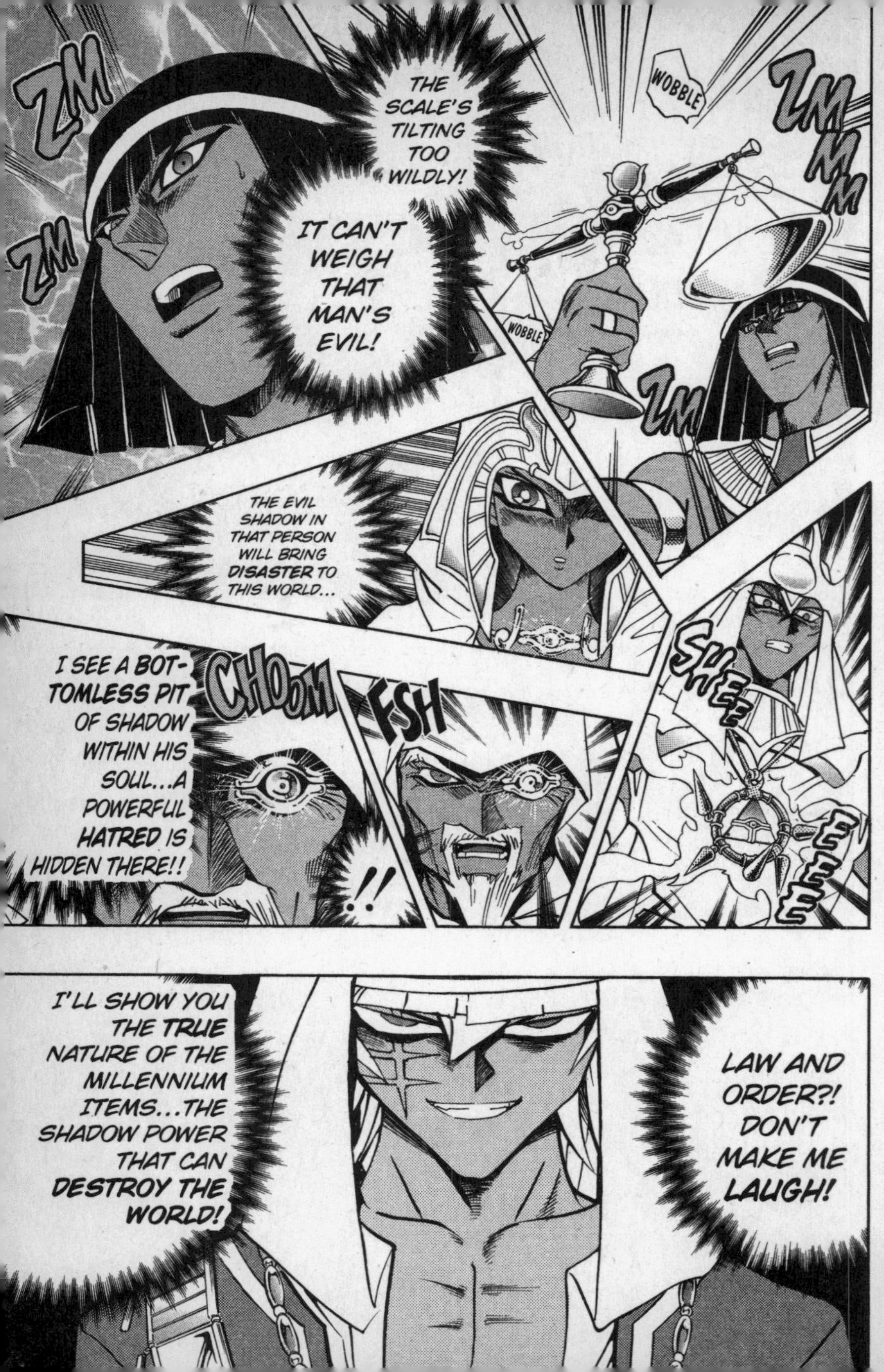
WOBBLE
ZMMM
WOBBLE
ZM
THE SCALE'S TILTING TOO WILDLY!
IT CAN'T WEIGH THAT MAN'S EVIL!
ZM
ZM
THE EVIL SHADOW IN THAT PERSON WILL BRING DISASTER TO THIS WORLD...
SHEEE-EEEE
FSH
!!
CHOOM
I SEE A BOT-TOMLESS PIT OF SHADOW WITHIN HIS SOUL...A POWERFUL HATRED IS HIDDEN THERE!!
LAW AND ORDER?! DON'T MAKE ME LAUGH!
I'LL SHOW YOU THE TRUE NATURE OF THE MILLENNIUM ITEMS...THE SHADOW POWER THAT CAN DESTROY THE WORLD!

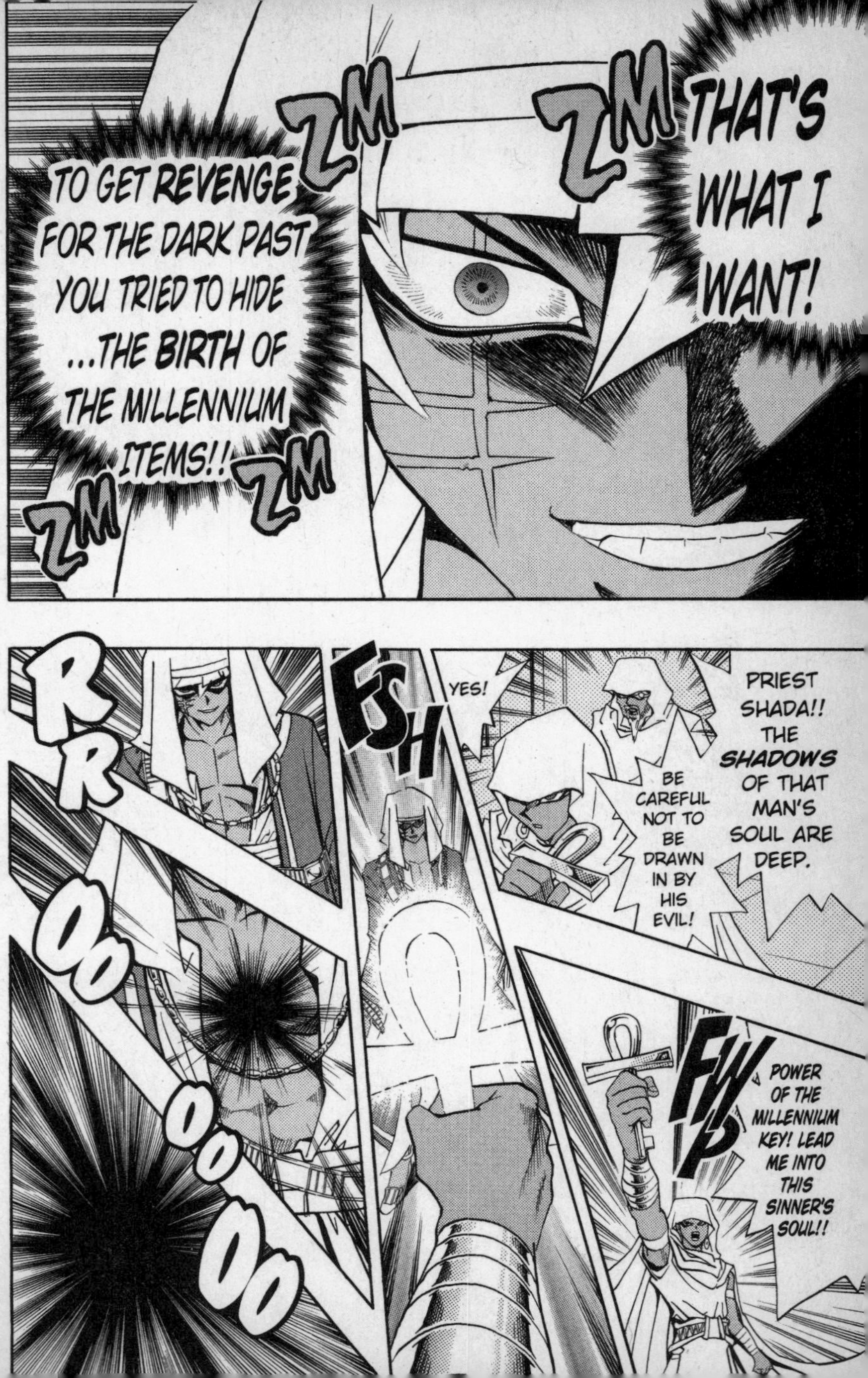
ZM
THAT'S WHAT I WANT!
ZM
TO GET REVENGE FOR THE DARK PAST YOU TRIED TO HIDE ...THE BIRTH OF THE MILLENNIUM ITEMS!!
ZM
ZM
PRIEST SHADA!! THE SHADOWS OF THAT MAN'S SOUL ARE DEEP.
BE CAREFUL NOT TO BE DRAWN IN BY HIS EVIL!
YES!
FWP
POWER OF THE MILLENNIUM KEY! LEAD ME INTO THIS SINNER'S SOUL!!
FSH
RROOOOOOOOOO

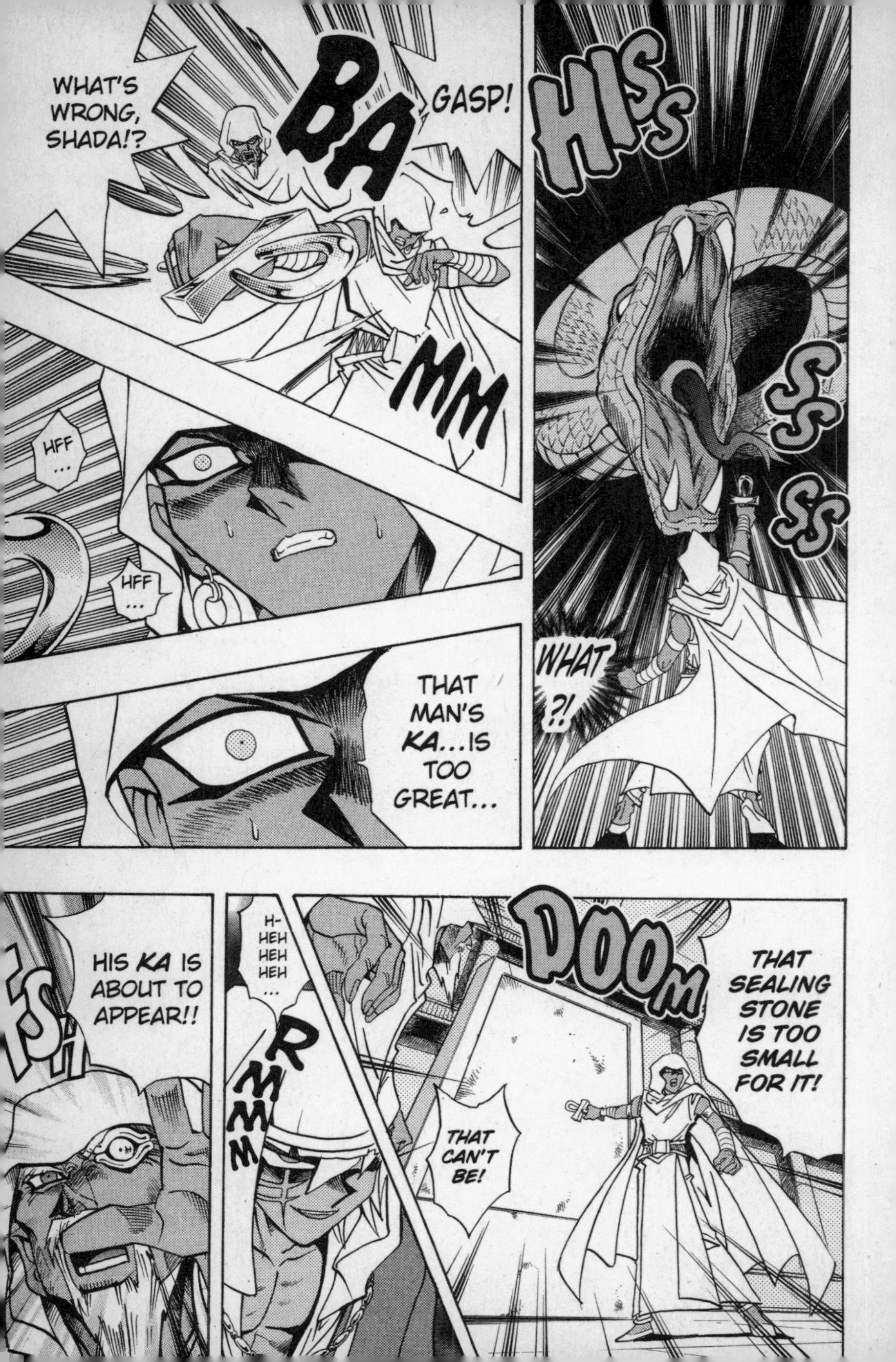
HISSS
SSS
SS
WHAT?!
WHAT'S WRONG, SHADA!?
BA
GASP!
MM
HFF...
HFF...
THAT MAN'S KA...IS TOO GREAT...
DOOM
THAT SEALING STONE IS TOO SMALL FOR IT!
THAT CAN'T BE!
H-HEH HEH HEH...
RMMM
HIS KA IS ABOUT TO APPEAR!!

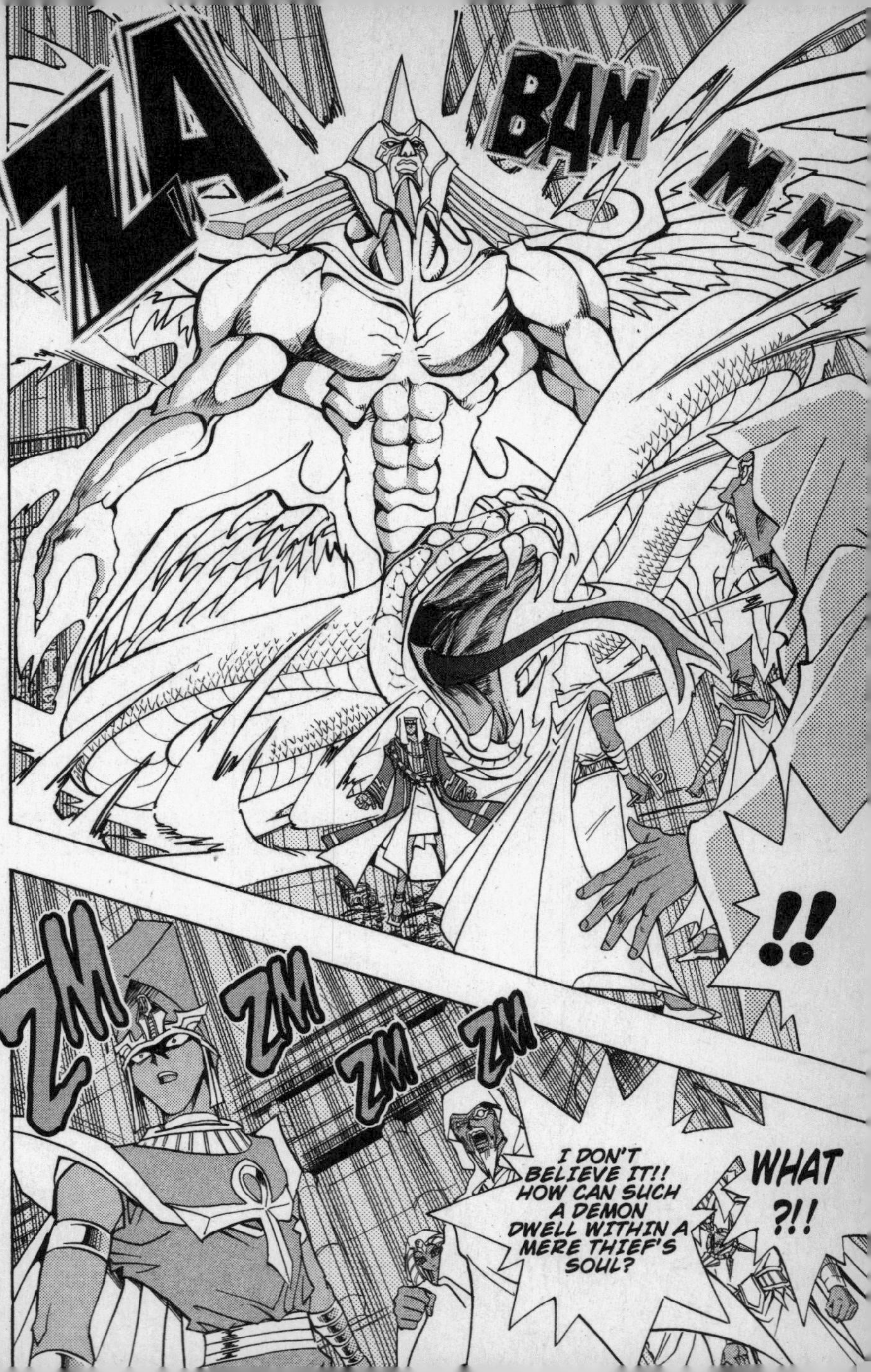
ZA
BAM
MMM
!!
WHAT ?!!
I DON'T BELIEVE IT!! HOW CAN SUCH A DEMON DWELL WITHIN A MERE THIEF'S SOUL?
ZM
ZM
ZM
ZM

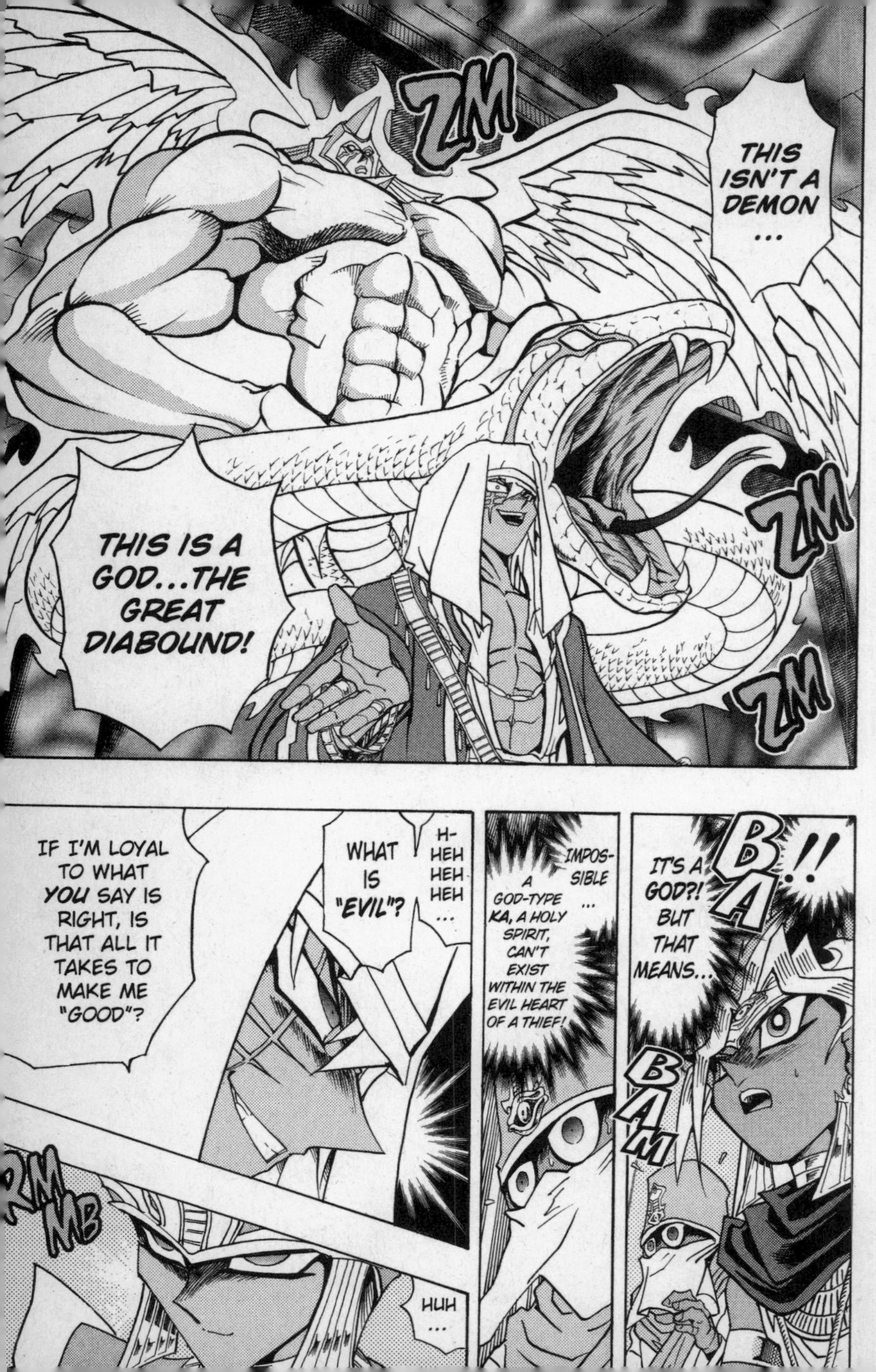
ZM
THIS ISN'T A DEMON ...
ZM
ZM
THIS IS A GOD...THE GREAT DIABOUND!
IT'S A GOD?! BUT THAT MEANS...
BA!!
BAM
IMPOSSIBLE ...
A GOD-TYPE KA, A HOLY SPIRIT, CAN'T EXIST WITHIN THE EVIL HEART OF A THIEF!
H-HEH HEH HEH ...
WHAT IS "EVIL"?
IF I'M LOYAL TO WHAT YOU SAY IS RIGHT, IS THAT ALL IT TAKES TO MAKE ME "GOOD"?
HUH ...

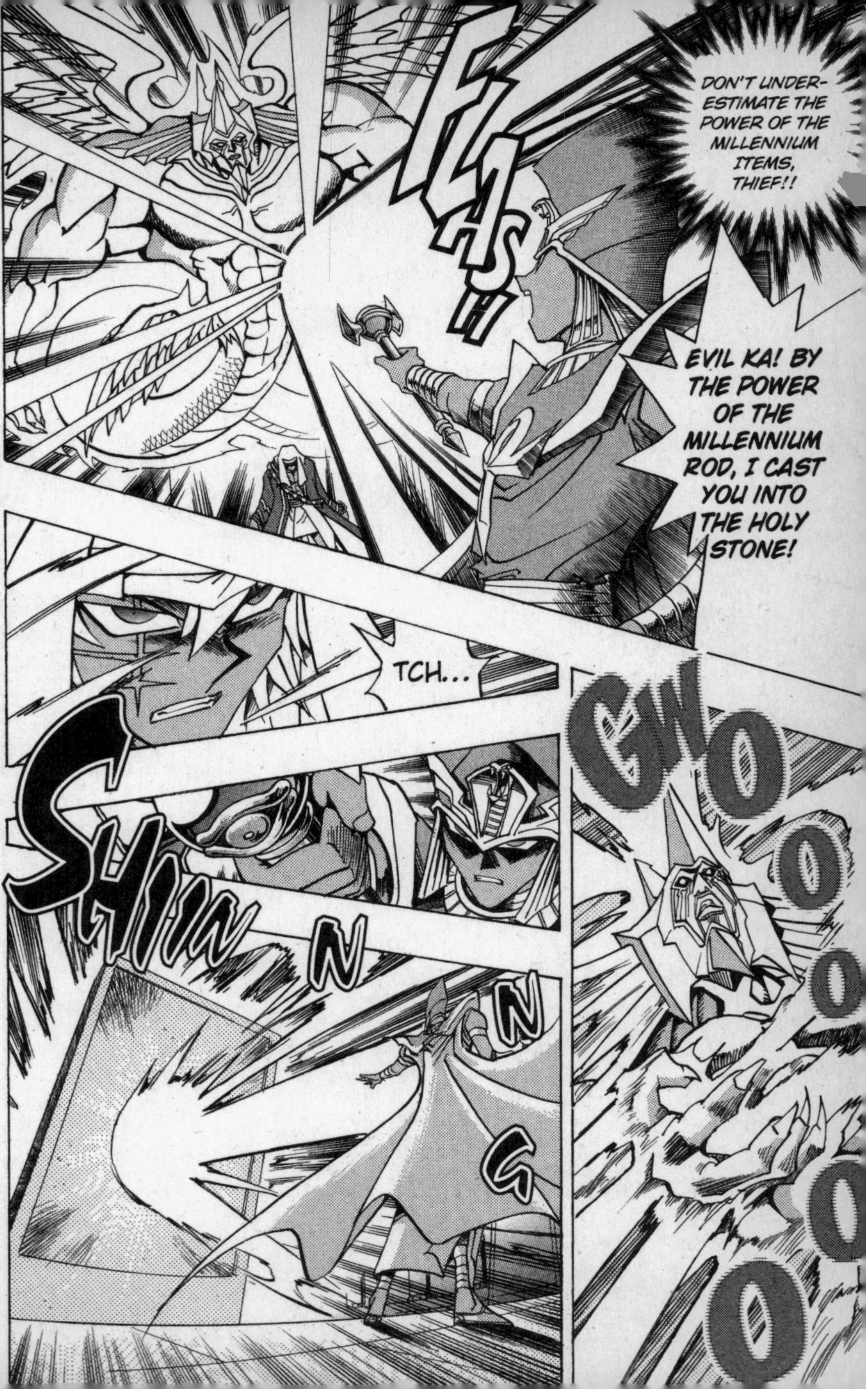
DON'T UNDER-ESTIMATE THE POWER OF THE MILLENNIUM ITEMS, THIEF!!
EVIL KA! BY THE POWER OF THE MILLENNIUM ROD, I CAST YOU INTO THE HOLY STONE!
FLASH
GWOOOOOOOO
TCH...
SHIINNNG

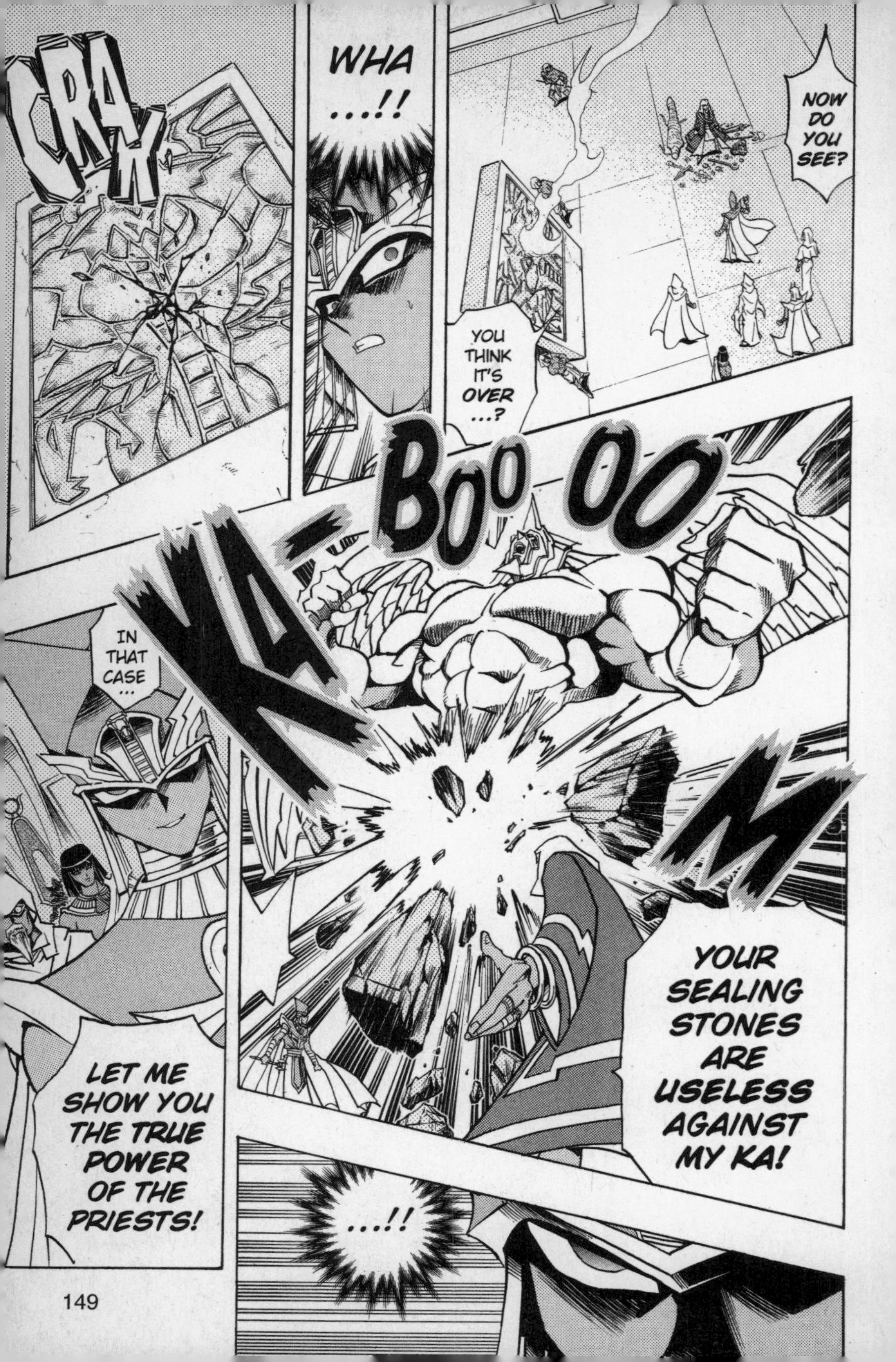
NOW DO YOU SEE?
YOU THINK IT'S OVER ...?
WHA ...!!
CRAK
KA-BOOOOM
YOUR SEALING STONES ARE USELESS AGAINST MY KA!
IN THAT CASE ...
LET ME SHOW YOU THE TRUE POWER OF THE PRIESTS!
...!!

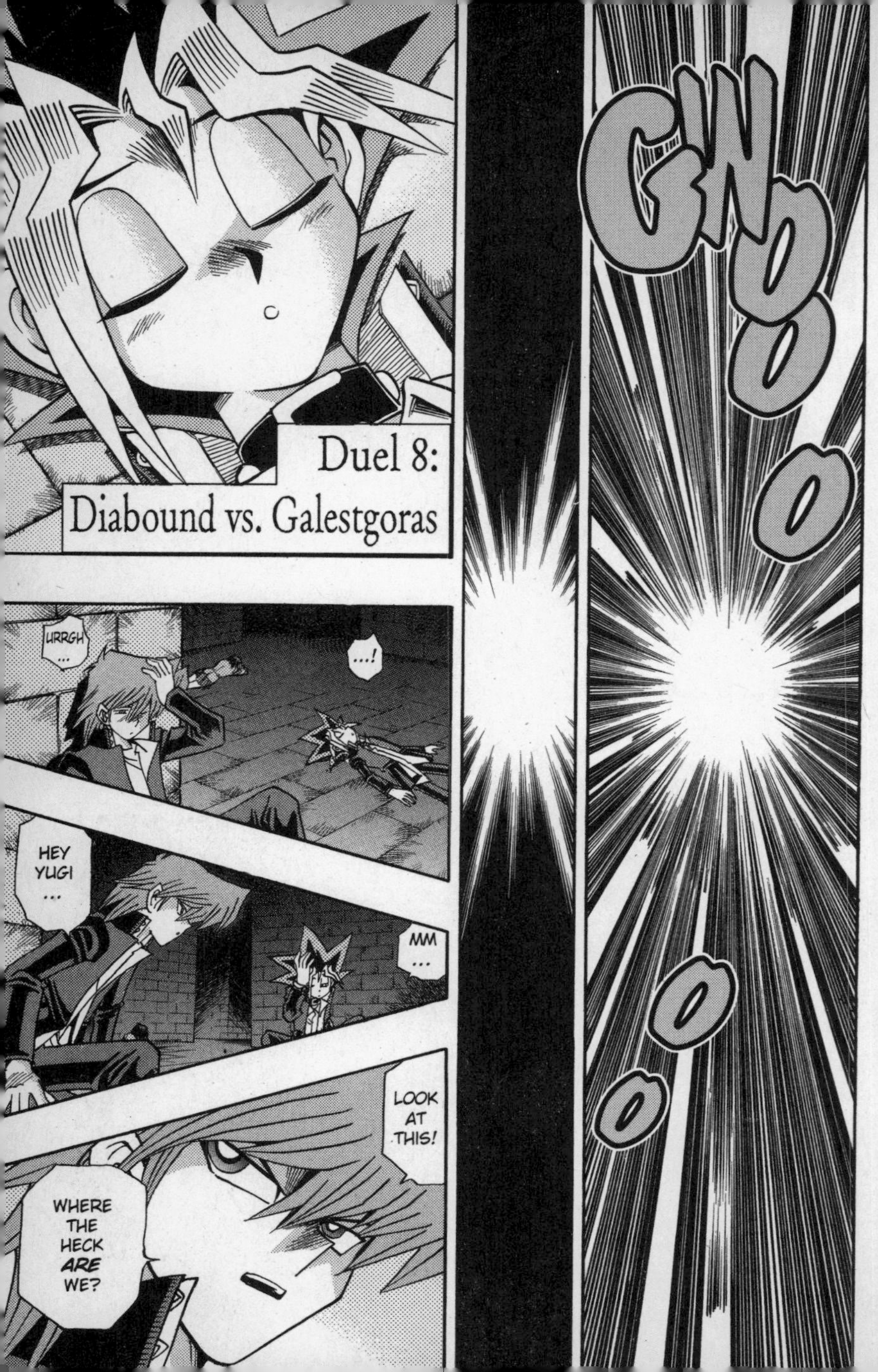
GINGOOOO
Duel 8:
Diabound vs. Galestgoras
URRGH ...
...!
HEY YUGI ...
MM ...
LOOK AT THIS!
WHERE THE HECK ARE WE?

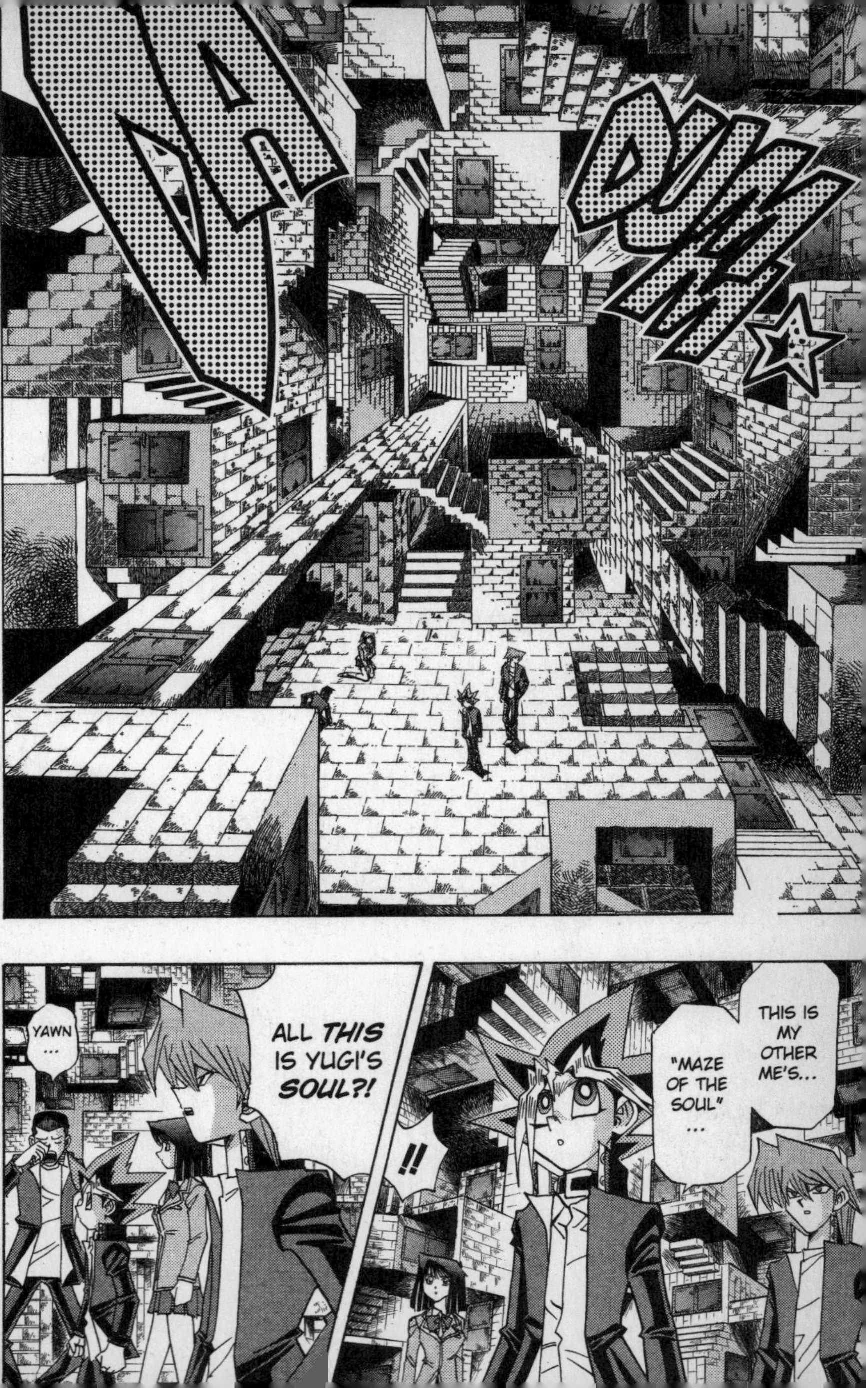
DA
DUM
THIS IS MY OTHER ME'S...
"MAZE OF THE SOUL" ...
!!
ALL THIS IS YUGI'S SOUL?!
YAWN ...

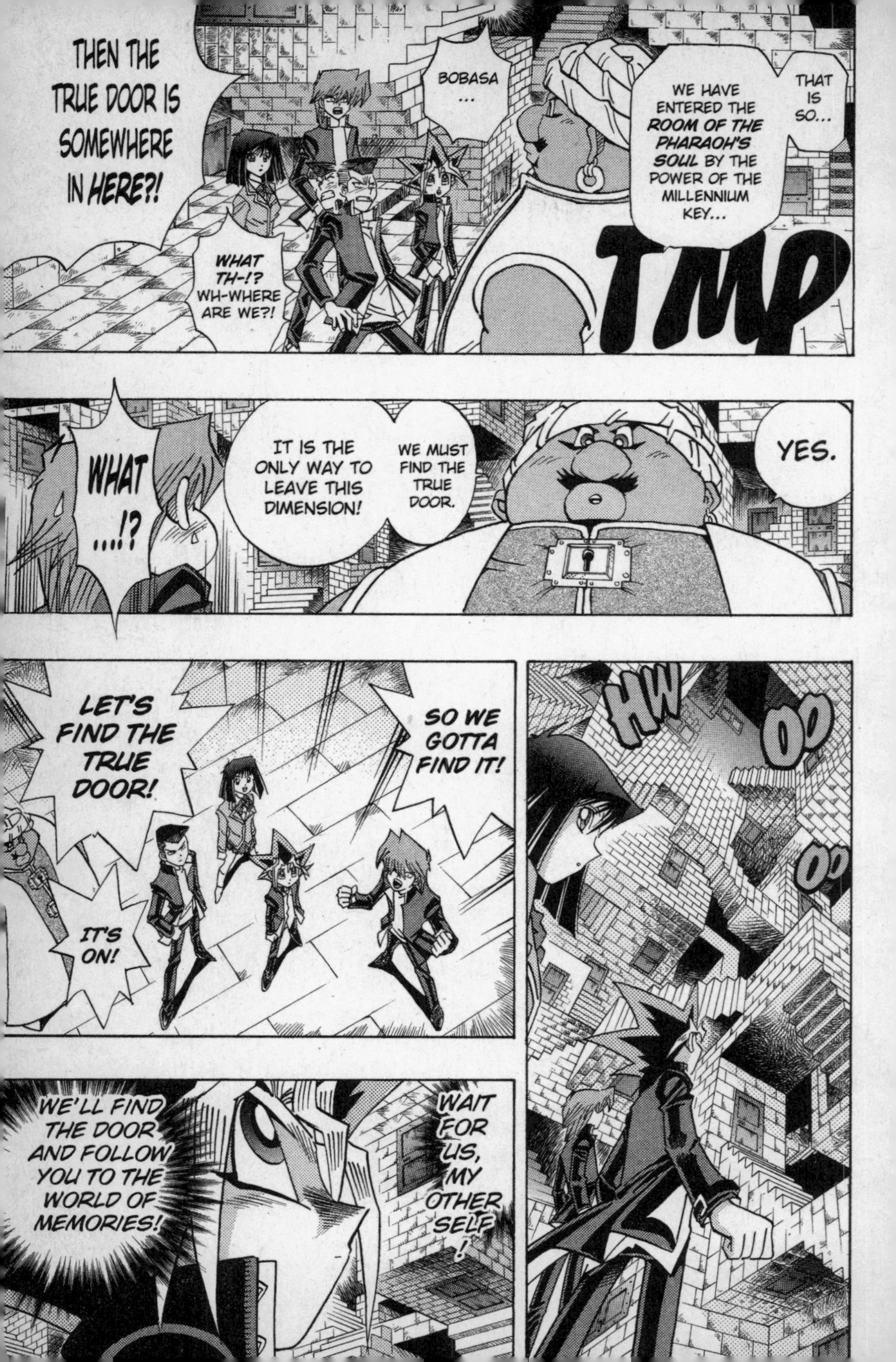
THAT IS SO...
WE HAVE ENTERED THE ROOM OF THE PHARAOH'S SOUL BY THE POWER OF THE MILLENNIUM KEY...
TMP
BOBASA ...
THEN THE TRUE DOOR IS SOMEWHERE IN HERE?!
WHAT TH-!? WH-WHERE ARE WE?!
YES.
WE MUST FIND THE TRUE DOOR.
IT IS THE ONLY WAY TO LEAVE THIS DIMENSION!
WHAT ...!?
HWOOO
SO WE GOTTA FIND IT!
LET'S FIND THE TRUE DOOR!
IT'S ON!
WAIT FOR US, MY OTHER SELF!
WE'LL FIND THE DOOR AND FOLLOW YOU TO THE WORLD OF MEMORIES!

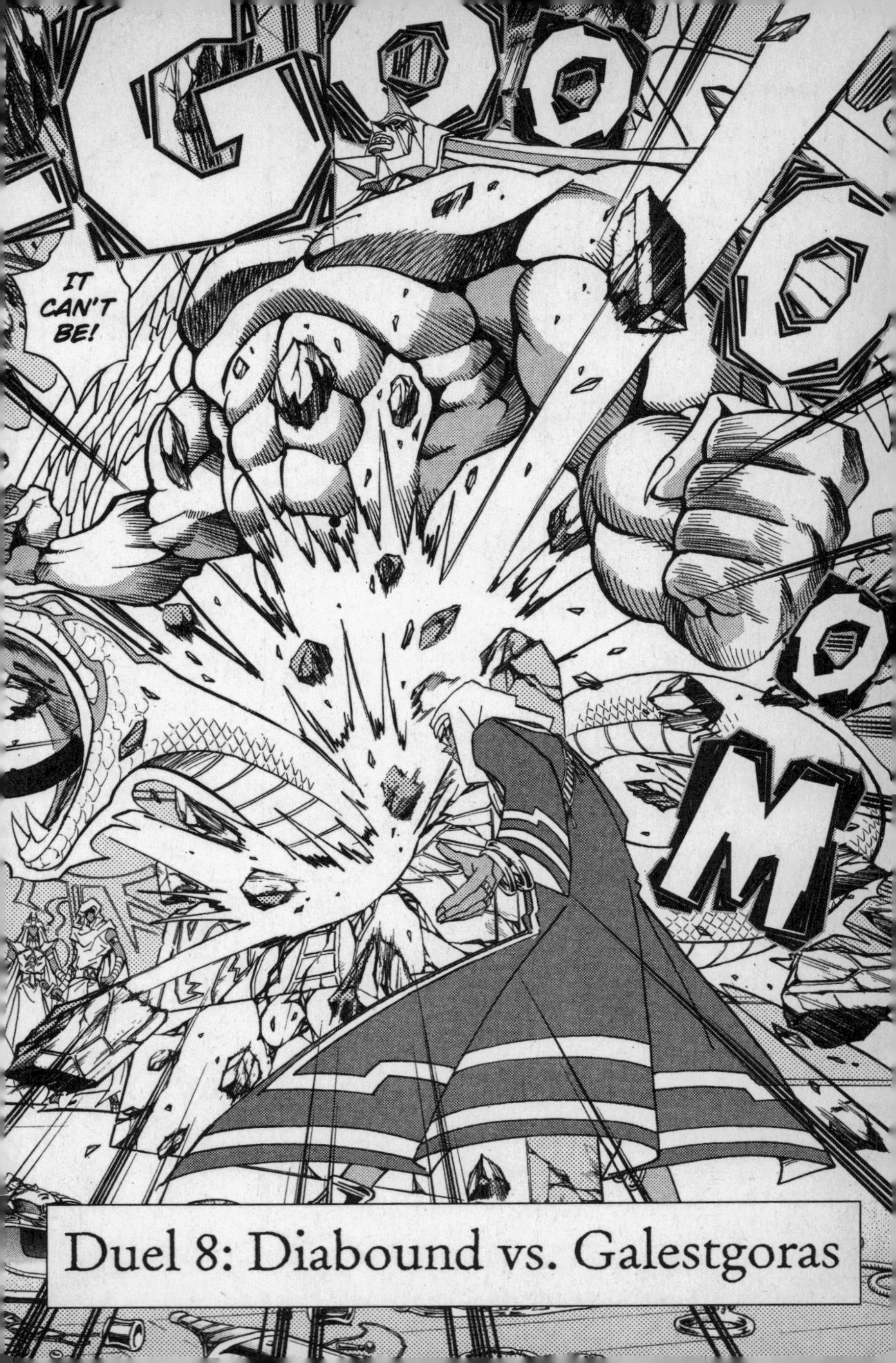
IT CAN'T BE!

Duel 8: Diabound vs. Galestgoras

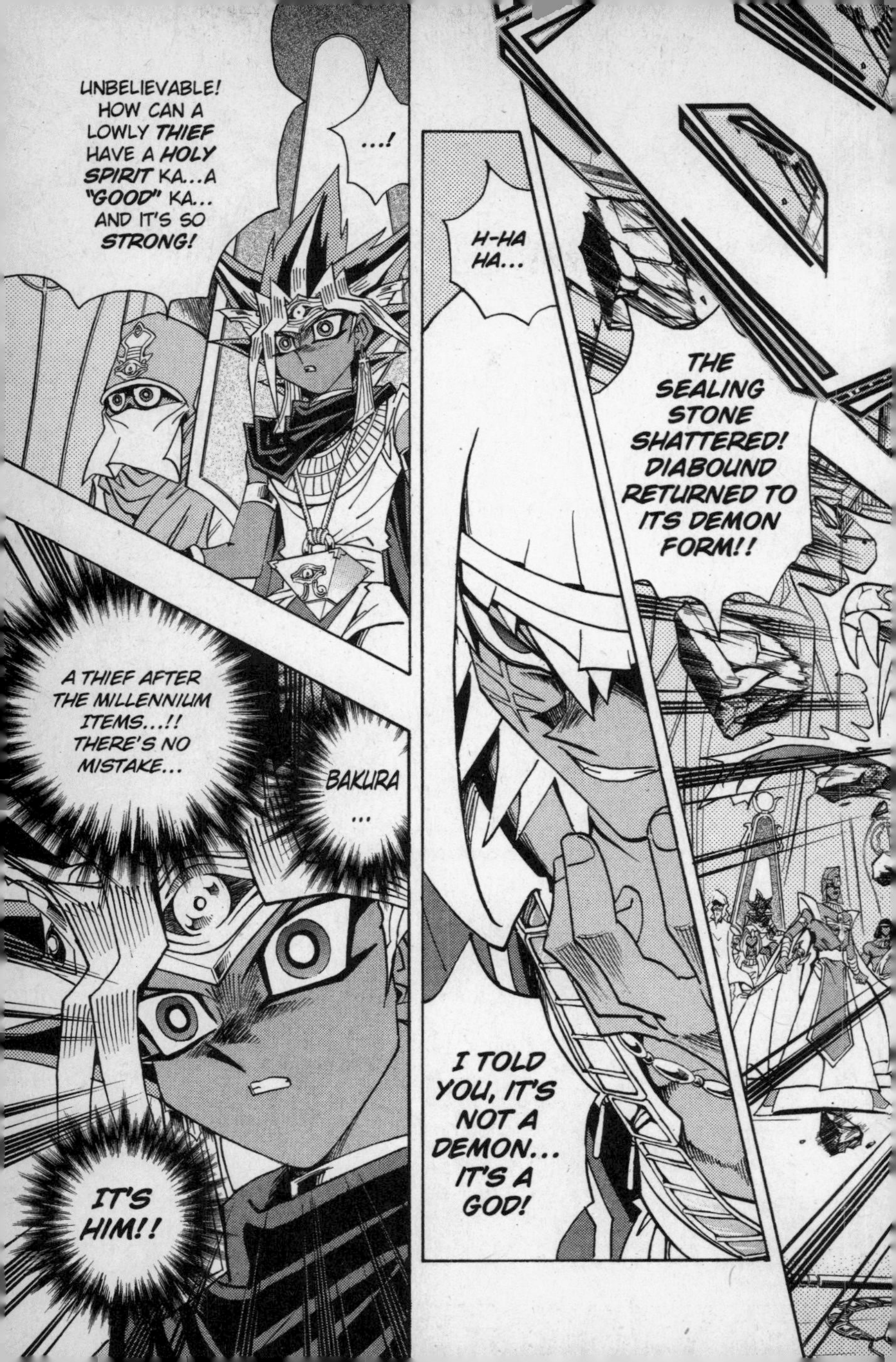
THE SEALING STONE SHATTERED! DIABOUND RETURNED TO ITS DEMON FORM!!
H-HA HA...
I TOLD YOU, IT'S NOT A DEMON... IT'S A GOD!
UNBELIEVABLE! HOW CAN A LOWLY THIEF HAVE A HOLY SPIRIT KA...A "GOOD" KA... AND IT'S SO STRONG!
...!
A THIEF AFTER THE MILLENNIUM ITEMS...!! THERE'S NO MISTAKE...
BAKURA ...
IT'S HIM!!

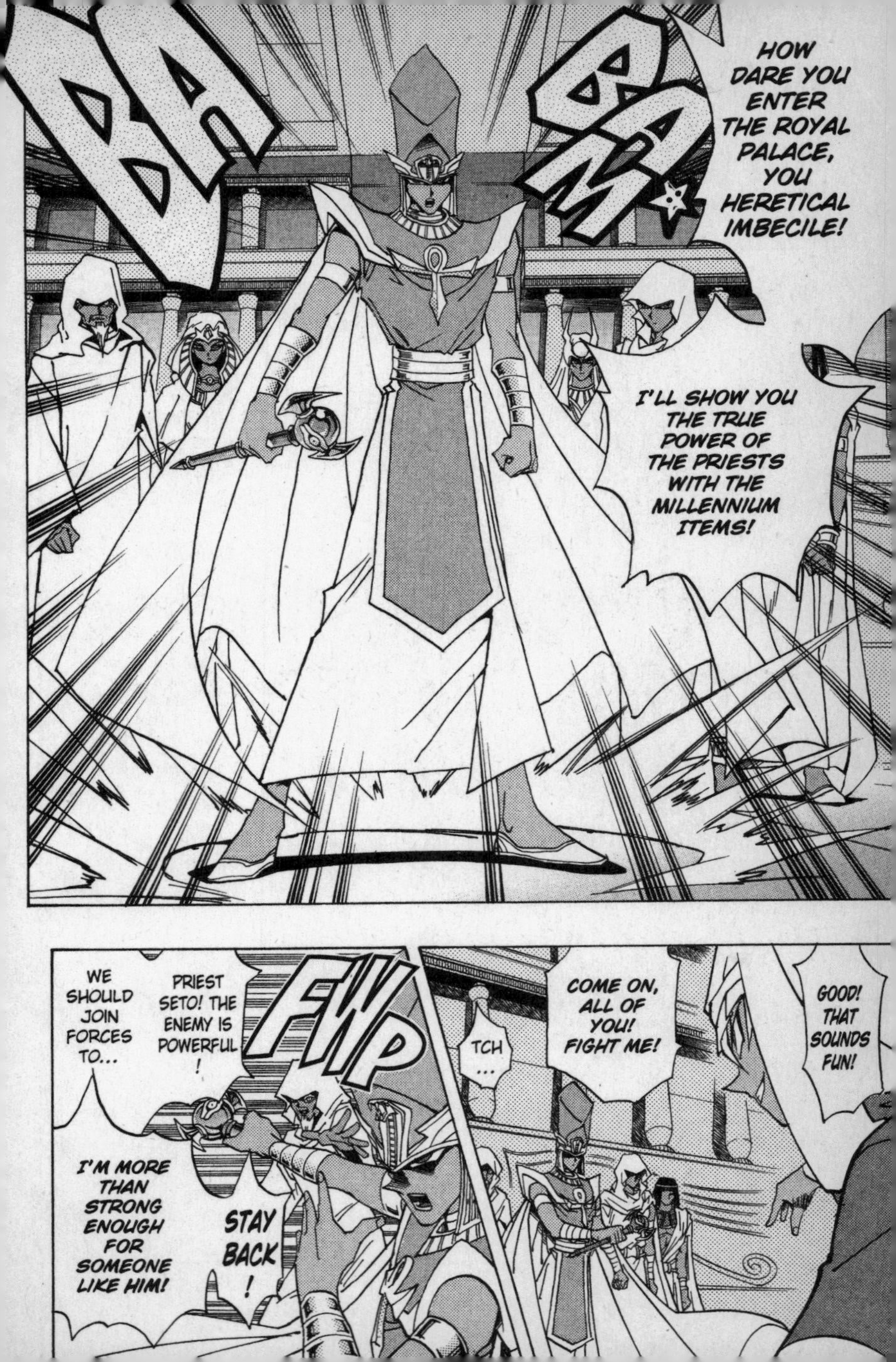
HOW DARE YOU ENTER THE ROYAL PALACE, YOU HERETICAL IMBECILE!
BAM
BA
I'LL SHOW YOU THE TRUE POWER OF THE PRIESTS WITH THE MILLENNIUM ITEMS!
GOOD! THAT SOUNDS FUN!
COME ON, ALL OF YOU! FIGHT ME!
TCH...
FWP
PRIEST SETO! THE ENEMY IS POWERFUL!
WE SHOULD JOIN FORCES TO...
STAY BACK!
I'M MORE THAN STRONG ENOUGH FOR SOMEONE LIKE HIM!

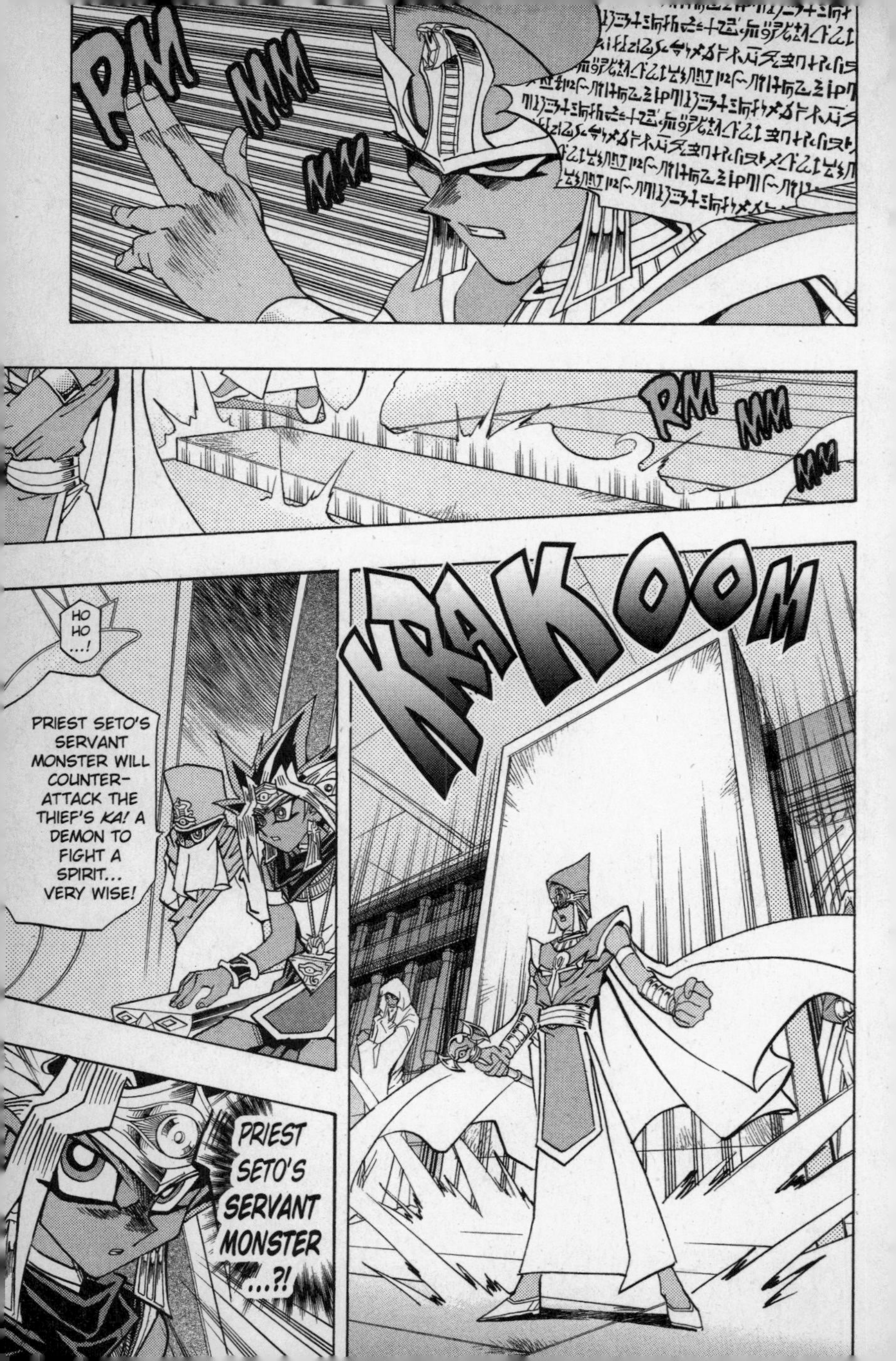
RM MM MM
RM MM MM
KRAKOOM
HO HO ...!
PRIEST SETO'S SERVANT MONSTER WILL COUNTER-ATTACK THE THIEF'S *KA!* A DEMON TO FIGHT A SPIRIT... VERY WISE!
PRIEST SETO'S SERVANT MONSTER ...?!

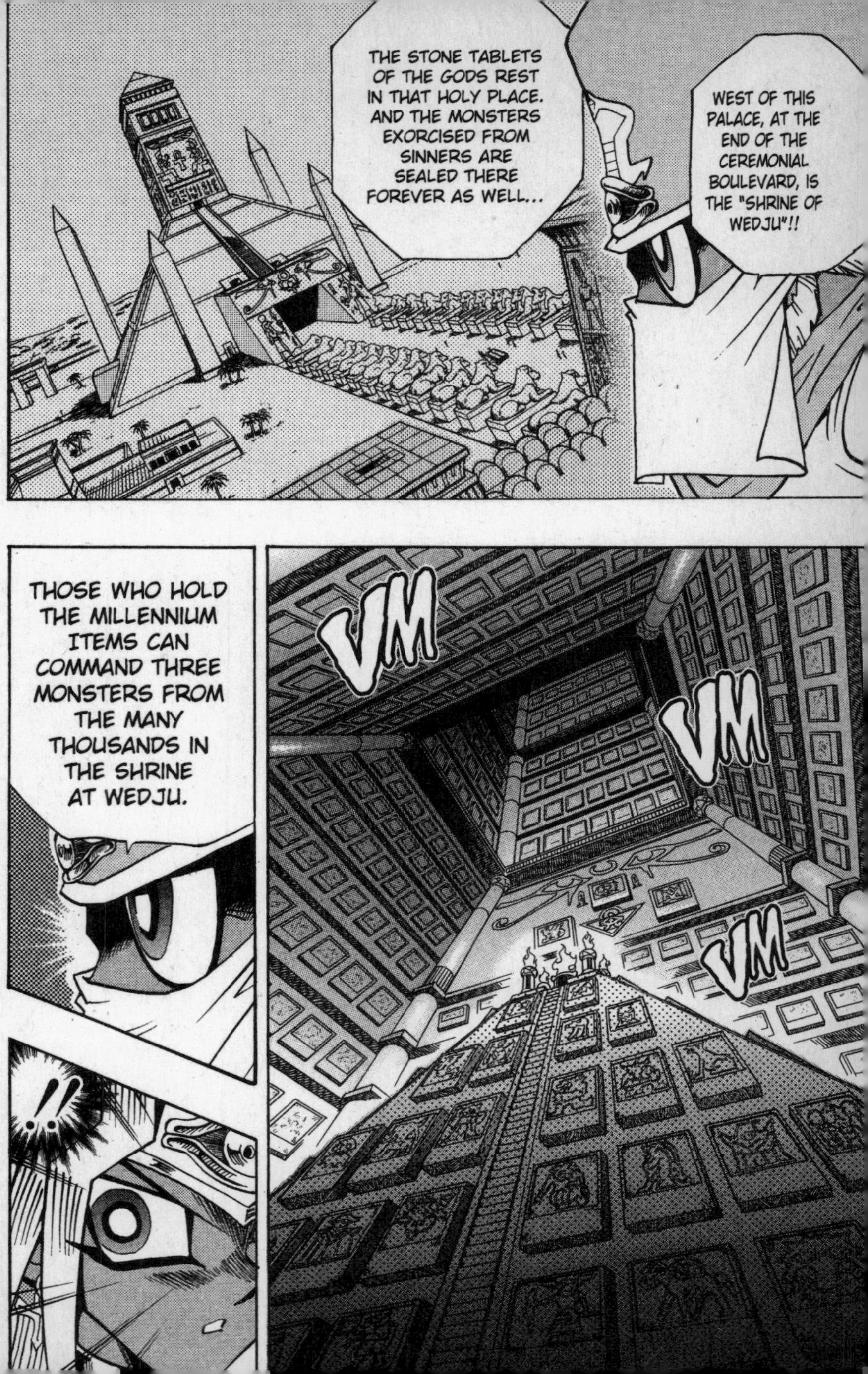
WEST OF THIS PALACE, AT THE END OF THE CEREMONIAL BOULEVARD, IS THE "SHRINE OF WEDJU"!!
THE STONE TABLETS OF THE GODS REST IN THAT HOLY PLACE. AND THE MONSTERS EXORCISED FROM SINNERS ARE SEALED THERE FOREVER AS WELL...
VM
VM
VM
THOSE WHO HOLD THE MILLENNIUM ITEMS CAN COMMAND THREE MONSTERS FROM THE MANY THOUSANDS IN THE SHRINE AT WEDJU.
!!

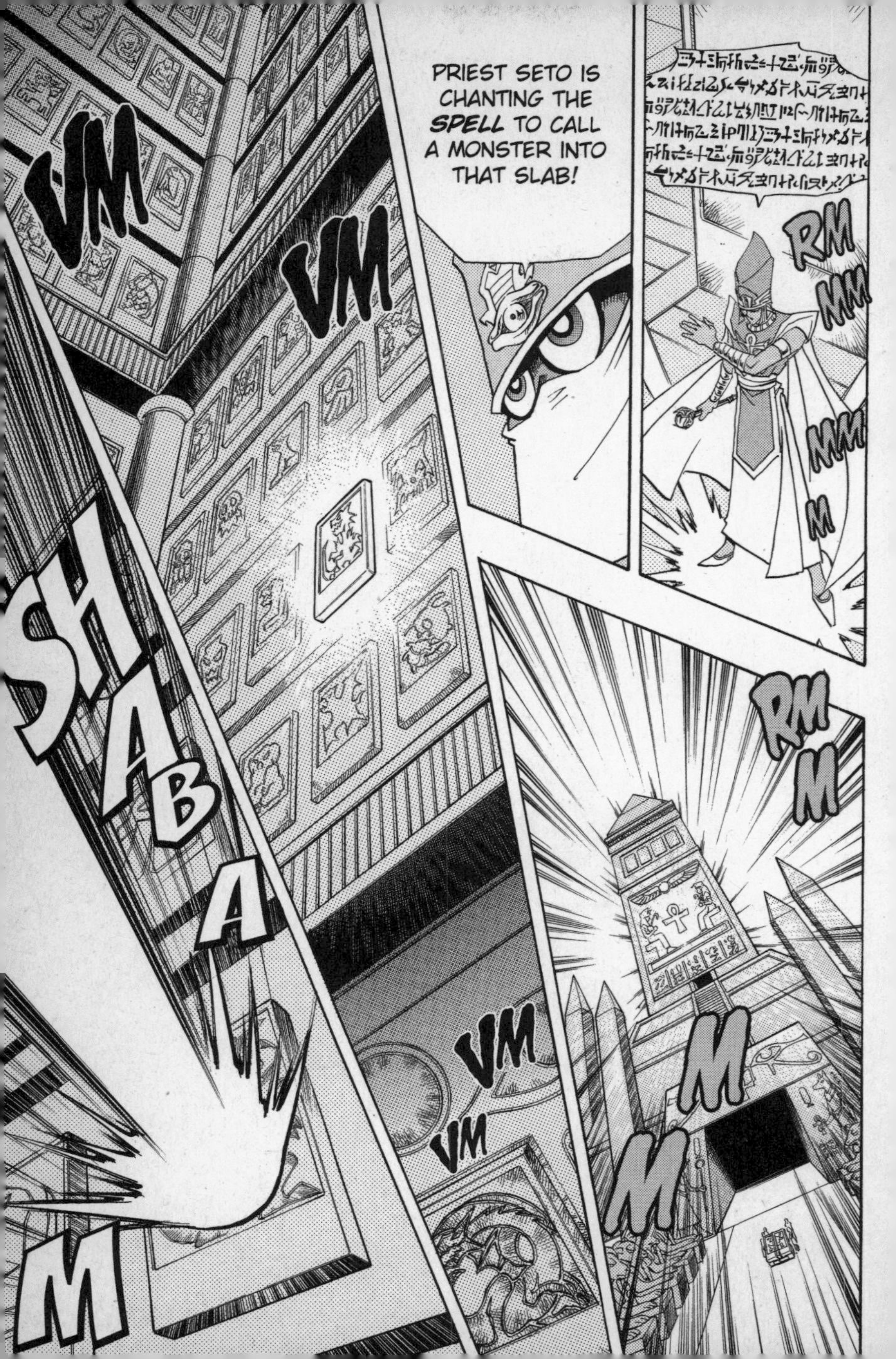
RM
MM
MM
M
PRIEST SETO IS CHANTING THE SPELL TO CALL A MONSTER INTO THAT SLAB!
VM
VM
RM
M
M
M
VM
VM
SHABAA
M

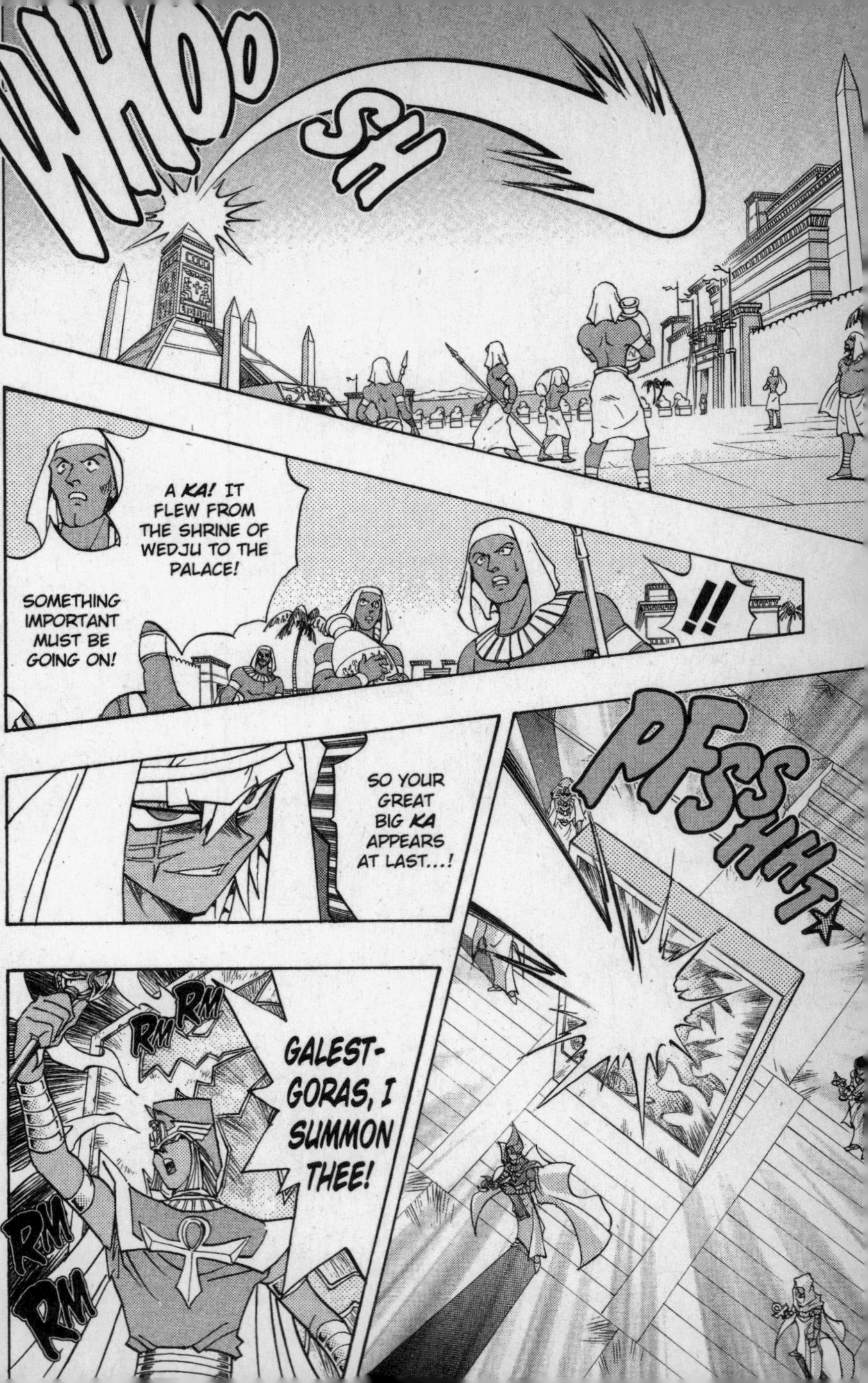
WHOOSH
!!
A KA! IT FLEW FROM THE SHRINE OF WEDJU TO THE PALACE!
SOMETHING IMPORTANT MUST BE GOING ON!
PFSSHHT
SO YOUR GREAT BIG KA APPEARS AT LAST...!
RM RM
GALEST-GORAS, I SUMMON THEE!
RM RM

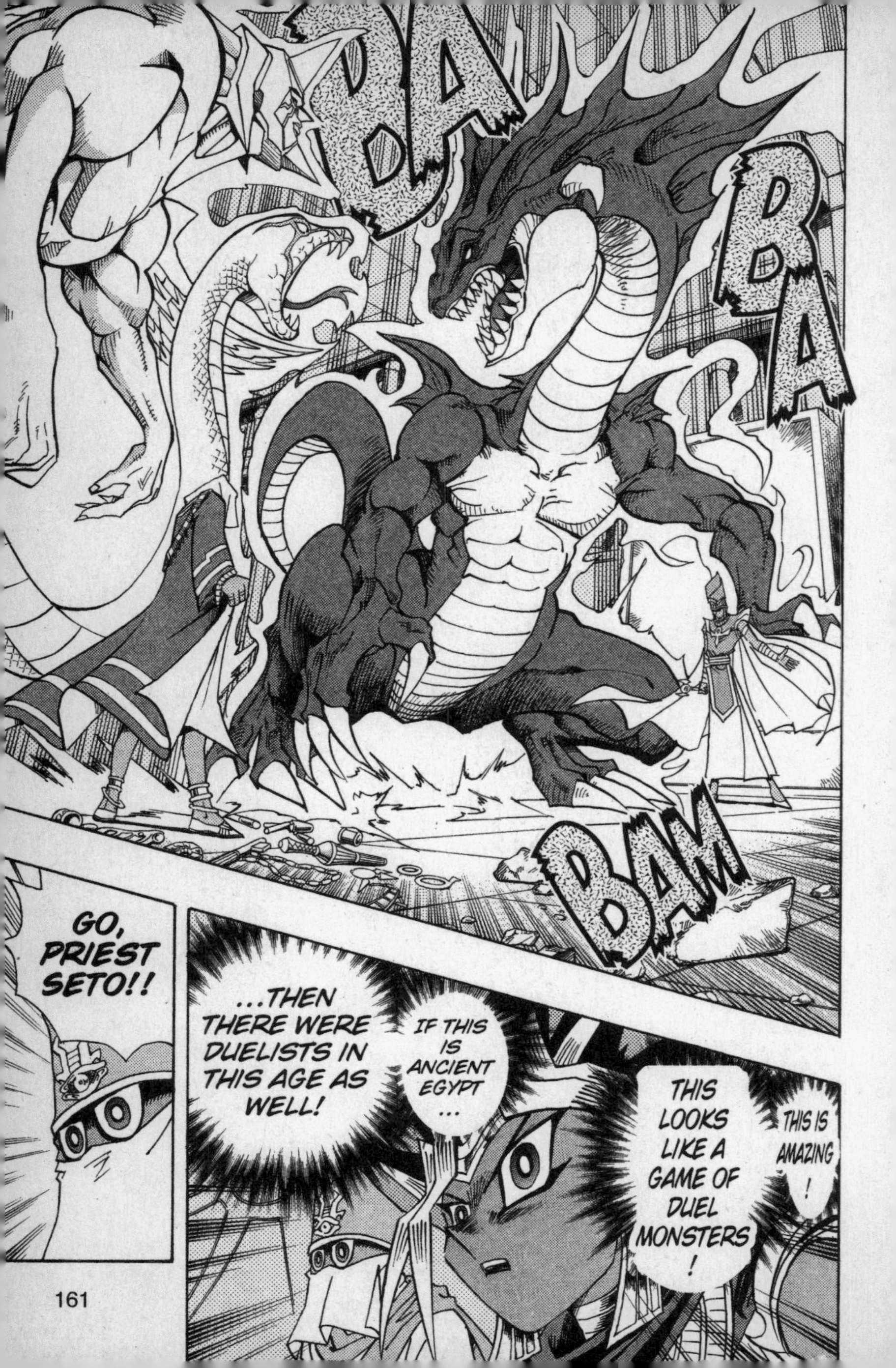
DA
BA
BAM
THIS IS AMAZING!
THIS LOOKS LIKE A GAME OF DUEL MONSTERS!
IF THIS IS ANCIENT EGYPT...
...THEN THERE WERE DUELISTS IN THIS AGE AS WELL!
GO, PRIEST SETO!!

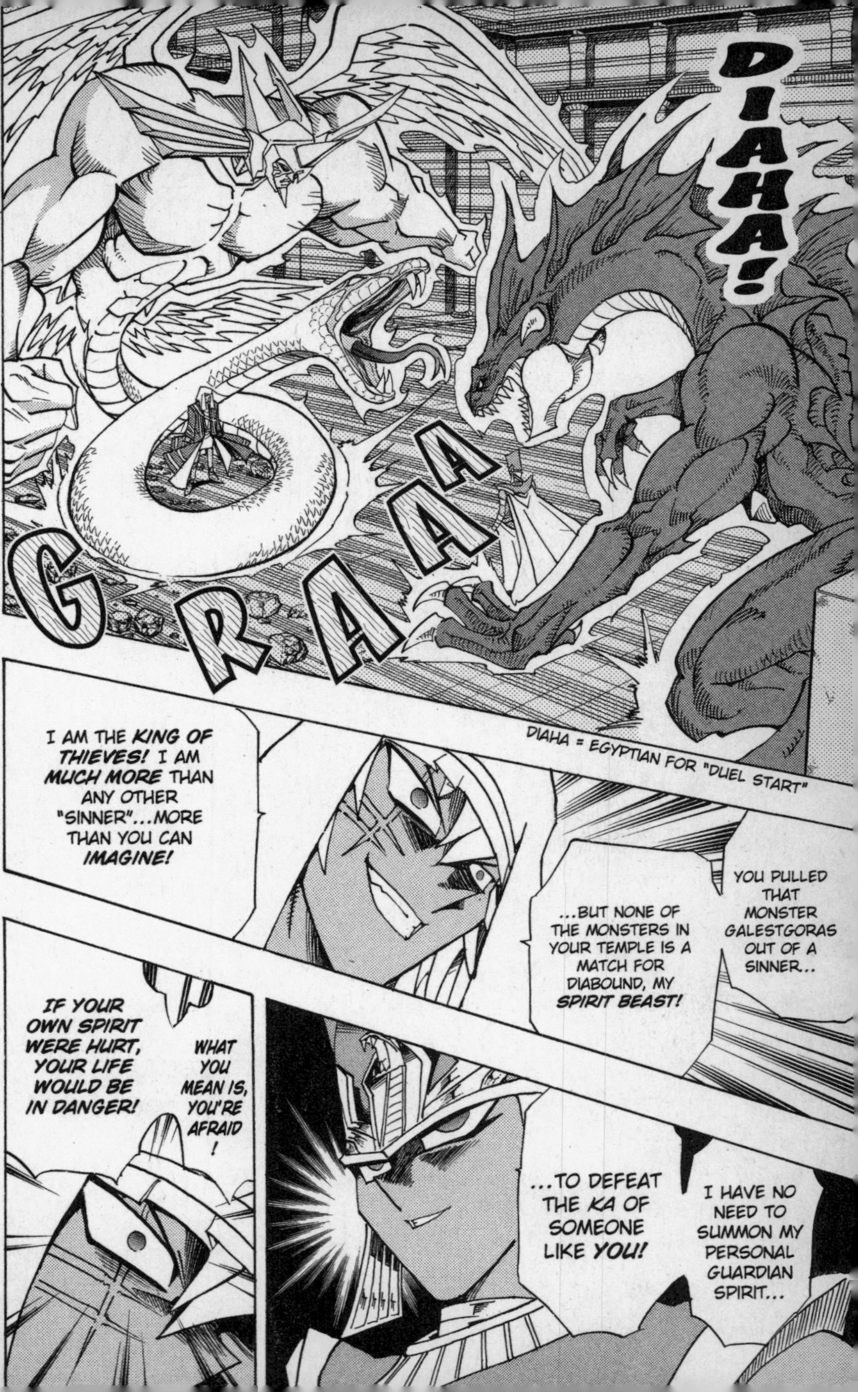
DIAHA!
GRAAA
DIAHA = EGYPTIAN FOR "DUEL START"
YOU PULLED THAT MONSTER GALESTGORAS OUT OF A SINNER...
...BUT NONE OF THE MONSTERS IN YOUR TEMPLE IS A MATCH FOR DIABOUND, MY SPIRIT BEAST!
I AM THE KING OF THIEVES! I AM MUCH MORE THAN ANY OTHER "SINNER"...MORE THAN YOU CAN IMAGINE!
I HAVE NO NEED TO SUMMON MY PERSONAL GUARDIAN SPIRIT...
...TO DEFEAT THE KA OF SOMEONE LIKE YOU!
WHAT YOU MEAN IS, YOU'RE AFRAID!
IF YOUR OWN SPIRIT WERE HURT, YOUR LIFE WOULD BE IN DANGER!

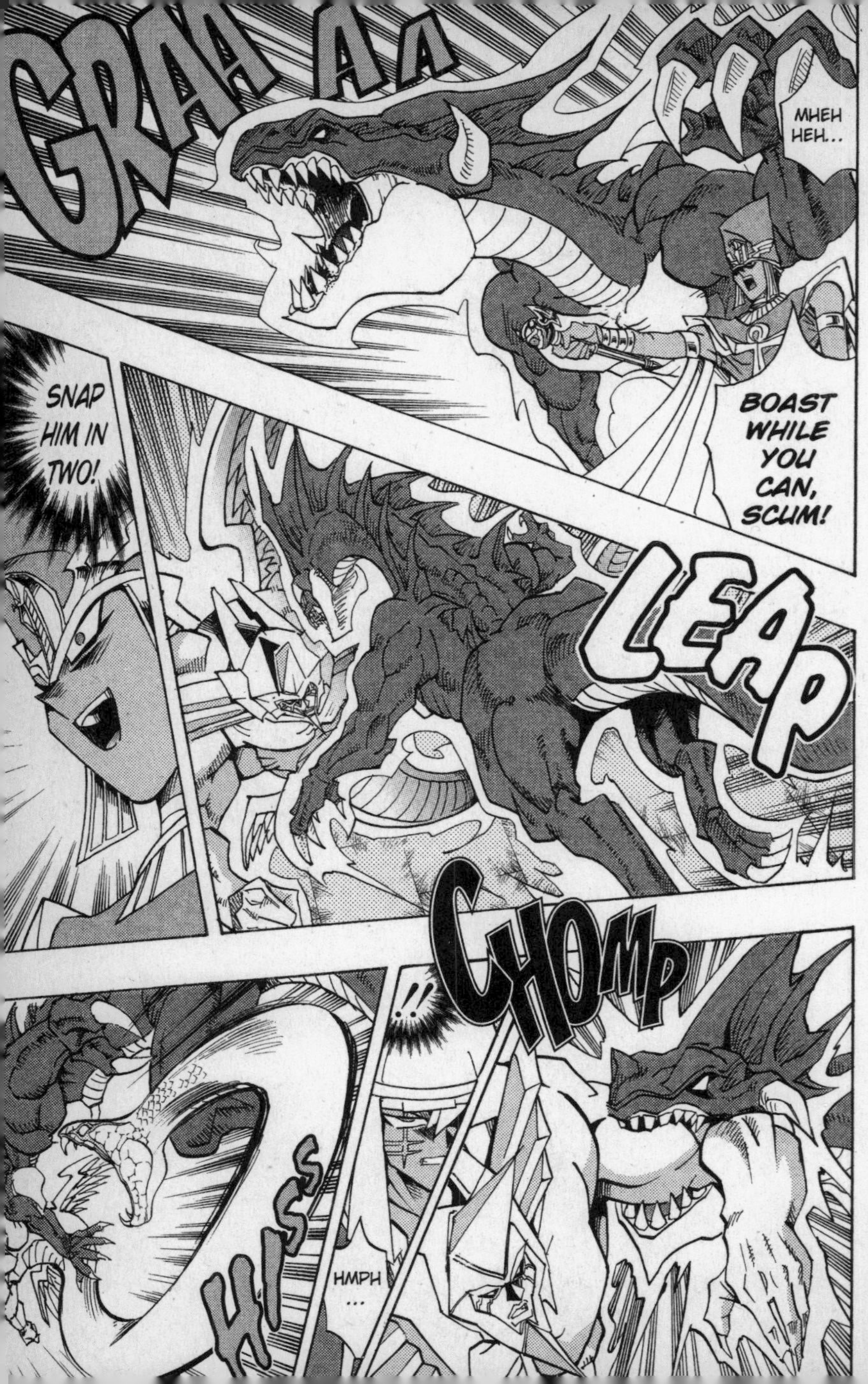
GRAAAA
MHEH HEH...
BOAST WHILE YOU CAN, SCUM!
LEAP
SNAP HIM IN TWO!
CHOMP
!!
HMPH ...
HISSS

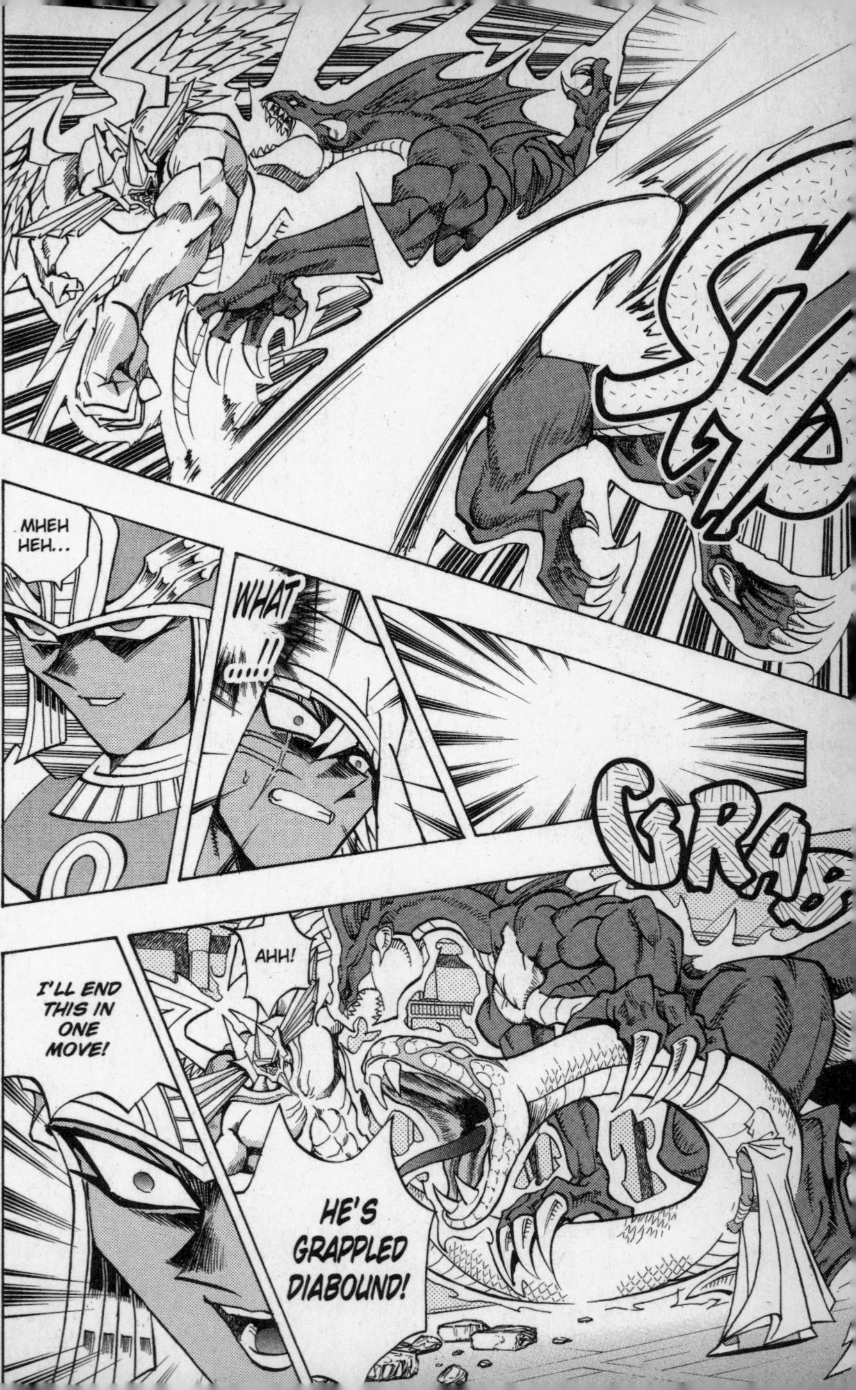
GRA..
WHAT...!!
MHEH HEH...
AHH!
HE'S GRAPPLED DIABOUND!
I'LL END THIS IN ONE MOVE!

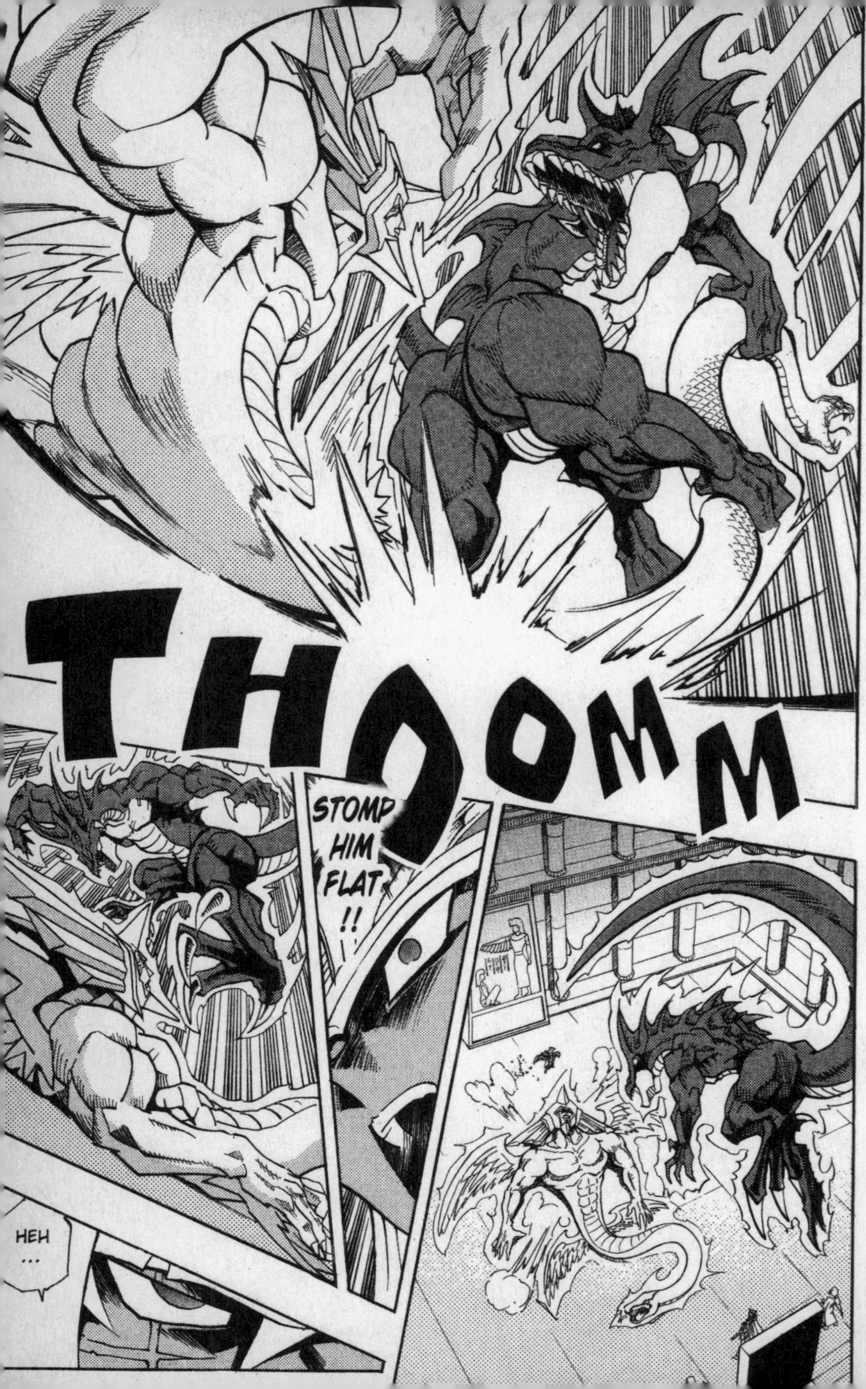
THOOMM
STOMP HIM FLAT!!
HEH...

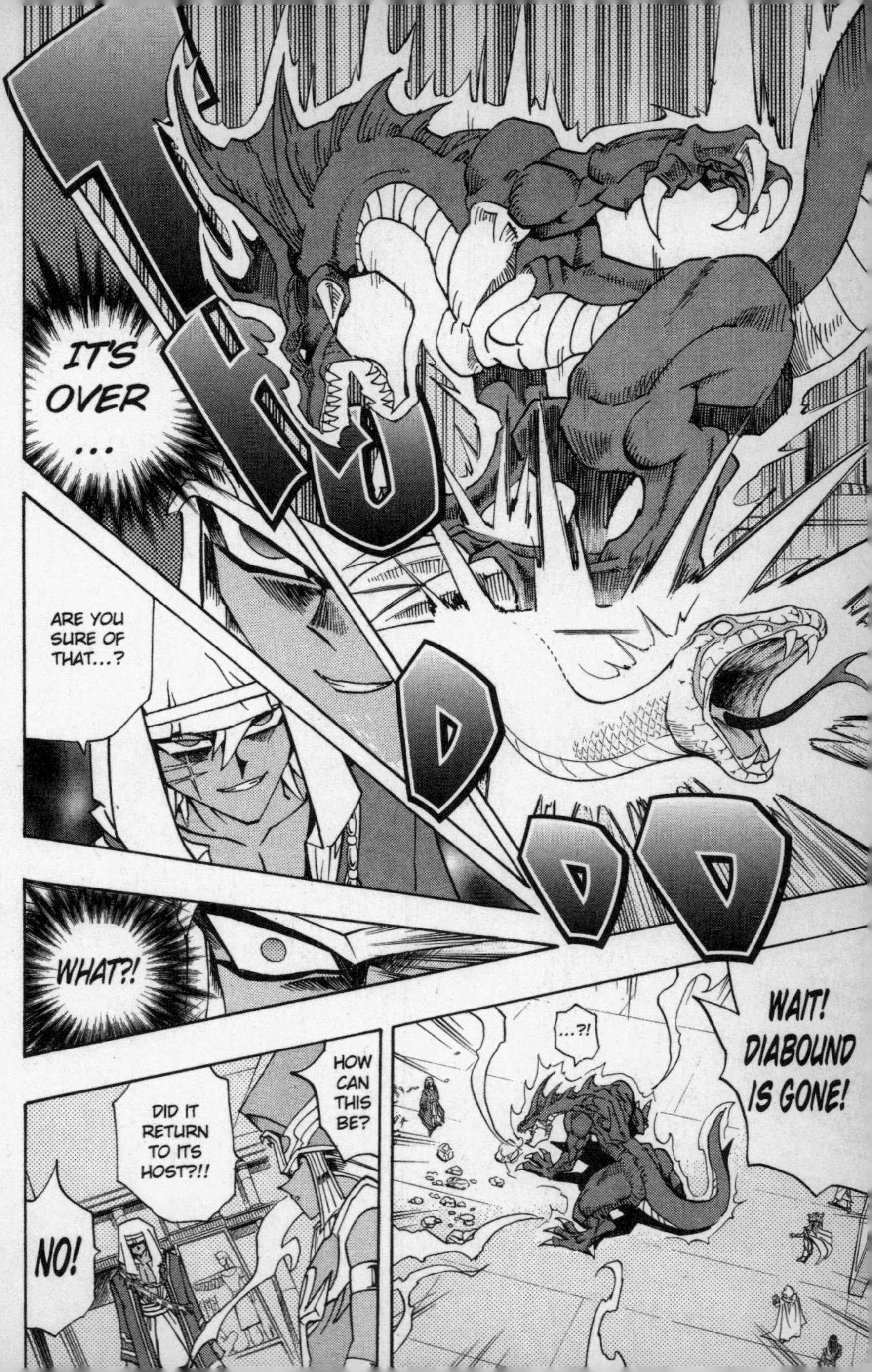

IT'S OVER...
GOOO
ARE YOU SURE OF THAT...?
WHAT?!
...?!
WAIT! DIABOUND IS GONE!
HOW CAN THIS BE?
DID IT RETURN TO ITS HOST?!!
NO!

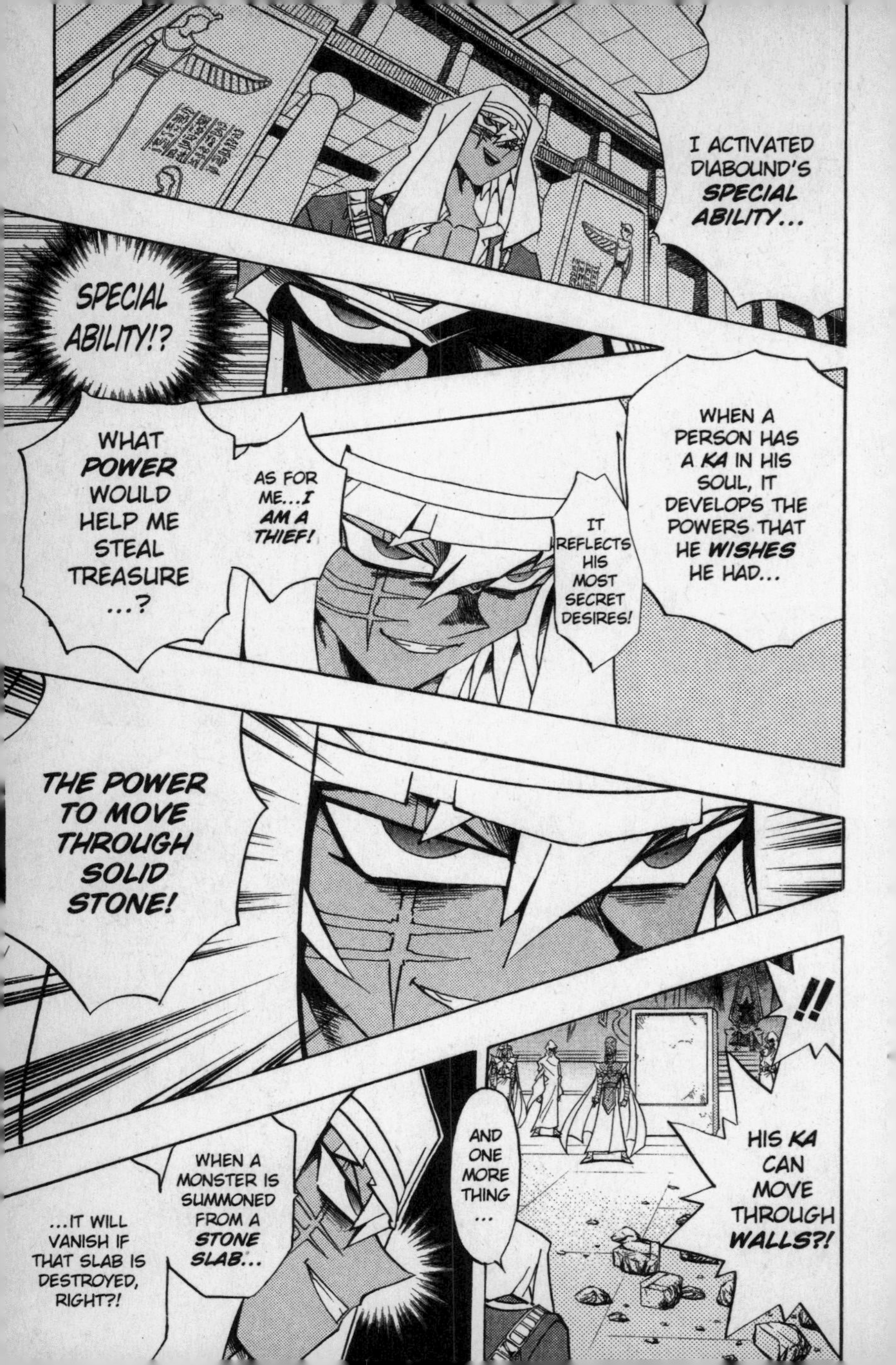
I ACTIVATED DIABOUND'S SPECIAL ABILITY...
SPECIAL ABILITY!?
WHEN A PERSON HAS A KA IN HIS SOUL, IT DEVELOPS THE POWERS THAT HE WISHES HE HAD...
IT REFLECTS HIS MOST SECRET DESIRES!
AS FOR ME...I AM A THIEF!
WHAT POWER WOULD HELP ME STEAL TREASURE ...?
THE POWER TO MOVE THROUGH SOLID STONE!
!!
HIS KA CAN MOVE THROUGH WALLS?!
AND ONE MORE THING ...
WHEN A MONSTER IS SUMMONED FROM A STONE SLAB...
...IT WILL VANISH IF THAT SLAB IS DESTROYED, RIGHT?!

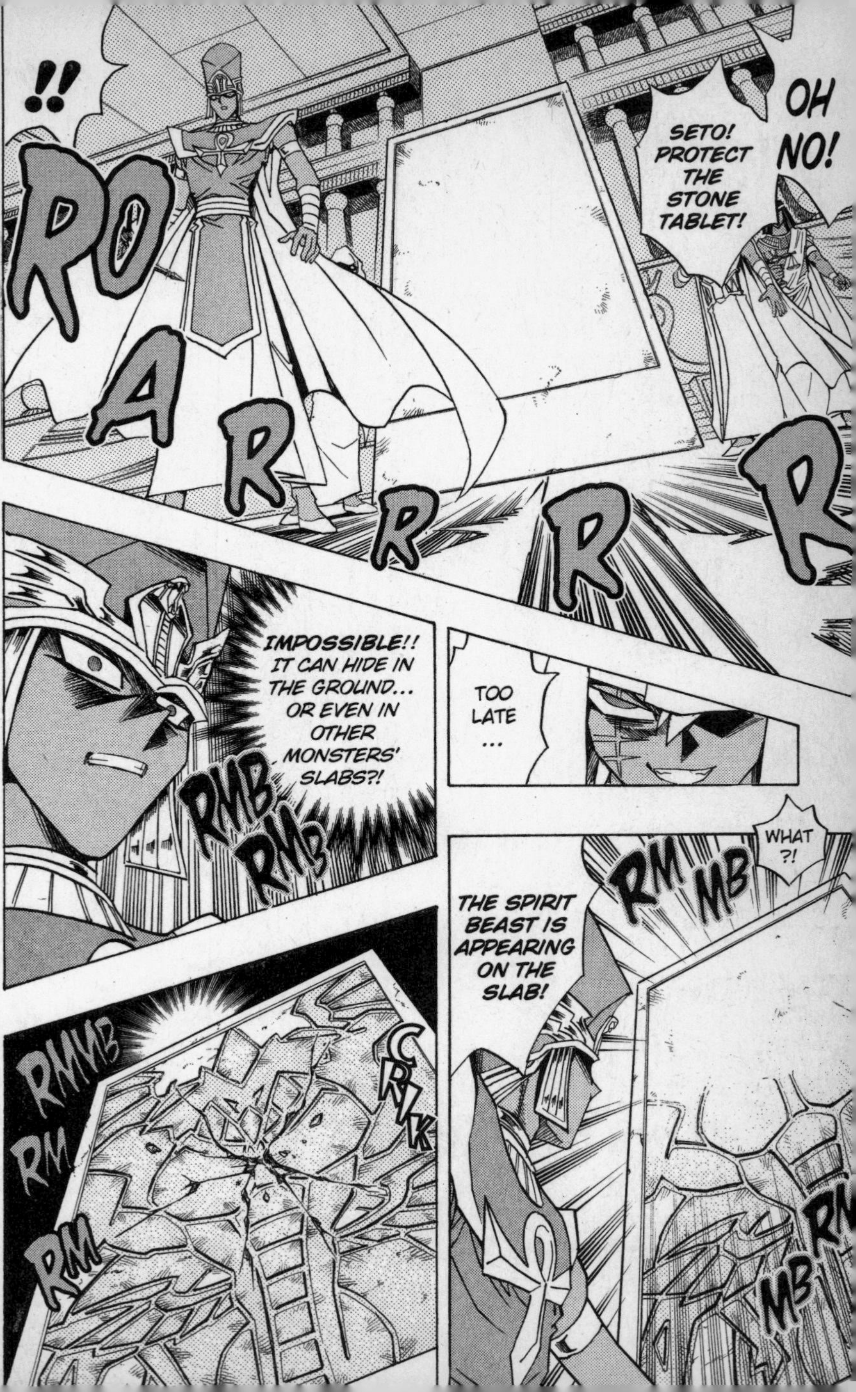
OH NO!
SETO! PROTECT THE STONE TABLET!
!!
ROARRRR
TOO LATE ...
IMPOSSIBLE!! IT CAN HIDE IN THE GROUND... OR EVEN IN OTHER MONSTERS' SLABS?!
RMB RMB
WHAT ?!
RM MB
THE SPIRIT BEAST IS APPEARING ON THE SLAB!
RM MB
CRIK
RMMB
RM
RM

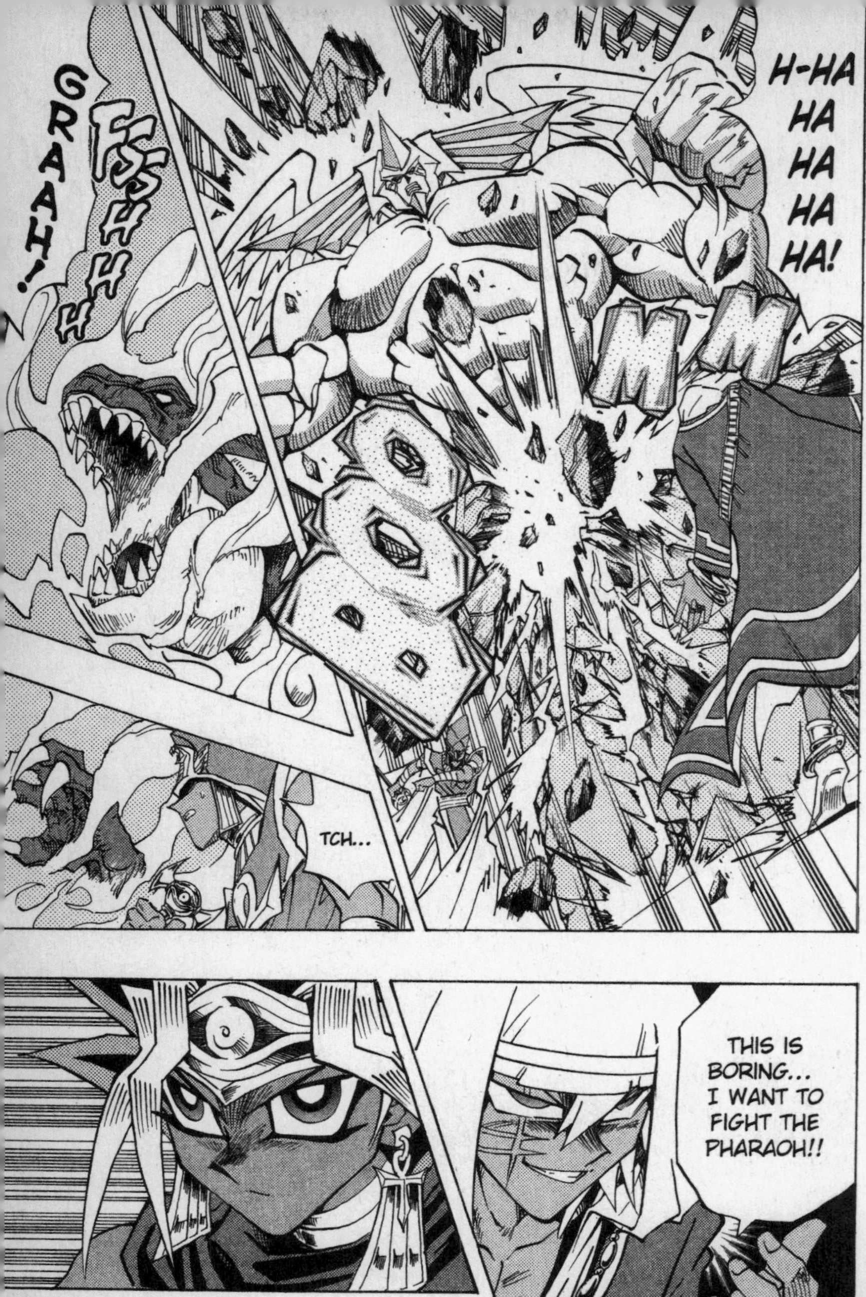
H-HA HA HA HA HA!
FSSHHHH
GRAAH!
TCH...
THIS IS BORING... I WANT TO FIGHT THE PHARAOH!!

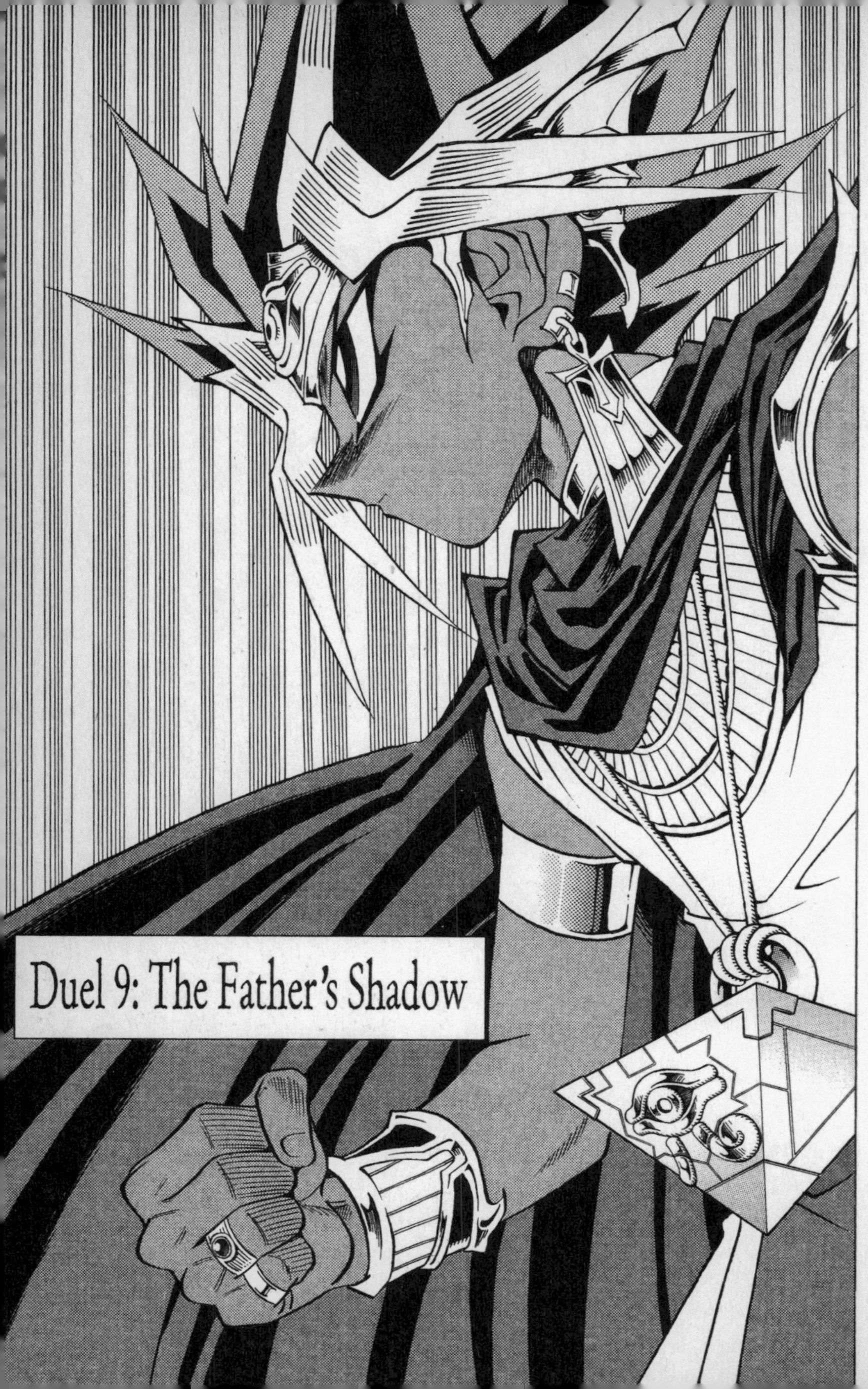
Duel 9: The Father's Shadow

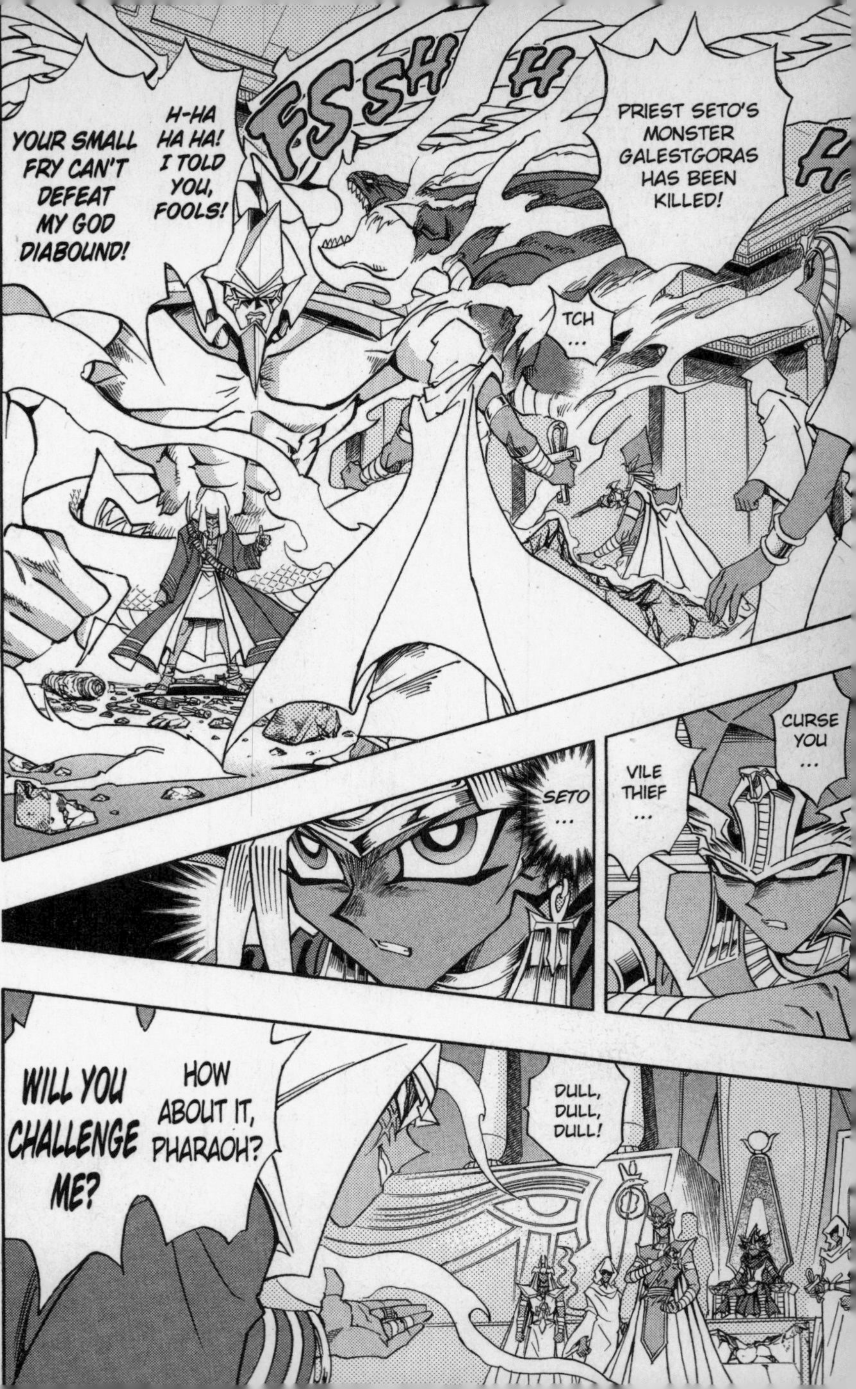
PRIEST SETO'S MONSTER GALESTGORAS HAS BEEN KILLED!
FSSH H H
TCH ...
H-HA HA HA! I TOLD YOU, FOOLS!
YOUR SMALL FRY CAN'T DEFEAT MY GOD DIABOUND!
CURSE YOU ...
VILE THIEF ...
SETO ...
DULL, DULL, DULL!
HOW ABOUT IT, PHARAOH?
WILL YOU CHALLENGE ME?

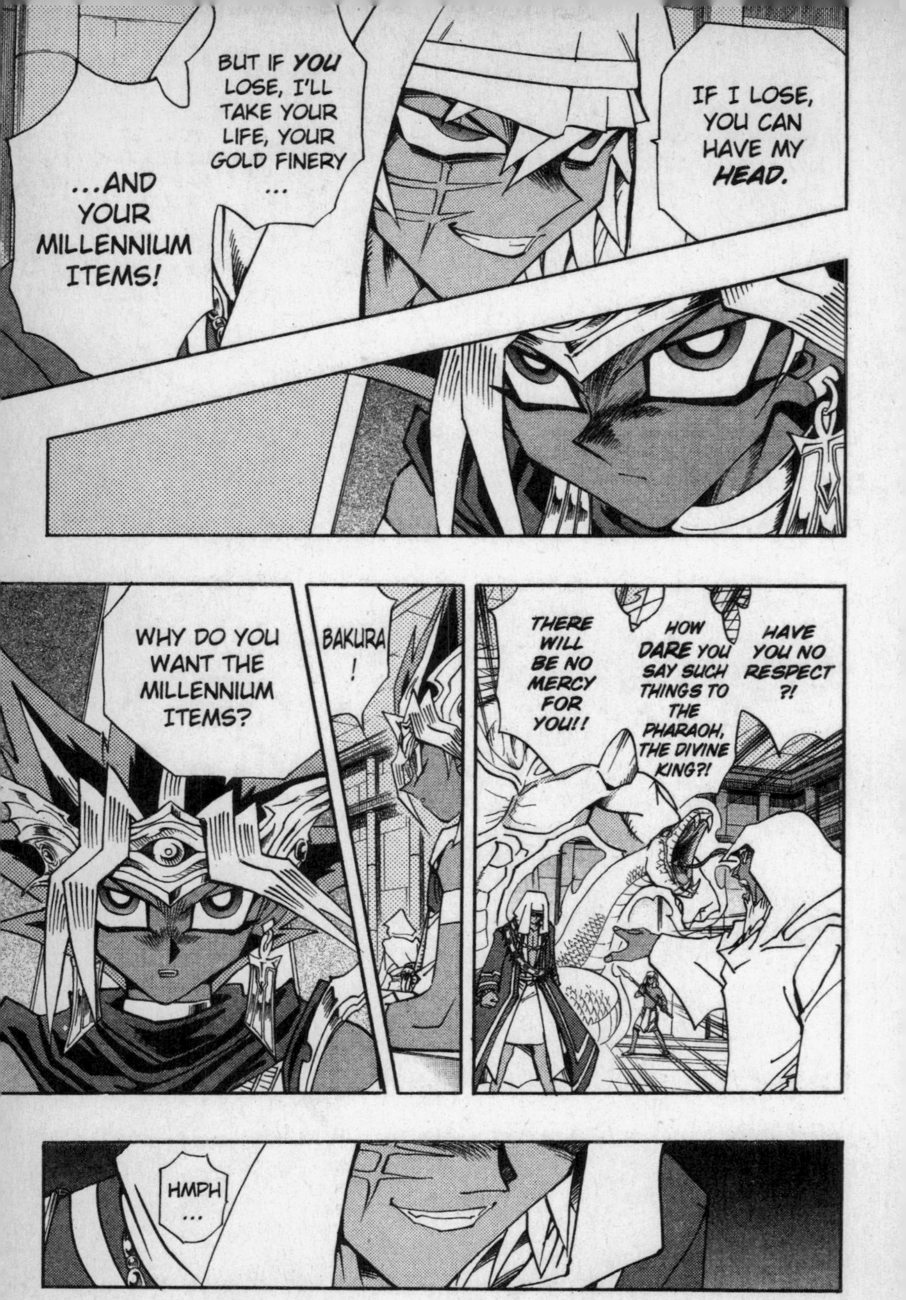
IF I LOSE, YOU CAN HAVE MY **HEAD.**
BUT IF ***YOU*** LOSE, I'LL TAKE YOUR LIFE, YOUR GOLD FINERY ...
...AND YOUR MILLENNIUM ITEMS!
HAVE YOU NO RESPECT?!
HOW **DARE** YOU SAY SUCH THINGS TO THE PHARAOH, THE DIVINE KING?!
THERE WILL BE NO MERCY FOR YOU!!
BAKURA!
WHY DO YOU WANT THE MILLENNIUM ITEMS?
HMPH ...

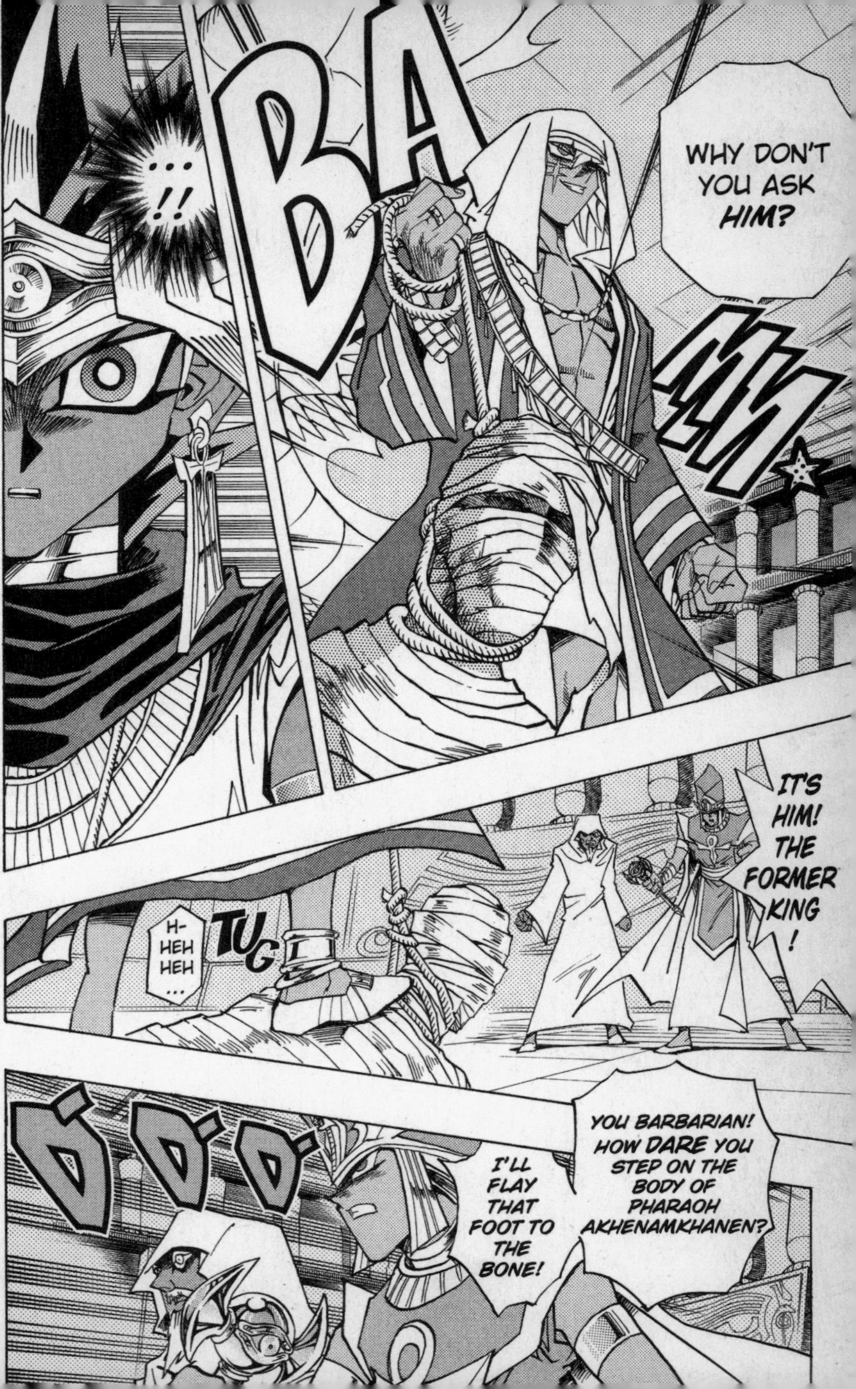
WHY DON'T YOU ASK HIM?
BA
...!!
IT'S HIM! THE FORMER KING!
TUG
H-HEH HEH...
YOU BARBARIAN! HOW DARE YOU STEP ON THE BODY OF PHARAOH AKHENAMKHANEN?
I'LL FLAY THAT FOOT TO THE BONE!

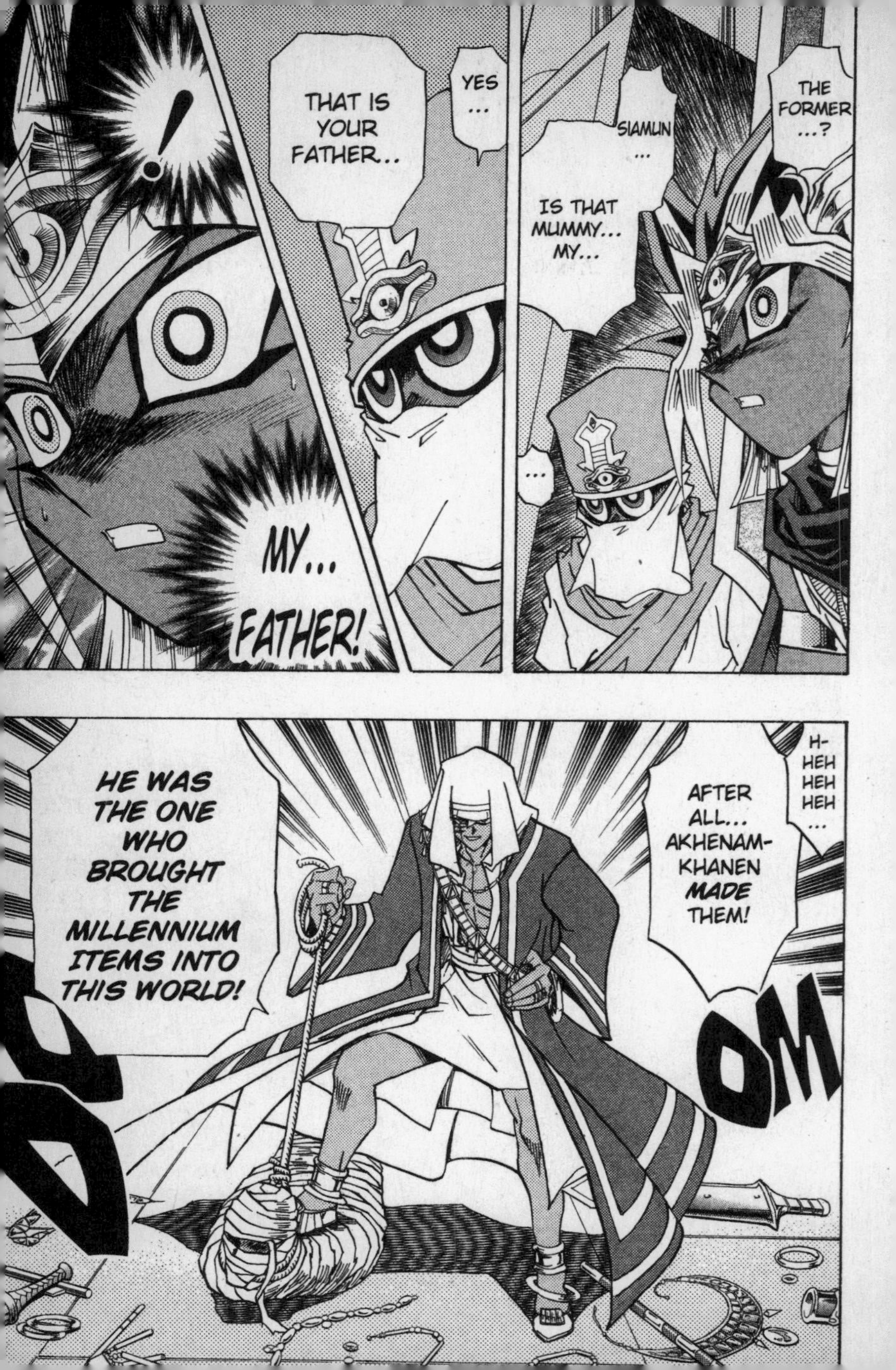
THE FORMER ...?
SIAMUN ...
IS THAT MUMMY... MY...
...
YES ...
THAT IS YOUR FATHER...
!
MY... FATHER!
H-HEH HEH HEH ...
AFTER ALL... AKHENAM-KHANEN *MADE* THEM!
HE WAS THE ONE WHO BROUGHT THE MILLENNIUM ITEMS INTO THIS WORLD!
OM

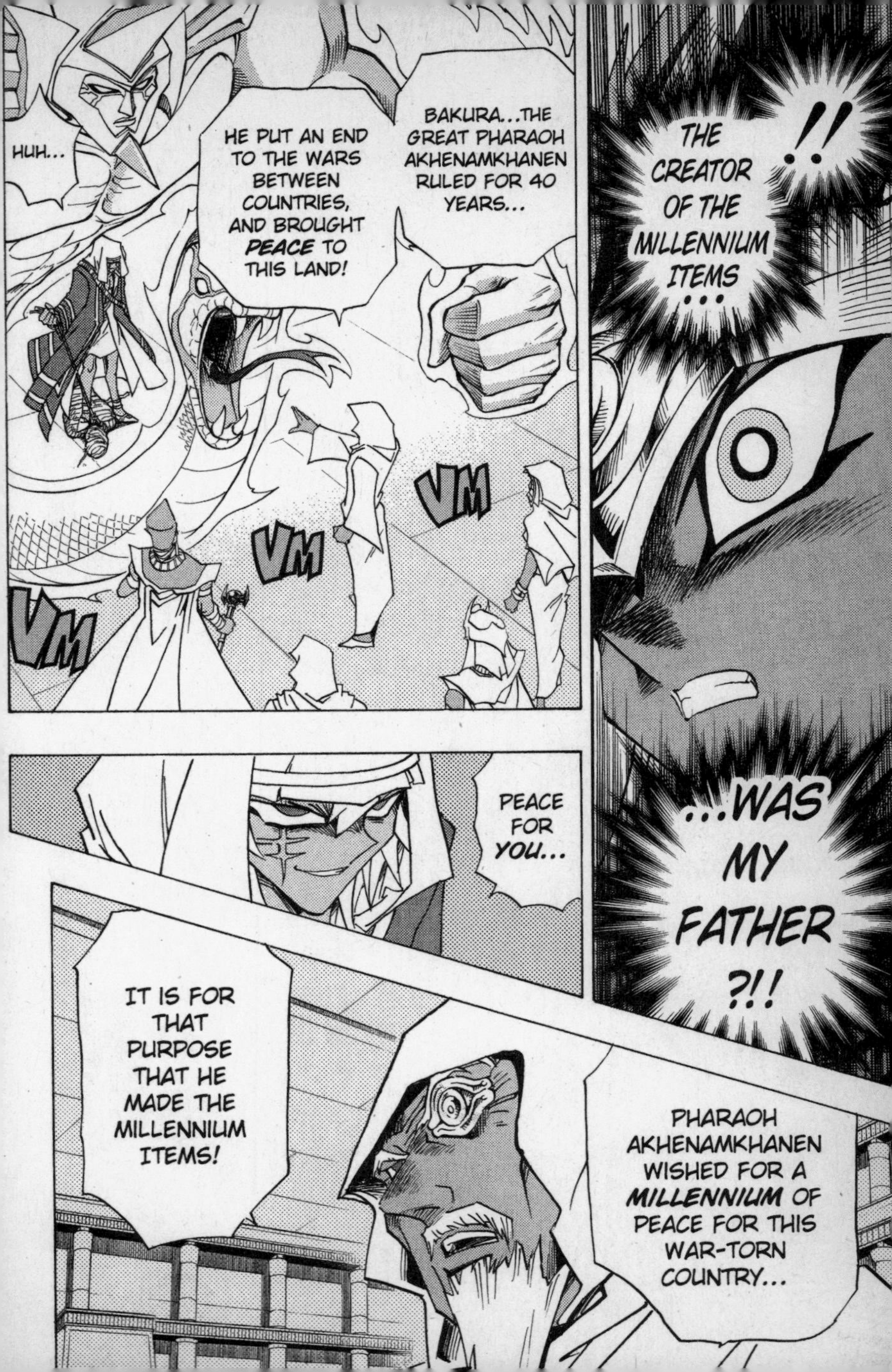

!!
THE CREATOR OF THE MILLENNIUM ITEMS...
...WAS MY FATHER ?!!
BAKURA...THE GREAT PHARAOH AKHENAMKHANEN RULED FOR 40 YEARS...
HE PUT AN END TO THE WARS BETWEEN COUNTRIES, AND BROUGHT *PEACE* TO THIS LAND!
HUH...
VM
VM
VM
PEACE FOR *YOU*...
PHARAOH AKHENAMKHANEN WISHED FOR A *MILLENNIUM* OF PEACE FOR THIS WAR-TORN COUNTRY...
IT IS FOR THAT PURPOSE THAT HE MADE THE MILLENNIUM ITEMS!

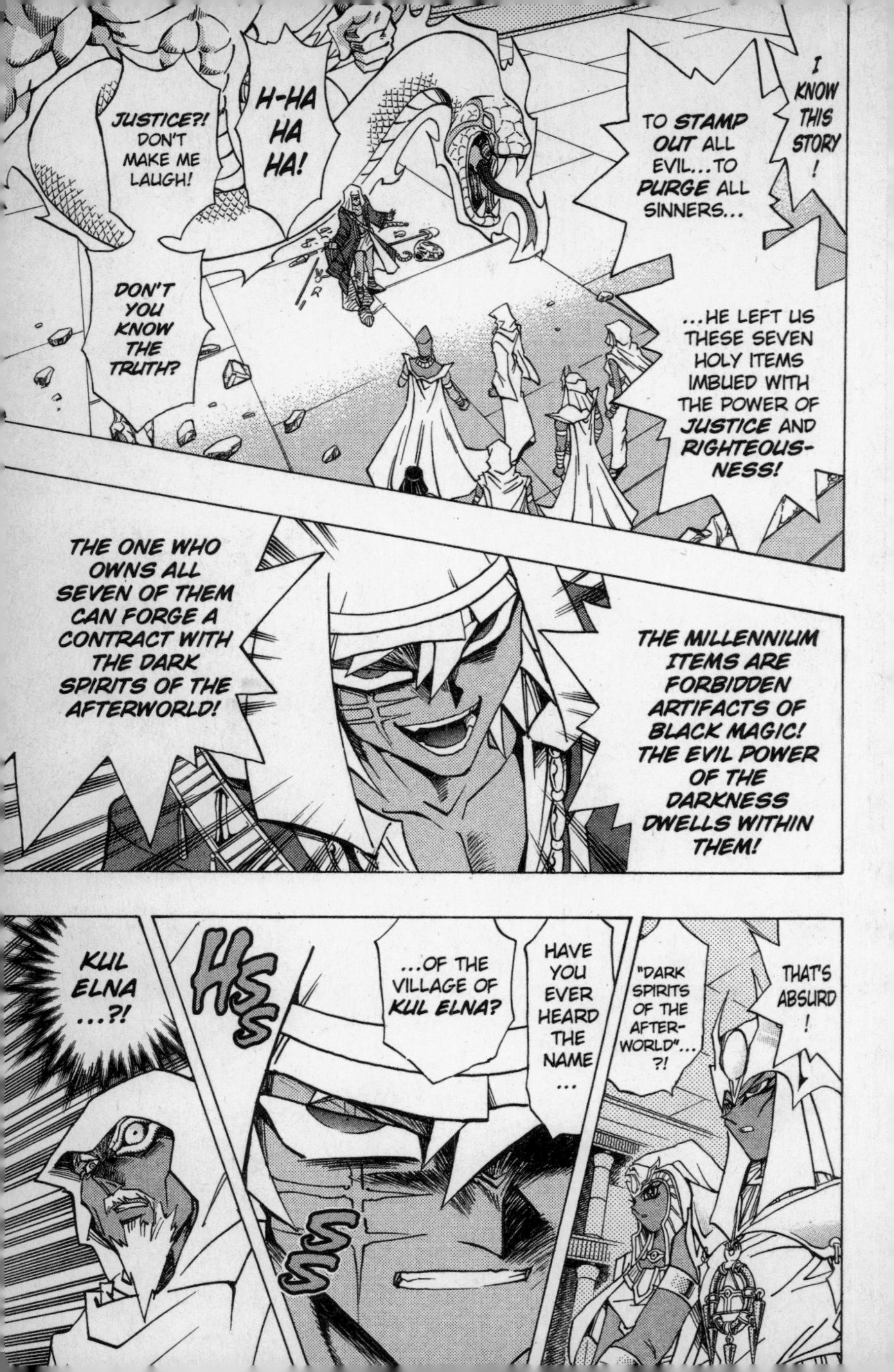
I KNOW THIS STORY!
TO STAMP OUT ALL EVIL...TO PURGE ALL SINNERS...
...HE LEFT US THESE SEVEN HOLY ITEMS IMBUED WITH THE POWER OF JUSTICE AND RIGHTEOUS-NESS!
H-HA HA HA!
JUSTICE?! DON'T MAKE ME LAUGH!
DON'T YOU KNOW THE TRUTH?
THE MILLENNIUM ITEMS ARE FORBIDDEN ARTIFACTS OF BLACK MAGIC! THE EVIL POWER OF THE DARKNESS DWELLS WITHIN THEM!
THE ONE WHO OWNS ALL SEVEN OF THEM CAN FORGE A CONTRACT WITH THE DARK SPIRITS OF THE AFTERWORLD!
THAT'S ABSURD!
"DARK SPIRITS OF THE AFTER-WORLD"...?!
HAVE YOU EVER HEARD THE NAME...
...OF THE VILLAGE OF KUL ELNA?
HSSSS
KUL ELNA...?!

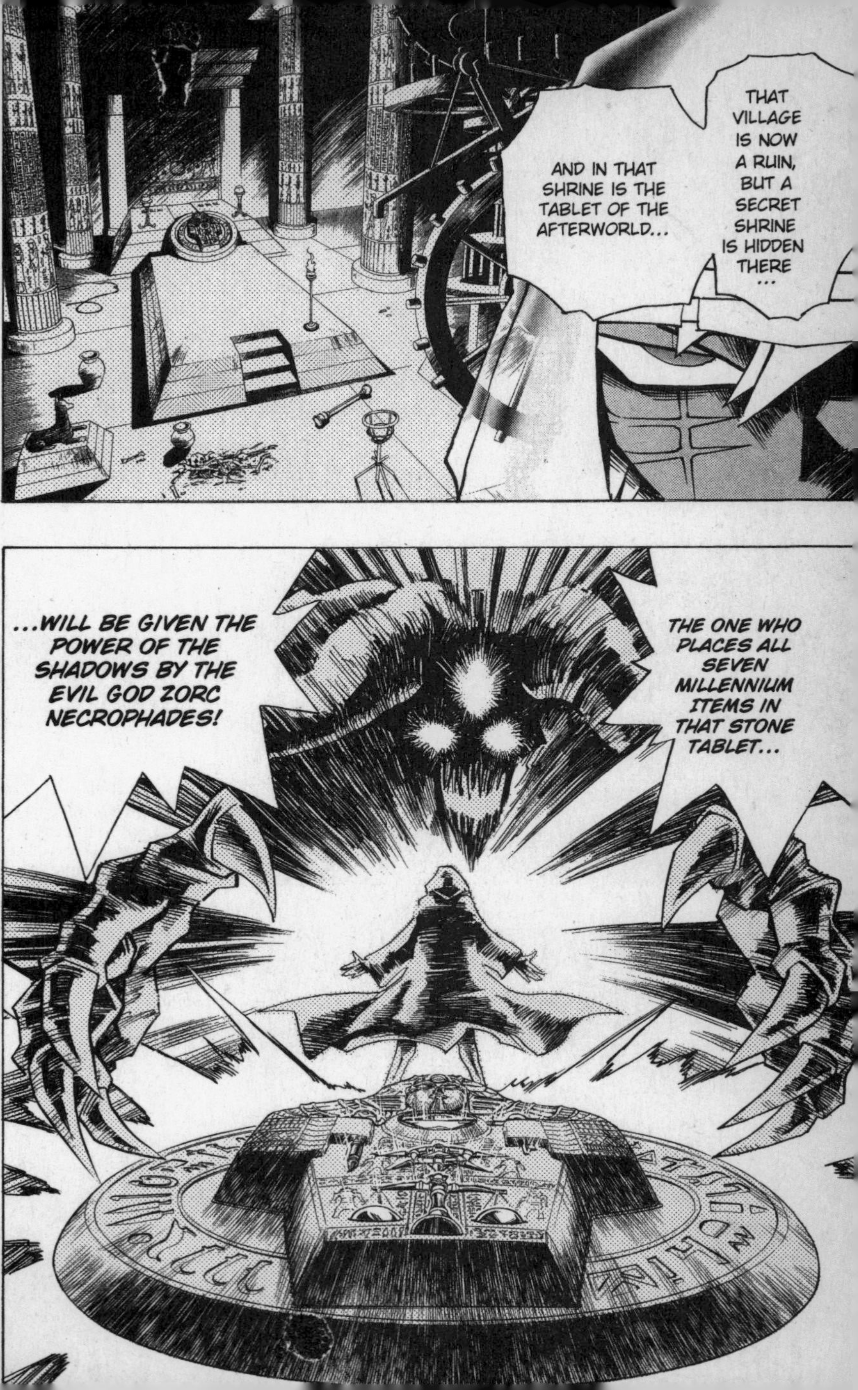
THAT VILLAGE IS NOW A RUIN, BUT A SECRET SHRINE IS HIDDEN THERE ...
AND IN THAT SHRINE IS THE TABLET OF THE AFTERWORLD...
THE ONE WHO PLACES ALL SEVEN MILLENNIUM ITEMS IN THAT STONE TABLET...
...WILL BE GIVEN THE POWER OF THE SHADOWS BY THE EVIL GOD ZORC NECROPHADES!

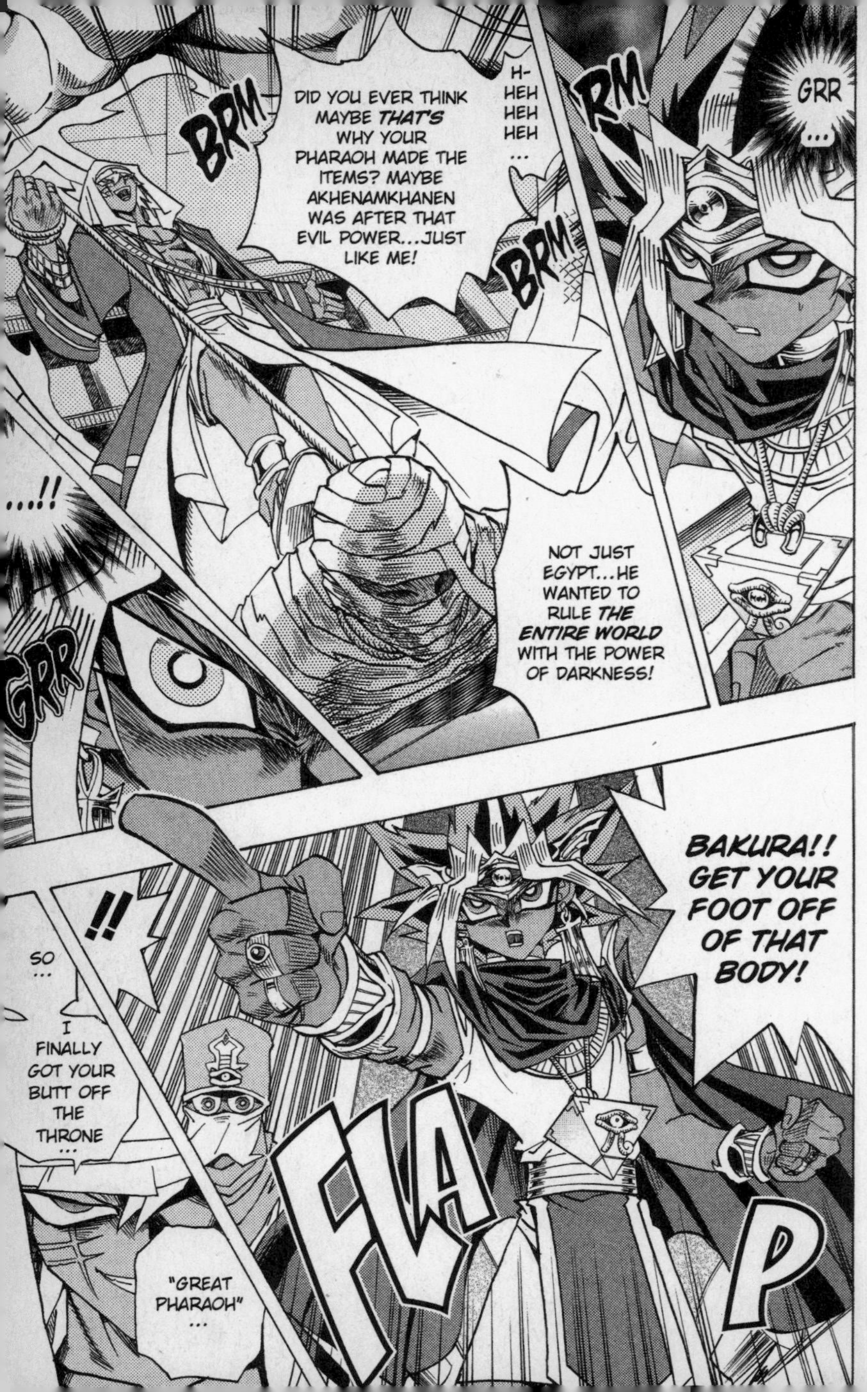

GRR ...
BRM
H- HEH HEH HEH ...
DID YOU EVER THINK MAYBE *THAT'S* WHY YOUR PHARAOH MADE THE ITEMS? MAYBE AKHENAMKHANEN WAS AFTER THAT EVIL POWER...JUST LIKE ME!
BRM
NOT JUST EGYPT...HE WANTED TO RULE ***THE ENTIRE WORLD*** WITH THE POWER OF DARKNESS!
...!!
GRR
BAKURA!! GET YOUR FOOT OFF OF THAT BODY!
FLAP
!!
SO ...
I FINALLY GOT YOUR BUTT OFF THE THRONE ...
"GREAT PHARAOH" ...

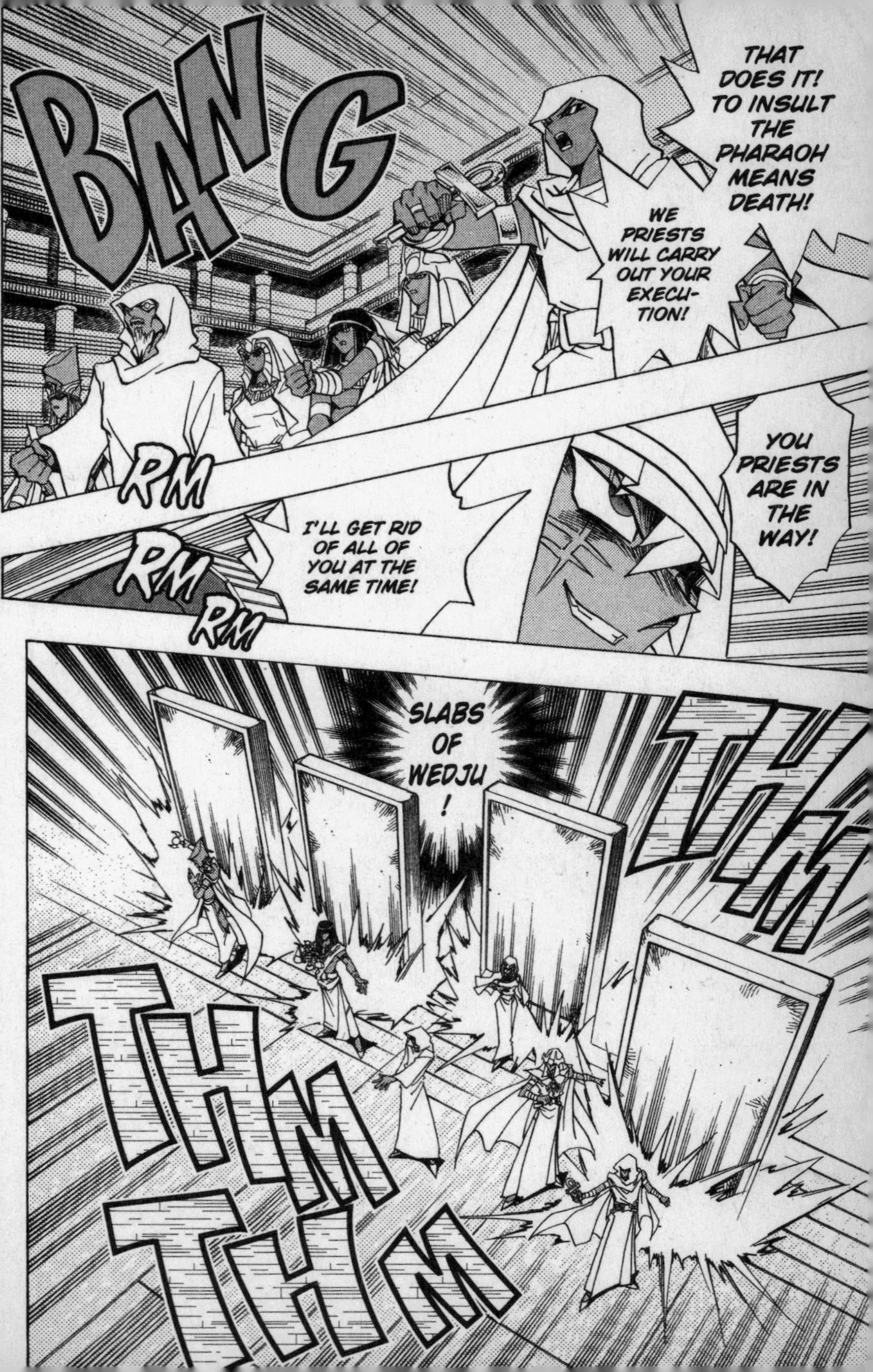
THAT DOES IT! TO INSULT THE PHARAOH MEANS DEATH!
WE PRIESTS WILL CARRY OUT YOUR EXECU-TION!
BANG
RM
YOU PRIESTS ARE IN THE WAY!
I'LL GET RID OF ALL OF YOU AT THE SAME TIME!
RM
RM
THM
SLABS OF WEDJU!
THM
THM

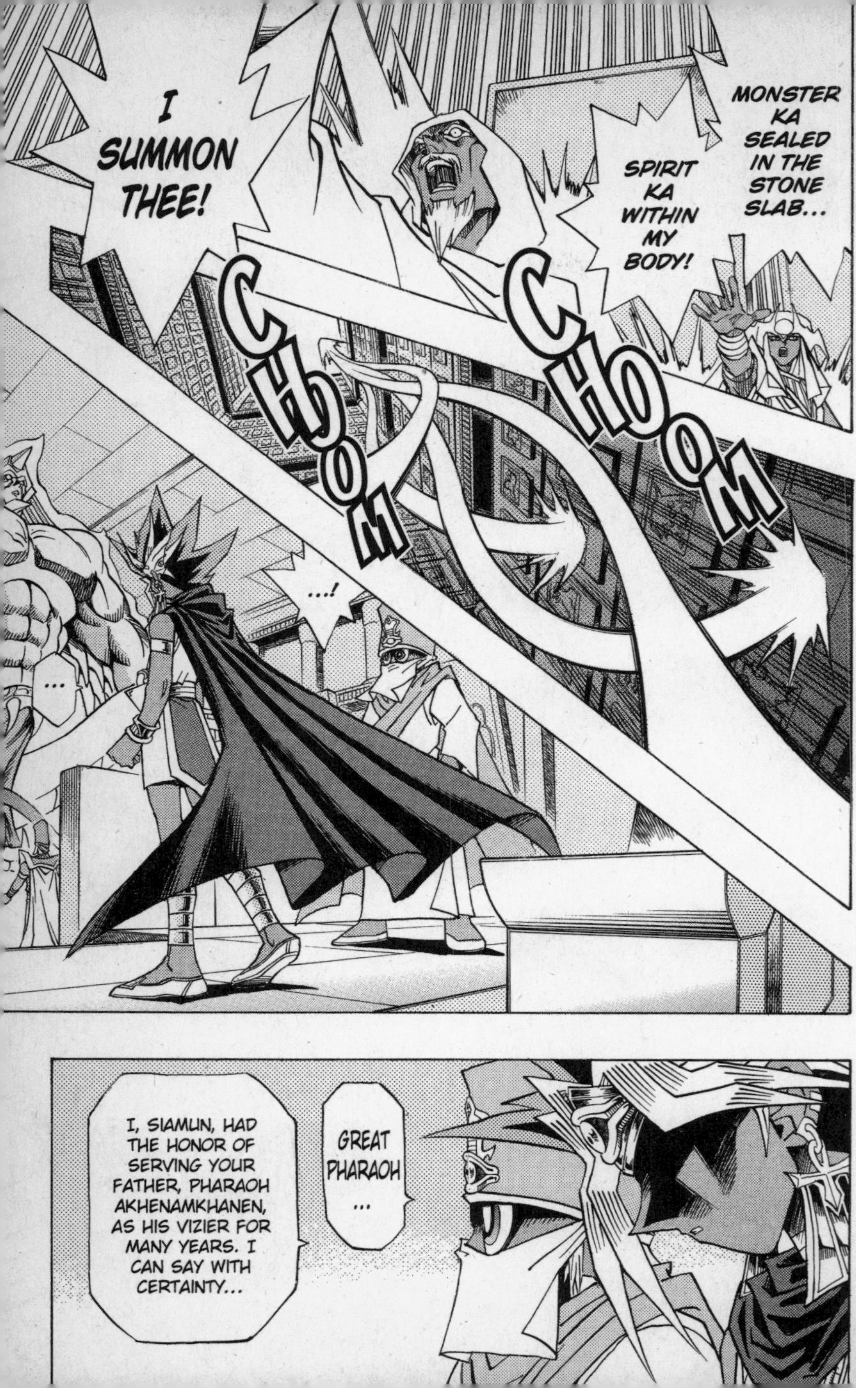
MONSTER KA SEALED IN THE STONE SLAB...
SPIRIT KA WITHIN MY BODY!
I SUMMON THEE!
CHOOM
CHOOM
...!
...
GREAT PHARAOH ...
I, SIAMUN, HAD THE HONOR OF SERVING YOUR FATHER, PHARAOH AKHENAMKHANEN, AS HIS VIZIER FOR MANY YEARS. I CAN SAY WITH CERTAINTY...

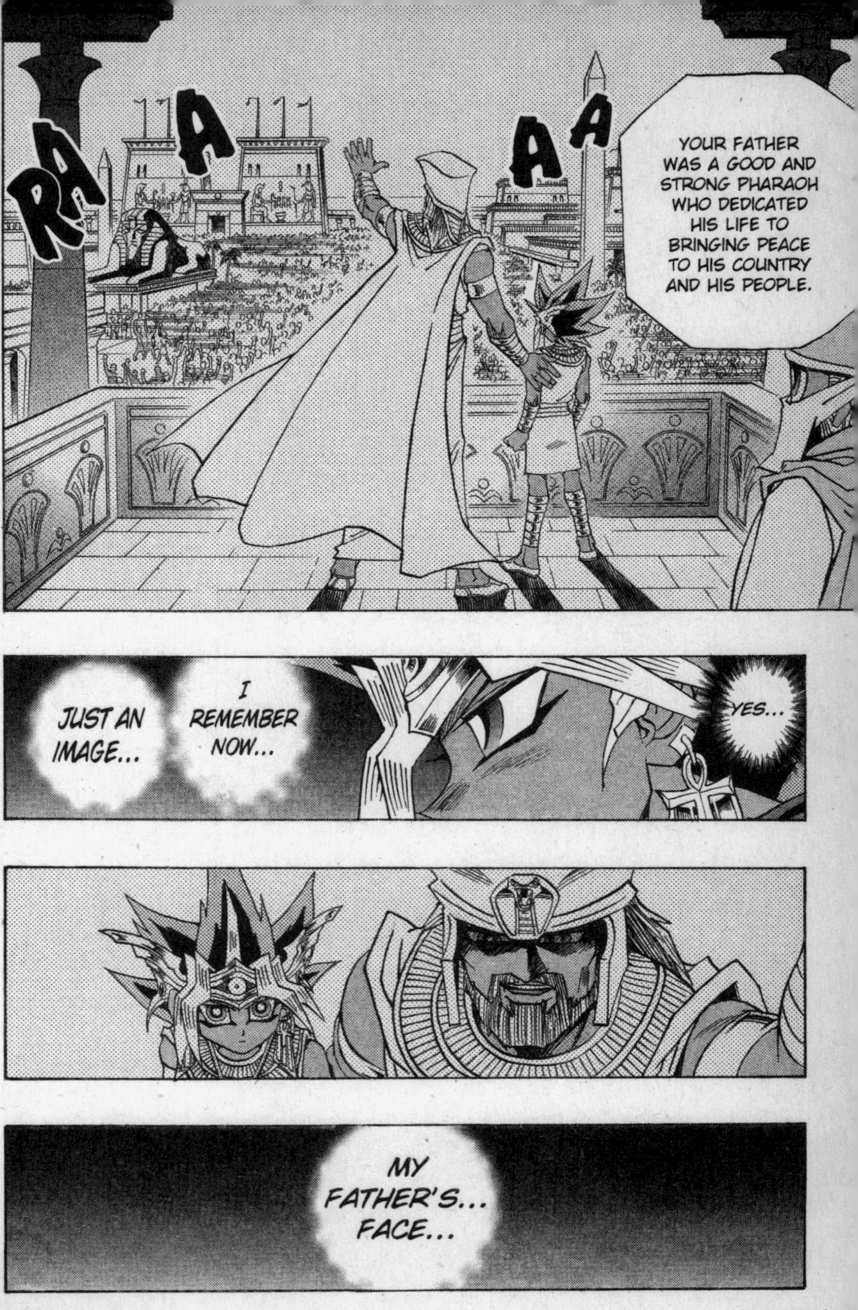

YOUR FATHER WAS A GOOD AND STRONG PHARAOH WHO DEDICATED HIS LIFE TO BRINGING PEACE TO HIS COUNTRY AND HIS PEOPLE.
RAAAA
YES...
I REMEMBER NOW...
JUST AN IMAGE...
MY FATHER'S... FACE...

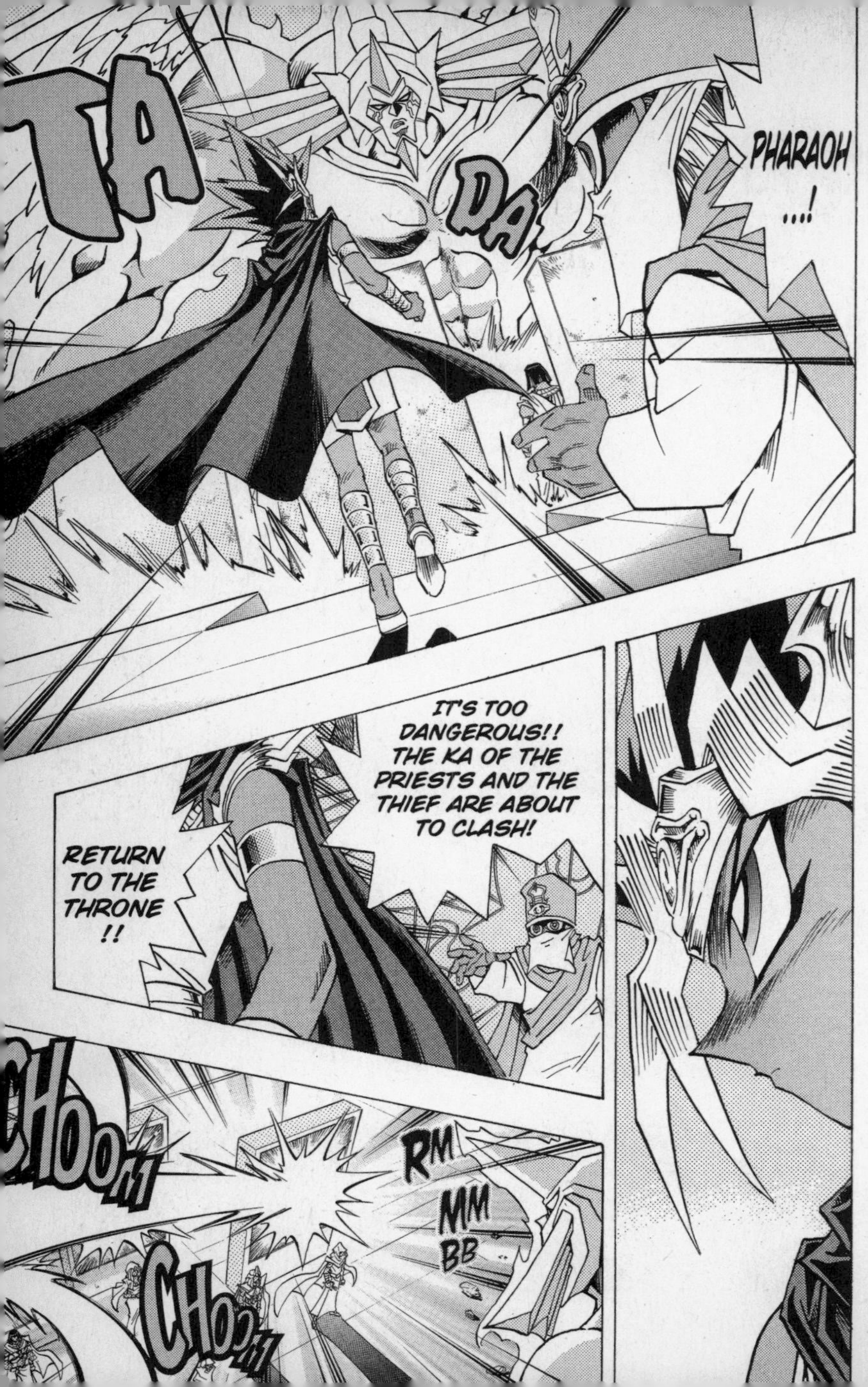
PHARAOH ...!
TA
DA
IT'S TOO DANGEROUS!! THE KA OF THE PRIESTS AND THE THIEF ARE ABOUT TO CLASH!
RETURN TO THE THRONE !!
RM MM BB
CHOO
CHOO

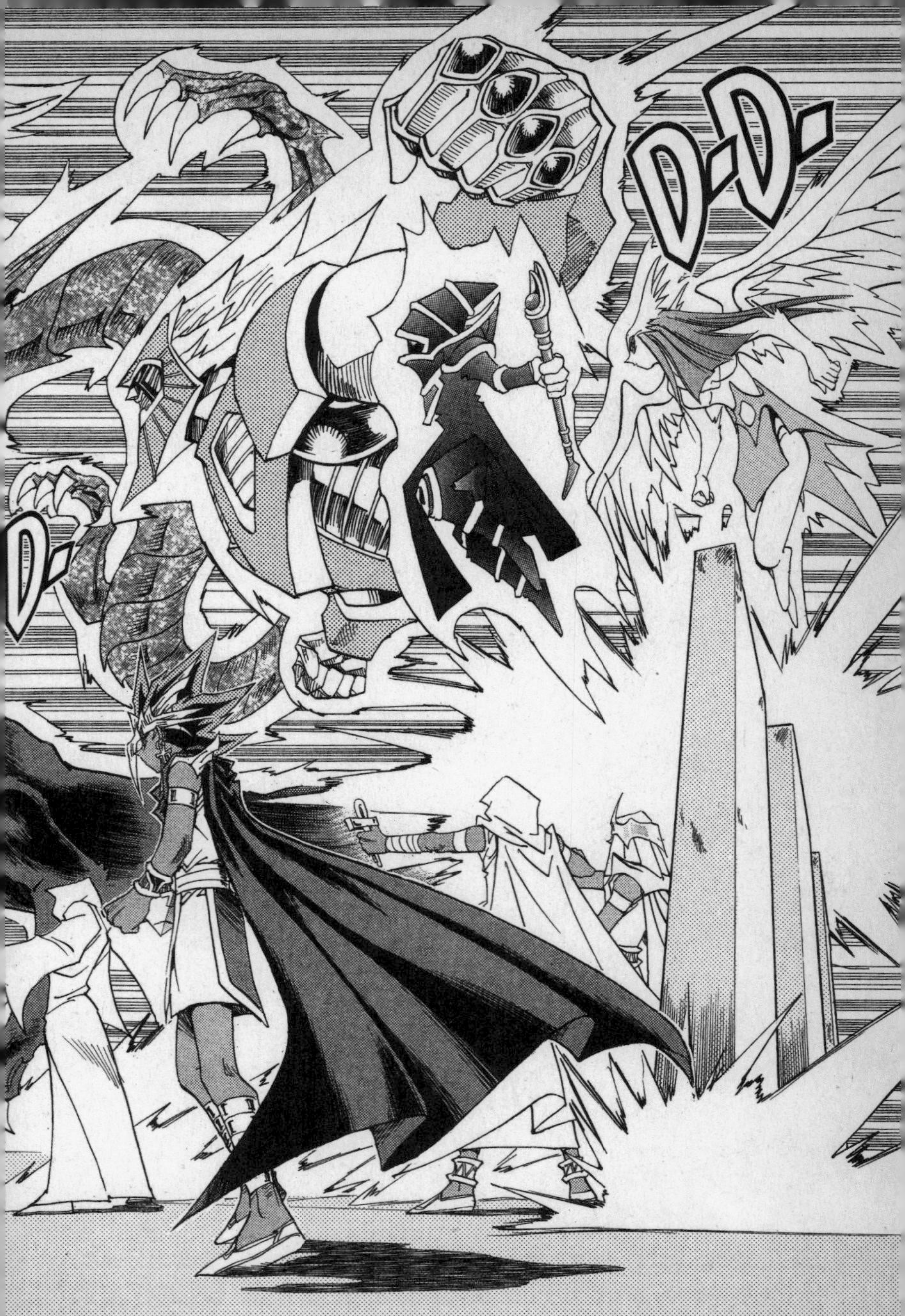
D-D-
D-

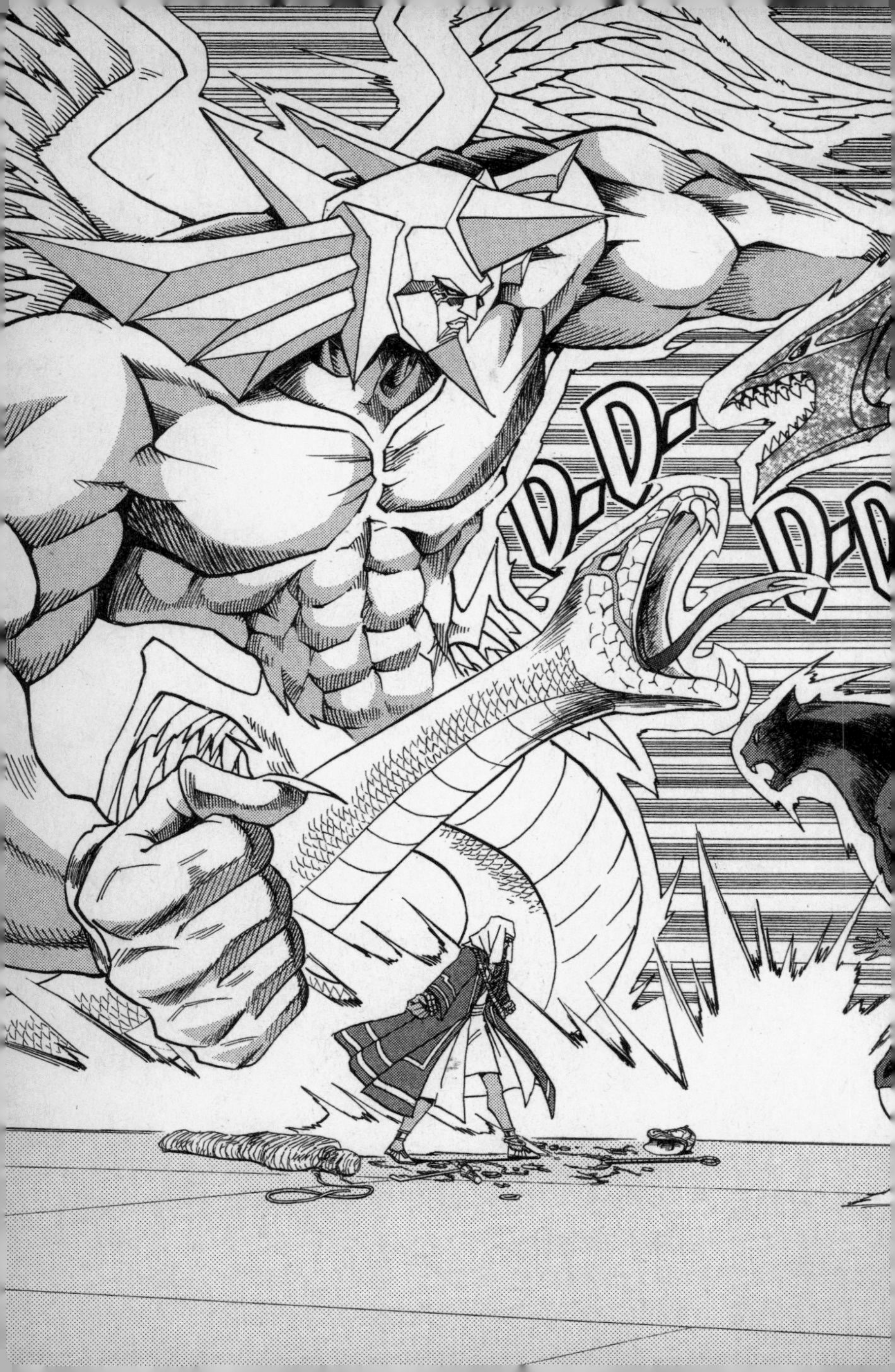
D-D-D-
D-D

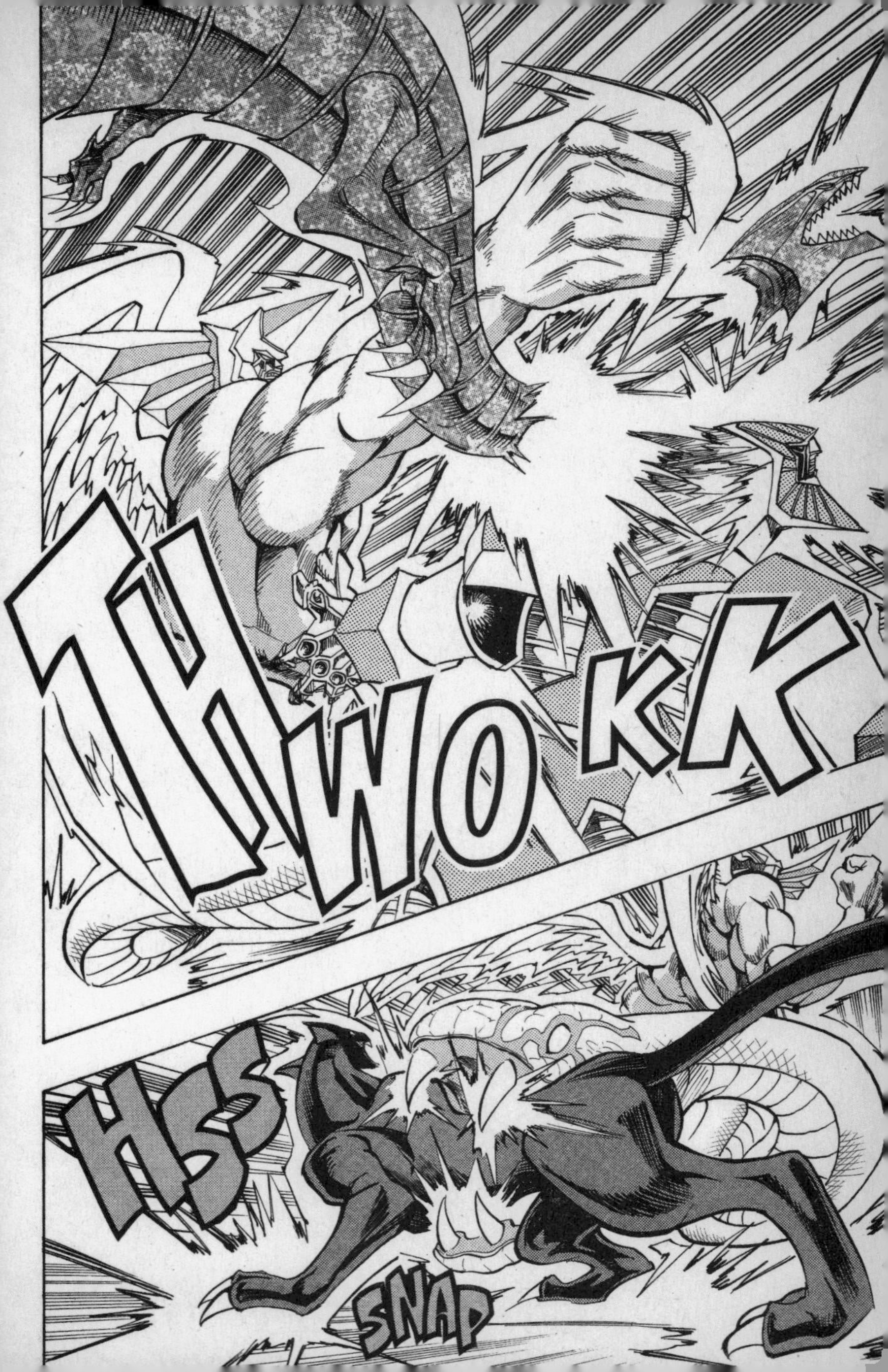
THWOKK
HSS
SNAP

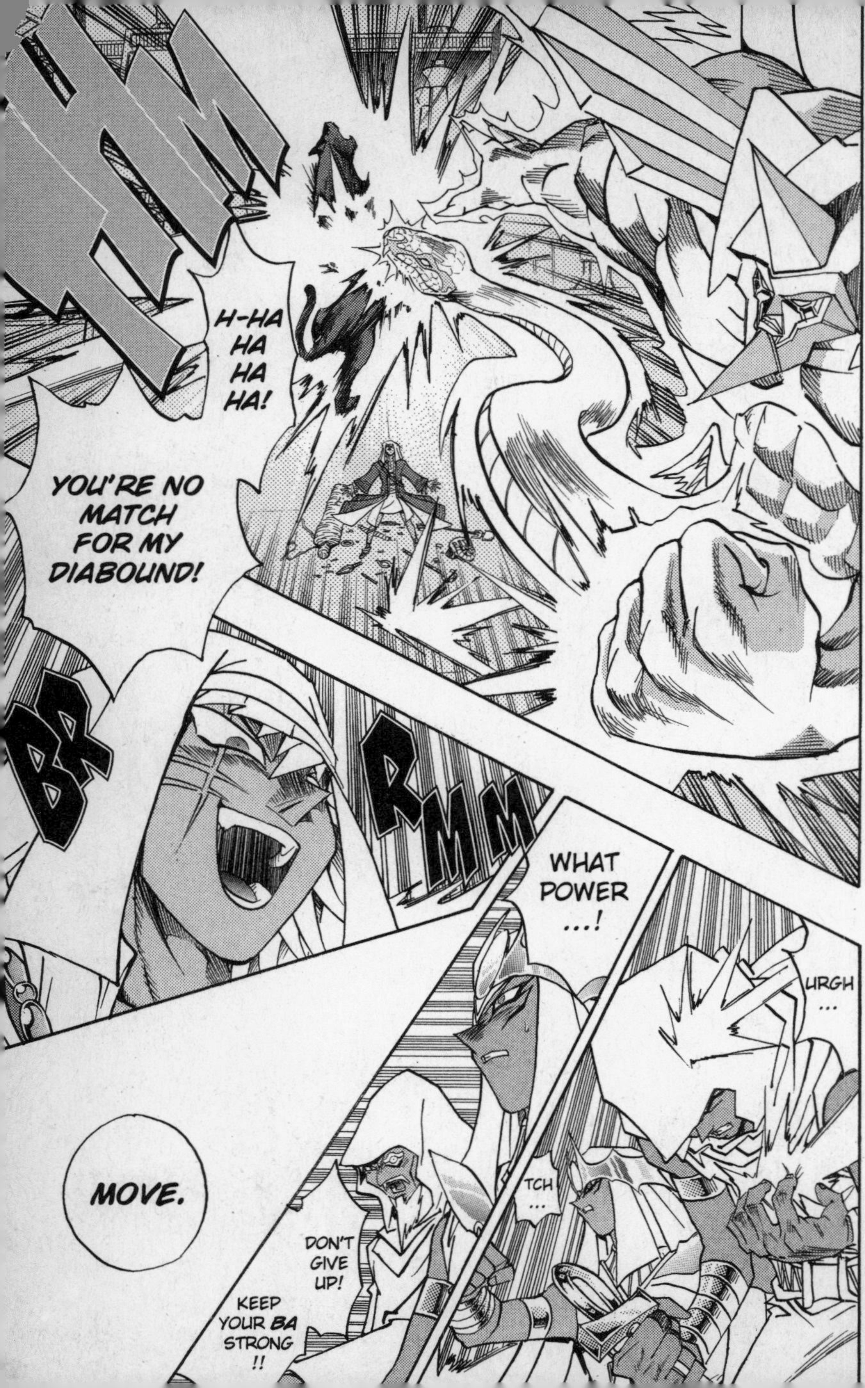
H-HA HA HA HA!
YOU'RE NO MATCH FOR MY DIABOUND!
BR
RMM
URGH ...
TCH ...
WHAT POWER ...!
DON'T GIVE UP!
KEEP YOUR BA STRONG !!
MOVE.

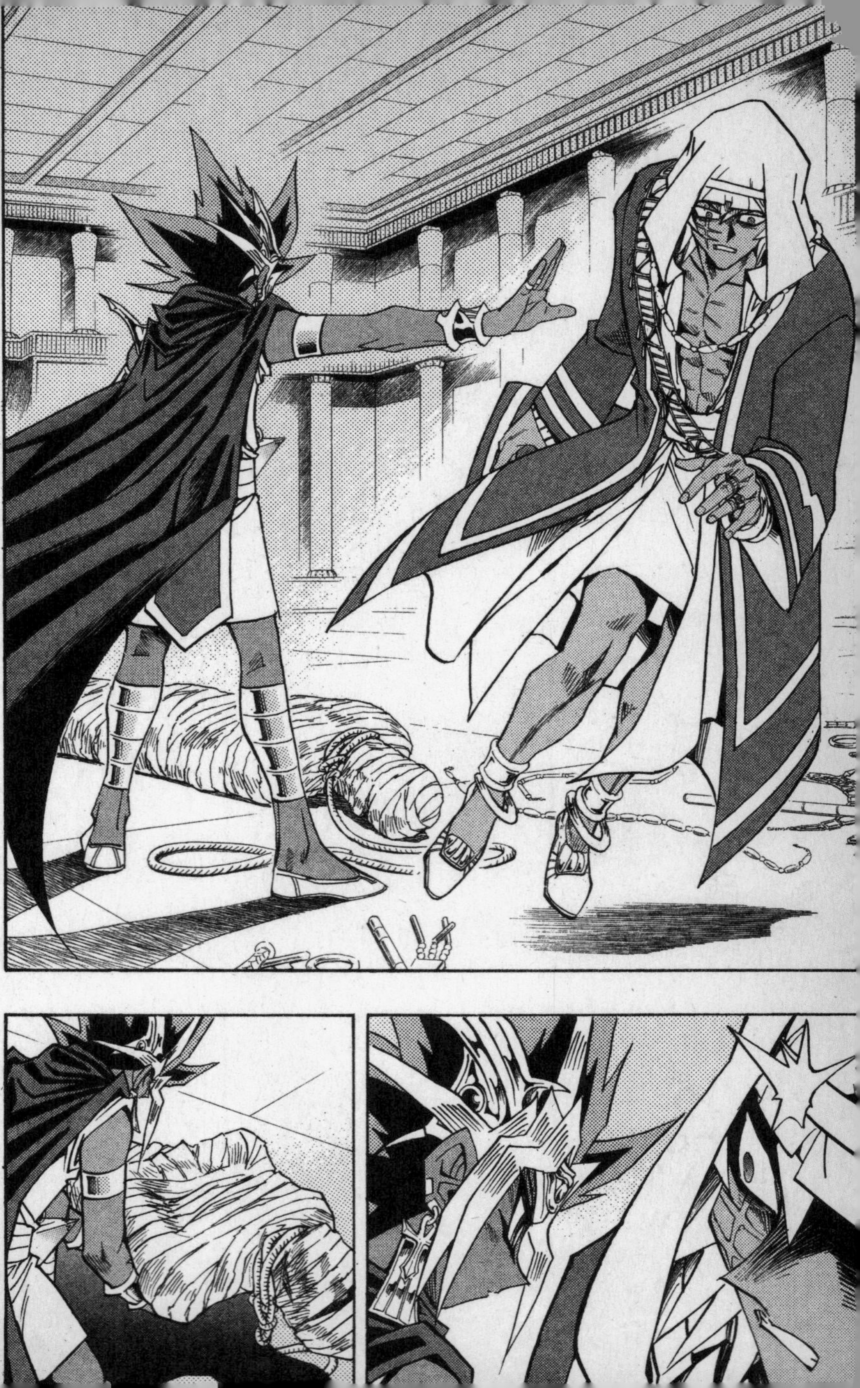

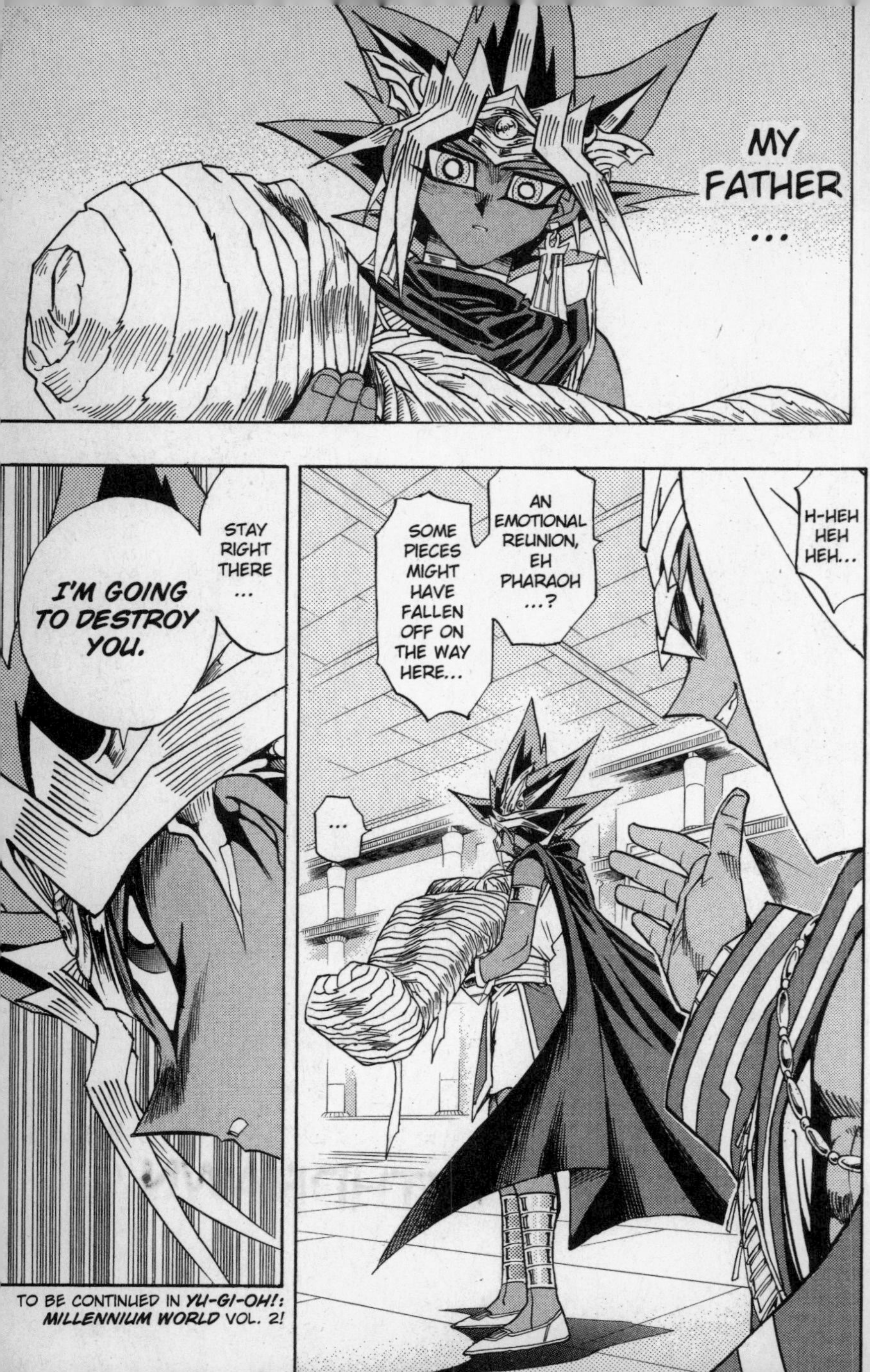
MY FATHER ...
H-HEH HEH HEH...
AN EMOTIONAL REUNION, EH PHARAOH ...?
SOME PIECES MIGHT HAVE FALLEN OFF ON THE WAY HERE...
...
STAY RIGHT THERE ...
I'M GOING TO DESTROY YOU.

TO BE CONTINUED IN *YU-GI-OH!: MILLENNIUM WORLD* VOL. 2!

IN THE NEXT VOLUME...

Yu-Gi-Oh fights Bakura! Can the three Egyptian gods defeat Bakura's spirit Diabound, or will the mad tomb-robber kill the pharaoh in his own throne room? As the archenemies clash, Yugi and his friends explore the Maze of the Pharaoh's Soul, trying to join their friend in the World of Memory. Meanwhile, High Priest Seto comes up with a ruthless plan to protect the kingdom from evildoers. But will the plan stop Bakura...or only spread the terror it tries to stop?

COMING DECEMBER 2005!

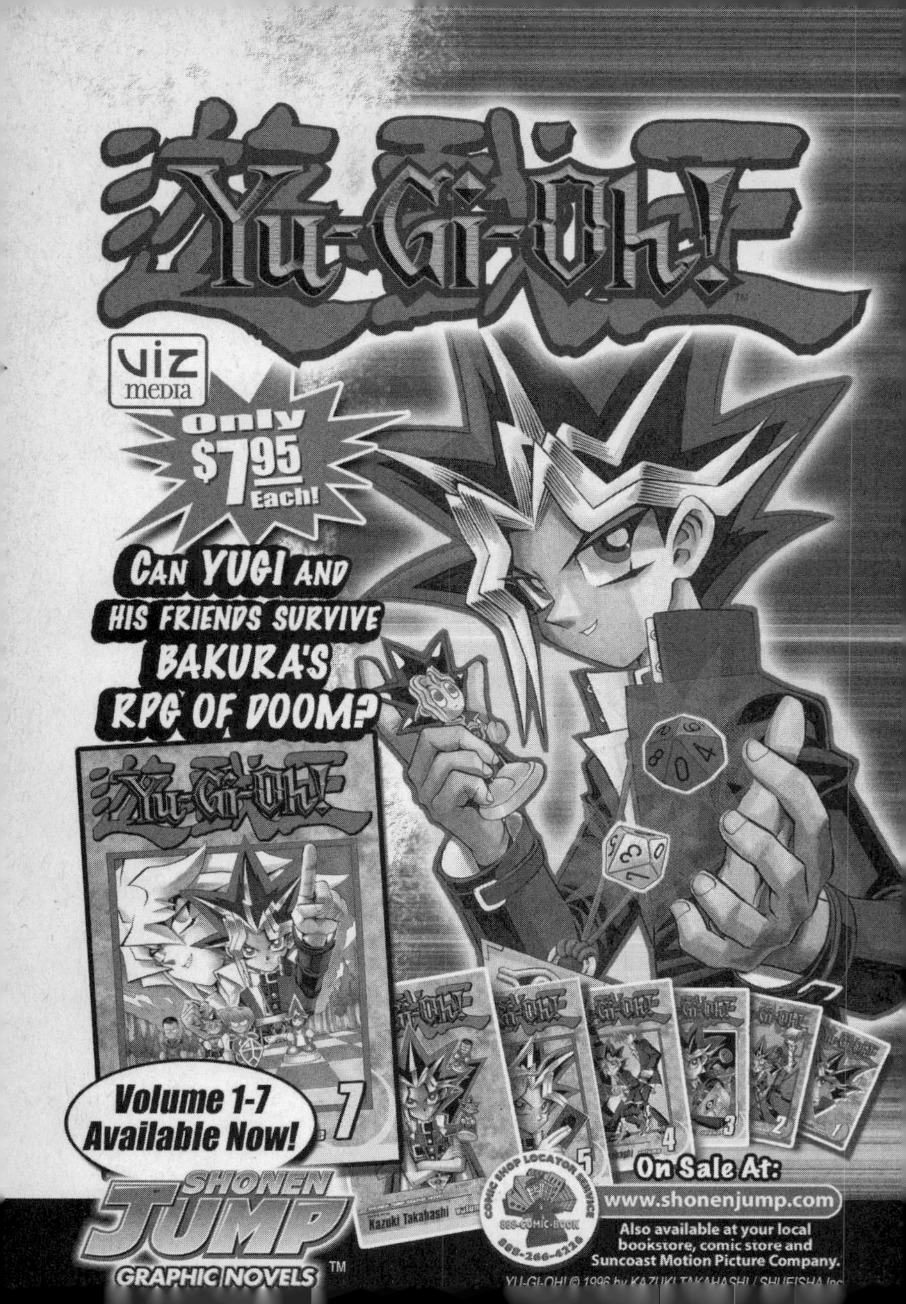

YU-GI-OH!
viz media
Only $7.95 Each!
CAN YUGI AND HIS FRIENDS SURVIVE BAKURA'S RPG OF DOOM?
Volume 1-7 Available Now!
SHONEN JUMP GRAPHIC NOVELS
Kazuki Takahashi
On Sale At:
www.shonenjump.com
Also available at your local bookstore, comic store and Suncoast Motion Picture Company.
COMIC SHOP LOCATOR SERVICE
888-COMIC-BOOK
888-266-4226
YU-GI-OH! © 1996 by KAZUKI TAKAHASHI / SHUEISHA Inc.

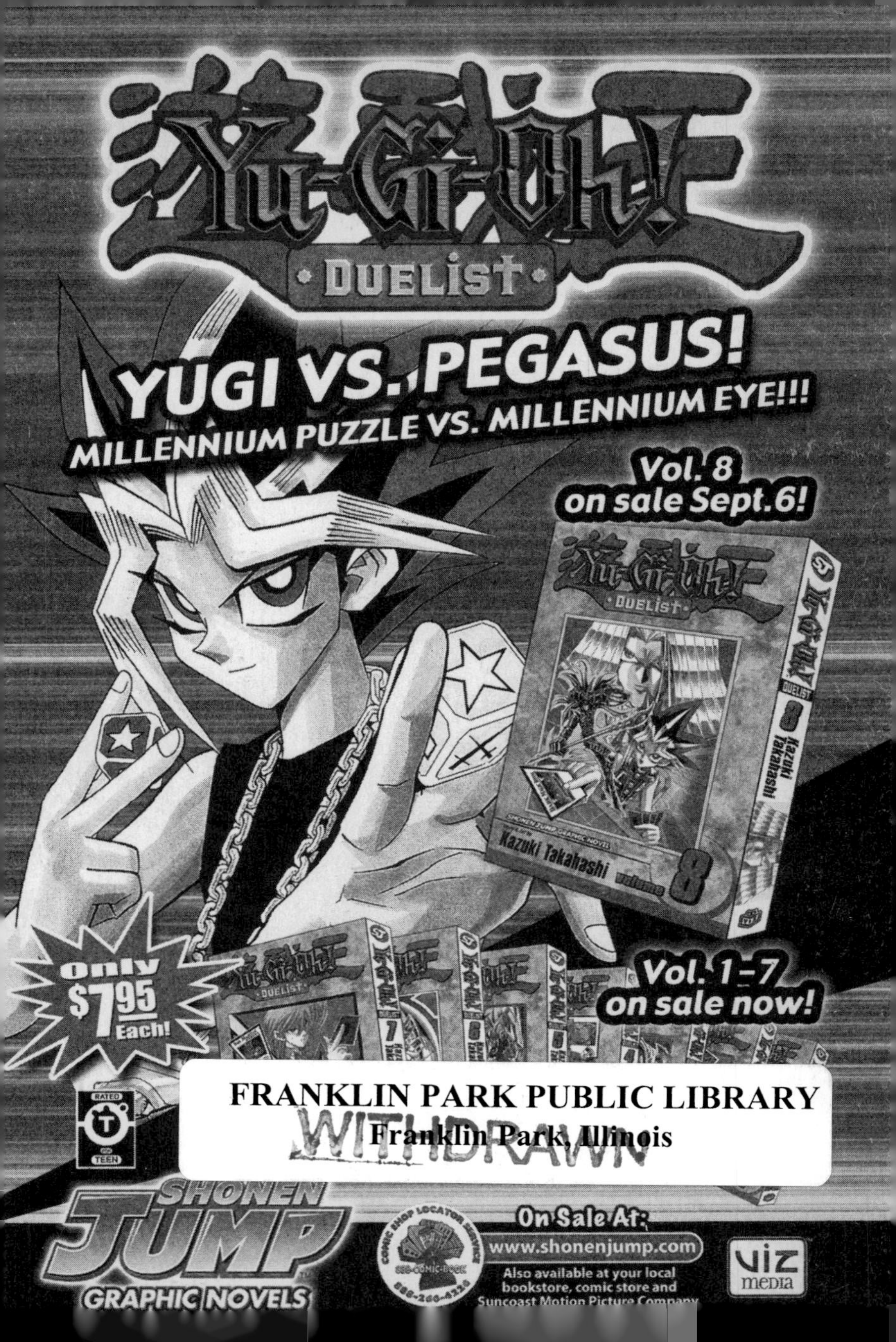
YU-GI-OH!
DUELIST
YUGI VS. PEGASUS!
MILLENNIUM PUZZLE VS. MILLENNIUM EYE!!!
Vol. 8
on sale Sept.6!
Kazuki Takahashi
volume 8
Only
$7.95
Each!
Vol. 1-7
on sale now!
RATED T TEEN
SHONEN JUMP
GRAPHIC NOVELS
On Sale At:
www.shonenjump.com
Also available at your local
bookstore, comic store and
Suncoast Motion Picture Company.
VIZ media